W9-ABN-419

PRAISE FOR CHRISTOPHER CLAREY AND

THE MASTER

"Roger Federer is the most beautiful and balletic player I've ever seen. In this entertaining and deeply researched book, Christopher Clarey, the top tennis writer of today, tells the story of how Federer became one of our sport's greatest champions and how much harder it was than he made it look."

—Billie Jean King, former world No. 1 professional tennis player

"Roger Federer plays tennis like Michelangelo painted: every stroke is perfection, the end result a masterpiece. Christopher Clarey captured just that."

—Martina Navratilova, former world No. 1 professional tennis player

"Christopher Clarey is a rare combination: the consummate insider with an objective lens. With THE MASTER, he delivers a deep and enlightening view of Roger's life and career that sports fans will be parsing for decades."

—Jim Courier, former world No. 1 and four-time Grand Slam singles champion

"An iconic master in his own field, Christopher Clarey is the perfect writer to wrap up the gift that is Roger Federer's career. You're not going to get a better look into his life, personality, and character. Christopher got close but not too close to Roger to compromise his perspective on this great champion. He shows sides and layers of Roger through conversations and stories that we have never been privy to before. I have deep respect for Christopher's fair and thoughtful journalism."

—Chris Evert, American former world No. 1 tennis player and winner of eighteen Grand Slam singles championships

"Christopher Clarey follows Roger Federer from insecure teen to mature champion who takes his family with him on the road and loves visiting new places. It takes a master to know a master. Among the many highlights of this valuable biography: informed glimpses of other great stars in Federer's long career."

—George Vecsey, *New York Times* sports columnist and bestselling author of *Martina* and *Coal Miner's Daughter*

"Perhaps no athletic figure of the past half century has so thoroughly captured the imagination of the worldwide public quite like Roger Federer. In this compelling book, the cerebral Christopher Clarey takes us behind the scenes to examine Federer across the board and up close as a man of deep sensitivity, a champion of singular creativity, and a transcendent sports figure."

—Steve Flink, leading tennis historian and member of the International Tennis Hall of Fame, author of *The Greatest Tennis Match of All Time*

"With the same elegance and excellence that defined Roger Federer's great career, Christopher Clarey has chronicled the making of a legend. THE MASTER is a truly enjoyable deep dive into the qualities that set Federer apart from the rest."

—Mike Tirico, host of NBC Sports

"Christopher Clarey, the longtime tennis correspondent for the *New York Times* and *International Herald Tribune*, has crafted a treat not just for Roger Federer fans, but for tennis aficionados who revel in behind-the-scenes details of life on the tour, strategy on the court, and the evolution of a tennis star. From his various conversations with and about Federer over more than twenty years covering him, Clarey zeroes in on the formative places, people, and matches in Federer's journey to the top. Through his coaches, his friends, his rivals, his idols, and Federer himself, THE MASTER travels the world creating time capsules for a golden era of tennis."

—Naila-Jean Meyers, former *New York Times* tennis editor

"Magnificent. THE MASTER is awash in absorbing stories, history and assimilation, and the kind of insider insights that only Chris Clarey could provide. His words are as elegant and graceful as his subject."

—Mary Carillo, Olympic correspondent and
tennis analyst, NBC Sports

"THE MASTER is a book we've been waiting for, for years. Clarey on Federer. A perfect match. The writer who for decades has documented Federer's artistry with lyricism and insightfulness owed us this definitive portrait. But it is far from an anthology of Clarey's greatest Federer hits. It instead delights with new revelations and fresh thoughts, from a writer uniquely qualified to deliver them. THE MASTER demonstrates clearly the mastery of both subject and author."

—Jeremy Schaap, host of *E:60* and *Outside the Lines*

PRAISE FOR
THE MASTER

"Style married with substance. Heft married with levity. Polished, detail-oriented, executed with grace. Roger Federer gets the biography he deserves."

—L. Jon Wertheim, *Sports Illustrated* executive editor and
bestselling author of *This Is Your Brain on Sports*

"A deeply reported and researched portrait of one of the greatest tennis players ever...A fine work of sports journalism, well worthy of its estimable subject."
—*Kirkus*

The MASTER

THE LONG RUN AND BEAUTIFUL GAME OF

Roger Federer

CHRISTOPHER CLAREY

TWELVE

NEW YORK BOSTON

Copyright © 2021 by Christopher Clarey
Cover design by Jarrod Taylor. Cover photograph © AP / Seth Wenig.
Cover copyright © 2021 by Hachette Book Group, Inc.

Hachette Book Group supports the right to free expression and the value of
copyright. The purpose of copyright is to encourage writers and artists to
produce the creative works that enrich our culture.

The scanning, uploading, and distribution of this book without permission
is a theft of the author's intellectual property. If you would like permission to
use material from the book (other than for review purposes), please contact
permissions@hbgusa.com. Thank you for your support of the author's rights.

Twelve
Hachette Book Group
1290 Avenue of the Americas, New York, NY 10104
twelvebooks.com
twitter.com/twelvebooks

Originally published in hardcover and ebook by Twelve in August 2021.

First Trade Edition: August 2022

Twelve is an imprint of Grand Central Publishing. The Twelve name and logo
are trademarks of Hachette Book Group, Inc.

The publisher is not responsible for websites (or their content) that are not
owned by the publisher.

The Hachette Speakers Bureau provides a wide range of authors for speaking
events. To find out more, go to www.hachettespeakersbureau.com or call
(866) 376-6591.

Library of Congress Control Number: 2021939246

ISBNs: 9781538719244 (trade pbk.), 9781538719251 (ebook)

Printed in the United States of America

LSC-C

Printing 1, 2022

For my dazzling mom,
who handed down her love of words and tennis

CHAPTER ONE

TIGRE, Argentina

Midnight approached, and so did Roger Federer.

We journalists do a lot of waiting, and this wait was in a chauffeured car in a Buenos Aires suburb with Eric Carmen's plaintive ballad "All by Myself" playing on the radio. That sounded right on key for me as I sat alone in the backseat with my notes and pre-interview thoughts, but not for Federer, who so seldom seems to be all by himself and certainly was not on this occasion.

It was mid-December 2012, the tail end of a resurgent year in which he had returned to No. 1 by winning Wimbledon, his first Grand Slam title in more than two years. Now, he had left his wife, Mirka, and three-year-old twin daughters at home in Switzerland and come for the first time to this part of South America to play a series of exhibitions that had sold out in minutes.

He was here for the money: $2 million per appearance, which guaranteed him more for six matches than the $8.5 million he had earned in official prize money in all of 2012. But Federer was also here for the memories: the chance to commune with new audiences in new places despite all the demands on his mind and body in the previous eleven months.

Other champions with their fortunes already secured would have been content to pass on the journey and the jet lag. But Federer and his agent, Tony Godsick, were thinking big picture: considering untapped Federer markets as well as untapped Federer emotions. The tour, which had taken him to Brazil and now Argentina, had surpassed their expectations, symbolized by the crowd of twenty thousand that had filled the makeshift stadium in Tigre this evening. That was a record for a tennis match in Argentina, proud land of tennis icons like Guillermo Vilas, Gabriela Sabatini, and Juan Martin del Potro, who had been Federer's opponent and to some degree Federer's foil.

"It was great but a little strange for Juan Martin," said Franco Davin, then del Potro's coach. "He's at home in Argentina, and they cheer more for Federer."

So it has gone in many a tennis nation. Federer gets to play at home just about everywhere, and even near midnight several hundred Federer fans were still waiting outside the stadium: adults standing on boxes to get a better view, children perched on their parents' shoulders, digital camera lights flashing as their owners kept fingers on buttons in order to capture the moment.

It was quiet and expectant, and then it was bedlam as Federer emerged from a side door and made his way to the backseat, moving lightly on his feet even after the three-setter against del Potro.

"Bye-bye. Bye-bye. Bye-bye!" he said rhythmically in a conversational tone to the fans before opening the car door.

"How are things?" he said to me in the same tone after closing it behind him.

I have followed Federer on six continents; interviewed him more than twenty times over twenty years for the *New York Times* and the *International Herald Tribune*. Our meetings have taken place everywhere from a private plane to a backcourt at Wimbledon to Times Square to Alpine restaurants in Switzerland to a suite at the Hôtel de Crillon in Paris with a ridiculously good view of the Place de la Concorde while his future wife, Mirka Vavrinec, tried on designer clothes.

One habit that separates Federer from most other elite athletes I have encountered is that he will ask about you first and not in a perfunctory manner: inquiring about your own journey to this particular place, your own perceptions of the tournament, the country, the people.

"The reason Roger is so interesting is because he's so interested," Paul Annacone, his former coach, once told me.

My family of five had embarked on a globe trot of our own in 2012: a school year on the road beginning with three months in Peru, Chile, and Argentina.

Federer wanted to hear the highlights (Torres del Paine and Chiloé Island in Chile, Arequipa in Peru). But he was most interested in the schooling and how our three children reacted and benefited. It was yet another hint that he planned to remain on the road with his own family indefinitely, that he wanted to keep his children part of his everyday life and show them quite a bit of the world along the way.

"We are sort of returning guests at most of the cities and tournaments, and we've also created a lot of friends around the world," he said. "It's that home-away-from-home feeling. I'm able to reproduce that quite easily now, especially now with the kids. I want to keep reproducing that for them so they always feel comfortable everywhere we go."

Federer's curiosity—be it polite or from the heart—sets the tone for a conversation rather than a structured interview. It is disarming, although that does not seem to be his intent. What it creates, most of all, is an air of normalcy amid the extraordinary, and that is something Federer projects very intentionally. Federer can handle being on a pedestal (he has had lots of practice), but he often emphasizes that he is happier seeing eye-to-eye. His mother, Lynette, might well have passed this on. When someone hears her surname or a shopkeeper sees it on her credit card and asks if she is related to *that* Federer, she answers in the affirmative but then quickly shifts the focus by inquiring if they have children of their own.

"Look at this, listen to this," he said in his distinctive nasal baritone, gesturing out the car window. "We're, like, snaking through the crowds with police escorts, and this is not what I usually have, you know?"

"Funny," I said. "I would think it would happen to you a lot."

"Thank God it doesn't, actually," he said. "I consider myself really like a regular guy with a fascinating life as a tennis player, because the life as a tennis player has become very much living it in the public eye, traveling the world, live audience. You get the review right away. You know if you are good or bad. It's like musicians a little bit, and I tell you, it's a good feeling to have. Even if you are bad, it doesn't matter. Go work at it. At least you know you have some work to do, and if you are great, it gives you confidence and motivation and inspires you. So it's a great life, I have to admit. It's hard at times, you know, because the travels can be hard. You know how it is. But I was thinking the other day, I entered the top 10 like ten years ago, and here I am now still experiencing things like this. It is like a total out-of-body experience, almost disbelief that it is really happening. I feel very fortunate, and I guess that's also one of the reasons I would like to play for longer, because these things are not going to come back around when you retire."

The surprise, even to Federer, was just how much more would come his way before retirement.

That night in Argentina, he was already thirty-one, the same age Pete Sampras, one of his role models, had been when he won a record fourteenth Grand Slam singles title at the 2002 United States Open. That turned out to be Sampras's final tour match and would have been one of the sport's ultimate walk-off home runs if Sampras had not waited another year to formally announce his retirement.

Stefan Edberg, another of Federer's boyhood tennis heroes, retired at age thirty.

But Federer was not late in his career in Buenos Aires, as most tennis experts and fans would understandably have imagined. He was still smack in the middle of his run and would play on effectively into the 2020s as his generational tennis peers moved into business, commentary, or coaching Federer's younger rivals.

Following Sampras in his final seasons in 2001 and 2002, it was clear that the grind and the pressure were taking a heavy toll on him. "Pete was done, but Roger is an entirely different animal," said Annacone, who has coached them both. "Traveling the world drained Pete's energy. Roger gets energy from it."

Annacone traveled with Federer to the ATP tournament in Shanghai.

On their second day in the city, Annacone and the rest of Federer's team were sitting at a table talking in Federer's hotel suite when there was a knock at the door. It was a Chinese woman.

Federer announced that their language teacher had arrived.

"Roger says, 'She's going to come over every day for like a half an hour, and we're going to try to pick up on a few words here and there so we learn some Mandarin,'" Annacone said. "And I was like, 'Dude, I can barely speak English.' And Roger was like, 'No, no, it'll be fun.' And he loved it. He wanted to learn some phrases so he could say thank you to the fans in Mandarin, but he was also in hysterics listening to us try to pronounce things. Roger just embraces the different aspects of traveling in a way that many others do not."

It was Federer's natural state with a father from Switzerland and a mother from South Africa, where Federer first visited when he was three months old and returned to regularly throughout his childhood. Sampras spoke no language other than English. Federer speaks French, English, German, and Swiss German, and also knows quite a few words of Afrikaans, thanks to his mother, and quite a few swear words in Swedish, thanks to his former coach Peter Lundgren.

As a Swiss in the border city of Basel, Federer was accustomed to switching cultural milieus from an early age. But being exposed to a way of life does not guarantee that you will embrace that way of life. Federer did so in part because, for a tennis champion, there was purpose to the globe-trotting, and what made him genuinely giddy in that car in Argentina in 2012 was the realization that the body of work he had created on the courts of Wimbledon and Roland Garros had translated and inspired more widely than he imagined.

"They are so passionate," he said. "I've had more fans break down here in South America than anywhere else in the world, you know. They cry, and they shake, and they are just so, like, not in awe, but so happy to meet you that it's disbelief for them. And that is something that has happened a few times before but it's very rare, and here I must have had at least twenty people probably hugging me and kissing me and so happy just to get a chance to touch me even."

As the Argentines shouted and pressed toward the car, he did not shrink from the window. He drew closer to it.

I asked Federer if he knew the English word "jaded."

"A little bit," he said, sounding hesitant.

"In French, it basically means 'blasé,'" I said. "You've been through it all before, things no longer give you the same rush. It's kind of how you imagine Björn Borg in the car leaving the US Open, never to return."

Borg was twenty-five then.

Federer considered that for a moment.

"It happens very quickly," he said. "You're just, 'I'm done. I don't want to do it anymore. I'm tired of it all.' And really, that's what I try to avoid by having the proper schedule and the proper fun and the proper change, because, like you mentioned, if you do the same thing, it doesn't matter what you do, too many times, all the time, too often you get bored of it. It doesn't matter how extraordinary your life might be, so that's where I think these kinds of trips, or a good buildup practice session or a great vacation or some amazing tournaments in a row, toughing it out, whatever it might be, it's in the mix that I find the resources for more, the energy for more. Really, it's pretty simple in a way."

Watching Federer stay fresh and eager deep into his thirties, against logic and against tennis precedent, it was intriguing to realize that his ability to remain in the moment was in fact about forethought. If he was relaxed and accommodating despite all the forces pulling at him, it was because he knew himself and his microcosm well enough to avoid the pitfalls that would likely snuff out his pilot light.

But then such intentionality is very much in harmony with his career as a whole.

He has often made the game look astonishingly easy through the decades: hitting aces, gliding to forehands, and, in his most gravity-defying act, remaining high above the waterline in a world rightfully flooded with icon cynicism. But his path from temperamental, bleached-blond teenager with dubious style sense to one of the most elegant and self-possessed great athletes has been a long-running act of will, not destiny.

Federer is widely perceived as a natural, and yet he is a meticulous planner who has learned to embrace routine and self-discipline, plotting out his schedule well in advance and in considerable detail.

"I usually have an idea of the next one and a half years, and a very good idea about the next nine months," he said in Argentina. "I can tell you what I'll be doing on Monday before Rotterdam or what I'm doing Saturday before Indian Wells. I mean, not hour by hour, but I pretty much talk it through day by day."

Though it is rare to see Federer sweat, there has been tremendous toil and ample self-doubt behind the scenes. He has played in pain far more than most of us realize. There has also been no shortage of bruising setbacks in the spotlight. One could easily argue that the two greatest matches in which he has played were the 2008 Wimbledon final against Rafael Nadal and the 2019 Wimbledon final against Novak Djokovic. Both ended in bitter defeats in tight fifth sets that extended past regulation.

He has been a big winner, racking up more than a hundred tour titles and twenty-three consecutive Grand Slam semifinals, but also a big loser.

That has no doubt contributed to his everyman appeal, helping to humanize him. To his credit, Federer has absorbed the blows, both public and private, and rebounded with the accent on positive energy and the long run.

He has transcended tennis, not by using it as a platform for higher or edgier causes but by remaining largely within the confines of the game. That is no small achievement for a sport with a dwindling and aging fan base in Europe and North America.

It is an old-school approach: low on controversy and on glimpses into his personal life, long on bonhomie and Corinthian spirit.

Boring? Hardly. How can anyone who unites in a divided world be a source of ennui? He has long had the beautiful game: balletic, often airborne as he leaps to strike a serve or groundstroke with his eyes on the contact point for a moment longer than any player I have watched in my more than thirty years of covering tennis. That ability to finish, truly finish, the stroke can make him appear nonchalant, but it is also integral to what makes him magnetic to the gaze. It is the equivalent of Michael Jordan hovering a little longer than everyone else in flight to the basket, of a dancer holding a pose for emphasis.

"He is the most beautiful and balletic player I've ever seen," Billie Jean King told me. "His kinetic chain stays very connected. That's where the elegance comes from."

Professional tennis has been put into a particle accelerator during the last quarter century, with more powerful rackets and polyester strings and with taller, more explosive athletes. Stroke technique and footwork have had to be adjusted to deal with the speed, but Federer still seems to have the time he needs to put a final coat of paint on his shots. How can he play this way and still recover before hitting the next polished stroke? Because of rare vision, mobility, and agility but also because of relatively compact strokes and the confidence that comes with knowing that while others must plan and grind and press, he can conjure solutions on the run or full stretch that others simply lack the tool kit—or Swiss army knife—to create.

Marc Rosset, the best Swiss men's player before Federer moved the goalposts to a faraway place, likes to talk about Federer's "processing speed."

Rosset remembers doing a drill in which someone would throw five balls of different colors into the air and ask players to catch the five balls in order according to color. "The maximum I ever did was four," Rosset said. "It was really tough for me. Rog, you gave him five balls, and he caught all five."

In Rosset's view, "People focus a lot on an athlete's talent with his hands or his feet. But there's a talent we don't talk about enough and that's reactivity, the ability of their brain to interpret what their eyes are seeing. When you look at the great champions, a football player like [Zinedine] Zidane or [Diego] Maradona, or you look at Federer, Djokovic, or Nadal in tennis, you have the impression sometimes that they are in the Matrix, that everything is going so fast, too fast for you and me, but they pick up on things so quickly that it is as if they have more time for their brains to process it all.

"Zidane, when he dribbled, there were four people around him, but he was calm. It's all in slow motion for him. These great champions are a fraction of a second ahead of everybody else, and that allows them to be more relaxed, because when you see some of the incredible shots that Roger could hit in his career, those are not shots you can practice."

To watch Federer on his finer days is to be swept away by the flow of his movement but also to be put on edge by the sense that legerdemain is surely on the way, but when? It is a double dose of intoxication: intensified by how little he has deviated from the challenge at hand for most of his career. Without tirades or banter and with his inner journey rarely reflected in his deeply set eyes on court, the focus has remained on the physical act of him practicing his craft.

"He plays the ball, but he also plays *with* the ball," his friend and longtime coach Severin Lüthi once told me.

It is a quality that appeals to insiders as well as outsiders. "Fed is the guy that probably more than anybody else still astounds other players," said Brad Stine, a longtime coach who worked with Kevin Anderson and No. 1 Jim Courier. "They watch him and they honestly say, 'How does he do that? I mean, really, how do you make that shot?'"

John McEnroe was an artist with a racket, too, but a tormented one. If Johnny Mac were Jackson Pollock, splattering paint in an attempt to express some internal struggle, Federer would be much closer to Peter Paul Rubens: prolific, well-adjusted, enduring, and perfectly accessible to mainstream tastes yet capable of giving chills to the experts with his brushwork and composition, too.

It is quite a school of performance art but also one that leaves ample white space on the canvas for others to find their own meaning in his work. Federer would rather not overthink the formula—"it's pretty simple in a way," he says—but he accepts that others will have at it, like a writer whose novels get parsed to the nth degree in a graduate seminar.

I remember talking with Federer about this before we boarded that private jet in the California desert in 2018 (it was my first and probably last ride in a private jet). He had played the final of the BNP Paribas Open the previous day against del Potro, blowing three match points on his own serve and losing in a third-set tiebreaker: his first defeat of the season. The margins had been so slim, the reaction time so compressed, even for him.

"Tactics? People talk about tactics," Federer said. "But a lot of the time at this level it just comes down to instinct. It happens so fast that you have to hit the shot almost without thinking. There's of course some luck involved."

Fortune has indeed played a role for Federer. He might not have become a champion, at least not a tennis champion, if an Australian journeyman pro named Peter Carter had not decided to take a coaching job in, of all places, a small club in Basel, Switzerland. Federer might not have had the staying power if he had not met a cerebral, sensitive, and gifted fitness trainer named Pierre Paganini or crossed career paths with Mirka Vavrinec, an older Swiss player who eventually became his wife, part-time press agent, and organizer in chief. There is no way he would have played on so long and so convincingly without her full support and her own ambition.

"She has a desire to succeed that is just as strong as Federer, perhaps stronger," said Paul Dorochenko, the French fitness trainer who worked with Vavrinec and Federer in their early years in Switzerland.

But in life and certainly in pro tennis it is really about what you do with your good fortune, what you make of your opportunities, and Federer built on many of them rather than squander them.

Federer is not as debonair as his marketers can make him appear. He is intelligent and intuitive but no master of the Bondian bon mot. He did, after all, stop school at sixteen and was not a particularly serious student. But he approached adulthood and the tour with much more rigor.

"I consider this life school," he said in Argentina.

Though Federer was undeniably gifted, one of the things that differentiated him from some of the other great talents of his generation was that he had both an abiding love of the game and the drive to demand more of himself. He believed that maintaining the same level in pro tennis was actually losing ground, a belief that rubbed off on his younger rivals.

"The number one requirement to succeed at this level is I think the constant desire and open-mindedness to master and improve and evolve yourself in every aspect," Djokovic told me recently. "I know Roger has talked about this a lot, and I think it's something most top athletes in all sports can agree on. Stagnation is regression."

Federer understood, or came to understand, his weaknesses and addressed them: anger management, mental toughness, concentration, endurance, a chronically sore back, and his single-handed backhand drive. He switched tactics, attacking more from the baseline than the net. He switched to a larger-headed racket to increase his chances of thriving in extended rallies and switched coaches repeatedly—but not impulsively—to get a fresh perspective and sometimes went without a coach at all. Throughout his life he has sought out people who could serve as mentors, even role models for his next phase: from Sampras to prelapsarian Tiger Woods to, more recently, Bill Gates, whose philanthropic approach Federer hopes to emulate in his later years.

His tennis skills have been the main ingredient in his success, but his people skills are also part of the recipe. Tennis superstars get a lot of free footwear, but it is rarer that they are able to put themselves in others' shoes. Federer is an empath, constantly registering the feelings and energy in the stadium, the street, the room, the backseat.

"He's extremely socially intelligent, and I think that's a huge reason why he's so popular," said Andy Roddick, the American star who became his friend. "He's a chameleon. He can work in kind of any room, and it's a genuine emotion. It's not like he's fitting the mold in a calculated sense."

———

About halfway between Tigre and downtown Buenos Aires, a car eluded the escort and pulled briefly alongside our vehicle at full speed. A young man, high on the thrill of the chase and perhaps on something else, extended his body halfway out the open window and waved a monogrammed RF cap at Federer.

"Well, at least you know your merchandise is moving," I said.

Federer chuckled and waved through the glass. "I hope he doesn't lose the cap," he said. "Bye-bye. Bye-bye."

Federer's finely tuned antennae are part of the explanation for his postmatch tears, much less frequent now but still inseparably part of his persona. They seem to be not just an expression of joy or disappointment but a release after all the input he has absorbed on court.

It is not just about what he has invested emotionally in a match or a tournament; it is about what everyone has invested emotionally in a match or a tournament.

"So, does it start to seem normal after a while?" I asked as the car carrying the fan with the RF cap accelerated out of view.

"This? No. No. No," he said, his voice rising to a higher pitch. "This is unbelievable. It's just nice to see happy people in general, right? And this is just another world here, and that's why I love playing exhibitions. Because it's different. You finally go to a country maybe you've never been to before or do things you normally don't have the time to do. You don't have to worry too much about how you are really going to play, even though there is a certain level I can always achieve. But it's about, really, how shall I say, making sure that you touch a lot of people's hearts in an exhibition and make them happy and make them not travel to come to see you but you come travel to see them."

At a press conference, Federer will answer queries at length and with a certain restraint. It is rare that he will stray off topic or volunteer information, but he respects the question and the questioner: quite a contrast with some of his predecessors (see Jimmy Connors) and his peers (see Lleyton Hewitt and, sadly in her later years, Venus Williams). In more intimate settings, Federer's natural exuberance and geniality often get him waving his arms and launching into rambling paragraphs. Thoughts expressed in English—his first language but not always his best language—can take him in unexpected directions that require him to double back and make a few detours to get to his intended destination.

He is less polished off-camera, even goofy at times, although he saves his pranks and surprises for friends and colleagues, not for journalists along for the ride.

I have taken quite a few rides through the years, and this book will examine Federer's career in part through the prism of those experiences. This will not be a Federer encyclopedia: Too many scores and match summaries bog down any tennis narrative, and he has given us biographers too much material, playing more than seventeen hundred tour-level matches and doing news conferences after most of them. Instead, this book aims to be episodic and interpretative, built with care around the places, people, and duels that have mattered most or symbolized most to Federer.

It is just one planet, and he has covered a great deal of it: pursuing trophies, paydays, novelty, fulfillment, and, increasingly through the seasons, communion.

Argentina was an unexpectedly meaningful stop on the journey, and as we approached his hotel in downtown Buenos Aires, Federer, winner of a record seventeen Grand Slam singles titles at that stage, was emphasizing how much he still wanted to improve.

"I'm going to take a vacation after this, rest and just get away from it all, because the last few years have been extremely intense," he said. "I feel if I keep on pushing at this pace I might lose interest like you mentioned, just get jaded."

Federer laughed.

"'Jaded.' That's the new word I have in my vocabulary, and that's the last thing I want happening," he said. "Hopefully next year is going to be a platform for many more years. That's the opportunity I want to give myself."

CHAPTER TWO

BASEL, *Switzerland*

Tennis, in many respects, saved me. During my childhood, my father, like his father before him, was working his way up the ladder to becoming an admiral in the United States Navy. We moved more than ten times before I went to college. From Virginia to Hawaii to California, tennis was one of my passports to inclusion in the next community, the next school, the next team. I never stopped appreciating the game and have been covering it with a critical eye but also great pleasure since the 1980s. I have written about all sorts of sports in thirty-five years, but tennis has held my interest like no other, in part because I have played, struggled, and choked enough to understand just how difficult it can be to hit the shots that virtuosos like Federer make look routine under pressure.

After finishing my studies at Williams College, where I played on the tennis team, I taught tennis for the summer in East Hampton, New York, at a modest club with an upscale clientele. Two of my pupils were Jann Wenner, the founder of *Rolling Stone*; and fashion designer Gloria Sachs. My goal was to give enough lessons to fund a low-budget world tour with my college roommate, and I managed it with help from Jann, Gloria, and others. I was so connected to the game that I strapped my Yonex racket to my backpack and brought it along, which seemed more than a little incongruous in places like Burma and rural China where there were no courts to be seen. But the racket was a security blanket amid the unknown, just as it had been throughout my youth.

Watching tennis is still, for me, closer to a physical act than a passive one: My body tenses, my right hand often clenches a notional grip. The first tournament I covered was a long way from Wimbledon. It was the United States Tennis Association's boys' twelve-and-under national championships in 1987—essentially a tournament for talented elementary school students—in my latest home city of San Diego.

I was a summer intern at the local newspaper back when people still got most of their news on paper. All I can recall from that long-ago championship is that Vincent Spadea, the father of future top 20 pro Vince Spadea, sang arias in the stands between his young son's matches; and that Alexandra Stevenson was there with her mother, Samantha, as a six-year-old spectator doing cartwheels on the grass. That was long before she reached the semifinals at Wimbledon in 1999 and long before anyone outside of her inner circle knew that she was also the daughter of NBA star Julius Erving.

It can seem random what sticks with you and what slips away. But I am sure of this: There have been only two occasions when I watched a young men's player and was certain, deep in my bones, that I was watching a future No. 1.

The first time was during the 1998 French Open, when eighteen-year-old Marat Safin upset Andre Agassi and defending champion Gustavo Kuerten in his first two Grand Slam matches. Safin was a combustible, telegenic, and phenomenally athletic Russian: an ethnic Tatar with swagger, sex appeal, and an explosive, often-airborne two-handed backhand that was unlike any shot I had seen.

The second time was on my first trip to Basel. I traveled there in February 2001 to cover Patrick McEnroe's debut as captain for the United States Davis Cup team and eighteen-year-old Andy Roddick's debut as a player. But I ended up writing a great deal more about a Swiss teenager instead.

I had watched Federer play (and lose) his first Grand Slam match at the French Open in 1999 to Patrick Rafter and had watched Federer some more the following year in the singles at the Summer Olympics in Sydney as he finished fourth, the bitterest place to finish at any Olympics. Now nineteen, he was widely considered a promising talent, but I had not grasped just how promising until those three days in Federer's home city.

The Davis Cup, the leading team event in tennis, was more prestigious at that stage: a mettle detector that generated a different, often more acute brand of pressure than the regular tour while testing the limits of players' endurance with matches played over best-of-five sets.

Federer, still ranked outside the top 20, already had experienced some thrills and crushing defeats in the competition, which he first played at age seventeen. But during that long weekend in Basel, he hoisted Switzerland's team onto his back and carried them to victory over the Americans in the first round, sweeping both his singles matches and a doubles match with partner Lorenzo Manta.

On opening day, Federer outplayed the veteran Todd Martin, who was a two-time Grand Slam finalist. Though the match was contested on a synthetic indoor surface, I kept imagining grass beneath Federer's agile feet as he sliced backhands, flicked forehand winners on the run, flowed from baseline to net, and cracked winning volleys and overheads. There was a liquid quality to his strokes and movement that was similar to both Sampras and Edberg: an ability to cover big spaces in a hurry with seemingly little effort. He could run around his backhand to rip his forehand with a speed and fluidity that I had never seen. His serve looked airtight and was clearly difficult to read, considering how often the six-foot-six Martin, a fine returner with a big wingspan, was far from reaching it.

"This guy is going to win Wimbledon, multiple times," I said to my neighbors in the press seats in the distant days when sportswriters bantered instead of tweeted.

That was out of character for me. By nature, I am much more an observer than a soothsayer, and that prediction could have seemed like a reach. Pete Sampras was still in his twenties and still an irresistible force at the All England Club. Pat Rafter, the net-rushing Australian, was in his prime and brilliant on grass. But if you watch enough elite tennis, you see the patterns and skills that are required to thrive and that can transpose a young player's game to grander occasions in your mind's eye. Federer's attacking style, all-court tools, deceptive power, and silken footwork transposed beautifully.

His game, replete with tactical options, had matured, which was marvelous for the Swiss and rotten timing for the Americans.

"We ran into a guy who dominated," McEnroe told us after the 3–2 defeat. "Federer is a great player, and he sort of came into his own this week, and we just couldn't get on top of him. But the guy's got a lot of game. He's certainly playing at a level within the top 10, if not higher."

Federer had just won his first ATP title the previous week in Milan on a similar indoor surface: a watershed moment for a young player. But winning in Basel for his country was an emotional breakthrough of a higher order.

He would go on to win ten singles titles in that same arena at the Swiss Indoors. But at that early stage, he was still unsure of his capacities, still uncertain whether he could shoulder the load of leading his team, particularly when he was on edgy terms with his captain, Jakob Hlasek. A former Swiss star, Hlasek had muscled his way into the role the previous year by displacing a man Federer and his teammates appreciated: Claudio Mezzadri.

"That match against the USA was an important moment in my career," Federer told me much later. "It helped me believe."

It was foreshadowing indeed. There were Federer tears in victory and Federer news conferences in three languages. His hair was long; his complexion still that of an adolescent; his face, with its strong features and prominent nose, more fit for a pugilist. As he arrived for an interview, he walked with a panther's rhythmic grace but looked self-conscious, as if he was still adjusting to being closely observed.

The American team also included two future stars—Roddick and James Blake—who would suffer at Federer's deft hands repeatedly in the years ahead.

Roddick, quick-witted and huge-hitting, made his Davis Cup debut in what is known as a "dead rubber," defeating George Bastl in the final singles match on Sunday after Federer already had clinched the Swiss team's victory by defeating Jan-Michael Gambill.

Roddick and Federer had their first conversation much later that night when the two teams crossed paths in a bar in Basel.

"You're curious to see how someone like that is going to handle the situation in his hometown with Davis Cup, and I watched him just dismantle our entire team," Roddick told me recently. "I think it had progressed past the point of 'Is this guy going to be really good?' I think that was a given. The question was: Is he going to be Roger or, I don't mean this in a disrespectful way, is he going to be a Richard Gasquet, who is someone who is really, really good? I'd say someone is probably lying to you if they say they can tell the difference at that stage because the difference is probably inward. I think it was a given Roger was going to be a top 10 guy, a top 5 guy, but there's a big difference between that and someone who is number one, wins a Slam, and is a relevant result maker for ten years. You definitely didn't think in the context of twenty years back then."

Blake, who had left Harvard after his sophomore year to play full-time on the tour, was a practice partner in Basel, which meant that he spent some time with Michel Kratochvil, the Swiss team's practice partner.

"We were so proud of Andy," Blake told me. "We were like, 'This kid is so good, you guys just wait, he's going to be amazing, he's going to be on our team for so long,' and I was talking to Kratochvil, and he was like, 'Um, maybe look at our guy. He's going to be pretty special, too.'"

Blake had a long look at Federer. His first realization was that once Federer took control of a point, it was a huge challenge to get the ball to his less dangerous backhand side. He was that quick.

"He moves so well that if he gets a forehand, you can't get him to hit another backhand," Blake said. "Once he hits a forehand, he is completely controlling the point. That was just incredible."

There was a second realization.

"We all watched him, and it looked like he was not sweating," Blake said. "It looked like his heart rate was thirty. It didn't look like anything was affecting him, like it was clear there were not going to be

AY/FIONA

BOSTON   TML C

DUBLIN   TML 2
    SAVR

I132 Y 17JUL 1745

21 1650 **20A** XXX

0

t's break point and he is nervous because
something."

ow far Federer had come in the behavior
t-chucking, self-berating episodes of his

what he was ready for and he could handle
," Blake said. "And then after the match to
that he really cared so much about play-
own, that was really cool."

ded home themselves, and I filed my col-
Herald Tribune. I didn't quite have the
ple Wimbledon champion in print.

Federer is a special player—precociously poised and complete, innately capable of raising his level under pressure and doing just about everything fluidly.

He can serve big. He can play scrambling defense and come up with a lob winner. He can play classic chip-and-charge tennis and smack away a stiff-wristed volley winner. He can dictate play with his forehand and hit his one-handed backhand with pace or a wicked, dipping slice that leaves less agile opponents huffing, puffing and digging for the quick-spinning ball.

For all that, it is impossible to know whether he will use his manifold gifts to become a consistent world-beater. Money, adulation and injuries can dull the biggest appetites and sharpest strokes, but there can be no doubt after the last two weeks that the Swiss have another potential champion in their midst. And unlike Martina Hingis, Federer actually spends more time in Switzerland than in Florida.

Federer's tennis was indeed made in Switzerland. He was born at the University Hospital of Basel on August 8, 1981, the youngest of two children of Lynette and Robert Federer, both enthusiastic athletes of modest height who began playing tennis relatively late in their lives.

Roger learned the game in Basel and later honed his game in other Swiss cities, but in a diverse country with four official languages, he also had plenty of foreign influences in his early life.

Lynette was from South Africa and had met Robert at age eighteen near Johannesburg, when both were working for the Swiss chemical company Ciba-Geigy. Though Lynette's first language was Afrikaans, she attended an English-language school at her father's insistence. After she and Robert moved to Switzerland and later started their family, she spoke English at first to Roger and his older sister, Diana.

"That was for the first few years," Lynette Federer told me in an interview early in her son's career. "Then I did switch to Swiss German. Living in Switzerland for such a long time, I picked it up very easily. Roger and I still speak English a great deal. We do speak a bit of a mix, depending on what we discuss."

Lynette and Robert chose "Roger" because they liked the euphony with Federer (he has no middle name). They also liked that it was easy to pronounce in English even though their son spent plenty of time in his early years reminding people that his given name was not pronounced "Roe-ZHAY" ("Roger" in French).

Federer's first significant tennis coach was Adolf Kacovsky, a Czech immigrant to Switzerland. Federer's most influential early tennis coach was Peter Carter, an Australian. Through the years Federer would also be coached by Swedes, Americans, and a cosmopolitan Croatian and former war refugee: Ivan Ljubičić.

But Federer, however global in his tastes and appeal, still considers himself a product of the Swiss Tennis Federation. That is not the case for Switzerland's other best recent players: Hingis, who preceded him at the top by reaching No. 1 in the women's game in singles and doubles; and Stan Wawrinka, who followed him and became the second-best Swiss men's player in history.

"Only Roger made it big through the federation," said Marc Rosset, the 1992 Olympic singles champion from Switzerland.

Basel is where Federer's story began: a cosmopolitan city on the Rhine River with Germany and France for next-door neighbors.

"I used to go shopping outside the country when Roger was a baby," Lynette Federer said.

For Rosset, Switzerland got lucky. "Five kilometers in either direction, and he could be German or worse yet French," said Rosset, who is from Geneva in Francophone Switzerland. "Can you imagine if he would have been French? That would have been too much to bear."

Federer was a very active child—"close to hyperactive," Federer says—and grew up in a middle-class home on a quiet street in the Basel suburb of Münchenstein, where he showed far more passion for sports than for academics.

"I didn't like school much," he said. "My parents had to push me very hard."

There is a picture of him holding a table tennis paddle even though he is barely tall enough to see over the edge of the table. His first tennis racket was made of wood, which likely makes him the last great player to have started with one. He began at age three and soon began hitting against walls, garage doors, cabinets, and closets.

"Boom, boom, boom," said Robert Federer in the 2008 documentary *Roger Federer: Spirit of a Champion*, describing the noise. "He would play for hours against the walls."

"Boom" seemed a particularly appropriate sound effect at that stage. The 1980s were the time of the tennis craze in Germany, which was sparked by Boris "Boom-Boom" Becker winning Wimbledon in 1985 at age seventeen and by Steffi Graf completing the first Golden Slam in 1988 by winning all four Grand Slam titles and the Olympics.

Just across the border in German-speaking Basel, young Federer and his friends took note, and Becker was Federer's first tennis idol.

Federer began playing on red clay at his parents' club, which was owned by their employer, Ciba, and located in the suburb of Allschwil. But at that early stage tennis was just one of Federer's many activities. He also played badminton, squash, basketball, and soccer.

"I'm not a big fan of running, of swimming, of riding the bike," he once said. "There's got to be a ball somewhere."

That did not hold universally true throughout his childhood.

Federer was drawn to Alpine skiing—he is Swiss, after all—but had to curtail his time on the slopes to reduce the risk of injury (more on that later). He also enjoyed hiking with his family.

But Federer's choice of a sporting career ultimately came down to a team sport with a ball and an individual sport with a ball. At age twelve, he chose tennis over soccer. That was late to commit compared with some tennis prodigies. Agassi, Sampras, the Williams sisters, and Maria Sharapova were all-in long before that stage. But it was not late compared to some of Federer's longtime rivals. Nadal, who grew up on the Spanish island of Mallorca, also chose tennis over soccer at age twelve. Wawrinka, considered a late bloomer in tennis, played the game just once a week until age eleven.

There has been an understandable backlash in recent years against early specialization, which can lead to overuse injuries and burnout. Federer has become one of the exemplars of the movement to encourage children to explore a range of sports for their long-term benefit. His longevity, durability, and enduring enthusiasm are rightly reassuring. Nadal's should be the same, even though he has had to deal with many more injuries, but the reality is that when it comes to producing great champions, both the extreme and the more balanced approaches can be effective.

The Williams sisters, after all, have endured beyond all expectations despite the master tennis plan crafted by their father, Richard: a cradle-to-greatness plan that, it should be noted, did allow them ample time to explore interests outside of sports.

Agassi, who had a tennis ball suspended over his crib to give him a head start on hand-eye coordination, also played and excelled deep into his thirties (despite chronic back pain) and was one of those who demonstrated to Federer that a long, fulfilling career at the top was possible.

As a father of three children and a longtime youth soccer coach, I know which approach I find healthier, but there is no sense in denying that a youngster with tunnel vision—or with tunnel-visioned parents—can grow up to be a Grand Slam champion. Early specialization just seems much closer to child labor than child's play. You wince to think of the attrition rate, of all the talented juniors who were programmed for tennis success based on the Agassi or Williams model and lost the taste for it, if they truly ever possessed it at all.

Federer, whose parents generally let him find his own path, has cited three reasons why he chose tennis over soccer.

"I had more talent in my hands than I did in my feet," he told me.

But he also sensed something in himself that many great athletes who chose tennis have sensed: a desire for control, for agency. "I wanted to have the victory or defeat in my own hands without having to depend on others," Federer explained.

But watching him through the years, it was clear that he was not a typical tennis individualist. He is gregarious and an extrovert, gaining energy from social settings rather being drained by them. He has often shown interest in the collective good, serving long stints on the ATP Player Council and launching a charitable foundation focused on early childhood education. When Federer and his agent, Tony Godsick, decided to leverage Federer's considerable political capital to create a new tennis competition in 2017, they started a team event—the Laver Cup—designed to honor the undervalued tennis greats of the past.

While it is hard to imagine a tennis star like Jimmy Connors finding fulfillment as a team-sport athlete, it is not difficult to imagine Federer doing so. But there was also something in him that wanted full ownership, a strain of perfectionism that made him realize he would have struggled to accept others' shortcomings when he already had so much difficulty accepting his own.

Nonetheless, if he had had a soccer coach with a different mentality at the local club Concordia Basel, he might have waited even longer to make a choice.

Federer was a fast and gifted striker, but he was juggling soccer training with tennis training. According to Federer, his soccer coach told him that it would not be fair to his teammates to play him in the games on the weekends if he could not attend all the practices during the week.

For Federer, it was the games that mattered, but he could not give up tennis. Soccer would have to go.

"No regrets," he said—understandably—many years later.

At age eight, Federer had begun playing tennis at Old Boys Basel, a leading yet modestly appointed club in a leafy section of the city within biking distance of the Federers' home. Lynette was already playing on the women's team at Old Boys and decided to move her children there because of the quality of the junior program, run by Madeleine Barlocher, a Swiss who had been good enough to play in the Wimbledon girls' tournament in 1959.

There were close to 130 juniors in the program.

"You could tell he had some talent, but I had a good group with a lot of young boys with talent, so I would never have guessed he would become what he would become," Barlocher told me. "But even at age eight, Roger was joking around with his friends that he was going to be number one."

Federer took group lessons at first but soon began taking private lessons with Adolf Kacovsky, a veteran coach nicknamed "Seppli," who quickly realized that the youngster was extraordinary.

"One day Seppli came to me and said that he had never had a junior who could apply his advice so quickly," Barlocher said. "Some students try it and it takes maybe a week or two, but Roger could just do it."

It was an observation many coaches would make of Federer through the decades. "Roger is really good at mimicking things, amazing actually," said Sven Groeneveld, the Dutchman who would work with him at the Swiss National Tennis Center.

But Federer sometimes had to learn the hard way, too. In one of his early junior matches at age ten, he was beaten 6–0, 6–0 by Reto Schmidli, a Swiss who was three years his elder and thus much more powerful. Schmidli never became a touring pro but was still giving interviews about that match and its unlikely score line nearly thirty years later.

But Federer's junior results rapidly improved as he worked closely at Old Boys with Peter Carter, a young Australian with a bowl cut, strong work ethic, and calm demeanor who was still juggling coaching duties with tournaments on the satellite tour.

"They got along very well, right from the beginning," Barlocher said.

It certainly did not hurt that Federer already spoke English. Carter's Swiss German would remain very much a work in progress, even though he eventually married a woman from Basel.

"Peter was a nice person, and he gave Roger a big boost," Barlocher said. "He really made Roger feel like a special player, and he helped him not only with his technique but with how to play matches."

Carter had a classic attacking game that included acrobatic volleys, fluid footwork, and a one-handed backhand.

If that sounds familiar, it should.

"A lot of what you see in Federer is very similar to what Peter was," said Darren Cahill, the leading coach and ESPN analyst who was one of Carter's closest friends. "But Federer has that explosive power and the ability to generate enormous amounts of spin, and Roger was a better mover. Peter was very good at everything. He was a good mover but not a great mover. He was good from both sides, but not great from both sides. He had a beautiful serve, but it wasn't big enough to win two or three free points every game."

David Macpherson, an Australian from Tasmania, played on the satellite circuit at the same time as Carter. Macpherson went on to coach the Bryan brothers and John Isner. "It was so amazing to me how much Roger's strokes looked like Peter's," Macpherson told me. "Maybe Roger doesn't even completely realize. Peter used to hit the forehand like Roger does. The ball's already left the strings, and he's still looking at the contact point. I've got a nice vivid memory of Peter doing that, and it was unique, and then all of a sudden we've got the best player in the world doing the same thing, like a golfer holding the finish. It's no coincidence, that's for sure. The serve is very similar, too, just the relaxed, fluid start to the serve. Peter had the prettiest game you've ever seen but, unlike Roger, wasn't able to get much pop on the ball."

Carter, nicknamed "Carts," was once one of Australia's leading juniors. He was coached by Peter Smith, who also worked with Cahill and many other future stars in Adelaide. Smith's pupils included Mark Woodforde and John Fitzgerald, both excellent singles players who made their biggest marks in doubles. Fitzgerald won seven Grand Slam titles; Woodforde won twelve, all but one of those with partner Todd Woodbridge.

But Smith's most prominent pupil turned out to be Lleyton Hewitt, a fleet and feisty baseliner who wore his cap backward and peaked early. Hewitt reached No. 1 in the world at age twenty and won the only two Grand Slam singles titles of his career—at the United States Open and Wimbledon—before he turned twenty-two.

Carter was raised in Nuriootpa, a country town in the booming wine-producing region of the Barossa Valley, home to Penfolds, Peter Lehmann, and other vineyards with global reach. Carter traveled frequently into Adelaide for tennis training and tournaments, but to cut down on the long commute he sometimes stayed overnight with Cahill and his family. Cahill's father, John, was a leading Australian rules football coach.

"Carts was a real stylish type of player, but just a real honest, simple, down-to-earth, hardworking bloke," Cahill said. "My dad, obviously, being a football coach and having some success, is pretty good at reading people. And he would always say, 'Mate, you end up turning out how you pick your friends and who you hang out with, and you've got a good one in Peter Carter. He is a good man, so you hang out with him as much as you want.'"

Carter eventually became a boarder with the Smith family at age fifteen before he and Cahill left Adelaide for the Australian capital of Canberra to live at the Australian Institute of Sport, a government-funded training center that has helped produce many leading Australian athletes.

"Carts was just a really good kid," Smith said. "We've had quite a few people live with us over the years, and usually the relationship sours a bit over a period of time because you learn a lot about people when they live with you. But for all the time Carts was with us, I don't think we had one cross word to say in that entire time."

Carter was a big enough talent to upset future Wimbledon champion Pat Cash on grass in the quarterfinals of the Australian Open boys' event, when Cash was the world's top-ranked junior. But Carter's most impressive performance came at age seventeen when, still a high schooler, he received a wild card into the 1982 South Australian Open and faced second seed John Alexander of Australia in the first round.

Alexander, an imposing figure and future politician, was ranked 34th in the world and had just won the tournament in Sydney. Carter was playing in his first ATP Tour–level event, but he surprised Alexander 7–5, 6–7, 7–6 with a polished display, looking out of his depth only when it came time for the postmatch interview, during which he kept the answers as brief as possible, eager to exit the court and the spotlight.

"Carts was a fairly shy, quiet sort of a kid," Smith said. "But if you knew him well, he had a strong voice, and he knew he could play."

Despite his early promise, Carter never broke through on tour, reaching a peak of 173 in singles and 117 in doubles. His lack of raw power was part of the explanation, but so were injuries. Smith said that Carter, who was slight of build, had stress fractures in his right arm, his playing arm, that long went undiagnosed. He also had back problems and more unusual issues, including a punctured eardrum suffered in a water-skiing accident that required surgery and later led to an infection.

He repeatedly missed significant playing time but continued to chase a career on tour. It is an against-the-odds struggle for most but can be even tougher psychologically on Australians, who must compete so far from home with the majority of the tour based in Europe and North America.

According to Cahill, who did manage to reach the elite and the semifinals of the US Open, Carter suffered from the lack of a major tennis weapon and from a procrastination streak that made it hard for him to be decisive.

"It was one of his downfalls," Cahill said. "We used to give him a hard time. It could be buying a car or an investment property or coaching opportunity or whatever. But that procrastinating did come onto the tennis court with him, and it held him back a little bit because he couldn't just make a decision and go with it. He was always thinking about what was the right thing to do, and that could transfer through to his shot selection as well."

Financial pressures were also a factor. Carter, like many lower-level professionals, decided to complement his meager tournament income by playing in European interclub competitions. Though he could have ended up at any number of clubs in any number of countries, life's roulette wheel landed him in Basel.

Teaching tennis in Switzerland paid relatively well, and Carter used his earnings to fund his travels. But it eventually became clear to him that his future was in full-time coaching and in Basel.

"I think finally the math hit home a bit," said Smith, who kept in regular contact. "But the good thing for all of us I guess is the coaching led to better things. And I guess we'll never know but there may not have been the Roger that we know, we may not have even heard of him, if it hadn't been for Carts."

Rosset suspects that Federer would have found another path to greatness. "I don't know," he told me. "I think when Roger was born there were quite a few gods hanging around the cradle who were sending out some good vibrations."

Smith, a schoolteacher as well as a tennis teacher, had a knack for producing excellent tennis coaches. Cahill went on to coach three No. 1s: Hewitt, Agassi, and Simona Halep. Roger Rasheed, another Smith pupil, later coached Hewitt and leading French players Gaël Monfils and Jo-Wilfried Tsonga. Fitzgerald went on to become Australia's Davis Cup captain.

Carter tragically did not get to explore his coaching gift for long. He died far too young in 2002 in a freak Jeep accident on his honeymoon in South Africa: a destination he had picked at the Federer family's urging. He was just thirty-seven.

But Carter left a precious legacy to the sport by molding Federer's tennis and psyche with care. When asked who has had the biggest influence on his game, Federer rarely mentions Kacovsky. He always mentions Carter.

"Peter brought me a lot, first of all, on the human side and of course with my tennis," Federer said. "People talk a lot about my technique. If it's so good, it's had a lot to do with Peter, although naturally others played a part, too."

There is nothing unorthodox about Federer's technique: His forehand grip is close to the classic handshake grip, known as an eastern grip. Many of his rivals use a semiwestern, with the palm of their hand much closer to the bottom of the grip, which can make it easier to produce topspin but more challenging to handle lower-bouncing balls and to switch grips in order to volley effectively.

As for the backhand, the two-hander already was the most popular choice for leading juniors internationally in the 1980s and 1990s, providing more punch from the baseline and increased stability and authority on returns. But it was no coincidence that Federer chose the one-hander.

His early professional role models—Becker, Edberg, and Sampras—all had one-handed backhands that they could rip or chip convincingly. Both Kacovsky and Carter were proponents of the stroke, and many of the older boys training at the club used it, too. So did Lynette Federer.

Among the one-hander's advantages is that it can make it easier to transition to net and hit a one-handed backhand volley. With Carter committed to playing classic attacking tennis, it is no surprise he wanted the same option for his star pupil, even if Federer needed time to become comfortable at net.

"I got that beautiful one-handed backhand from Peter," Federer said, managing to sound cocky and deferential in the same phrase.

But the shot was more irresistible to the eye than to the opposition in those formative years. Cahill visited Carter in Basel in 1995 when Federer was thirteen. He came out to the Old Boys club to watch them hit together. It was Cahill's first look at Federer in person.

"Back then Roger had a little bit of that John Travolta strut that he had in *Saturday Night Fever* in the way he walked around the court," Cahill said. "Roger actually doesn't have it as much now, but it was kind of a 'Hey man, I own this court, and this is where I want to be' kind of look. You smiled as you watched him. I don't know if he knew me, but he knew I was a friend of Peter's, and so Roger was showing off a little bit to me as well. He was zipping the forehand all over the place and sliding like a guy who obviously had grown up on clay and looked incredibly comfortable."

Cahill said Carter kept looking over at him expectantly after high-velocity rallies.

"I was impressed, for sure, but I wasn't that impressed with Roger's backhand," Cahill said. "Because he took a big step. We teach as coaches basically little steps, get yourself in a position so you can get that ball right into the sweet spot where you can hit it. Everything starts on the back foot. You transfer the weight through to your front foot, and you drive with as much power as possible. It's like throwing a punch. The bigger the step with a punch, the less powerful that punch is going to be. And Roger took this big step into the backhand. He had a nice slice back then, but every time he tried to come over it, he would shank half of the backhands he hit."

After the coaching session, Carter asked his friend for feedback.

"I said, 'Well, firstly, I reckon I got a kid in Adelaide who is a bit better than this guy, and that's Lleyton Hewitt,'" Cahill recalled.

Cahill told Carter that Federer's forehand and movement were impressive. "But I said, 'Mate, that backhand, you're going to have to do some work,'" Cahill said. "'Because that looks like it might be something that could hold him back.'"

Cahill told me he would have viewed that practice session through a different lens later in his coaching career.

"It's where coaches go wrong a lot, because we spend too much time looking for the areas that are bad or average," Cahill said. "And then we concentrate on those areas too much instead of working on strengths. So that was kind of me as an early coach. I was looking for areas that were going to hold him back, and I ignored a little bit the stuff that was going to make him great."

The greatness would be in the forehand, footwork, serve, timing, court sense, planning, and appetite for more. But there was another undeniable weakness in those early years: Federer's mentality.

"I was a terrible loser, I really was," Federer said.

Barlocher remembers him losing in an interclub match at Old Boys and sitting under the umpire's chair and crying long after everyone else had left the court.

"Usually when we have these team matches, then we also eat something together, and we were already eating sandwiches, and he wouldn't come," Barlocher said. "So half an hour later I had to go get him underneath that umpire chair, and he was still there crying."

The tears were Federer's reflexive response to defeat. He knocked over a few chessboards after losing to his father, too. His competitiveness was extreme, and his sensitivity left him vulnerable to his and others' expectations.

But though Federer's self-control was lacking, he was hardly alone.

"He wasn't really unusual at that age," Barlocher said. "One child was crying. Another one was shouting. But Roger did have a problem realizing that other people could play good tennis, too. We had to remind him of that."

He did know how to have fun, however. Before one interclub match, Barlocher remembers searching for him when it was his turn to play and not being able to find him. It turned out that he was hiding in a tree that he had climbed.

"He loved these kinds of jokes," she said.

Lynette and Robert were not helicopter parents, and Robert traveled often for work with Ciba.

"Of course they came around when he had a match, but for the trainings, they were still working, so they would never show up or tell me what he has to do or how to play or how to practice," Barlocher said. "I had parents that thought their children were much better than they really were. You get those kind of people, but I didn't have any trouble with the Federers."

Though the Federers were not the types to deprive their son of dinner when he lost a match, they did feel compelled to act when he lost his cool.

Federer tells the story of when his father had heard and seen enough during one of their hitting sessions. Robert expressed his disapproval, placed a Swiss 5-franc coin on the bench, and told Roger that he could find his own way home.

One of Federer's best explanations for what he was experiencing at that stage came in an interview with the *Times* of London.

"I knew what I could do, and failure made me mad," Federer said of his youth. "I had two voices inside me, the devil and the angel, I suppose, and one self couldn't believe how stupid the other one could be. 'How could you miss that?' one voice would say. Then I would just explode. My dad used to be so embarrassed at tournaments that he would shout at me from the side of the court, telling me to be quiet, and then on the way home in the car he might drive for an hour and a half and not say a word."

At least Federer got a ride home. But for those who saw him implode, Federer's combustibility was the biggest reason he was not a can't-miss prospect. He clearly had the talent and seemed to have the ambition, but the mental game is often what makes the difference between mediocre and good, between good and great.

"I don't think Roger was an automatic," said Peter Smith, who sometimes discussed Federer's behavior with Carter. "Roger was temperamental, and he needed someone with a firm hand, and most people would have thought that wasn't Peter Carter, but I think it was the Peter Carter that I grew to know. I think he learned to coach in a very disciplined way."

Changing Federer's on-court behavior turned out to be a long-term project rather than a quick fix, but fixing it would be crucial to Federer's development and to the on-court persona that would prove so appealing.

Carter was a coach and confidant with a good sense of humor. He was also a bridge to tennis history with his Australian accent. He spoke with Federer about the Australian greats of the past: men like Rod Laver, Ken Rosewall, and John Newcombe. Meanwhile, Federer had the chance each year to get a close-up look at the best players of the present.

A men's tournament, the Swiss Indoors, was held in Basel each autumn. Roger Brennwald, the tournament's founder and director, used big appearance fees and an advantageous spot on the calendar to attract fields that were remarkably robust for an event that was then part of the lowest category of the ATP Tour.

From 1987 to 1997, the roll call of winners included Grand Slam champions like Yannick Noah, Edberg, Courier, John McEnroe, Becker, Michael Stich, and Sampras.

Lynette, deeply involved in the Basel tennis community, volunteered in the tournament's accreditation department. Her son soaked it all up, working as a ball boy for the first time in 1992, the same year in which he was presented with an award during the tournament for being a promising sportsman in the region. Jimmy Connors and Iranian player Mansour Bahrami exchanged a few shots with the young, bristle-haired Federer and posed for a photograph with him at net.

In 1993, Federer was sixth in the line of ball persons to shake hands with Stich and receive a medal after Stich beat Edberg in the final. In 1994, Federer was back in line to greet champion Wayne Ferreira, who as a South African had Federer's support.

Federer was observing the life he would eventually lead, and the champions whose paths he crossed briefly in Basel as a boy later reentered his orbit in a much more profound way: Edberg as his coach; Ferreira as his friend and occasional doubles partner.

For Federer to grow up in the city that staged the most significant Swiss tournament was one more ingredient in his success. Geography may not quite be destiny, but it can drop a few hints, and through the years, Federer would pay back the tournament where he got his first exposure to the professional game.

Just four years after his final stint as a ball boy, Federer played in the Swiss Indoors himself, losing 6–3, 6–2 to Andre Agassi in the first round as a wild card. Two years after that, Federer reached the final, losing in five sets to Thomas Enqvist.

Lifted by Federer's popularity, the Swiss Indoors moved up in category on tour in 2009, doubling its prize money.

"We had organized our tournament for thirty-five or thirty-six years and more or less knew what to expect," said Brennwald in an interview with the Swiss journalists Simon Graf and Marco Keller. "Then suddenly something happened that changed everything we thought we knew from experience. The interest in Federer was simply overwhelming."

Brennwald, once the most influential figure in Swiss tennis, had to adjust to being usurped by Federer. It has not always been seamless. In 2012, a dispute about Federer's future appearance fees became public. Brennwald suggested that Federer and his agent, Tony Godsick, were being greedy even though Federer had played for several years for a fee of $500,000, which was below his usual rate. Federer was taken aback by the criticism but chose not to push the point or skip the tournament. He played the Swiss Indoors in 2013 without receiving any appearance fee at all: a deft move in what amounted to a public relations joust.

"It is my hometown, so it just kind of hurts me," he said to me shortly after the 2012 tournament. "It was just strange to see the dynamics it took because the goal was to sign a long-term deal before the tournament exactly for those reasons: so we would not talk about stupid stuff like that. And then the next thing you know it dominates the press during a tournament that everybody works hard at to try to make it successful and fun for everybody."

Federer, no fan of controversy, was in the midst of a rare one, but he chose to let the kerfuffle pass.

"What's important is down the road you maybe set the record straight," he said. "I think the people trust me that what I do is the right thing, and that when I do take decisions, I thoroughly think them through and that the last thing I want is this kind of thing. There have been some bumpy moments along the way, but those are part of you. They make you grow and make you stronger, and honestly, you can't fight it all anyway."

Federer signed a new agreement with Brennwald in 2014 and has remained committed to his roots and the tournament. From 2006 to 2019, he won the title ten times and lost in the final three times. Though small in scale, it is an event that has brought him a great deal of delight and meaning. He has been as loyal to the Swiss Indoors as he has been to Wimbledon.

His appearance in Basel has been his most visible annual connection with Switzerland, all the more so since he stopped playing Davis Cup in 2015. But Switzerland remains a place where discretion is valued and where Federer fever has been a decidedly low-grade affliction compared to what it might have been if Federer had been, say, Brazilian or American.

A recent petition to rename the St. Jakobshalle arena in his honor failed to attract enough signatures for it to be considered formally by municipal authorities. That could certainly change, but for now signs of his achievements and stature are hard to come by in Basel. The only court that bears his name in his home city is at the Old Boys club.

It is easy to visit. You can stroll unimpeded through the club gate; there is no security guard. On your left is a large chalkboard on which the day's reservations for each of the nine courts are handwritten. Only two of the courts are named for players: Roger Federer Center Court, which is adjacent to Marco Chiudinelli Court.

To an outsider, it seems particularly Swiss that Chiudinelli, who never broke into the top 50 and had a career tour singles record of 52-98, should get essentially equal billing here with Federer, one of the greatest players of all time.

But this was Chiudinelli's home city and club as well: the place where he started his climb, even if it stopped well short of the snow-capped heights that Federer reached.

"Besides Roger, Marco was the only one from our club who played internationally on the ATP Tour, so why not name a court for him, too?" Barlocher said.

Chiudinelli is only about a month younger than Federer. Both grew up in Münchenstein, and though Chiudinelli first played in another Basel club, he soon moved to Old Boys.

"Those two were always together; they played together and did everything together," Barlocher said. "Marco was Roger's big junior friend."

Both loved soccer and tennis, and they played against each other in soccer first. But they eventually faced each other in a tennis tournament when they were eight years old. It was aptly called the Bambino Cup, and Federer described the match in a background interview for the documentary film *Strokes of Genius*.

"It was up to nine games," Federer said. "And I would go up 3–0, and he would start crying, like, 'Oh, I'm playing so bad,' and I'd be like, 'Agh, it's okay, Marco, you'll come back, you watch. You're a good player.' Then he'd be in the lead 5–3, and I'd be crying, and he'd be like, 'Don't worry, you'll be fine. I'm just playing so good, the last few games, you know.' And then I'd be up 7–5 and he'd start crying again. We were comforting each other while the match was going on."

Chiudinelli went on to win, which did not turn out to be a sign of things to come. But he and Federer played plenty of tennis, cards, and pranks together in their youth, and despite Federer's rise to great wealth and fame, they have remained good friends.

"When we both made it on tour, it was like a fairy-tale story," Federer said.

They returned to Old Boys to face each other in a charity exhibition in 2005. Federer remains a member even if he has not played at the club since then, and he has contributed to a fund to build a permanent indoor facility at the club.

On the day of my visit, two young men from Basel—Jonas Stein and Silvio Esposito—were training in the sunshine on Court No. 1: the same court where Federer cried under the umpire's chair.

"You kind of expect more, right?" Stein said after he and Esposito had finished. "This is the most Federer place to be in Basel, but not everyone knows that this is his club here. Everyone knows he's from

Basel, but the club isn't that prominent. I think the management ten years ago here missed the opportunity to promote it. They could have made a tourist attraction out of it, and every Chinese person could have come by and taken a picture in front of it. But I guess that's not how we are in Switzerland."

The only photo of Federer on the grounds is a mural inside the modest clubhouse restaurant that shows him leaping high to hit a serve at Wimbledon with the words "Home of a Legend" written underneath the Tennis Old Boys Club Basel logo. For Switzerland, that is about as ostentatious as it gets.

Esposito has some Federer memorabilia of his own. He said Federer's parents gave one of their son's early rackets to Esposito's grandfather, and Silvio later received it as a gift.

"I started playing with it, but I didn't get that energy," Esposito said with a laugh.

It takes rather more to convincingly channel Federer. It requires exceptional talent and drive, a solid support structure, plenty of luck, and sound decisions.

One of Federer's smartest was leaving Basel, at least for a little while.

CHAPTER THREE

ECUBLENS, Switzerland

"*Arrête*, Roger. *Arrête!*"

The voice belonged to Christophe Freyss, a French coach at the Swiss national training center, and he was telling Roger Federer to stop hitting a tennis ball against an equipment container.

"It was making so much noise that it was hard for everyone to concentrate," Freyss said.

Federer, an impulsive teenager with energy to burn, would heed the request but not for long.

"He stopped for maybe five minutes, but then he got his racket and started again," Freyss said. "And I said, 'Roger, stop now!'"

Federer, then fourteen, was in his first year as a boarding student in Ecublens, a suburb of Lausanne on Lake Geneva. He was still in his home country but very much an outsider as a youngster from German-speaking Basel. The primary language in Lausanne is French, and Federer arrived in August 1995 with a problem.

"He could maybe say *bonjour*, *merci*, and *au revoir*, but other than that his French was nonexistent," said Yves Allegro, a fellow student and future Davis Cup teammate.

Federer was living with a local French-speaking family, the Christinets, and attending a local secondary school, the Collège de la Planta, where the language of instruction was French. It was a steep learning curve on an emotional roller coaster.

As one of the younger students training at the national center, Federer practiced in the afternoon while the older students had a training session from 10:00 a.m. to noon. But on this occasion Federer finished school around 11:00 a.m., which meant that he arrived at the tennis center while the older group was still playing.

"Roger was a bundle of nervous energy, and knowing that, I told him to go do his homework," Freyss said. "But that was a lost cause, and voilà, that's when he starts hitting the ball."

After warning him twice, Freyss hatched a plan with his players. If Federer came back a third time, they would teach him a lesson.

"I was nearly certain he was coming back," Freyss said. "He really could not sit still."

Sure enough, Federer returned, and this time Freyss and the players descended on him and carried him upstairs to the locker room, giving every indication that they were going to put him under the shower fully clothed.

"We wanted him to believe even though we knew we weren't going to do it," Freyss said. "I even turned the shower on. It stopped there because that's where it was always going to stop. But I'm sure it's a moment that stuck with him."

Federer definitely remembers. It was part of a turbulent, trying time.

"I was the Swiss German kid that everyone was making fun of," he said. "I couldn't wait for the weekend when I could take the train back home to Basel."

But the move to Ecublens was also a choice that he had made freely, leaving behind not only his parents and sister but coach Peter Carter, the Old Boys club, and his comfort zone in an attempt to take his tennis to another level.

"We wanted it to be Roger's decision," Lynette Federer told me. "We were very much in the supporting role, and I think that was one of the reasons he stayed with it and persevered: because it was his decision."

Talk to Federer now, and he has no regrets. Quite the contrary. He sees the two years he spent in Ecublens as vital to his maturation and critical to his later success.

"I'd have to say now that those were probably the two most influential years I had in my life," he said.

When he gives advice to young players, he often recommends that they take the opportunity to leave home for a stretch to build their sense of self-reliance, a key trait in a brutally competitive individual sport where trusting yourself can be every bit as important as trusting your forehand.

Federer did not face the obstacles encountered by many great modern tennis players. He did not have to cross an ocean at age six like Maria Sharapova in pursuit of her father's long-shot goal in the academies of Florida. Federer did not have to find a way to train and improve through a war, like Novak Djokovic.

But viewed through the prism of Federer's comfortable middle-class existence, Ecublens was adversity: self-imposed and minor, but still adversity. It was a big part of his growth, both as a person and as a player.

"At home I was the favorite, the champion, but in Ecublens I was around other champions, and I had a hard time coping with that," he said. "My host family was very nice, but it wasn't my family. After three months, I really hesitated about staying. But I did the right thing by pushing through it."

More than twenty years later, the training center in Ecublens and the small club at which it was based are long gone. The eight courts, tiny gym, and adjacent running track have been redeveloped and replaced with apartment buildings.

It is not the only touchstone in Federer's career to have disappeared. The Ciba club, where he started to play in Basel, was demolished and replaced with senior housing and a public park. Federer often sends video messages, and he sent one to the Ciba club members in 2012 for their farewell party shortly before the demolition, sharing his recollections of matches and barbecues past.

Ecublens stirs more mixed emotions for him, but there is still a sense of loss when he thinks about what is no longer there.

"It's bittersweet for me," Federer said. "It was such an important place in my life."

Others who trained there feel a similar sense of nostalgia.

"Nothing left; it breaks my heart," said Manuela Maleeva, the women's star who reached No. 3 in the world rankings.

"Always tough," Allegro said. "I go by there maybe once a year, and I try to pass by because it's part of our youth. It's still painful to see that the tennis center is not there anymore."

But even without a brick-and-mortar trace, a rich legacy remains for Federer from the Ecublens years.

There is his fluent, often flowing French. Mastering the language has broadened his perspective and social circle and increased his appeal both internationally and in his polyglot home nation, where he can bridge the cultural divide.

"I think for the French-speaking Swiss it's really important and appreciated, because a lot of German-speaking Swiss don't speak good French," Swiss author Margaret Oertig-Davidson told me. "People in the German-speaking part of the country generally learn much better English than French, so it's very valued that Roger can speak French that doesn't hurt your ears."

The Ecublens legacy is also there in the friendships Federer formed with players like Allegro, Lorenzo Manta, Ivo Heuberger, Alexandre Strambini, and Severin Lüthi, a long-underestimated figure who would become part of Federer's inner circle and his coaching staff.

In Ecublens, Federer also developed his affinity for indoor tennis and fast playing conditions. The four indoor courts in Ecublens, which were the primary courts during the cooler months, were low bouncing and quick. "Lightning quick," Federer said.

The Ecublens legacy is also there in Federer's deep connection with a much older man who never played tennis competitively but who played a major role in Federer's long-running success, perhaps the decisive role.

Pierre Paganini is Federer's fitness coach. He met Federer in Ecublens in 1995 and joined his personal staff in 2000, which makes him by far Federer's longest-serving team member.

He helped Federer remain free of major injuries until late in his career and helped him sustain quickness and agility with an innovative program. But Paganini, a former decathlete who likes to do drills with his athletes and run when they run, has been much more than a clever and hyper-fit taskmaster. He has been Federer's sounding board, occasional spiritual guide, and final word on scheduling: a subtle yet convincing lobbyist for the benefits of dedication and moderation.

From the start, Paganini had a long-term view of Federer's health and path and had the confidence and credibility to help him implement it.

The central message was that tough, consistent work was necessary but so were rest and escape if Federer wanted to last in a sport whose repetitive rhythms and patterns can wear down a player's joie de vivre in a hurry. Fresh legs were vital, but no more vital than feeling fresh in the head.

"The most important guy in Federer's career is Paganini," said Günter Bresnik, a veteran Austrian coach.

That is a bold statement, and Bresnik is not alone in putting so much emphasis on Paganini.

"For me, it's Mirka number one and Pierre number two," said Allegro. "If there's a big decision, Pierre would always be involved, because I think Pierre has always had the big picture in mind. Roger trusts him like crazy."

Stan Wawrinka, the other Swiss star who has trained with Paganini for more than a decade, says he owes more to Paganini for his own career than anyone.

But Federer is not quite prepared to take that leap publicly. He has had too many influences and has too much diplomacy to elevate one key contributor above the rest. What is clear is that Paganini is on his short list, his very short list.

"A big part of the reason that I'm here where I am today is definitely because of Pierre," Federer told me late in his career.

It has been a close working relationship that has grown richer rather than stale.

"He's made fitness workouts so enjoyable, if they ever can be,"

Federer said. "I just follow his beat. Whatever he tells me, I'll do it because I trust him. People ask me, do you still do your physical tests and stuff? I don't have to do any tests because I work with Pierre and he knows and sees if I'm moving well or not, if I'm slow or fast, all these things. He's had a huge part of this success, and I'm happy I called him way back when."

Bresnik, one of tennis's deeper thinkers, has been coaching for more than thirty years. He has known Federer since the mid-1990s, and he met Paganini several years earlier when Bresnik was coaching Swiss player Jakob Hlasek.

Bresnik trusts Paganini enough that when his star student, Dominic Thiem, was still in his midteens, Bresnik invited Paganini to Vienna to offer his opinion on whether Thiem had the requisite speed and physical ability to succeed on tour.

The answer was yes, and Thiem grew up to become a Grand Slam champion with multiple victories over Federer as well as the other members of the Big Three: Nadal and Novak Djokovic.

Bresnik admires Paganini's commitment and intuition, and in a Darwinian world where players, including Federer, often get edgy about sharing their methods, Bresnik values his discretion, too.

"Paganini is a smart guy who has no desire to showcase himself, to put himself in the limelight," Bresnik said. "He will always be in the background. Federer is the guy who is out in front, but the brain behind the scenes over probably the last twenty years is Paganini."

Federer appreciates discretion—he is half-Swiss, after all—and Lüthi has a similarly self-effacing approach.

"He's also very modest, low-key, never wants to be in front," Bresnik said.

Paganini, with his polished bald head and wire-rimmed glasses, has an academic air, and he does not come from a family of athletes. Both his parents were musicians and educators and, despite the surname, no relation to the Italian virtuoso Niccolò Paganini, known as the "Devil's Violinist" in the nineteenth century because, people said, he surely must have sold his soul to be able to play so sublimely.

Pierre, born in Zurich in 1957, also played the violin in his youth but was drawn to sports from an early age.

"He and I often joked that he was the not-so-intelligent one in the family because he got involved in sports," said Magdalena Maleeva, another of his longtime clients.

Paganini played soccer and competed in track and field, gravitating to the decathlon, the ten-event endurance test that is the most labor-intensive of the sport's disciplines.

But Paganini sensed quite early that he wanted, above all, to play a role behind the scenes.

Watching the 1966 World Cup of soccer, he was less interested in what the players were doing on the field than in what they might be doing off the field.

"I was eight, and I wanted to know what was going on in the locker room, what the manager was saying to them when we couldn't see them on television," he said in an interview with the Swiss newspaper *24 Heures* in 2011. "Even at that age, I was fascinated by the hidden side of it all. In my job, we work often in the shadows, and I really love that."

He had long wanted to be a fitness trainer but, uncertain of the job market, he hedged his bets: getting a business degree and even taking some classes at a Swiss hotel school. He eventually listened to his inner voice, which was closer to an inner shout, and earned a coaching degree from the Swiss Federal Institute of Sport Magglingen, the only Swiss university focused exclusively on the study of sports. He was taught by Jean-Pierre Egger, a former Swiss shot-putter who coached Werner Günthör and Valerie Adams to world championships and Olympic medals in the shot put but also worked in other sports, including wrestling, sailing, and Alpine skiing. In 2020, Egger was voted the best Swiss coach of the previous seventy years at the national sports awards. Egger taught Paganini the importance of matching the fitness work to the specific needs of a sport.

Paganini graduated in 1985, and his plan was to train soccer players, but he was instead offered work at the tennis center in Ecublens despite having no tennis background. He was part-time at first, unable to support himself without taking a second job as a teacher at a nearby school, but he eventually became an integral part of Swiss tennis.

Two of the first players to benefit were Marc Rosset and Manuela Maleeva.

Rosset was a lanky six-foot-seven power player with an ironic wit and a complex, sometimes contrarian personality. He was the best men's player in Switzerland when Federer emerged, but movement was not Rosset's innate strength.

"The first time I saw Pierre, he had come from the decathlon and knew nothing about tennis, and then he started to play the game to understand the details," Rosset said.

Bresnik said Paganini felt guilty about those early years.

"He told me once that he should be fined for what he did to guys twenty-five years ago when he had no idea about the needs of tennis," Bresnik said with a chuckle. "He said with what he knows today, he's embarrassed. But he can never stop learning, and he adjusts to players."

Consider the contrast between Federer and Wawrinka. Federer is of medium build, light on his feet, quick off the mark, and inclined to attack. Wawrinka is barrel-chested and nicknamed "the Diesel" because it takes him time to reach full speed. He possesses bullish power and endurance.

"To work with Federer and Wawrinka at the same time, who are completely different kinds of tennis players and athletes and are physically completely different, shows that Pierre understands the physical needs of a tennis player like nobody else," Bresnik said. "Whatever the guy says, I would take for guaranteed. Other trainers are still tapping around in the dark."

Despite the guilt, Paganini's lack of tennis knowledge in the early years was also an advantage. Like a traveler arriving in a new country, he was attuned to the incongruities in a way a longtime resident could not have been. He applied his track-and-field background to his work in tennis but ultimately did not lean heavily on it. Following up on his work with Egger, he focused on creating tennis-specific fitness drills. That meant doing a lot of work on the court instead of in the gym and meant that heavy weights and distance running were of little use.

"You have to be strong, fast, coordinated, and have endurance in tennis and you have to do drills for that," Paganini told me. "But you also should never forget you have to use this on a tennis court, not on the road or in the pool. So you always have to create a link between the speed and the athletic way it's used on the court. Nine times out of ten on the court, the speed is in the first three steps and then you're playing the tennis ball. So you have to train to be particularly strong in the first three steps."

With Grand Slam singles matches routinely stretching past three hours, you also have to train to be strong in the first three steps in the fifth set, not just the first set.

What is required is what Paganini calls "explosive endurance." That might read like an oxymoron at first. It is not, but it is definitely a challenge for a fitness trainer.

"In track and field, the guy who has endurance does the marathon and the guy who is explosive does the sprints," Paganini said. "But in tennis you have to have endurance and explosion, and these are two antagonistic qualities. That's why tennis is fascinating, and also why I think it is much tougher than people usually imagine."

In tennis, longer hauls are sometimes required. There is the pursuit of a drop shot, the retreat from the net to retrieve a lob, the corner-to-corner journey along the baseline to hit a passing shot at full stretch.

But it bears remembering that the length of the baseline in singles is only 27 feet, about 8 meters, and that the distance between the net and baseline is just 39 feet, about 12 meters. Even if a player starts running very deep behind the baseline, they are not going to cover more than 60 feet, or 16 meters, in a straight line.

"In tennis, you don't do one sprint like a guy who does the hundred meters," Paganini said. "You go for three hours or more, stop and go. That's very tough but you have twenty-five seconds or ninety seconds to recover. In all the work you do, you have to stay aware of that. We don't ask you to beat a speed record. We ask you to be fast repeatedly for a long time. That's what makes tennis interesting. You don't run forty kilometers when a match lasts five hours. You run perhaps six kilometers at most."

Short bursts of movement are the staple of the game, so Paganini logically decided to focus on training the burst, often while asking Federer and his athletes to perform a complex task requiring hand-eye coordination.

They would do intense tennis footwork while catching and throwing a medicine ball, then grab a racket and do the same footwork sequence while hitting a tennis ball.

Paganini would place numbered sticks in the four corners of a square and place a player in the middle with a medicine ball. Paganini would call out a number, and the player would have to sprint to the corresponding stick and hold the medicine ball aloft.

It was about mental agility as well as physical agility, and he would also test players' ability to maintain the integrity of their technique under duress by having them do quick and intense sessions of cardio work on court, sometimes on a stationary bike, and then immediately transition to all-out, two-on-one hitting drills.

He also favored interval training—a classic method for runners—but in shorter intervals than usual: thirty seconds or less of intense effort followed by thirty seconds or less of rest. The goal was to increase a player's quickness, not just their VO_2 max, or maximum rate of oxygen consumption, the traditional measure of endurance.

"For me, Pierre's the best fitness trainer in the world for tennis, because he's the first one who really did drills and exercises that were completely specific, down to the detailed footwork," Rosset said. "Even me at my height, I moved relatively well with no big injuries, and if you look with Paganini and all the players he trained, they really had relatively few injuries."

That is quite a feat considering that training athletes to be explosive carries a greater injury risk. But Paganini navigated the shoals remarkably well, even if Federer and Wawrinka both ended up having knee surgeries in their thirties.

Rosset, long retired but still in touch with the game as a commentator, often sees today's fitness trainers working with players at tournaments or in videos posted to social media.

"*Putain*," Rosset said, deploying a French expletive. "It's practically the same thing I did with Pierre twenty-five years ago. Of course, there are things that have improved, but lots of fitness trainers have been influenced by Pierre. His results speak for themselves. If tomorrow, somebody asked me to coach them, I would say, okay, do four months with Paganini, and then we'll talk."

Manuela Maleeva is the oldest of three sisters from Bulgaria who were taught the game by their mother, Yulia Berberian. All three siblings—Manuela, Katerina, and Magdalena—became top 10 players despite limited means and the significant obstacles they faced as Bulgaria transitioned from communism.

The Maleevas, hardly household names outside Bulgaria, were one of tennis's most remarkable success stories, anticipating the Williams sisters.

"You know, if we were American we would be huge," Yulia once, quite rightly, said to the *New Yorker*.

One of Yulia's daughters did become Swiss. Manuela married Swiss tennis coach François Fragnière in 1987 when she was just twenty years old and began training in Ecublens, where she and Paganini crossed paths.

"I'm actually the first professional tennis player that he started following for work," Manuela told me. "He pushed me very, very far but without me hating him for this. That is a difference with a lot of the other coaches."

Manuela and Fragnière, who was her coach as well as her husband, had determined that she needed to improve her physical conditioning to improve her chances against the likes of Steffi Graf, Martina Navratilova, and Gabriela Sabatini in the late 1980s.

One of Paganini's first priorities was to assess her level of fitness.

"Probably the only time I thought that I would smack him on the head was the first time we went for a run," Manuela said with a laugh. "He wanted to see what kind of shape I am in and to know where to start with me. So we went out and started jogging around the club."

Maleeva and Paganini soon headed for the nearby forest to run on the trails. Maleeva was hurting, close to vomiting after the endurance work they already had done. But Paganini was in a much more upbeat mood: running backward slightly ahead of her so he could speak to her face-to-face.

"I thought, 'No way, my tongue is dragging on the ground and the guy is running backwards and talking to me,'" Maleeva said. "This I will never forget."

But she did forgive and would work with Paganini for seven more years until she retired in 1994, just after winning her final WTA tournament in Osaka, Japan. She was still in the top 10.

"I improved so much with him," she said. "The difference is I used to cramp a lot when I would go to three sets, and this was something that was always worrying me. Once I started practicing with Pierre, little by little I got in such shape that I felt that I could stay on the court for five hours, and I was not afraid."

By the time Manuela retired, Paganini was already working in Ecublens with Magdalena, nicknamed Maggie, who is eight years younger than Manuela.

"The important point with Pierre was always the quality of the footwork," Magdalena said. "You had to be very precise with where you put your feet."

Manuela Maleeva, who had turned pro at fifteen, retired just before her twenty-seventh birthday. Magdalena, who turned pro at fourteen, retired at thirty. Both sisters felt they had had long careers and were weary of traveling, but both remember Paganini telling them that the tour players in the next generations would play much longer.

"Nobody at that time was saying that," Magdalena said. "Most people were saying the opposite, that tennis is very tough, very tough on the body; that the players don't have an off-season and they will be more and more injured."

But Paganini believed tennis-specific training, smarter scheduling, improved recovery methods, and better, bigger support teams would lengthen careers. His vision has proved correct, looking at the number of players on both the men's and the women's tours deep into their thirties still playing and even improving their rankings.

"Pierre didn't believe in the stereotype that once you're over thirty, your athletic ability declines," Magdalena said. "He really believed if you work the right way you can play much longer."

Magdalena, who began working with Paganini at age seventeen, would stay with him until she retired in 2005, which is the way relationships often work with Paganini. He inspires damp-eyed loyalty, even if some other fitness trainers feel he has limitations.

Paul Dorochenko, the Frenchman who later worked with Federer and other juniors for the Swiss Tennis Federation, hesitates when asked to describe Paganini and ultimately settles on the word "unusual."

That is in part because Paganini never felt compelled to get a driver's license, relying instead on trains, taxis, car services, and his second wife, Isabelle, who does drive.

"I would say Pierre has very set ideas, he's not easily flexible, and it's not easy to speak with him," Dorochenko said. "He's very introverted, but he's someone who I think works very well in terms of developing strength and coordination. When you do a session with Pierre, he holds your attention and doesn't let it go. He knows how to do that very well. He's more someone who works in the field than a conceptual thinker."

But Paganini's ability to hold his players' attention and keep their loyalty is linked to his creativity and his talent for crafting highly individualized programs: hardly the sign of someone who lacks flexibility.

Federer, who craves variety in many aspects of his life, would surely not have settled for twenty-plus years of routine.

Though Paganini shuns the limelight and is shy by nature, Federer and others have found him easy to communicate with.

"You can imagine the impact that he's had on my career as a fitness coach but also a little bit as a mentor, to be honest, because we do a lot of talking besides working," Federer once said. "You always count an extra forty-five minutes where we just talk about everything."

To interview Paganini, which is a rare feat, is to get deep quickly. He is intense, speaks in long paragraphs, and gravitates to metaphor. We talked at length in 2012 and in 2017, both times in French: the same language he uses when he trains Federer.

I asked Paganini if conventional wisdom was correct and if Federer's bone structure and natural grace made it easier for him to stay healthy.

"I hear that all the time," Paganini answered. "To have a potential is one thing but to express it for seventy matches a year is something else. That is Roger's goal: to be consistent in each match he plays and each training session he does. I think we underestimate all the work Roger does, and it's a beautiful problem he has. We underestimate it, because when we see Roger play, we see the artist who expresses himself. We forget almost that he has to work to get there, like watching a ballet dancer. You see the beauty, but you forget the work behind it. You have to work very, very hard to be that beautiful a dancer."

It takes time to acquire the muscles and muscle memory, but it also requires time to acquire the polish and poise. While Federer has spent decades in the global spotlight making tennis look easy, he spent his early years reminding a much more limited audience of just how frustrating the game could be.

Consider Magdalena Maleeva's first impression in Ecublens, when Federer was fourteen.

"At the time he was a little guy, and the impression was that he gets very mad," she said. "He was throwing his racket quite a lot."

Maleeva, six years older and already entrenched in the WTA Top 10, won a set against Federer at one stage in practice.

"He came across a bit like a spoiled boy, because he would just be so angry so often," she said. "But I guess he wasn't feeling great about things."

Freyss, the director of the Ecublens center and the national technical director of men's tennis in Switzerland, could understand Federer's distress. He had been at an academy himself in his youth: boarding at the French Tennis Federation's training center in Nice in the 1970s along with Yannick Noah, the future French Open champion.

Freyss went on to play on tour and break into the top 100. He did not go deep at the majors, but he did defeat four former or future major champions: Arthur Ashe, Andres Gomez, Manuel Orantes, and Ivan Lendl.

Freyss later became a no-nonsense coach, one with an acute awareness of how much sacrifice and self-discipline were required to succeed. Like many, Freyss could see Federer's potential: the fast-twitch forehand, the quickness, the innate sense of anticipation. Normally reluctant to talk up a young prospect, Freyss told Georges Deniau, his mentor and predecessor at Ecublens, that Federer was a special talent. He also told his friend Régis Brunet, a tennis agent with IMG, to keep an eye on Federer, and Brunet eventually signed him to his first management contract.

But Federer's struggle within was also glaringly apparent.

"Emotionally, Roger was on a razor's edge," Freyss said. "First of all, to be a teenager is not easy, and when Roger left his family for Ecublens that was already a tough transition. Having to learn French and go to school in French was also complicated, and then there was the tennis.

"It was a very, very difficult time on many levels for him. I didn't cut him any slack. It's not in my nature. I treated him like all the others. I didn't look to see who was number one in their age-group or whatever. I didn't give these young players any room to breathe. I wanted to get to something that resembled a good tennis player, and I put my heart and soul into it."

Freyss did not work with Federer day to day. Alexis Bernard, a young Swiss who coached the younger players, had that role. But Freyss supervised the process and often worked directly with Federer on his technique, tactics, and attitude.

"I don't know if I did things the right way with him," Freyss said. "But I know I was clear that we were not going to deviate much from an acceptable way of behaving. We clashed, but he accepted it and swallowed it. He had to swallow a lot, and it surely was not something he enjoyed."

Federer, for all his natural sociability and empathy, was not easy to communicate with at that stage, and Freyss was in no mood to hold back.

"He had very little capacity for confrontation," Freyss said. "He needed to play, and that was how he expressed himself. I'd say to him, 'Roger, listen, look me in the eye. I need to understand if you understand what I'm trying to say to you. You are walking around. You are hitting the ball. You are bouncing the ball between your legs. Stop it.'

"Even that part was not easy for him. It was like he was overflowing with emotion and energy. He had to play, had to move. Above all, he's a player."

Paganini remembers Federer releasing pent-up energy at the start of practice sessions by shouting repeatedly.

"He was the youngest, and I remember watching him and thinking how spontaneous he was," Paganini told me. "In just a few minutes he could go from laughter to tears."

Federer was not the only future No. 1 who was struggling to manage his emotions and expectations. In September 1996, Federer played for Switzerland at age fifteen in the World Youth Cup in Zurich. Switzerland's opening-day opponent was Australia, which meant that Federer faced Lleyton Hewitt.

Darren Cahill was the captain for Australia; Peter Lundgren, a former top 25 player from Sweden, was the captain for Switzerland; and Peter Carter also was in attendance.

"Roger and Lleyton had never played before, but both guys knew each other's reputation, so there was a lot of pride on the line," Cahill recalled. "It was on from the very first game. They were trying to get into each other's heads: the gamesmanship, the bouncing of the rackets, the swearing, the arguing with the umpires, just everything. I didn't know what had hit me because it was the first time that I'd ever really watched Lleyton play a match, certainly the first time I sat on the court with him. And this was like McEnroe and Connors, two fifteen-year-olds going at it.

"Both guys ended the match basically in tears. I think Lleyton threw his racket into the back fence at the end."

Federer won in a third-set tiebreaker and remembers Hewitt punching his strings so hard that his hand started to bleed. Cahill walked off court a bit dazed and upset: not because of Hewitt's loss but because of the young combatants' comportment. Cahill walked up to Carter, who was smiling, not because of Federer's victory but because of the future.

"Mate, these two guys are going to be great," Carter said.

Cahill's response: "These boys both need a good kick up the backside. You can't behave like that."

Carter kept smiling. "Well, all right, you be the one to give it to them," he said. "But they're going to be special players."

It was the first of many meetings between Federer and Hewitt. None would be as fiery in the future, but their rivalry was launched, and it would prove pivotal for both in their long careers.

In Zurich, Cahill was more impressed with Federer's game than he had been in Basel. Federer's backhand had improved, even if the big step was still there.

"He had stopped shanking and missing it nearly as much," Cahill said. "I just thought this guy had unbelievable hand-eye coordination. He made it work, and it's turned into the shot it has today. He has improved his little steps, but every now and then he'll just take a massive big step with the right leg to his backhand side and smack a backhand down the line, and you go, 'Where does that power even come from? And how do you even make that?'"

Back in Ecublens, Federer's technique was a regular source of discussion among the coaching staff.

He had arrived with strong fundamentals, courtesy of Kacovsky and Carter, but there were sources of concern. The forehand was not one of them.

"The way he prepared the shot and dropped his racket head and accelerated with his wrist, that was magical," Freyss said. "That's him. He was born with that. All we did was focus a bit on the finish. We wanted him to keep the contact with the ball on the strings a bit longer."

On the backhand, Federer still needed to master the topspin drive.

"That was the big construction site for us," Freyss said.

Freyss sometimes fed him the ball by hand, stopping when the result was satisfactory and asking him to memorize the path he had just made through the air with his racket.

In Freyss's view, Federer was not stable enough through the stroke, bringing his left shoulder forward too quickly as he finished the shot. "Keeping the shoulders in line longer is really important for consistency, so we worked a lot on that," Freyss said. "There were some sessions where the balls were going a bit all over the place."

The other focus on the backhand drive was getting him to make contact farther in front. But the one-handed backhand slice, another Federer strength during his career, also needed fine-tuning.

"His head went a bit backwards as he sliced," Freyss said. "So we needed to change that."

On the serve, the priorities were getting more shoulder rotation and making the toss more consistent, emphasizing the importance of disguise by hitting different serves from the same toss location.

"Sampras could hit all the different serves with one toss, so then as you go about your career you also try to incorporate some of his things while making it your own," Federer told me. "I was always playing around with my toss, seeing if I could hit the other way with a kicker toss or hit a kicker with a flat toss. And I actually realized I can do it all."

Paganini, who was also in charge of coordinating players' schooling and housing, was the one who matched Federer with a local family, the Christinets: parents Cornélia and Jean-François and their three children. Federer spent his weekdays at the Christinets' before traveling by train back to Basel to spend the weekends and holidays with his parents and sister.

"If he won, it was because of corn flakes," said Cornélia Christinet in an interview with the Swiss magazine *L'Illustré* in 1999. "He ate entire bowls and all day long. He didn't like meat or fish. He only liked pasta."

Nor did Federer like to rise and shine. "Sometimes he slept through the alarm, and I had to go get him," Cornélia Christinet said. "But he was up in five minutes. I never saw anyone that quick."

Schoolwork was the major challenge, but he learned French quickly, in part because he plunged in and was not overly concerned about making grammatical mistakes when he spoke. He was not alone in the struggle. Sven Swinnen, another German-speaking Swiss, was also a novice at French and shared the same classes and tutors with Federer. Swinnen, who was a very promising player as well, routinely defeated Federer in their early teens and later received a tennis scholarship to the University of Oregon.

"At the beginning it was tough for both of us in Ecublens," Swinnen told me. "With the language, we were both outsiders. It was like, 'What are you doing here?' But it also helped us. We got to learn a language, which was obviously positive and certainly helped Roger down the road to be the kind of person who speaks many languages. It contributed to his popularity."

Philippe Vacheron, a teacher who tutored them both at the Collège de la Planta, remembers Federer well and even practiced with him once.

"He had this wild side that I would call instinctive," Vacheron said in an interview with the Swiss newspaper *Le Temps*. "All of a sudden he would shout out in class, 'Monsieur Vacheron! What does that mean?' because he did not understand something. Certain teachers would not have stood for it, but I found it endearing. Sven, his Swiss German comrade, was more by the book, while Roger said what he thought. He had strong reactions but was never disrespectful. He could also be extremely sensitive when he had some real difficulty.

It was the frustration of not being able to understand combined with the difficulty of being far from home. Even if he had not become a champion, I would remember him. But of all the players that came through our school, he was the only one where I said to myself that he had to go all the way. After that, it could be make or break. But he had a talent."

There was no doubt, and in his second year in Ecublens, his tournament results began to improve as he found his equilibrium and confidence and integrated new elements into his game.

Allegro remembers all the players in the program filling out a form in which they were supposed to state their tennis goals. Allegro wrote down that he hoped to break into the top 100 in the world. "Roger was the only one of us to write that he wanted to become number one," Allegro said. "I'm not sure he believed it 100 percent, but he put it out there."

So much can go awry in a young player's attempt to climb to the top of the tennis heap. But Freyss, who had played against and coached so much talent, liked Federer's chances of success when Federer left Ecublens for good at age sixteen. For Freyss, Federer's game was exceptionally promising because it was so sound and free-flowing.

"I could see no barriers when he played," Freyss said. "He could be two meters behind the baseline. He could be inside the court. There were no brakes to keep him from shifting into higher gears. For me, the sky was the limit."

But Freyss, after watching Federer closely for two years, did see one obstacle.

"The only thing that could stop him was his head, his nerves," Freyss said. "And at the end I said to him, and I remember this very well, 'Roger, listen, you can hold up the biggest trophies in the world, but try not to be your own enemy, because then it will be more complicated.'"

CHAPTER FOUR

BIEL/BIENNE, Switzerland

Over lunch in the Alps, Roger Federer dropped his own name.

He was suggesting a list of places I should visit that have mattered most to him in Switzerland: Basel, of course; Ecublens; Zurich and its lake; Lenzerheide and its spectacular mountains and ski runs, where he and his wife, Mirka, built one version of their dream house in Valbella.

Then he mentioned Biel.

"I have a street named there for me now," he said matter-of-factly. "Roger Federer Street."

Upon further inspection after a scenic train ride to Biel, it was not quite the street most of us would have envisioned. It is a straight stretch of tarmac off a highway in a modern zone that bears much more resemblance to a late twentieth-century business park than anyone's vision of cobblestoned Helvetic charm.

Still, it is tough to get on the map in Switzerland: The authorities discourage naming any public place or thoroughfare after living Swiss. Federer, the most famous living Swiss, was deemed worthy of an exception in 2016 even though he was hardly lobbying. The uninspiring setting is definitely appropriate in one sense. The road runs next to the national training center known as the House of Tennis, where Federer spent several formative years after it opened.

"My adult life basically began in Biel," Federer said.

His street actually has two names, which are both on the signs: Roger-Federer Allee and Allée Roger-Federer. That is because Biel is bilingual: a bridge between the German-speaking and the French-speaking regions of Switzerland.

Biel is its German name, Bienne its French name, and Biel/Bienne became its official name in 2005. The city's website reflects the duality—www.biel-bienne.ch—and Federer reflects it, too, referring to the city as "Biel" when speaking German or English and "Bienne" when speaking French.

Bilingualism is one of the reasons the Swiss Tennis Federation chose to relocate its national training center to Biel/Bienne from Ecublens in September 1997.

"A very politically correct location," said Sven Groeneveld, the Dutchman hired to oversee the coaching program in 1997.

Unlike French-speaking Ecublens, Biel/Bienne allowed school-age prospects to be educated primarily in the language of their choice.

Federer, fluent in French after all his toil, was ready for whatever his new training base could throw at him, but he no longer needed to be concerned about homework. At age sixteen, after completing the compulsory number of years of instruction, he decided to stop his formal schooling and focus entirely on becoming a tennis professional.

It was a bold move in a conservative, education-oriented society like Switzerland, one where sports, even in the late 1990s, were rarely viewed as a serious career pathway.

"The mentalities have evolved, but Switzerland is not what I would call a true country of sport," said Marc Rosset, the best Swiss men's tennis player when Federer emerged. "It's not the USA. It's not Australia. It's not Italy. Sometimes the path is really tough for athletes in Switzerland."

Rosset remembers winning the Swiss junior championship at eighteen and finding out that the Swiss Tennis Federation did not intend to send him to the 1988 Orange Bowl, one of the world's premier junior competitions, in Florida.

"I said, 'Why not? Normally each guy who becomes Swiss champion at eighteen plays in the Orange Bowl,'" Rosset recalled. "But they said, 'You are not good enough; there's no point.'"

Rosset, wounded but determined, told the federation to enter him anyway because his family would pay for the trip. He made the most of the journey by becoming the first Swiss to win the Orange Bowl boys' eighteen-and-under title. (Federer would be the next.)

"That gives you a sense of how it too often works in Switzerland," Rosset said. "It's not nice what they did to me, but in another way, it also helped me mentally. It was, 'Okay, you don't want me. I'll show you.'"

Federer faced skepticism almost immediately after his decision to leave school. When he visited his regular dentist in Basel, the conversation began, as many conversations with dentists do, in the middle of a cleaning.

"He's in my mouth, and he's like, 'So what are you doing now?'" Federer remembered. "And I'm like, 'I'm playing tennis.' And he goes, 'Okay, what else?' And I'm like, 'That's it.' And he looked at me like, 'That's it?! Just tennis?!'"

Federer changed dentists.

"I never went back, because I just felt like he's not really understanding what I'm trying to do here," Federer told me. "I'm chasing a dream. I'm trying to aim for the stars, and he's trying to pull me back. And you know what? I don't want to be surrounded by people like this."

It was an approach that Federer carried forward with him as he built his own professional and private circles. He valued positive energy and people who empowered him. That approach, of course, runs the risk of attracting sycophants who will tell you what you want to hear rather than what you need to hear, particularly if they are on your payroll. Professional tennis is awash in entourages, sometimes euphemized as "teams." There is no shortage of sycophants in a microcosm where many of the best people are understandably resistant to providing the kind of 24/7 support and ten months of travel that the stars often require as they search for ranking points and an edge. The coaches and physiotherapists want, after all, some life of their own, too.

Federer, according to those who have worked closely with him through the years, would come to value internal debate and constructive criticism. But at sixteen he was craving backslaps and faith.

"I wanted to hear, 'That's awesome, Roger, that's a great plan,'" he said. "I think people can really help young people by telling them, 'All right, go for it! I'll support you whatever path you choose.' But of course you also have to be realistic. When you're no good, you have to realize it's okay to stop, because some people go too far, and then they get blindsided by it."

The most influential voices of reason at this stage belonged to his parents. Yes, they recognized that their son had considerable potential and had shown commitment to his game in Ecublens. But the Federers were also well aware by this stage that many promising juniors never reach the highest level. They wanted a backup plan.

Robert Federer told Roger that they would help finance his career but that if he was not in the top 100 by age twenty, he would have to return to school and pursue a degree.

"I had no problem with that, no problem making that promise," Roger told me. "I liked my chances, but I was also realistic."

The stopwatch started in earnest in Biel/Bienne, little more than an hour's drive south of Basel. As so often on and off the court, Federer's timing was excellent.

The new "House of Tennis" belonged entirely to the Swiss Tennis Federation, unlike the center in Ecublens, where the federation had only been renting facilities and paying for court time in a private club. The move also allowed the federation to centralize, basing its coaching and administrative departments in the same place for the first time.

Swiss tennis was at a new high-water mark. A few months earlier, Martina Hingis had cemented her status as one of the game's great prodigies by reaching the top of the women's singles ranking at age sixteen, making her the youngest No. 1 in history. The 1997 season would be her finest as she won the Australian Open, Wimbledon, and the US Open, and she might have completed the Grand Slam if she had not been upset in the final of the French Open by another youngster: Iva Majoli of Croatia.

Hingis briefly reigned supreme before the Williams sisters took the game to a new level. She was an all-surface threat with polished technique and exquisite court sense who had more guile and self-belief than power. She was nicknamed predictably "the Swiss Miss" and, in journalistic circles, "Chucky," after the grinning slasher-film child doll who terrorizes his elders.

The Hingis smile was indeed cryptic: a sign of fulfillment or menace, depending on the circumstances. But her tennis talents were unmistakable, and like Federer, she had international roots. Her parents were from the Slovakian part of the former Czechoslovakia. Hingis, coached astutely by her mother, Melanie Molitor, emerged from an independent structure, like most of Switzerland's best players before Federer, but she proved it was possible to both dream big at a young age and make it big at a young age.

Federer, a sensitive sixteen-year-old brimming with ambition and nervous energy who once had been a ball boy for Hingis in Basel, took note and inspiration, even if the men's and women's tours were and remain very different realms.

"It's like you're a mountain climber and you're looking at this wall, thinking, 'Can this be done?'" said Heinz Günthardt, a former Wimbledon junior champion and the best Swiss men's player of the 1980s. "And suddenly somebody climbs it. So, are you more inclined to go and try to climb that wall? Yes, you are, absolutely. And even if you fail the second time, the third time, the fourth time, you know there's a way up because somebody has done it. Martina definitely opened up a pathway, mentally if nothing else. It certainly would have helped me in my time to have someone who showed me that it was possible."

Günthardt, a singles quarterfinalist at Wimbledon and the US Open but probably best known for coaching Steffi Graf, emerged as a leading player when it was considered a success for a Swiss to compete in a Grand Slam tournament, much less win one.

Federer would hold himself to a higher standard and, in the wake of Hingis, be held to a higher standard.

"I did feel it was possible to aim for the stars, and thankfully there was Martina and others who did great in sports in this country," Federer told me. "I think we can do a little bit better job to believe, like, in America that anything is possible and, you know, dream big. I feel sometimes we don't believe because we are kept in education, a job and safety and security. I feel that can sometimes block us from going all out and saying, 'Let's take a chance, let's go for it, let's follow our dreams for two or three years and see what happens.' But half and half doesn't cut it. If a guy in China or Russia or America or Argentina or wherever trains five hours and you can only train two, how is that going to work? It's not realistic then to become the greatest ever or the best. It's not by dreaming that you're going to be top 250 or that you're ever going to win Wimbledon."

Federer was fortunate that the well-equipped center in Biel opened just in time to play a major role in his development, providing him with a solid training base and brain trust at a very reasonable price, with the federation covering much of the cost.

His parents were spending about 30,000 Swiss francs ($21,000) a year on his tennis at this stage: significant but hardly a fortune compared to some other tennis families in countries that lacked federation or government support.

In Biel, Federer was surrounded by fresh and deeply familiar influences. One of the new voices was Groeneveld, a tall and handsome young Dutchman who already had coached Mary Pierce to the 1995 Australian Open title and Michael Stich to the 1996 French Open final. He would go on to coach Ana Ivanovic and Maria Sharapova to Grand Slam titles as well.

Groeneveld had been hired by Stephane Oberer, Rosset's longtime coach who was also the Swiss Davis Cup captain and was overseeing the new training center.

One of their first recruits in Biel was Peter Lundgren, a good-natured Swede who had once been ranked as high as 25 and as a coach had managed to survive the experience of guiding Chile's truculent and ultratalented Marcelo Ríos into the top 10.

Lundgren told me he took the post in part because of what he had heard about Federer.

"My agent called me and said there's a job in Switzerland and this young, promising player, Roger Federer, that they want you to take care of," Lundgren said. "It was a tough decision. My family was living in Sweden. We had just had a daughter, so I moved down there by myself first, and when I came down it was tough."

No lodging had been organized for him at first. Groeneveld was a friend, but the language barrier was often a challenge otherwise.

"When I got there, I had this funny feeling in my stomach," Lundgren said. "I will never forget that. Just a very awkward feeling. It was, 'Have I done the right thing?'"

Swiss Tennis soon hired another Peter: Peter Carter, lured from Basel and the Old Boys club by the prospect of reuniting with Federer. Carter, who had made a good life for himself in Basel, had not made the decision easily.

"Peter was really quite hesitant to leave, but I told him about my vision and my plan of him taking the lead in Roger's development," Groeneveld said.

While Lundgren focused at first on older players like Ivo Heuberger who were already entering the professional tour, Carter focused on younger players who were in transition. They included Federer, Allegro, Michael Lammer, and Marco Chiudinelli, Federer's boyhood accomplice in tennis and mischief from Basel, who rejoined him in Biel.

It was a promising group, and though only Federer would become a global phenomenon, the others would experience at least some success as professionals, as would Michel Kratochvil, who also was training in Biel.

They would all push each other at a formative stage, which is often the key to the fortress in tennis. Players cannot become great in isolation. From the Bollettieri Academy in Bradenton, Florida, in the 1980s to the clay courts of Barcelona in the 1990s to the clubs of Moscow in the 2000s, the ability to bring talented youngsters together to test their limits and psyches on a daily basis has proved to be a successful formula.

Lundgren knew this as well as anyone. He was part of the Swedish wave that came after Björn Borg, the long-haired, poker-faced teen idol turned serial champion. Borg was the epitome of Nordic cool despite having a fiery temperament in his youth (sound familiar?) and became one of the Open era's first superstars.

Lundgren, born in 1965, is from the same Swedish generation as Mats Wilander and Stefan Edberg, who both reached No. 1, along with Anders Järryd, Joakim Nyström, Mikael Pernfors, Henrik Sundström, Jonas Svensson, and Kent Carlsson, who all were in the top 10 (Järryd was also No. 1 in doubles).

At the 1987 French Open, with Borg already retired, there were eighteen Swedish men in the 128-player main singles draw—astounding for a country with a population of just nine million with long, dark winters and a shortage of indoor courts.

"I was ranked 25 in the world at my best and was only ranked 7 in Sweden," said Lundgren. "That tells you a lot."

The Swiss who gathered in Biel would not rival the collective achievements of the Swedes, but they, too, found strength in numbers.

"This peer spirit we had was very important," Michael Lammer told me. "We had great coaches. It was a relaxed atmosphere, but it was important for us younger players that every day you saw the top players in Switzerland practicing from different generations. I think this was a big motivation."

Federer did not live with a host family this time. At sixteen, with his parents' benediction and financial backing, he moved into a small apartment near the House of Tennis that had been rented by his friend Allegro, who was nearly three years older.

The apartment was on Henri-Dunant-Strasse (Rue Henri-Dunant on the bilingual Biel/Bienne map). Dunant was the Swiss cofounder of the International Red Cross, and he shared the first Nobel Peace Prize in 1901.

Federer was still a few years from becoming a philanthropist and far from imagining at that stage that he would have a street named for him in the same neighborhood.

For the moment, he was struggling just to make it to practice on time and keep his room clean.

"Not his strength," said Allegro with a laugh. "There was a lot of PlayStation."

Allegro, who later became a coach of juniors at the federation, spoke with me over lunch at the training center in 2019, more than twenty years after he and Federer arrived.

He pointed out the picture window of the Topspin Restaurant to one of the six outdoor clay courts.

"Roger and I were the first ones to practice here," Allegro said. "It was the fifteenth of August 1997, and we were with Peter Lundgren on that court."

Much has changed at the House of Tennis in Biel since Federer's time. There is now a four-story office building and an academy dormitory on-site with balconies that look out on the red clay just below. There is an arena, completed in 2017, with room for twenty-five hundred spectators, that can be used for Swiss Davis Cup and King Cup matches and other events.

It is an expansion that Federer's success and visibility helped facilitate, and though he rarely returns, he is still a presence. Large photographs of him adorn the walls, as do large photographs of Stan Wawrinka, who would follow his lead as a Swiss major champion.

A billboard-sized photo of Federer, Wawrinka, and their triumphant Davis Cup teammates from 2014 is mounted on the exterior of the tennis hall, visible from Roger-Federer Allee.

Only one other street is named for him. That is in Halle, Germany, at the grass court tournament he dominated for more than a decade.

"It is a very little street, hardly one hundred meters long," Federer said at the ribbon-cutting in Biel in 2016. "But Germany is not Switzerland. To have one here is a much stronger feeling.

"I hope there will always be lots of action here, with young players who are conscious that they are not here on holiday and are not afraid to have big dreams. Not just becoming a pro—one ATP point is all you need for that—but young players who dream of winning

Wimbledon or the Davis Cup, or why not having a street with their name on it?"

You have to start from zero at some stage, however. Less than two weeks after Allegro and Federer arrived in Biel, they were not just housemates and practice partners but rivals as they took part in a series of satellite tournaments in Switzerland: the lowest rung on the professional tennis ladder.

In those years, satellites were often like mini circuits with three tournaments played back-to-back over three weeks, followed by a "masters" event for the top performers.

The first stage of this satellite, from August 23 to September 21, was in Biel on red clay at a small club. Federer recorded his first victory at the professional level in the first round by winning 7–5, 7–5 against Igor Tchelychev, a Russian already ranked in the top 400 at age twenty.

"Tchelychev was a tall guy, athletic, and really Russian, you know," Allegro said. "He was a guy with a deep voice, and we were making fun of that. Roger winning that match kind of set up his whole satellite, and he started to play really well."

Federer won two more rounds in Biel before losing in the semifinals to Agustín Garizzio, a twenty-seven-year-old Argentine based in Switzerland who was a terror in local tournaments, particularly on clay. He would reach a high of 171 in the ATP rankings in 1998.

Garizzio, the No. 1 seed, went on to beat Federer in the second round the following week in the next stage of the satellite in Nyon. But he was still deeply impressed with the youngster. Both matches had gone three sets, with Garizzio twice forced to rally from losing the first set.

"In Nyon, in the middle of the match, I went up to an Italian friend who was watching and said to him, 'This kid, the day he will be able to hit through his backhand, will be number one,'" Garizzio told the Swiss newspaper *Le Matin Dimanche*. "I was playing a guy who was dancing on the other side of the net."

Federer went on to reach the semifinals in the third stage of the satellite in Noës. One of his opponents was Joël Spicher, a young Swiss who lost to Federer in three sets, 6–3, 0–6, 6–4, in the second round.

"It came down to one or two points in the third set," Spicher told *Le Matin Dimanche*. "I was struck by his capacity to take incredible risks on important points. He went for shots that I did not consider reasonable with a success rate that ended up driving me crazy."

Spicher would not be the last to make that observation through the years.

Federer qualified for the Masters, the final phase of the competition in Bossonnens, near Lausanne. Allegro qualified as well, and the two housemates made the round-trip journey daily from Biel with Peter Lundgren in Lundgren's blue Peugeot 306.

"We called it the Blue Flame, because the car had no power," Allegro said. "We were laughing a lot about that, too."

After Allegro and Federer won their opening rounds, they faced each other in the quarterfinals. They warmed up together and then walked on court to play for real. There were no ball kids. Allegro and Federer called their own lines, and it turned into quite a tussle, with Allegro winning 7–6, 4–6, 6–3.

Allegro recalls Federer getting something in his eye early in the third set and losing his rhythm and cool down the stretch because of it.

"Roger cried pretty badly at the end of the match," Allegro said. "But he cried for like twenty minutes, and then it was over. That night we ate dinner together."

Allegro said the only people in attendance at the match were Lundgren; Federer's father, Robert; and Claudio Grether, the tournament referee.

"Claudio was a longtime supervisor," Allegro said. "And he came up to me after the match and said, 'Well done, Mr. Allegro, but that's the last time you're going to beat Federer.' And you know what? He was right."

From then on, Allegro had to be satisfied with a few scattered victories in practice matches, where Federer was seldom an irresistible force.

"In practice, I even beat Roger when he was number one in the world," Allegro said. "That was not very difficult sometimes, but in official matches that was a different story."

Qualifying for the Masters in Bossonnens was a reward on multiple levels. Above all, it guaranteed that a player would earn ATP ranking points.

For any player, earning those first points is a major moment. "Like getting your first car," Jim Courier, the American star, once told me.

Federer, just a few weeks past his sixteenth birthday, did not even have a driver's license, but on Monday, September 22, he had his first points: twelve, to be exact.

That put him in a tie for 803rd in the ATP rankings with Daniel Fiala of the Czech Republic, Clement N'Goran of Cote d'Ivoire, and Talal Ouahabi of Morocco.

Federer remembers looking at the ATP website to find his own name.

"It's like a milestone," Federer said to me, many years later, of those first points. "Like top 100, top 10, No. 1 in the world. It's one of those big things you look forward to."

But precious few get to experience all of those milestones. Fiala, N'Goran, and Ouahabi never managed to break even into the top 250 in the rankings. Federer, however, was at the beginning of an extraordinary tennis journey. And when the ATP rankings were released that week, he was not the only then-obscure teenager listed on page nine.

There at No. 808 was Lleyton Hewitt, another future No. 1 and future US Open and Wimbledon champion.

Hewitt acquired his first points at age fifteen, just as Rafael Nadal did several years later in 2001. But Federer is still in very good company. Novak Djokovic, Andy Murray, and Wawrinka are among those who also acquired their first points at sixteen.

Even before that satellite circuit, Lundgren was confident that he had come to Biel/Bienne for the right reason.

"When I saw Roger the first time, I thought, 'This guy is going to be a superstar, 100 percent,'" Lundgren said. "It was a no-brainer, because I had worked with Ríos before, who was a little bit similar when it comes to talent but not personality."

I laughed at this, which made Lundgren laugh, too.

"I'm trying to be diplomatic," he said.

It should be noted that Lundgren also kicked Federer out of their first practice for misbehavior, but not before he took good note of his elastic, explosive forehand.

"Okay, he was lazy, but he had an incredible forehand," Lundgren said. "And I said that forehand is going to be a monster when he gets older and stronger."

Lundgren was not as impressed with other elements of the sixteen-year-old Federer's game.

"Physically, he was weak," Lundgren said. "And the backhand was a nice swing but no legs, nothing."

Before accepting the job with Swiss Tennis, Groeneveld had attended a federation training camp and also had a long look at Federer. He quickly saw the upside and the challenges.

"I saw how stubborn he was and also how playful he was: very, very, very playful," Groeneveld told me.

It is a word that was often used to describe Federer in the early years and is still used to describe Federer by those who know him well and have experienced him hiding behind doors and surprising them.

But what did "playful" mean, exactly, to Groeneveld?

"Competitively playful is how I'd describe him at that stage," he said. "Everything was a game, whether it was on the court, off the court, or in conversation. And still today if you have a casual conversation with him, just having a guys' talk, there's always an element of competition to it, whether it's a joke or more serious. But because of his playfulness, it was hard for him to keep his concentration and to really stick to one thing in those days. He needed a lot of variety, and if you didn't give him variety, he would become a nuisance, like right away."

The solution? Variety for everyone.

"I'm not saying that Roger was driving our entire group, but because it was a group stationed in one national tennis center, Roger could be the disrupter," Groeneveld said. "So we had to tailor the entire group to a lot of variety."

That meant "PC" and "PL," as Peter Carter and Peter Lundgren soon became known, often would opt for creative and quick-shifting drills and have their charges cross-train in a number of sports.

They integrated squash, badminton, soccer, table tennis, and even floor hockey into the schedule in some form to keep things fresh and above all to keep young Federer's focus from meandering.

Groeneveld has kept a Polaroid photo from those early days of Federer looking underwhelmed during a practice session. Federer signed the photo with the phrase: "I'm not in the mood."

"He would get bored," Groeneveld said. "He would rather play PlayStation or do something else. And if he was getting bored or was not in the mood, most likely you were better off not getting him on the court because it would ruin everybody's day. But he's such a good kid that you couldn't really get mad at him."

You could discipline him, however, and during that first year in Biel, the players had been warned not to damage the new, custom-designed backdrop on the indoor courts: a heavy and costly antinoise curtain printed with the names of the Swiss federation's sponsors.

All was well until Federer chucked his racket after a frustrating half hour of practice and to his surprise and dismay watched as the racket sliced through the backdrop and clattered off the back wall, leaving a slit in what had looked, at least to Federer, like a much sturdier object.

"Like a hot knife through butter," Federer remembered.

His first thought was "What a poor-quality curtain." His second thought was that he was in big trouble.

Federer walked to his chair, grabbed his gear, and left with Lundgren shaking his head and reminding him that a deal was a deal.

"I thought I was going to get kicked out because we had been warned about it," Federer said.

Groeneveld was loath to suspend or banish a young player, but he did believe in punishment. Federer, a night owl and famously late riser, was ordered to wake up early for a week that winter and clean the courts and the facility, including the toilets.

This story has become a central element of the Federer narrative: a tough-love tale that helped remind him that the rules, in Switzerland at least, also applied to young tennis geniuses.

"That was the kind of teenager I was, always testing the boundaries," Federer said nearly twenty years later in Biel. "It's what my children are doing with me now. It's only fitting."

It seems only fair at this stage to put Federer's behavior in perspective. He was no bad boy off the court and frankly no worse on court than a lot of youngsters with a perfectionist streak trying to navigate their way through a game that does not allow for perfection. Most of his outbursts were directed at himself, even if his disgust at losing a point could sometimes be interpreted as a slight on his opponent's abilities.

Lammer, who has known and played Federer since boyhood, acknowledges that there was a self-control issue but is also convinced that it has been magnified by what Federer became.

"He of course did make a big evolution in his career, but a lot of young guys who are also very talented and really are into the sport and really want to do something are also very emotional," he said. "They also cannot accept how they lose or why they lose. Roger was maybe throwing rackets, but others were, too. It's not like he was the worst ever, not at all. I would say it has been exaggerated to say he was completely out of his mind."

But the concern was undeniably there, for Federer and his family and also for his coaches. Groeneveld said he, Carter, Lundgren, and Federer's parents concluded that Federer would benefit from a sports psychologist.

"It was decided that it would be best if it was somebody not too old, somebody from his own region and with an interest that Roger had as well, which was soccer," Groeneveld said. "The idea was that there would be very, very many connecting areas that he could relate to."

The search led in 1998 to Basel and to Christian Marcolli, a twenty-five-year-old who had played professional soccer in Switzerland for several seasons, including three with Federer's favorite club, FC Basel, before a series of knee injuries and surgeries ended his playing career in his early twenties. Marcolli was forced to, in his own words, "rethink my entire life plan."

He transitioned to performance psychology: a relatively new field in Switzerland despite psychology's famously deep roots in the country (see Carl Jung and Jean Piaget).

Marcolli was studying for his master's at the University of Basel when he began helping Federer. He would later get his doctorate in applied psychology from the University of Zurich.

"Of the players, I'm the only PhD in the whole history of FC Basel, 190 years," Marcolli said with a laugh when we spoke by Zoom in 2021.

He went on to work with a number of prominent athletes, including Swiss national soccer team goalkeeper Yann Sommer and Alpine skiers Dominique and Michelle Gisin, both Olympic gold medalists.

Federer and Carter learned about Marcolli's new line of work after reading a newspaper article about him. Federer remembered Marcolli from his playing days.

He became one of Marcolli's early clients. The idea, according to Groeneveld, was to provide Federer with some tools to change his patterns and manage his emotions more systematically, above all when matches got tight.

Federer was hardly trailblazing. *The Inner Game of Tennis*, Timothy Gallwey's now-classic book about defeating the demons within, had been published nearly a quarter century earlier, in 1974.

Ivan Lendl, on his way to No. 1 in the 1980s, worked with Alexis Castorri, an American sports psychologist he met late one night in a Denny's restaurant in Boca Raton, Florida, when Lendl was in a downbeat mood after a loss to Edberg. Lendl went on to embrace techniques that were avant-garde at the time: using visualization and self-talk even during matches to deepen his ability to focus and encourage flow ("Ivan Lendl is grabbing his towel. Ivan Lendl is wiping his face. Ivan Lendl is holding the ball in his hand and preparing to serve...").

Marcolli is a charismatic interlocutor and fine storyteller, even in his second (or third) language of English. I asked him what separates tennis from other sports from a performance psychology perspective.

"It's probably the toughest sport mentally, maybe with golf," he said. "When you're confident, every sport is easy. Tennis, when you're not confident, it's very lonely. It's very brutal, because it's not over soon. In skiing, in one minute your race is over and you can go home, but from a net time perspective, tennis is brutal."

What also makes it challenging is that coaching is not officially allowed during matches on the men's tour, even if it happens plenty on the sly.

"In other sports they can call time-out or shout to give you instructions," Marcolli said. "Of course there's great teamwork in tennis in the preparation and the strategy and everything, but during the match you really have to do this alone."

There is also much more downtime than action. A point might last five to ten seconds, but there are twenty to twenty-five seconds between points. In a five-set match, that adds up to a great deal of time to think dark thoughts.

"The downtime is a good thing if you use it well," Marcolli said. "It's a huge, huge opportunity. I would even go as far as to say you can make a difference in the downtime."

Marcolli focuses on intentionality between points: on players managing breathing patterns and controlling where they look to maximize focus.

"The big thing to me is always how you use your eyes," he said. "But there is another fundamental component to me, which is beyond that, which is: Are you at peace with yourself? Is your overall life plan more or less in place which gives you the fundamental joy to be here in that moment? Or would you rather be somewhere else and solve a problem somewhere else?"

Federer, to his credit and benefit, chose to address his mental weaknesses when he was still quite young. He was not yet seventeen when he began collaborating with Marcolli.

As a teenager, Marcolli had struggled to manage his own emotions in competition. "I had yet to learn that grace under pressure," he wrote in his 2015 book, *More Life, Please! The Performance Pathway to a*

Better You. "At the age of 17, when things got hard, I got very hard-headed. I had the passion for the game, but I wasn't using it in a controlled way."

That was precisely what he saw in Federer.

"Roger always had the passion to win," Marcolli once explained to *L'Équipe*, the French sports publication. "At a certain moment of his career, he made the choice to learn how to use this energy in a constructive way so he could reach his maximum potential. That was the focus of our work together."

Their collaboration would last approximately two years, and though they hardly resolved Federer's issues entirely, the tools that Federer acquired with Marcolli allowed him to shift into a higher gear.

"That gave him the keys," Lynette Federer told *L'Équipe* in 2005. "I think he is still using these processes on the court. I've never spoken to him about it. It's his world, not mine, but it seems obvious to me."

Groeneveld agrees. "It became very powerful, almost like a strong friendship, like a brother that he never had," he said of Federer's relationship with Marcolli. "He really embraced it."

Federer has never gone nearly that far publicly and has spoken little of Marcolli through the years, but he did acknowledge some benefits in one of our early interviews. Lundgren certainly noticed a difference.

"Of course it helped," Lundgren said. "It's up to the player also to take it. Either you believe it or you don't. When it came to Roger, I don't think he really liked it, to be honest, but he did it, and I think he took the best out of it. To listen to this kind of stuff is not too easy, especially when you're that young with the personality he had or has. It was tough for him."

Consulting a performance psychologist was then still widely viewed as a sign of vulnerability. It also did not dovetail with the rugged individualism that Federer adopted and enjoyed projecting once he reached maturity, going significant stretches without a formal coach or an agent.

"It was seen more like a weakness," Groeneveld said of sports psychology. "We just saw that we could not deliver what Roger needed as coaches. His parents couldn't deliver that either. We needed independent counsel, somebody just on his side."

It is striking to see the evolution in sports and tennis with a player like 2020 French Open champion Iga Świątek employing a full-time sports psychologist, Daria Abramowicz, who sits in her player's box and openly discusses some of their methods.

Marcolli has written books with the Gisin sisters, two of his other star clients. But neither Marcolli nor Federer has publicly explained their work in detail because that is Federer's wish.

"We agreed to that relatively early and then over time we talked and reconfirmed it," Marcolli told me.

What is clear is that Federer, already a successful junior player, soon became a phenomenal one.

Until then, he had not won the biggest titles, even in Europe. Not Les Petits As, the prestigious fourteen-and-under tournament in Tarbes, France, where he was beaten in the round of 16 in 1995. Not the European junior championships, where he was beaten in the semifinals of the sixteen-and-under event in 1997.

But the second half of 1998 was his time to take flight. After losing in the semifinals of the Australian Open junior championships in January and losing, disappointingly, in the first round of the French Open junior championships in June, he arrived at Wimbledon to play in the juniors for the first time with renewed confidence and more equanimity.

Playing and serving irresistibly on the grass, he did not lose a set on his way to the final, where he faced Irakli Labadze, a gifted yet streaky Georgian left-hander.

The final was played on the No. 2 court, yet another court from Federer's youth that no longer exists. Before it was demolished and replaced, it was nicknamed "the Graveyard" because it had been the scene of so many upsets, including John McEnroe's loss to Tim Gullikson in 1979.

Federer, soon to turn seventeen, played at breakneck pace in the sunshine, taking precious little time between points and ripping through nearly all his service games in a hurry. He won the first set 6–4 in just twenty-two minutes after holding serve at love in just under a minute.

His brown hair was short at this stage, with no bandanna. His outfit from Nike, with whom he was already under contract, was baggy and similar to the gear worn that year by one of his tennis idols: Pete Sampras.

When Federer served, he sometimes stuck his tongue out the edge of his mouth, like one of his other idols: the NBA star Michael Jordan. He had another habit that he would later discard: bouncing the ball between his legs between points and serves with a flick of his racket, then catching it behind his body before bouncing it back through his legs again.

It was an eye-catching, fast-twitch trick, typical of Federer's need to play with the ball, not just play the game. It would have become one of his trademarks if he had kept it at the professional level, but it turned out to be only a youthful indulgence.

It was also striking that Federer did not serve and volley in the final even though that was still the status quo for his role models on grass at that stage. Federer and Labadze might as well have been playing on a hard court. It was a hint of the way Wimbledon would be won in the future.

Federer's lateral quickness already was exceptional, allowing him to surprise Labadze by extending rallies or ending them with a flick of his wrist on the stretch. And yet he was more upright in his footwork than he would be in his prime. His split step between shots was not as wide, his flexibility less apparent, his changes of direction less precise.

His serve, already a major weapon, was also noticeably different. The motion was quicker, requiring nearly a second less from initiation to contact than it would in the 2019 Wimbledon final against Djokovic. Federer's weight was not on his front foot for quite as long, his takeback was not as low and far behind the body, his knee bend not as deep, and the leap toward the ball not as explosive.

As expected, he often deployed the backhand slice, but the surprise, more than twenty years later, was that even at this early stage he already was hitting plenty of flat or topspin backhands under duress.

His sole break of serve in the opening set came off a classic Federer pattern as his skidding backhand chip landed short and forced Labadze to move forward and hit an unconvincing approach shot from a stooped position. Federer seized the opportunity he had created by ripping a backhand passing shot winner.

There were other soon-to-be-familiar flourishes, including the most telegenic shot of the day: a forehand topspin lob winner off the back foot that landed just inside the baseline.

A pity that hardly anyone was there to savor it. No more than two hundred fans were in attendance and one middle-aged spectator was stretched out in the stands with his bare feet resting on the top of a nearby seat: not the image most of us have of the elegant All England Club. It was all quite a downbeat contrast to the packed house in nearby Centre Court, where Sampras was fighting through a five-set victory over Goran Ivanišević and tying Borg's modern men's record with a fifth Wimbledon singles title.

Despite his volatility, Federer's temper was largely, if not entirely, in check against Labadze. He picked at his strings often—a classic method of staying in the moment—but he also exited the bubble on occasion by gesticulating and muttering to himself in Swiss German.

The one hint of implosion came early in the second set when, at 1–1, Federer missed a backhand at deuce on Labadze's serve and let his racket fly, shouting at himself. He was up a set, on serve, in command. Why get negative and risk tumbling into an all-too-familiar trap?

But instead of surrendering his edge and rhythm, Federer was able to rein himself in. It was Labadze, not Federer, who later received a code-of-conduct warning after tossing his racket in the fifth game of the second set on his way to being broken.

The title was in reach and Federer snatched it, serving out the 6–4, 6–4 victory without facing a break point down the stretch.

Though it was an impressive performance, there were skeptics, but then so few people could see what was coming for grass court tennis.

"So is Federer a future Wimbledon champion?" asked Guy Hodgson in the *Independent* newspaper in Britain. "Probably not unless he learns to vary his tactics. He has been brought up on clay and it showed, his trips to the net being about as frequent as a blue moon."

Still, the most important match of Federer's young life had required just fifty minutes of his time. Perhaps the biggest surprise, knowing what we know now, was the absence of tears on court. Instead, he raised both arms and flashed a big grin and then produced another satisfied smile when he later received his trophy from the Duchess of Kent in the Royal Box on Centre Court.

BBC commentator Bill Threlfall observed the scene and confidently told his viewers: "We'll be seeing him again."

That was prescient, no doubt, but also risky. Grand Slam junior champions are hardly guaranteed safe passage to greatness. As of 2020, there had been sixty-nine different boys' singles champions at Wimbledon. Only six of them went on to win a Grand Slam singles title, and only four of them went on to win Wimbledon: Borg, Pat Cash, Stefan Edberg, and Federer, who is the only Wimbledon boys' champion to win a major in the last thirty-five years.

Long odds indeed. It is a brutally competitive sport, where the pyramid gets so narrow at the top, and where the most luminous talents have not always prioritized junior competition. But Federer, who also won the Wimbledon boys' doubles title with Olivier Rochus in 1998, definitely headed home to Switzerland with more cachet and greater faith in his capacities.

He left London without joining Sampras and the other winners at the official Wimbledon champions dinner—something he would come to regret—in order to focus immediately on his next challenge.

That was in Gstaad, the upscale Swiss Alpine resort, where he had a timely wild card into the main draw for his ATP Tour debut. It was a quick transition back to clay and high altitude after the grass and sea-level conditions of Wimbledon, and Federer faced Lucas Arnold Ker, an Argentine veteran, in the first round on July 7.

Arnold Ker, ranked 88th, had made it into the main draw only as a lucky loser after young German star Tommy Haas had withdrawn with food poisoning.

"They told me I was playing a local junior," Arnold Ker told Argentine publication *La Nación* twenty years later. "You couldn't get luckier. In that time, Switzerland had Marc Rosset and not much more. If it had been a Spanish wild card, I would have said, 'Okay, watch out,' but a Swiss guy didn't worry me."

Arnold Ker, a strong doubles player who volleyed well, capitalized on Federer's weaker wing: hitting kick serves high to his backhand and coming to net successfully in the fast Alpine conditions. Arnold Ker won 6–4, 6–4 in an hour and twenty minutes.

"The match was close, but when it ended, it never crossed my mind that 'this guy is going to be great,'" Arnold Ker said. "I never thought this junior would become a legend."

Federer had been looking forward to playing Haas, a rising star who would later become one of his closest friends. But the match with Arnold Ker was still on the second-biggest show court, still a big focus for the Swiss fans and news media.

David Law, a young Briton, was assigned to work at Gstaad that year as an ATP Tour communications manager, helping Federer navigate the press.

Law, now a host of the *Tennis Podcast*, was new at this, just like Federer, but he quickly realized that Federer's debut was the big story of the week.

"They wanted to have a press conference from the moment he arrived, basically," Law remembered. "So I got to meet up with him before his tournament started and just figure this out, and I remember how utterly clueless he was about it all. He had no idea who I was, what I was there for, and what I remember is how amused he was by it all. He was just amused people were taking so much interest in him. I immediately liked that about him: the playfulness, the fact that he didn't take it all too seriously. He wasn't stressed out about it."

He was soon switching between Swiss German and French with the press: just as he would for decades to come.

"Everything seemed very easy," Law said. "There was no pretense, no acting, no awkwardness. He didn't seem like a teenager in that way that so many of them do."

Marc Rosset noticed the same quality when he invited the sixteen-year-old Federer to train with him in Geneva.

Rosset, then twenty-seven, expected Federer to be nervous, ready to run through walls to impress his elder, just as Rosset had been when French star Henri Leconte had asked Rosset to serve as a sparring partner in his youth.

"Roger was very relaxed, very at ease, pretty much nonchalant," Rosset told me. "I think it was a bit of the South African side he got from his mother. There was nothing Swiss about that. What fascinated me about Roger then and still is that he manages to live in the present. He has a great ability to take things as they come. He lives a moment, experiences it fully, takes pleasure in it and finishes it and then moves on to the next. It's for that reason you have the feeling that things happen very naturally with him. It's a talent, and to be honest it's a talent that even today fascinates me more than his tennis."

Marcolli thinks it also comes down to trust. "You can train to be in the moment, there are techniques for this," he said. "But the other component is to trust that life is going in the right direction, to trust that the close people around you do a great job and that you don't need to worry or think about something else. And I think Roger always had the ability to surround himself with people he can trust and he does fully trust. It takes a while to get that trust but once you're in, nothing is second-guessed.

"'Are you sure about what you do? Is this the right technique?' I never had a question like this."

There was still plenty of teenager in Federer, however. Shortly after playing in Gstaad, Federer joined Rosset and the Swiss Davis Cup team for their match against Spain in La Corogne in July to serve as a practice partner. It was his first time with the squad and a reward in part for his Wimbledon junior victory.

Rosset, well aware that Federer had the potential to be a fixture on the team for years to come, asked that he be put in an adjoining room at the hotel with a connecting door.

"I wanted to take him under my wing, make him feel part of the squad," Rosset said.

Rosset had brought his PlayStation, which was of course catnip to Federer. It quickly became difficult to tell whose room was whose.

"One time I left to train," Rosset said, "and I came back, and he was in my room playing again, and I said, 'Do you mind? Can you leave me in peace for a little while?' And Roger came out of his trance and said, 'Hey, sorry,' and left to go next door. He could be oblivious, but it was also cool and fun. After that week, I always thought of him as something close to a little brother."

Paul Dorochenko, the French fitness trainer and physiotherapist, arrived in Biel in August 1998. Like many at the House of Tennis, he had been drawn to Switzerland in part by the chance to work with Federer.

Dorochenko, born in Algeria when it was still part of France, was forty-four and had trained a number of leading players, including Rosset. Most recently he had been in Spain and on tour with Sergi Bruguera, a two-time French Open champion, and Bruguera's father and coach, Luís.

Dorochenko has a strong personality: egocentric according to some who know him. He also has a scientific bent. He has focused recently on helping athletes change long-held techniques, like service tosses or forehand windups, through the use of low-frequency sounds.

Through his work with the Brugueras in the 1990s, he had a deep understanding of professionalism.

Federer needed work, lots of work.

"You have to say it like it was," Dorochenko told me. "Roger was fragile emotionally. He could not accept defeat, and he was mediocre in training. He was not a big worker. He was fooling around most of the time. In terms of fitness, I demanded a lot from him and had him do a one-hour run that had frankly no utility for tennis, but it was good for the mental side, to toughen him up."

Like the other coaches in Biel, Dorochenko cooked up ways to keep Federer engaged and amused.

"We hired a guy who came from a circus school to come in and do juggling with the players," Dorochenko said. "Federer was spontaneous and very talented, but he had no continuity. For fitness training, I had to go find him sometimes because he forgot to come. It was a pain, and his apartment was a disaster zone. You cannot imagine. In the morning, when I went in there, we could not even tell if he was in there or not. It was that messy."

Meanwhile, Peter Carter and the other coaches in Biel were focused on structuring Federer's game for the long run: refining the technique and the style of play that would allow him to maximize his gifts.

Groeneveld, concerned about Federer's low margin for error on his groundstrokes, tried stringing a rope three feet above the net and having Federer clear the rope with his shots while still keeping the ball in play. Tremendous topspin was required, and though Federer got the message, in typical fashion he also took the exercise to the next level, finding a way to marry massive spin and velocity. The forehand he learned to hit at full rip was dubbed "the cliffhanger."

"A ball with so many RPMs that it would look like it was going out but then at the last minute it would drop onto the baseline," Groeneveld said. "I know we always speak of Rafa Nadal's racket-head speed, but Roger has an incredibly fast arm. Rafa has mainly developed it due to the racket he uses, and the technique that was developed around the racket. Roger stayed for a long time with a traditional frame and could never have physically sustained the RPMs that needed to be generated to hit the cliffhanger or he would have had major injuries."

Federer, at this stage, was using a Wilson Pro Staff Original with an eighty-five-square-inch head, the same racket being used by two of his idols: Sampras and Edberg. The frame was comparatively heavy at twelve ounces, thin in the beam and small in the head, which could make it unforgiving on off-center hits.

But Federer loved the feel of the racket when he did get the timing right. The sweet spot was sweet indeed, and Federer was, after all, not planning on waging long battles of attrition from the baseline. He wanted to attack from all over the court and keep the points relatively short.

Dorochenko said he spoke often with Peter Carter about Federer's game. One of Dorochenko's areas of interest is laterality, the dominance of one side of the brain in controlling body functions. He is particularly focused on eye dominance and how it might impact a player.

Dorochenko determined that Federer, who is right-handed, is left-eye dominant, which means that his left eye relays information more quickly and accurately to his brain than his right eye.

Typically, a person's dominant eye corresponds with their dominant hand. Federer was cross-dominant—the case in only about 30 percent of the population.

For Dorochenko, it meant that Federer's most natural shot was the forehand, because with his shoulders turned, his dominant left eye could track the ball from an advanced position.

"When you are right-eye dominant and right-handed, the backhand is the natural shot, like with Richard Gasquet or Stan Wawrinka," Dorochenko said.

Dorochenko, a strong club-level player in France, recalls playing tennis with Federer at the training center on the weekends in Biel and keeping it interesting for both men by having Federer play with his left hand.

"I worked a lot with him on his left hand, and by doing that you improve the overall coordination, and your brain becomes more symmetric," Dorochenko said. "Federer was a creative type, a guy who did not have much concentration and who had lots of ups and downs. He broke rackets and threw away matches. He was really not good in mental terms, and so we said, okay, let's construct a tennis for Federer that fits Federer, and Peter Carter was really the constructor in chief. I don't think Federer knew all that was done for him, but it led to developing a technique that was totally made for him. Nobody made Federer fit into a mold. A mold was made to fit Federer."

Attacking, forehand-centric tennis required excellent mobility and powerful legs in order to run around the backhand whenever possible and drive through the ball. With Federer now in his late teens, they worked on his diet and his strength. By the time Dorochenko left the Swiss federation in early 2000 to rejoin Bruguera's team, Federer could bench-press more than 100 kilograms (220 pounds) despite his unimposing frame.

He also had, for a young tennis player, a solid VO_2 max, which boded well for his five-set future.

"The error people made looking at him was thinking that he was somewhat fragile," Dorochenko said. "But he was strong, quite strong, and had a VO_2 max of 62 at that stage, which for an attacking player was a high aerobic level. Marc Rosset, to give you a comparison, was at around 50. A good cyclist would be at 75 or 80. Bruguera, a baseliner, was 72, but Federer was above the level of the typical attacking player. So you knew he would have no problem in terms of surviving in a long match, and you can see how many five-setters he went on to win in his career. He never collapsed."

But for Dorochenko the most striking aspect of Federer as an athlete was how dynamic and quick-footed he was. Federer was exceptional in plyometric training, where the focus is on repetitive, explosive exercises like box jumps.

"He would shatter the records," Dorochenko said. "While others in thirty seconds could do perhaps fifty-five jumps, Federer would do seventy. Really, he was a remarkable athlete, but because the mental side was fragile and the backhand had a tendency to break down, Peter Carter felt the focus needed to be on shortening the rally lengths. It's all about finding the number of shots that correspond best to you. For a guy like Bruguera, the ideal rally was eleven shots or more. For Federer it was three, four, five shots."

If that sounds like a straightforward formula, it was not. Federer, with his mental combustibility and manifold tactical options, would need more time than some of his peer group to learn how to make the right shot selections and experience consistent success.

Peter Carter understood this perfectly and often defended Federer in Swiss federation meetings from those who thought his progress was too slow and who pointed out that tennis's greatest men's champions had typically won major titles by age twenty (see Sampras, Borg, McEnroe, and others). But Carter was adamant that Federer was on a different timetable, that he was trying to focus not on two or three big shots but on all the shots.

Andre Agassi, one of the best and most intuitive players of the modern era, sensed this as well. Back in the top 10 in October 1998 after a resurgent year, Agassi faced Federer in the first round of the Swiss Indoors in Basel. That was the week after Federer had qualified for the main draw at the ATP event in Toulouse and won two rounds against established tour players Guillaume Raoux of France and Richard Fromberg of Australia before losing to Dutchman Jan Siemerink.

Agassi, the first top 10 opponent of Federer's career, defeated him 6–3, 6–2. After the match, Agassi's coach, Brad Gilbert, went to the locker room after what had looked, in many respects, like a routine victory.

"Andre's like, 'Shit, this kid Federer has got some serious skills, and he's going to be good really quickly,'" Gilbert said.

In the next round, Agassi defeated Federer's twenty-two-year-old Swiss compatriot Ivo Heuberger, 6–2, 6–2. David Law, working the event for the ATP, escorted Agassi to his news conference, and on the way he asked Agassi who would win if the two rising Swiss, Federer and Heuberger, were to play.

"Agassi said, 'Well, if they played now, Heuberger would win,'" Law told me. "'But the kid who will have the career is Federer.'"

It would be a career like no other, certainly greater than Agassi would have imagined, but first there would be plenty of learning-curve moments like the one in Küblis, a picturesque Swiss mountain village near the Austrian border.

It was the week after the Basel event, and though Federer was still in his country, he was in another world and struggling to readjust. Instead of facing Agassi, one of global sports' luminaries, on the main tour, he was facing Armando Brunold, a little-known twenty-one-year-old Swiss ranked 768th, in the first round of a satellite tournament in a town with fewer than one thousand inhabitants. The pressure was all on Federer.

Peter Lundgren, one of the very few in attendance, was seething as he watched Federer essentially throw the match after losing the opening-set tiebreaker, missing groundstrokes wildly.

"He was tanking, and I was going crazy inside," Lundgren said.

The tournament referee arrived: Claudio Grether, the same official who earlier in the year had informed Allegro that he would not beat Federer again. This time, Grether told Lundgren that he intended to give Federer a warning for lack of effort.

"I said, 'Go right ahead! Do it!'" Lundgren said.

Grether went on court and followed through, stopping the match to make the announcement. Federer, chastened but still off-kilter, went on to lose in straight sets.

Lundgren, who had to field a concerned call from Federer's parents, said Federer was fined $100: a pittance considering the more than $100 million in prize money that he would go on to earn. But at that stage, $100 was more than the first-round loser's check. Above all, it was an embarrassment: one that did not pass unnoticed in Switzerland, generating a few critical headlines and reports from media outlets that had just finished covering Federer's run in Toulouse and duel with Agassi in Basel.

Lundgren and Carter told Federer that if there were any similar shenanigans in the next tournament, they were done traveling with him.

Federer absorbed that ultimatum and proceeded to win two of the next three tournaments in the satellite series and reach the final in the other. He beat his housemate and doubles partner Allegro twice along the way.

"That's typical Roger," Lundgren said with a chuckle. "He got, you know, squeezed in the corner and then won the satellite."

It is hard not to see such moments as big positives for the man and player Federer would become.

Rip the practice curtain in an act of petulance? Clean the courts and toilets at the crack of dawn.

Disrespect a tournament and the sport with lack of effort? Face the fine and the backlash.

These are the pivot points, like Robert Federer requiring his temperamental son to find his own ride home in Basel or, in a move that would certainly raise an eyebrow in some cultures, stopping the car and rubbing young Roger's head in the snow to cool him off during one of his son's post-tournament rants.

Despite his solid family and empathetic nature, Federer could have turned out quite differently if he had been enabled more often in his youth, coddled in light of his potential.

No doubt he was cut some slack. Consider the circus performers in Biel/Bienne and concessions to his short attention span. No doubt he was not entirely in touch with reality. Signing a contract with Nike in your teens and being told repeatedly that you have the talent to reach No. 1 can render that difficult.

"People told me that all the time," Federer said.

But Federer was also put in his place, not just Swiss-style but, because of his coaches, Australian-style and Swedish-style, too.

All three of those countries have an egalitarian streak that might have diminished in fervor in recent years but remains an element of their national identities. The Australians still use the term "tall poppy syndrome," meaning that the tallest poppy gets cut down to size. The Swedes, like other Scandinavians, make frequent reference to the "Jante Law," a social-democratic ideal of equality.

Federer, a human antenna, had to pick up at least some of the signals.

But equality has its limits in tennis. Only one player emerges a champion at any singles tournament, and only one boy finishes the year as the top-ranked junior in the world.

Federer got there in 1998, securing the spot after winning the Orange Bowl despite coming perilously close to elimination in the first round against a Latvian named Raimonds Sproga.

That was not all due to Sproga's brilliance. Before the tournament, Federer was jumping rope and ended up spraining an ankle quite badly.

"As usual, he was fooling around," said Dorochenko, who was along for the trip. "His ankle blew up like a potato in a few seconds. So, I treated him for three days and in the first round he played on one leg basically but still won. Then it got better every day after that."

That was for the best, because Federer had to beat Jürgen Melzer of Austria in the second round and then face David Nalbandian of Argentina in the semifinals. Nalbandian had beaten Federer in the US Open boys' final earlier in the year, but Federer would win this duel and then beat another talented Argentine, Guillermo Coria, in the final.

It was quite a run, and it would look even better a few years later when Melzer reached No. 8 in the ATP singles rankings and Nalbandian and Coria went on to reach No. 3 and play in Grand Slam singles finals.

But Federer would finish on top of that exceptional class as a junior, clinching the spot after Andy Roddick, another of his future pro rivals, defeated Julien Jeanpierre of France in the last ITF tournament of the year in Mexico to eliminate Jeanpierre from No. 1 contention.

Federer was already back in Switzerland: his junior career over and his pro career about to start in earnest. Coria, who retired young at twenty-seven, was still amazed many years later at how that career played out.

"I can put my hand on my heart and say that I would never have imagined that Federer would become who he is," Coria told the Argentine radio program *Cambio de Lado* in 2019. "The work that people close to him did, above all the one who worked on Federer's head, deserve the Nobel Prize.

"He was crazy. He listened to heavy metal at full volume with his headphones. His hair was dyed blond. He was a personality. Nothing to do with who he became."

Many of us had a look in our youth we would rather bury deep in the archives. This surely was Federer's. He had acne. He had a deeply compromised fashion sense and, as Coria remembers correctly, the peroxide-blond hair that he acquired during the Orange Bowl. He also had that prominent nose, inherited from his father. Dorochenko recalls him saying in those early years that "it's big, but when I'm number one, people won't notice it anymore."

Twenty years later, Federer posted a photo of himself on Instagram from that self-conscious period with the hashtags #teen and #premirka and the caption: "Reminding everyone there are better days ahead."

That certainly proved true in his case, but that was also because he was focused on self-acceptance and self-improvement: with Carter, with Marcolli, and, above all in his quiet moments, on his own.

It was a long-term project. To date, no Nobel Prizes have come from it, but Federer did find a form of peace.

"When I see Roger today, I always tell him, 'What you do on the court is extraordinary, but how you handle your life to me is out of this world,'" Marcolli said. "When you have everywhere, all the time five-star-plus luxury, people who look into your eyes and bring you stuff you don't even order, and then you go on the court, and the game doesn't care. The game doesn't care where you slept, what you did, how many people you met. The game is pure, and he managed over twenty years to come out and play it with humility and that same amount of connection it takes to be able to keep winning matches. The way he approaches work, and yes, we can call it work: the dignity, the level of concentration. To me, he's a role model from that perspective."

CHAPTER FIVE

———◁▷———

SYDNEY

For all the talent, for all the commitment, achieving and sustaining greatness can also come down to luck.

Marc Rosset still gets shaky thinking about his ski trip with Federer in January 2000. Federer had just returned to Switzerland after losing in straight sets to Frenchman Arnaud Clément at the Australian Open. Next up was the Davis Cup against Australia at home in Zurich, but before tackling that challenge, Federer decided to enjoy the Swiss winter. He joined Rosset and his brother in the mountain resort of Crans-Montana.

It was getting late in the day, and they were skiing the same run where the women's World Cup downhill is raced each year.

"It was the thing where you do the same run a bunch of times," Rosset remembered. "At the beginning you are careful and then you start going faster and faster and then there's the moment where you go too fast."

There were back-to-back jumps, and Federer absorbed the first well enough but miscalculated and carried too much speed into the second. He went into something resembling low-earth orbit. Rosset watched in horror as the future of tennis disappeared from view.

"He lost control and went really high, and I didn't see him land," Rosset said. "It looked bad. He was way down the hill, and the skis had come off, everything. Nobody was wearing helmets in those days, and I was afraid, really afraid."

Careers can turn or stay the course at such moments. Federer could have torn up his knee or worse, could have missed months on tour or worse. Instead, he shook off the snow and the fright and assured the wide-eyed Rosset that he was okay.

On course to Zurich, where Federer won two of his three matches but could not prevent the Swiss from losing 3–2 to an Australian team featuring Mark Philippoussis and Lleyton Hewitt (him again), who defeated Federer in four sets on the final day.

Half a world away in Adelaide, Darren Cahill pulled up a chair on the eve of his wedding to watch the match alongside Peter Carter, who had made the long trip back to Australia to celebrate as one of Cahill's groomsmen.

"We just sat up and had a couple of beers and watched the boys play," Cahill said. "To us, it didn't matter who won or lost. It was like our two kids playing, and we savored it."

Carter would project with Cahill, envisioning their teen protégés meeting one day in a Grand Slam final. It would not take long for that to become a reality, but for now the stakes were still lower, the learning curves still steep.

Federer headed south to Marseille, where he reached his first ATP singles final and faced none other than Rosset, whom he had recently passed to become the top-ranked Swiss man.

"Marc is a true friend," Federer said on the eve of the final. "He gives me precious advice for matches because he knows all the players on the circuit. This time, however, I'm going to have to manage on my own."

The first ATP singles final between Swiss men was an intergenerational tussle but also a stylistic contrast: Federer, a smooth mover even at eighteen with beads around his neck and his long dark hair pulled up in a samurai-style topknot; Rosset, twenty-nine, with a scraggly beard and a rough-hewn game that looked more like hard labor than poetry in motion.

But both played power tennis, eager to rip their forehands and attack the net on the quick indoor surface. Federer saved three match points, two with bold backhand passing shots, as Rosset served for the match at 5–4 in the third set. It came down to a third-set tiebreaker, and at 5–6, Federer ran around his backhand and whipped an inside-out forehand that hit the tape and fell back.

Rosset had the title: 2–6, 6–3, 7–6 (7–5).

The friends met at the net, and the six-foot-seven Rosset—the tallest man in elite tennis before genuine giants like Ivo Karlović and John Isner arrived—bent down and gave Federer a fraternal peck on the top of the head.

Federer, being Federer, was soon in tears again.

"He was thinking it might be the only chance for him to win an ATP tournament," Rosset said. "And I told him, 'Calm yourself.' "

Rosset, who had now won fourteen tour singles titles, was convinced Federer was going to win plenty, and he said as much in the postmatch ceremony when he thanked Federer for letting him win this one.

Rosset stopped himself from sharing his belief that Federer was going to win a Grand Slam title.

"I couldn't say that then, because everybody would have thought I was crazy," Rosset said. "For me, it was sure he would win one, but it's also true that you can have all the talent and still there is so much work that goes into it."

There has long been debate: Are champions born or made or, more logically, a bit of both?

When it comes to tennis, I favor Martina Navratilova's hybrid formula: "Champions are born, and then they have to have the right environment to be made."

No matter how sound the plan, how high the work rate, or how wealthy the parent, a player of modest height and below-average hand-eye coordination and quickness is not going to be hoisting any Grand Slam trophies.

No matter how fleet, deft, and driven, a player who does not receive some quality instruction and some level of opportunity is not going to fulfill what looked like their destiny.

"It takes a village, you know, and so many good things have to happen," Navratilova told me. "So, it's a total combination, and then they also grow into it.

"Look at Roger and Björn," she said, referring to Federer and Borg. "They were hotheads when they were young, and then they had, like, this come-to-Jesus moment, and they were total control freaks of their emotions the rest of their careers."

How many would-be tennis champions, with all the requisite ability and resilience, never even get the chance to play the sport? How many are drawn to a different game, a different passion?

For years I heard professional tennis coaches openly wonder how Michael Jordan or LeBron James would have transformed the men's game if they had picked tennis.

Federer could certainly have chosen a different path. Soccer was his first passion and long his Plan B. Perhaps if he were coming of age in this era, he would have aimed for e-sports stardom instead.

"The guy's a master," said Peter Lundgren. "I will never forget when he bought the James Bond Nintendo game, and we went to some tournament, and he had to go through a gate in the game, and he called me and said, 'Peter I can't get through this stupid gate!' And I said, 'Why are you calling me? I have no clue.' And then he calls me an hour later and he goes, 'Yes! I did it!' He finished the whole game in one day, and it would take a normal person maybe a month. The guy is scary when it comes to games. That's something you're born with: that ability to solve problems. And very often when he was under pressure in matches, when he was the mouse and the other guy was the cat, he found the hole to escape and survive."

Happily for tennis, a nineteenth-century game with a diminishing hold on twenty-first-century European youth, Federer was able to find what he was searching for with a racket in hand instead of chasing it elsewhere. He pursued his goals with passion and an increasingly clear sense of daily purpose, but there were still moments when fortune played a decisive role.

His crash in Crans-Montana was one example, but what happened later that year in Sydney at his first Olympics would have perhaps the biggest impact on his staying power at the top.

It was a memorable Summer Games, the best overall of the many I have covered. Australians love their sport, and Sydney, with its shimmering harbor, provided a grand backdrop in late September.

Tennis, usually an attention magnet in Australia, was hardly top of mind. The country's focus was on the pool, where seventeen-year-old Australian swimmer Ian Thorpe set a world record in his opening race. But above all, Australians had their eyes on the track and Cathy Freeman, an indigenous Australian sprinter. Freeman had become a genuine icon at home and was the gold-medal favorite in the 400-meter race.

I had interviewed Freeman twice in the years leading up to the Games for the *New York Times,* once in a Melbourne coffeehouse, and she was as down to earth as the expectations were lofty: a gentle soul in an extraordinary position. She understood why she had become a symbol and had played a role in becoming one by celebrating her victories with both the Australian and the Aboriginal flags. But as the Olympics approached, she was resistant to having her achievements politicized even if it was too late to turn down most of the heat.

"I'm just really keen on having a good time, and making the most of this time," she told me. "The time will come when I can be more instrumental in politics and Aboriginal affairs. But now I think I'm playing a big part just doing what I'm doing."

Freeman lit the Olympics cauldron during the Opening Ceremony, and on the night of the 400-meter final, she donned a hooded green-and-gold bodysuit that was designed to make her more aerodynamic but also seemed useful as a protective barrier from all the electricity and expectation in the massive Olympic stadium.

From my vantage point high in the stands, she looked tiny in the midst of all that humanity, but she held firm with the record crowd of 112,524 roaring her on. It was the loudest 49.11 seconds I have experienced, and the din could have lifted her or weighed on her. Perhaps it did both. When she crossed the finish line and dropped to the track after winning the gold medal, she looked more disoriented than elated, like a free diver who had just resurfaced, blinking in the fresh air after plumbing the depths and the limits.

Nothing that happened in the nearby tennis complex at Homebush Bay could compete with that, but the tournament was a chance for Federer to experience the Olympics when he was still out of the spotlight.

He would be front and center after that: carrying the flag for Switzerland at the Opening Ceremonies in 2004 in Athens and in 2008 in Beijing. He would be back under the microscope in London in 2012 on the familiar grass of the All England Club. But Sydney was his time to be a rank-and-file Olympic villager, the one gawking at the stars instead of the one being gawked at.

While Venus and Serena Williams felt compelled to seek refuge in a downtown Sydney hotel in their first Olympics to escape the attention from their peers, Federer and the rest of the Swiss tennis players and officials, including Lundgren, shared a house in the village in Homebush Bay with other Swiss Olympians.

"Luckily, I was on the second floor, and the wrestlers were on the first so I was safe," Federer joked in an interview with *L'Équipe*. "We had a blast. It's hard to explain just how much fun I had at the Games."

Federer, a big NBA fan who had grown up watching the Olympics, somehow did not make it to the basketball games but was able to attend swimming races and badminton matches. He also spent quality time with his tennis teammates, including another Swiss Olympic rookie: Miroslava Vavrinec, then twenty-two.

Vavrinec, nicknamed Mirka, had broken into the top 100 earlier in the year. But she had made it to the Olympics only because the leading Swiss women, Martina Hingis and Patty Schnyder, had decided not to play. Vavrinec, whose ranking was outside the cutoff for automatic qualifying, also had required a wild card entry from the International Tennis Federation in order to compete.

She lost 6–1, 6–1 in the first round in singles to Elena Dementieva, the eventual silver medalist, and lost in the first round of doubles with partner Emmanuelle Gagliardi. But at least Vavrinec got to play doubles. Federer, who had planned to join forces with Rosset, was left without a partner when Rosset withdrew from the team at the last minute.

That deprived Federer of his most likely chance at a medal and also, because of the lateness of the decision, deprived another Swiss men's player like Lorenzo Manta or Michel Kratochvil of the chance to replace Rosset.

"I didn't see it coming," Federer said upon arrival in Sydney, sounding miffed at being left in the lurch despite his friendship with Rosset.

As Federer was well aware, the Olympics had played a central role in Rosset's career: He won the singles gold in 1992. But his and Hingis's absences were reminders that the Games were still not a primary objective for many tennis players in a sport with an overstuffed calendar and no shortage of big events and paydays.

Pete Sampras and Andre Agassi, long the dominant figures in the men's game, both skipped the Sydney Games as well: Agassi for family reasons; Sampras because he preferred to focus on the regular tour and had never had an Olympic medal on his list of career goals.

Tennis was part of the modern Olympics from the start in 1896 in Athens but was out of the Games from 1928 until 1984, when it returned in Los Angeles as a demonstration sport before being fully reintegrated in 1988. The comeback was the result of successful lobbying by the International Tennis Federation and its French president, Philippe Chatrier, a clever journalist and administrator who would also play a major role in the renaissance of the French Open.

There was no denying that tennis failed to meet the pinnacle test. A gold at the Olympics was not the ultimate achievement in a sport where the four Grand Slam tournaments remain the biggest prizes. But then winning Olympic gold in basketball has never been the pinnacle for the best NBA players, and they still rejoined the Games in 1992.

The Olympics were changing, becoming more commercial and increasingly focused on bringing together as many global sports stars as possible. Rugby, golf, and surfing would eventually join the qua-drennial summer circus as well.

Unlike Sampras and his generation, Federer, who was born in 1981, had never known the Olympics without his sport.

"When I grew up, the Olympics was there in tennis," Federer said. "It was for me always a goal. It's an event that has always fasci-nated me."

All the more so because of his affinity for Australia and Sydney, which he visited with his family in 1995, shortly before he joined the Swiss national training center in Ecublens. His father, Robert, had even briefly entertained the possibility of taking a job in Australia but decided against it.

The Australian culture suited Federer's extroverted personality: his love of the beach, sun, and open space, a combination that he had also embraced on his childhood visits to South Africa.

But that did not mean he came to Sydney without tennis ambitions.

"I would very much like to come back home with a medal, prefer-ably a gold," he said before leaving for Australia—strong words from a nineteen-year-old who was ranked 43rd and had yet to win an ATP Tour title.

It is often reported that Federer and Vavrinec met at the Olympics, but they already knew each other after crossing paths at tournaments and in Biel/Bienne at the National Tennis Center, where Vavrinec sometimes attended camps or trained with her private coaches.

Vavrinec, poised and more than three years older than Federer, did not appear particularly impressed with the teenager at first.

"I was rather calm and disciplined; Roger made a lot of noise," she told the Swiss newspaper *Le Matin* in one of her rare interviews. "He sang Backstreet Boys songs at the top of his lungs."

But she found him amusing despite the contrast in their personalities.

"He was funny, full of life, he made me laugh," she said. "The coaches sometimes had to kick him off the courts to get some peace."

They were opposites at that stage in their approach to training: Vavrinec was never a clown, never a hothead. But they both had grand dreams and immigrant roots. Federer's mother was from South Africa, Vavrinec's parents from Czechoslovakia.

An only child, she was born on April Fools' Day, 1978, in Bojnice, a small town best known for its historic castle in what is now independent Slovakia. For a city of only five thousand inhabitants, it has had an outsized influence on tennis. Miloslav Mečíř, one of the best men's players of the late 1980s, was born there and later reached the US Open and Australian Open finals, and won the Olympic gold medal in singles in 1988 in Seoul. Nicknamed "the Big Cat" for his feline grace, he was a bewitching player with a deft touch, feathery footwork, and an uncanny ability to read the flow of play and avoid wasted effort. Asked once for his 100-meter time, Mečíř joked he didn't know because he had never run one hundred meters. Karina Habšudová, who was ranked No. 10 on the women's tour in 1997, also was born in Bojnice.

Vavrinec was not long for the city, however. Her parents immigrated to Switzerland when she was two and settled in Kreuzlingen, a small city on the shores of Lake Constance, where her father continued to work as a goldsmith and jeweler, launching a company named Mir'Or.

She became a tennis player in earnest when her father sought out Czech-born superstar Martina Navratilova and her stepfather, Miroslav Navratil, for advice in the late 1980s. Navratilova was also a Czechoslovakian expatriate and had fled the Communist regime for the United States.

It has often been reported that a nine-year-old Vavrinec and her father showed up unannounced at the WTA event in Filderstadt, Germany, in 1987 and succeeded in securing an audience with Navratilova after Vavrinec's father, a Navratilova fan, talked his way past the security guard and had his daughter present Navratilova with a pair of handmade earrings for her birthday.

Navratilova then reportedly told the Vavrinecs that Mirka had a good athletic build and might make a fine tennis player. She put them in touch with Jiří Granát, a Czech coach based in Switzerland with whom she had played junior tennis.

And so it all began, supposedly.

But that remarkable origin story was perhaps a little too remarkable. Though Vavrinec, who has not given a formal interview in over a decade, did not confirm it, Navratilova told me that Vavrinec's father had, in fact, previously consulted with her stepfather in Czechoslovakia for an expert opinion on his daughter's potential.

"My dad had a session with her and said yeah, she had the potential to play on the tour," Navratilova said. "I just know my dad gave the green light and said she's going to be good. That I know. That I'm sure of. So that's what happened, and then I met the family when they came to the tournament. My parents were there, because at that point they could travel, so we all had like a lunch or dinner and hung out, and that was like a year later."

Navratilova's parents divorced when she was four and her biological father, who later died by suicide, did not play nearly as big a role in her life as Navratil, her stepfather. He met Navratilova's mother through tennis and introduced young Martina to the sport, becoming her first coach and a strong paternal figure before his death in 2001.

"I don't think of him as not my blood," Navratilova said. "I think Mirka's father knew that my father called it like he sees it, kind of like what I do even though I don't have his DNA. I got that from him. He wouldn't bullshit. He would have told them you are wasting your time, or this is possible, so that's what happened. My father is a straight shooter, and you can see talent. You know if a kid has something, you know it early on. You just don't know how far it's going to go."

Navratilova maintains that you can tell if a young person is a good athlete simply by looking at their walk. Vavrinec, a dancer in her early years, had the walk—the natural, rhythmic grace—and she quickly developed into a formidable junior player, winning the Swiss eighteen-and-under girls' title at age fifteen.

The bar in Switzerland was now remarkably high. Hingis, who also emigrated from Slovakia as a young child, was two years younger than Vavrinec and already had reached No. 1 in the world and won multiple major singles titles. Vavrinec was the same age as Schnyder, a future top 10 player whose brother had been one of Federer's early junior rivals.

But Vavrinec was committed, and she eventually secured both a Swiss passport and some precious private backing from Walter Ruf, a Swiss businessman who invested in her career. Such an arrangement is not uncommon for talented juniors and their families as they search for funds to pay for coaching and travel.

Vavrinec developed into a solid professional player, but her game was limited.

"She did not have the quality to be a top player, but for sure she could have been top 50," said Eric van Harpen, who coached Grand Slam champions Arantxa Sanchez Vicario and Conchita Martinez.

"She was a good baseliner, very athletic, very powerful, very strong, but kind of mechanical," Groeneveld said. "She had no big weapons, but she was compensating with her ability to keep the ball in play and run all day. She would bite into a match, and she would fight."

Navratilova's early contact with Vavrinec was not the last time she would play a role in the rise of a young player. In 1993, she spotted the talent of six-year-old Maria Sharapova at a clinic in Moscow and told Sharapova's father, Yuri, that they should find a way to train abroad. They moved to Florida with less than $1,000 and gambled on Maria becoming a professional. She managed that and much more: winning Wimbledon at seventeen, reaching No. 1, and becoming for many years the top-earning female athlete in the world.

Did this sort of thing happen often to Navratilova: changing life paths and tennis history through brief encounters?

"No," she said with a laugh. "I think Maria and Mirka are the only two."

Vavrinec never reached remotely the same heights as Sharapova as a player. She effectively retired in 2002 because of chronic foot problems. But two years earlier in Sydney, as she and Federer reveled in their first Olympics, it seemed likely that they both had long careers ahead of them.

For Federer, 2000 had turned into a trying season, full of setbacks and first-round defeats and some weighty decisions.

He had determined early in the year that he would break away from the Swiss federation and create his own private team after the Olympics. The problem was choosing a coach. Would it be Carter, his long-time mentor; or Lundgren, who—unlike Carter—had played regularly on the main tour and been ranked in the top 30?

"The problem is I like working with both of them," Federer explained. The choice could have been neither Peter.

Groeneveld said he was approached by Federer and his family to take on the role in 2000. Groeneveld declined.

"Robbie, Roger's dad, always kind of makes fun of me, saying I'm the only guy to turn down the job with Roger," Groeneveld said.

Groeneveld had left his managerial position at the national training center in Biel/Bienne in 1998 after just one year to coach British star Greg Rusedski. Groeneveld said he told the Federers that the opportunity should go to Carter or Lundgren.

"Both Peters had invested so much time in Roger, and I had such a good relationship with both, and I felt I couldn't take the job because these two guys deserved it," Groeneveld said.

The Federers then asked Groeneveld which Peter he would choose.

"It seemed clear to me that Roger was going to face so much criticism in his years starting out, and I felt that Peter Lundgren had more of an international reputation and that the Swiss media could not break him down," Groeneveld said. "They could break down Peter Carter easier because he had not been ranked in the top 50. He never won an ATP tournament. He came from a small town in Australia. He didn't have that status Lundgren had. And because of that background and Lundgren's experience with Marcelo Ríos and his own playing experience himself and all his connections with the Swedish player group, I picked Lundgren over Carter because I knew it was going to be so tough. And those three years did turn out to be really, really tough."

Groeneveld was not the only person to be consulted. There was also

Paul Dorochenko, the outspoken French fitness trainer and physio-therapist who had worked and traveled with Federer frequently before leaving the Swiss federation in early 2000.

"Roger came to see me one day and said, 'What do you think, Paul? Who should I travel with?'" Dorochenko remembered. "And I said, 'Listen, I sincerely think you would travel much better with Lundgren than Carter.' For me, Lundgren had this high-level experience, and he's a guy who is always in a good mood, a jovial guy, very pleasant. He's not a technician, like Peter Carter was, but he's a coach who knows how to motivate you."

Federer announced his choice in a communiqué that his father faxed to the Swiss press on Easter Sunday, April 23. After much thought, it would be Lundgren.

"It was fifty-fifty," Federer later explained. "I've known Peter Carter since I was eight years old. It was the toughest decision of my life, and it really came down to a gut feeling."

Carter, the architect in chief of Federer's game, expressed some dismay but was generally supportive of the decision in public. According to those who knew him well, he was devastated.

Peter Smith, Carter's boyhood coach and close friend, said Carter telephoned him in Australia after an emotional Federer informed him of the decision in March well ahead of the announcement. "We had a really long conversation, and he was gutted," Peter Smith said of Carter. "He'd spent a good chunk of his life working with Roger. He loved him, I think."

Carter was convinced that he would be a better influence on Federer, but Federer, who had spent plenty of time with Lundgren in his nearly three years based in Biel/Bienne, clearly saw a different, more reassuring side.

Lundgren said the decision did not create tension between him and Carter, who had become a friend. But Lundgren could certainly sense Carter's disappointment and was appreciative of the way he handled it. So was Federer.

"When Roger decided to go with me, Peter said, 'If you need my help, I'm here. I'm behind you. One hundred percent,'" Lundgren said.

But Smith said Carter did feel bitterness, and Dorochenko, who was working closely with Carter at that stage, confirmed it.

"He never was quite the same Peter Carter after that," Dorochenko said. "He really had a hard time processing the decision."

It was not the first time Federer had left Carter's orbit: He had made the move from Basel to Ecublens at age fourteen. But this decision was much harder for Carter to accept with Federer on the verge of becoming one of the best players in the world.

Carter did what he could to move on, asking Swiss Tennis for a raise and a promotion and continuing to coach young players at the National Tennis Center. Meanwhile, Federer assembled his team. It would include Pierre Paganini, the Swiss fitness trainer whose rare blend of rigor, creativity, and compassion had impressed Federer in Ecublens.

The plan was to start work as a group after the Olympics. Meanwhile, the losses kept piling up. Federer conceded that he was struggling with the pressure of his own expectations, magnified by his decision to break away from the federation.

He also had stopped working with the psychologist Christian Marcolli in early 2000.

"Everything I do is focused on the idea that there will be one day you don't need me," Marcolli told me. "I never want to create dependency, never want to create a relationship where people say I can only be good when you are there. My mantra, and I'm very transparent with them, is 'I want you to tell me one day, "Thank you, I get it. I can do it without you."' Of course that day is an emotional day, but I see this as my ultimate responsibility."

Federer was hardly thriving, however. Beginning in April, he lost in the first round on clay in five straight tournaments, including a 6–1, 6–1 defeat to Sergi Bruguera in Barcelona. Dorochenko had been back with Bruguera for only about two weeks after leaving the Swiss federation.

"I said to Sergi, 'Listen, you play high topspin to Roger's backhand, and don't worry about a thing,'" Dorochenko said. "Bruguera was coming back from shoulder surgery, and it was his first match, but playing on clay, if you know how to hit high topspin to Federer's backhand, you win. But there are honestly not a lot of players who know how to do that well, because Federer's shots go so fast that it doesn't leave you the time to get organized."

Rafael Nadal, still in his early teens at this stage, would attack Federer's backhand to devastating effect in the years and French Open finals to come.

But for now, Federer had other concerns.

"It just wasn't happening," said David Law, an ATP communications manager at the time. "He lost to Jiří Novák in Monte Carlo, 7–5, in the third, and I remember going up to the press conference, and on the way, Roger said, 'Why do I lose all the close matches?'"

He made a good run at the 2000 French Open, winning three rounds before losing to Àlex Corretja, another excellent Spanish clay courter with plenty of topspin. But Federer was soon back in a funk with six more opening-round defeats in Nottingham, Wimbledon, Gstaad, Canada, Cincinnati, and Indianapolis.

Law could sense Federer was at a crossroads: one where fulfilling his tennis potential was at risk.

"I have to say that he could have gone the other way, because he did like the life of being a tennis pro and traveling about and having a laugh," Law said. "Being in the locker room he'd be playing practical jokes in a really nice way but there was so much energy. And it's really a question of 'Where are you going to expend that energy? How are you going to use it up?'"

John Skelly, an American who coached Vince Spadea and Bob and Mike Bryan and other players, remembers crossing paths with Federer and Lundgren socially at that stage.

"Federer was pretty chill at that time," Skelly said. "He definitely partied and liked his beer, as did his coach. I remember in 2000 at Wimbledon, Federer was drunk as hell at a bar in Wimbledon village. He was definitely a happy drunk, loved the player parties in his younger days."

Federer once had unwittingly played a role in Skelly losing his job. Spadea had beaten Federer convincingly in Monte Carlo earlier in 1999 but then lost to him in a hurry in Vienna later in the season. Skelly said Spadea's father, Vincent Sr., was upset enough to make one of the poorest predictions in tennis history.

"Papa Spadea said right after the match, 'You're fired! This guy sucks! He's never gonna be anything!'" Skelly said.

Skelly, who later reunited with Spadea, certainly did not hold it against Federer.

"Really a class guy," he said. "He never changed a bit with all his accomplishments. He always treated me well and with respect, always a big smile whenever we crossed paths."

At the Olympics, the smile returned for Federer as he won four straight matches in straight sets to reach the semifinals, beating David Prinosil, Karol Kučera, Mikael Tillstrom, and Karim Alami.

There were no true tennis greats on that list, although Kučera, a smooth-moving Slovakian, had once been in the top 10. But it was still a reaffirming run, and Federer entered the medal round with renewed confidence to face Tommy Haas, a German with a one-handed backhand and flowing all-court game of his own. Haas, unlike Federer, had left Europe as a youngster to train in the United States at the Bollettieri Academy in Bradenton, Florida, growing particularly close with the academy's founder, Nick Bollettieri, a gregarious, perma-tanned force of nature who married eight times but was above all married to his work. Bollettieri had a bottomless need for self-promotion but also a genuine love of the game that he coached much better than he ever played.

Haas, then twenty-two, already had reached a Grand Slam semifinal at the 1999 Australian Open and would go on to rank No. 2 in the world in 2002 before major injuries stopped his ascent. But Haas, like Federer, had had a disappointing season in 2000 until the Olympics.

He dispatched Federer with relative ease, winning 6–3, 6–2 as Federer struggled with consistency and even kicked his racket into the air in frustration in the final game as Haas served out the victory to reach the Olympic final and guarantee himself a medal.

It was all too easy to flash back to a Lundgren comment from earlier in the tournament: "When he's behind, Roger sometimes still has a hard time fighting."

But Federer still had a chance for a medal because of the Olympics' unusual tennis format. He played another surprise—twenty-one-year-old Arnaud Di Pasquale of France—in the bronze-medal match.

Di Pasquale, ranked just 62nd, and Federer were on friendly terms, but their unexpected duel in Sydney was tense from the start. Di Pasquale prevailed, 7–6 (7–5), 6–7 (7–9), 6–3, failing to convert a match point in the second-set tiebreaker but rebounding from an early break of serve to win the third.

"I was afraid, very afraid, but I told myself that I could not come off the court the loser," Di Pasquale said. "It's the biggest moment of my career."

There was no predicting then, but it would remain the biggest moment of his career: Di Pasquale retired in 2007 with a losing record on tour in singles.

Federer had to settle for finishing just off the podium in fourth, the most frustrating spot at any Olympics. He had struggled to recover emotionally from the loss to Haas and had plenty of regrets about the Di Pasquale match as well.

"Honestly, it's so frustrating," he said, his ball cap pulled low to shield his eyes at the postmatch interview. "I played very badly in the semifinal against Tommy Haas. Today my tennis was better. It came down to details, to peanuts. To lose a medal like this, having it within reach, really hurts."

But Federer's first Games would actually end on a happier note. On his final evening in Sydney, he kissed Vavrinec for the first time.

That they had had this extended opportunity to spend so much time together was against the odds: Vavrinec could easily have missed the Olympics altogether.

They would not see each other again until December, keeping in touch by phone, but they had found something special in each other, and nobody would play a bigger role in Federer making the most of his transcendent tennis skills for so long.

"She was on a mission," Groeneveld said.

Chance certainly was a factor in the beginning, but so much hard work and so many smart choices would be required for Roger to become Federer, as Swiss journalist Laurent Favre cleverly phrased it.

"Mirka was a big believer in me not wasting any sort of talent," Federer told me many years later. "Because she knew herself that she was limited to a degree. She was extremely hardworking, but she knew with my talents I could achieve so many more things, and that belief was very influential."

CHAPTER SIX

———⊃○⊂———

WIMBLEDON

"Are you familiar with the Centre Court traditions?" an official asked Roger Federer as he prepared to enter Wimbledon's tennis temple.

Federer said that he had watched many a Centre Court match on television but had never played there, so the official reviewed the unwritten rules, including the custom of players walking on and off together and bowing to the Royal Box (this still happened in 2001).

While the nineteen-year-old Federer was happy to respect protocol, he was about to break with tradition in dramatic fashion. His fourth-round match was against Pete Sampras, the powerful and self-contained Californian who had lost just once at Wimbledon in eight years, and that was back in 1996 to Richard Krajicek.

At this stage, Centre Court belonged as much to Sampras as it did to the All England Club. But Federer, after years of observing from a distance, was now prepared to trespass, ready to show an unsuspecting global audience his panoply of tennis skills and newfound cool under pressure.

Those of us who followed the sport year-round understood the threat. We had seen Sampras struggle by his standards throughout the 2001 season, failing to win a title.

"I just wonder if he is getting to that time of life when you are still trying hard, and it's just not quite happening," said Martina Navratilova, one of the few who could relate to Sampras's serial success at Wimbledon with her nine singles titles.

We had also seen Federer develop into a more reliable force:

winning his first ATP title in Milan, excelling in the Davis Cup, reaching the quarterfinals at the French Open on clay and the semifinals at the grass court event in 's-Hertogenbosch. At Wimbledon, where he had not won a match since taking the boys' singles and doubles titles in 1998, he was on a run: beating Xavier Malisse in five sets in the second round and then sending a stronger signal by winning in straight sets against Jonas Björkman, a Swedish veteran with formidable returns who relished playing on grass.

British tennis fans already were looking ahead to Sampras's potential quarterfinal match with Tim Henman, the perennial English striver. But the cognoscenti were looking closely at Federer as he walked onto the rectangular lawn, where the good are separated from the great.

"I've arrived at where I wanted to be: playing Pete for the first time and on the Centre Court at Wimbledon," Federer told the Swiss press. "I'm not going out there just to win a set. I'm going out there to win."

Wimbledon really should have lost its luster. It is an anachronism. Who plays tennis on grass anymore? It was once the game's preeminent surface, with the Australian Open and US Open also contested on it. But grass court tennis occupies only five weeks on the tour calendar now. Synthetic surfaces rule, and yet Wimbledon remains essential, the tournament where players reconnect with their sport's past and predominantly white clothing while becoming stars in the present.

It is the only one of the four majors that is played in a private club, but the All England Lawn Tennis & Croquet Club is far from private during a normal Wimbledon, much as Augusta National is far from private during a normal Masters.

Wimbledon's passageways and concession stands get overcrowded during the championships, but the tournament rarely disappoints. The club is hillier than most imagine, more modern than most imagine, but Centre Court matches up well with the mind's eye. It feels like a theater more than a stadium with its concert-hall acoustics and dearth of advertising.

It has lost some of its symmetry with the installation of an imposing retractable roof in 2009, but it was still in its traditional state when Federer stepped onto its grass for the first time.

He and Sampras were not strangers. Federer had been a ball boy for Sampras during the ATP event in Basel. They had later met and practiced together on tour after Sampras had taken note of Federer's nearly single-handed destruction of the American Davis Cup team in February.

But Sampras was still the No. 1 seed, still the most successful men's grass court player of the Open era, and still eager to become the first man to win the Wimbledon singles title for the eighth time.

There had been a flashing yellow light in the second round, however, when he was pushed to five sets by Barry Cowan, an affable Englishman ranked a lowly 265th.

"I mean, a normal Pete Sampras would beat him in three," Federer said.

Normal or not, Sampras had rebounded quickly to trounce Sargis Sargsian in the third round and was rightfully confident against Federer.

"I felt good," Sampras told me twenty years later. "I knew Roger a little bit and knew he was an up-and-coming player, so it wasn't like I was saying I had a great draw here. But I did feel I had a match I should win, and I was caught off guard a little bit."

Federer felt good about his game, but his body was sending him signals that this was not a normal match. He said his hands felt "ice cold" during the five-minute warm-up session on Centre Court. But he started the match in style, slicing an ace on the opening point and then another ace later in the game as he held at love in just over a minute.

As the match developed, he picked at his strings between points, rather like Sampras, instead of harping on his errors, and offered precious few clues to his inner dialogue.

This was progress indeed: the result of years of work on himself and of constructive criticism from everyone from his parents to sports psychologist Christian Marcolli to his coaches to his girlfriend, Mirka Vavrinec, who was sitting in the player's box on Centre Court.

Peter Lundgren had warned Federer once, "Everybody knows you're the best tennis player, but they fight because if you lose your mind, they have you."

Federer's poker face also was the product of understanding that as he became more prominent, his on-court antics and negativity risked defining his image.

At the Italian Open in Rome in May, he had beaten Marat Safin, the fiery Russian star, in a tight three-setter full of shouts, pained looks, and tossed rackets: much of which was replayed on European sports highlights shows. Federer did not like what he saw.

A week after playing Safin, Federer played Argentine veteran Franco Squillari in the first round in Hamburg in what turned out to be another ill-tempered performance. Facing match point on his serve, he badly misjudged a volley and then broke his racket in disgust.

"Smashed it as hard as I could," he said.

But this time, Federer walked off the court angry at his own behavior rather than simply disappointed with another early defeat. He told himself that it was time to change in earnest, to muzzle himself for the greater good, above all his own. Despite all the lobbying from those closest to him, the decision had to come from him.

"That was a career-defining moment for me," he told me many years later. "I started to feel uncomfortable after a while when you're on TV like this. It's just a bad look when you see yourself throw the racket in the corner and you're like, oh my God, and you're looking around, and you're so frustrated and disappointed. And I just said, 'This just looks stupid and silly. Let's get your act together a little bit.' It took me a long time, you know. It was interesting. It took me a long time."

Federer had reverence for the increasingly grand settings in which he was playing, but he also recognized that his outbursts were impacting his performance as he advanced deeper into draws.

"I knew I was getting so drained from my behavior so I would come

to, like, the quarters of a tournament and be like, 'Ah, I'm so tired,'"
Federer said. "It wasn't because of the matches but because of the way
I *felt* during the matches. It was so emotional. The funny thing was
when I was twelve or thirteen everybody behaved like me. Marco
Chiudinelli and Michael Lammer, we all did it. We were all grunt-
ing and trying to piss the other guy off, and I honestly don't know all
that we were doing. It was normal to behave like this, and all of a sudden one thing leads to another and you are on the big stage, and you
can't behave like this anymore because now you're playing Pat Rafter
or Pete Sampras or someone you actually admire. You know what I
mean? It just can't be the same."

Actually, it can. The transition to the big stage has hardly stopped
other tennis stars from continuing to throw tantrums, rackets, or
chairs: see John McEnroe, Safin, and Nick Kyrgios.

But it was enough to finally calm Federer, at least on the outside.

Inside, the blood still boiled.

"Yep, you could say that," Federer confirmed.

It was about learning to control the flames instead of extinguish-
ing them, about converting them into slow-burning fuel rather than a
bonfire of distraction.

He showed plenty of staying power against Sampras, even if he
sometimes felt like he was in the midst of an out-of-body experience.

Federer would never play his other boyhood idols, Boris Becker
and Stefan Edberg, and he had not yet faced Marcelo Ríos. But here
was Sampras, the American star whom Federer used to cheer from
afar, aiming his fearsome serve in Federer's direction amid the hush
of Centre Court.

"In the beginning, that's how it is," Federer told me. "You play
against your heroes from TV. You have to work your way through
that."

Sampras had worked his way through it quickly when he was nineteen, defeating Ivan Lendl and John McEnroe back-to-back on his way
to winning the 1990 US Open, where he also beat Peter Lundgren,
Federer's future coach, in the second round.

That was the first US Open I covered, and I will always remember the self-conscious look Sampras often wore in the latter stages of that breakthrough, like a kid who had been handed the test questions before the exam and was well aware that he was going to succeed.

Now Sampras was the veteran champion, almost exactly ten years older than Federer, whose game was, in many respects, a tribute to Sampras's success, from the one-handed backhand to the devastating running forehand and acrobatic improvisational moves (consider both men's leaping backhand smash).

Both had a rhythmic "no-step" service motion in which they kept their feet apart as they tossed the ball and then bent their knees and leaped as they struck the serve. Many other players, including Rafael Nadal and Andy Murray, take a step with their back foot after the toss.

Sampras and Federer were the same height (six foot one) and same listed weight (176 pounds). They even used the same racket: the Wilson Pro Staff 85 with its comparatively small eighty-five-square-inch head, which had so much feel on well-timed shots. I played with it recreationally for many years and always felt the best description for hitting volleys with it was "buttery."

Tom Gullikson, the twin brother of Sampras's deceased former coach Tim Gullikson, was one of those who was struck hard by the similarities as he watched Sampras and Federer from the stands.

"I'm kind of rubbing my eyes here," he told me then.

They were not carbon copies. Federer's erect bearing contrasted with Sampras's slight stoop. Federer was the more fluid mover. Sampras was the more intimidating presence with superior service power, more explosive moves in the forecourt, and no qualms about ripping his second serve at first-serve pace. But the commonalities were unmistakable, and though contrasts in style generally produce the most watchable tennis matches, this strawberries-to-strawberries duel at Wimbledon would prove an exception because of the no-nonsense quality and variety of the shot making, the pure athleticism, the brisk pace and neck-and-neck score line.

There were plenty of complaints before and during the Sampras era about bang-bang tennis on grass and the patterns being too predict-ably brief. But to watch Sampras-Federer many years later in the midst of a long-running era of baseline domination is a bittersweet reminder that pure attacking tennis, with its quick points and staccato rhythm, still had its charms when two supreme practitioners were trading aces and fast-twitch blows.

"It was like old-school tennis," Federer's coach Peter Lundgren told me recently. "You don't see that anymore. Now the Wimbledon court is bare around the baseline. That match it was like it used to be: bare like a T from the baseline to the net. So much fun to watch, and it's still fun. Whenever it comes on, I enjoy it."

Sampras had to fend off three break points from 0–40 in just the fourth game before holding serve. He was characteristically bold under pressure, but as the match wore on, there were also uncharac-teristic gaffes: some straightforward backhand passing shots dumped into the net; volleys that he seemed slow to appraise; even a mishit on one of his trademark shots—the "slam dunk" overhead leaping forward.

This, sadly, would be their only official match. But at least it was a classic duel, hinging on just a few shots. Like the Federer first serve at 5–6 in the first-set tiebreaker that appeared to be long but was called good to the dismay of Sampras, who rightly voiced his skepticism after missing the return on his only set point. Like the high forehand volley that Federer nervously shanked to lose his serve and the second set. Like the biting body serve that the surprised Federer magically found a way to return with the head of his racket pointing toward the grass, allowing Sampras the chance to muff another overhead and lose the third set.

But Sampras would force a fifth by dominating the fourth-set tiebreaker before heading off court for a bathroom break. Federer remained in his chair with ample time to consider the situation as he folded a fresh bandanna and wrapped it around his head.

From my vantage point in the press seats on Centre Court, I thought Sampras had him. The American was not at his best, but he was still quite a force, and he had the momentum in the match and the deep faith that comes from having seen so many Wimbledon challengers crack under his pressure.

But then we already knew what Sampras was capable of. We did not need to imagine it or think creatively. He had been proving it for years. Federer was the unknown.

Sampras had never lost a fifth set at Wimbledon. Federer, perhaps for the best, was unaware of that statistic. Despite a nagging tightness in the adductor muscle of his left leg, he felt fresh and, just as important, calm.

He held serve quickly when play resumed, and neither man would face a break point in the final set until Federer served at 4-all.

Sampras, rarely a consistent returner, had long followed the template of coasting through most of his opponents' service games only to lift his level and hit enough quality returns in a flurry to get the one break that was often all he needed to win a set with his devastating serve.

The 4-all game felt like one of those moments, and Sampras would indeed get two break points to put victory in reach. But in atypical fashion, he squandered both. At 30–40, Sampras hit an uninspired backhand pass from inside the court that Federer quickly volleyed away for a winner. At ad out, Sampras missed a running forehand pass into the net that was hardly child's play but likely a shot he would have found a way to make at the peak of his powers.

"It just felt like usually I come through in those situations on that court," Sampras told me. "For me, one break point is a match point in my head. If I get one of those, to me the match is mine, but it wasn't meant to be."

Federer held serve to 5–4, held again to 6–5, and then took quick command of Sampras's next service game with a backhand return winner off a second serve.

On the next point, Sampras, moving a bit stiffly, punched a low forehand volley long to go down 0–30. He got back to 15–30 and then lost the next point with another missed forehand volley, this one into the tape.

It was 15–40. Match point for the teenager. Sampras, true to his Centre Court habits, flicked sweat off his brow with his index finger and ripped a first serve into play. It sliced wide but not wide enough to escape Federer.

"The thing about Pete is he can hit all the spots with his serve, and at big moments that's what made him so good," said Paul Annacone, then Sampras's coach. "I remember thinking as soon as Pete hit the serve that he had missed his spot by about eight inches, which is not Pete at a big moment."

Federer stepped to his right and smacked a forehand return winner down the line that the onrushing Sampras was nowhere near reaching. Sampras's thirty-one-match winning streak at Wimbledon was over, and Federer dropped to his knees and rolled onto his back, hands covering his face, before jumping to his feet for the handshake as the tears started to come.

"I had the feeling I really could beat him," Federer told us. "I had that feeling all the way. That's why I won."

He had played like a Centre Court regular.

"I thought the moment would get to Roger a little bit, and it wouldn't get to Pete," Annacone said. "In a weird way, I kind of felt like it didn't really get to either one. Roger just played a little bit better, which was surprising. That was a welcome-to-the-big-time moment."

It was only when the match was over that Federer looked like a rookie again: continuing to walk toward the exit while Sampras stopped for the traditional bow. Federer, grinning and sheepish, quickly reversed direction to rejoin the seven-time champion for a hasty bow of his own.

He dedicated the victory to Björn Borg, Lundgren's Swedish role model and close friend, whom Lundgren could impersonate astonishingly well. In the days before caller ID, Lundgren could fool his fellow Swedish players with crank calls. He once conned Jonas Björkman into believing that Borg had invited him to dinner. Björkman learned the truth only when he arrived at the fancy Monte Carlo restaurant where he had reserved a table.

"He's better than Borg at being Borg," Björkman said.

The voice was so familiar to Federer that he had a hard time keeping a straight face when he finally met the real Borg in Monte Carlo earlier in 2001.

One of the greatest to play the game, Borg had won forty-one straight singles matches at Wimbledon and five titles in a row. Sampras had been pursuing those records.

Federer had stopped him short, and now he wanted to speak with Borg directly. A phone call was quickly arranged. Federer's agent Bill Ryan was also Borg's longtime agent. "Roger was like a little kid in a candy shop when he was talking to Borg," Ryan told me. "His eyes were like plates."

Federer had beaten Sampras by hitting an equal number of aces (twenty-five), by returning more consistently, by producing clutch second serve after clutch second serve, and even by striking the ball more authoritatively, often surprising Sampras with the pace of his passing shots.

"It's true," Sampras told me. "I don't want to say I was overpowered, but there was definitely a bit of weight behind it that I guess I wasn't used to. It was my first time playing him. If I played him the next day, I'd be more prepared, but I was just a little bit uneasy. At that point he was very good. A couple years later he became great. I knew he had talent and was going to be around for a while, but I don't think anyone could have predicted he was going to dominate for the next twenty years and do all the things he would do. It's not like Tiger Woods or LeBron James, where since they were twelve you knew they were going to be superstars. For me and Roger, you just didn't know. It's not so clear-cut in tennis. It takes time to evolve."

There was a reminder of that two days later when Federer lost to Henman in four sets in the quarterfinals: 7–5, 7–6 (6), 2–6, 7–6 (6).

Federer would not be able to channel Sampras completely by winning his first major title at nineteen. His leg hurt, and he had required painkilling medication to get through the tournament. His margin over the opposition, even on grass, was not yet abundantly clear, but he had made quite an impression. Nothing elevates a young player like beating a superstar on one of the game's biggest stages. That would prove true for Naomi

Osaka in the tumultuous 2018 US Open final in which she defeated Serena Williams. It certainly proved true for Federer at Wimbledon.

"I think the Pete Sampras match changed everything," Lundgren said. "Because then everybody knew who he was. If you beat Pete Sampras on Centre Court in Wimbledon, then you know you can play, and after that he was on the map, basically. I mean, he had results before that, but you know managers and people around would say, 'What is wrong? Why doesn't he win more?' And I told them, 'He's not ready yet.' His game is big. He's got a huge game, and it takes time to choose the right weapon for the right shot. He had so many tools in his bag. He probably had fifteen on each shot."

The Sampras victory justified Lundgren's faith, as well as Peter Carter's, and calmed the concerned agents and sponsors. While it was unquestionably a coming-of-age moment, it did not yet signify a true changing of the guard.

"Let's not get carried away," Sampras said the day of his defeat. "I mean, I just lost. I plan on being back for many years. I mean, this is why I play: for these tournaments. I feel the reason I'd stop won't be because of my ability; it will be because I don't want to do it anymore. There's no reason to panic and think that I can't come back here and win here again. I feel like I can always win here."

Sampras would never win another Wimbledon, but he would silence his own skeptics by winning a fourteenth Grand Slam singles title at the 2002 US Open in what turned out to be his final match. As for Federer, he would not head straight to the top. Despite his sangfroid and all-court brilliance at the All England Club in 2001, he was not yet ready to dominate, not yet ready to live comfortably with the expectations generated by the Sampras upset. At that stage, he was also injured, and after a brief appearance in Gstaad, where he lost to his future coach Ivan Ljubičić in the first round, he took a forced six-week break to heal in Biel/Bienne.

During his hiatus, he became a chauffeur. Michael Lammer had taken over as Federer's housemate after Yves Allegro and then Sven Swinnen had moved on. Lammer was trying to rehabilitate an ankle injury but still needed to get to his high school classes.

Federer, who now had his driver's license, volunteered to be of service.

"Roger was like, 'Okay, I'll come pick you up at school, and I'll bring you to school, because I'm also injured, and my schedule is very flexible. I'll be the taxi driver for you,'" Lammer said.

Mirka Vavrinec, who was in Biel trying to recover from her own injuries, was also spending considerable time with Lammer and Federer.

"Mirka started to run the apartment for us thankfully, so that was lucky," Federer told me with a chuckle. "Michael and me, we still laugh about it. Michael came to visit me, and we had dinner and we were talking about it again, how good it was to have Mirka in our life. Finally, we could find stuff, and finally we could breathe normally again from all the dust being cleaned up."

Consistent excellence remained elusive, however, and Federer finished the year ranked 13th—a significant improvement on 2000 but not enough to qualify for the elite eight-man tour finals in Sydney, Australia, which were won by Lleyton Hewitt.

The 2002 season began auspiciously for Federer with a title in Sydney, more Davis Cup brilliance in Moscow, finals in Milan and Miami, and then another title on clay in Hamburg after victories over clay court master Gustavo Kuerten and Safin. But Federer still lost in the first round of the French Open to Hicham Arazi before returning to Wimbledon as the No. 7 seed and one of the betting favorites after his performance the previous year.

John McEnroe, aggressive during his playing days and bold with a prediction, picked Federer to win the title. The All England Club, clearly a believer in Federer's style and prospects, put him right back on Centre Court against a qualifier from Croatia: Mario Ančić, who was tall, skinny, and intelligent and, like Goran Ivanišević, from the lovely coastal city of Split. At age eighteen, Ančić was two years younger than Federer and making his first appearance in a Grand Slam tournament. Attacking with conviction, Ančić trounced him 6–3, 7–6 (2), 6–3, proving again that Centre Court experience was no prerequisite for Centre Court excellence.

It was the most deflating loss of Federer's career to date. It came at a sensitive time, with his Nike agreement up for renewal and his management situation with IMG in flux because of disputes about some contract details.

Tennis is a sport where off-court earnings dwarf prize money for the biggest stars, and in the sports business world, which is so often a futures market, there were genuine doubts if Federer was the next No. 1 or merely one of a talented group of young contenders.

Lleyton Hewitt, nearly the same age, already was the world's top-ranked player and would win Wimbledon in 2002, defeating another of Federer's junior rivals—David Nalbandian of Argentina—in a sea change final devoid of serve-and-volley (at least traditionalists could take solace in the fact there was a rain delay). There was also Andy Roddick, the fast-serving and quick-witted American teenager who came from a much more important commercial market than Federer and was pounding on the door of the top 10.

It was an anxious, uncertain period for Federer, and it was about to get worse, much worse.

———⊂⊃———

In early August, Federer and Lundgren traveled to Toronto for the Masters Series event and the start of the summer hard court season.

Late on the night of August 1, Lundgren's phone rang. It was Darren Cahill, who was coaching Andre Agassi.

"I thought Darren was calling me because Agassi wanted to hit with Roger," Lundgren said. "And then Darren said, 'Sit down.'"

Cahill told Lundgren that Peter Carter had been killed in an automobile accident in South Africa on his honeymoon while traveling to Kruger National Park. Carter was just thirty-seven years old.

Federer's mother, Lynette, had helped arrange the trip, and Federer often had urged Carter and his Swiss wife, Silvia, to make the journey. But South Africa, for all its charms and natural beauty, remains one of the most dangerous places on the planet to drive. And on August 1 Carter had been in a Land Rover driven by a friend who had to swerve to avoid an oncoming vehicle. A bridge was just ahead, and the driver could not regain control in time. The Land Rover plunged over the side of the bridge and landed on its roof, crushing and killing Carter and his friend.

Silvia was in a separate vehicle and unharmed. The honeymoon had been intended to be a celebration of her return to health. She had been diagnosed with Hodgkin's lymphoma shortly after their wedding in 2001, but her treatment had been judged a success by the summer of 2002, and she and Carter were finally able to take their delayed trip to South Africa.

It ended in tragedy, and it was up to Lundgren to tell Federer.

He left him phone messages and finally got a call back. Federer, already eliminated in singles, was out in the city and was soon sprinting through the unfamiliar streets in tears, trying to process what Lundgren had just told him.

"He did what little boys do when faced with something huge and dark: He ran," wrote S. L. Price, the intuitive American sports journalist, in a piece for *Sports Illustrated*.

Federer ended up in Lundgren's hotel room.

"He came in, and he was looking at me, and I looked like shit, which was of course normal in that situation," Lundgren said. "I was empty. It was so tough for both me and for Roger. Peter and I were extremely close. We spent a lot of time together. Roger lost his former coach and friend and everything. I knew how much Peter meant to Roger. It was the first time for both of us to go through something like that."

Sven Groeneveld, who was in Toronto coaching Greg Rusedski, also got a call from Lundgren to come to the hotel room.

Lundgren, not Federer, told him about Carter. "Roger was devastated," Groeneveld remembers. "He couldn't talk. He was totally out of it."

For Federer, a week short of his twenty-first birthday, the powerful emotions were compounded by the role he and his family had played in encouraging Carter's trip. There was guilt mixed with the grief.

"I think that's what hurt him the most," Groeneveld said.

Federer barely slept that night but somehow still played the quarterfinals of the doubles the following day with South African partner Wayne Ferreira. They lost in a third-set tiebreaker to Sandon Stolle and Joshua Eagle, both Australian, which was a further reminder of Carter.

By sad coincidence, Federer's father, Robert, was in South Africa on business at the time of the accident.

"Peter had a special place in our lives," he told the Basel newspaper *Basler Zeitung* the week of Carter's death. "You realize at such a moment just how close he was to all of us."

Federer and Carter had remained on good terms despite Federer's surprise decision to hire Lundgren as his traveling coach. Federer had pushed successfully in the summer of 2001 for Carter to lead the Swiss Davis Cup team after Federer had led an insurrection that forced out former captain Jakob Hlasek. Carter, who was not yet a Swiss citizen, was not allowed to formally take on the role of captain by the International Tennis Federation, but he had directed the Swiss team in Moscow in February when it faced Russia in the first round of the 2002 Davis Cup.

"I love the Davis Cup, but it never would have been possible for me to have this role in Australia," he told the Swiss press. "I really believe Switzerland can win the Davis Cup in the next five years if its leading players can stay healthy."

In Moscow on an indoor clay court, the inspired Federer defeated former No. 1 players Marat Safin and Yevgeny Kafelnikov in straight sets in singles, but Federer and Marc Rosset could not win the doubles against the two Russian stars and the Swiss went on to lose the tie, 3–2.

In his Davis Cup role, Carter traveled more frequently to tour-level events than in the past, and he saw Federer at both Wimbledon and Gstaad before heading to South Africa.

"I will always remember what Peter gave me," Federer said shortly after Carter's death. "He taught me so much that is still inside me."

Federer chose to play on but lost in the first round to Ivan Ljubičić in Cincinnati. "I'll never forget," said Bill Ryan, Federer's agent at the time. "It was 1,000 degrees. Lundgren and I went and sat with Roger outside the players' lounge in the shade under a tree because it was so fricking hot, and Roger said, 'I don't feel like playing tennis anymore.'"

He withdrew from the Washington, DC, event and flew home to Switzerland for the funeral, the first he had attended.

"I knew that I had to get back," he explained later. "America was just too far away at that moment. I wanted to be with my friends, though I certainly could not help much. I will always miss Peter Carter, but he will be with me on the tennis court my whole life."

Emotions were still raw as he joined the more than two hundred mourners at the church of Saint Leonhard in central Basel along with many of Switzerland's leading players, including Yves Allegro.

"Roger was completely destroyed," Allegro said. "You could see in his body language, and he could not stop crying. I think he cried for the whole funeral, an hour and a half straight. It was tough to see that kind of grief. But I really think Roger became a man at the moment of Peter's death. That's basically the first time he really had to face something tough or horrible. He was quickly in the top 100, quickly making good money. His family was healthy. His parents were together. Sure, he and his sister had some fights because he had money she didn't have or whatever, but that was not a big problem. He met Mirka and was happy there as well. So everything was going smoothly, you know? And then he lost one of the most important people in his life."

Cahill, so close to Carter since boyhood, made the journey to Basel as well. When the service was over and Silvia Carter and others had spoken, Cahill went up to the red-eyed Federer and told him, "Mate, Peter would be damn proud of everything you've done. And your only job now is to continue to make him proud."

"That's really all I said," Cahill told me many years later. "And boy, has Roger lived up to those words. Peter would be upstairs smiling every single day about what Roger has been able to accomplish, and those of us who were Peter's mates, we are proud in a secondary sort of way to watch Roger and what he's been able to do, because it means something to us as well."

For Federer, the funeral was an epiphany. His evolution from talented prospect into one of the greatest players of all time involved many elements, but Carter's death was a major factor, perhaps the decisive factor. From that point on, Federer understood that his success validated Carter's efforts and honored his memory. Carter's life had been far too short, but at least if Federer could achieve what Carter had envisioned on court, then that life had served some part of its purpose.

"I did find a new motivation," Federer told me.

In Carter, he had a cause greater than himself: one without a clear finish line.

"That was the turning point," Allegro said. "It's tough what I'm going to say, but seriously I don't know if Roger would have had the same career if Peter would still have been alive. But there is also the possibility he would have become an even better player, because in my mind it was clear that at some point he was going to take Peter back as a coach."

Allegro believes that after choosing the more experienced Lundgren to guide him through the early years of his professional career, Federer would have gone back to Carter once he had become established.

Federer has never confirmed this, but he had certainly created an opportunity to see much more of Carter by helping to place him in the Davis Cup post.

Nobody knew his game better, from the foundation to the superstructure. Now Federer would have to go forward without that reassuring link to his past. So many of his boyhood courts were gone and now his boyhood coach was gone, too.

"It keeps hitting me in waves," Federer told the Swiss press when he returned to competition after the funeral at the ATP event on Long Island in Commack, New York. "This is the first time a close friend of mine has died, and there were so many more things I wanted to tell him. I can't do that anymore. I feel most of all for his wife, Silvia, who I also know well, and his family and friends."

Federer lost in the opening round to Nicolás Massú in Commack. But he pulled out of his tailspin the following week at the US Open, winning three rounds before losing to Max Mirnyi in straight sets. After beating thirty-year-old American star Michael Chang in the second round, Federer was asked if it might be a wise idea to resume working with a therapist to help him through this challenging emotional phase. It was a reasonable thought. Marcolli, the performance psychologist who had helped Federer in his teens, knew Peter Carter well.

"I don't need one anymore," Federer said in New York. "I have to deal with the ups and downs myself."

More mixed emotions awaited him in Casablanca, where the Swiss Davis Cup squad traveled to play a strong Moroccan team in a World Group qualifying match on clay that would determine which nation took part in the top division in 2003.

Carter had helped plan the particulars of the match before his death. Lundgren agreed to replace him as team leader at the request of his players and Swiss tennis officials. As a Swede, he, too, could not be the official captain, and he arrived after his players following a trip home to Sweden to be with his daughter Julia, who had been diagnosed with diabetes.

The Swiss team included Federer, Marc Rosset, Michel Kratochvil, and George Bastl, who had upset Sampras at Wimbledon himself earlier that year in the second round in what turned out to be Sampras's final Wimbledon match. Lundgren asked Severin Lüthi to help as an assistant coach and named Rosset, the veteran, as the playing captain. Lundgren made the objective abundantly clear.

"We can do it," he said. "For Peter Carter."

Federer did not drop a set in three matches: beating Hicham Arazi in singles after losing to him on clay at that year's French Open, teaming with Bastl to win the doubles, and then defeating Younes el-Aynaoui on the final day to clinch the 3–1 victory.

Federer dedicated it to Carter. "I thought of him often," he said. "He was just there, even on match point."

Rosset could sense a change in Federer, using the French word *déclic*, which translates roughly as "eureka moment."

"I think Peter's death made him grow up very quickly," Rosset said. "And it made him feel like he was on a mission."

Less than a month later, Federer tearily dedicated another victory to his former coach: this one at the ATP event in Vienna, where he beat Carlos Moyá in the semifinals and Jiří Novák in the final.

Both Moyá and Novák were top 10 players, and the title proved critical to Federer's qualifying for his first year-end championships, reserved for the top eight singles players. It was known then as the Tennis Masters Cup, and it was being held in China for the first time in an exposition hall in Shanghai. There were concerns that Chinese fans, new to the sport, might not understand the rules, so a pamphlet was handed out to spectators explaining the basics.

But no guidebook was required to sense the transcendent intensity of the semifinal between Lleyton Hewitt and Federer.

Hewitt was the defending champion after winning the event in Sydney in 2001. Federer had beaten him in Miami earlier that season, but this was their most significant duel yet.

Hewitt had already clinched the year-end No. 1 ranking for the second straight season before facing Federer, but he threw his wiry frame into each exchange. The court coverage from both twenty-one-year-olds was routinely exceptional, the shots in extension often spectacular. There is a recency bias in tennis. It is tempting to see the newer material as the best material, but some of the all-court points that Federer and Hewitt collaborated on in this classic three-setter were as good as any they would ever play.

Federer could not serve out the first set. Hewitt was unable to convert a match point before losing the second and then failed to serve out the victory at 5–4 in the third. But Federer, still a gusting wind at this stage of his career, lost his serve again at love, double-faulting on the last two points.

Hewitt, so tenacious and consistent from the baseline, closed out the 7–5, 5–7, 7–5 victory in the next game and went on to win the title in Shanghai.

At this stage, he held a 6–2 edge over Federer in their tour matches. Cahill, who coached Hewitt until the end of 2001, had helped him establish that early dominance. What did young Hewitt have that young Federer did not?

"Look, they both had so much," Cahill said. "But Lleyton certainly had the ability to play the score much better than Federer. He would sense an opportunity, and he would lock down and just wouldn't miss. Whether that be a break-point opportunity or a chance to get a double break or a 15–30 point when you're up 3–2 in the first set serving. Some young players would play a lackadaisical couple of points and drop a quick service game. Lleyton would sense that the 15–30 point is a massive point in the match, make sure that he got that first serve in, wouldn't miss that point, bring it back to 30-all, and then get a sneaky free point for 40–30, and then problem solved."

Federer's insistence on attacking the net also played into Hewitt's deft hands at that stage, in part because of the revolution in string technology, which was allowing players to generate more spin and precision with full-force swings.

"Lleyton loved a target," Cahill said. "But Lleyton also had, especially back then, a burning desire to compete and to be great. It was unrelenting, and I think that was really rare. I think the only player that really you can compare it to is someone like Rafa [Nadal]. Lleyton had that before Rafa arrived on the scene, and there was no deviating for him. Even as a seventeen-, eighteen-, nineteen-year-old, you could have World War Three happening around Lleyton outside the court. He could be having problems with the ATP or it could be problems in his house or a girlfriend problem or whatever. But once he stepped onto the court, that was his safe place. That was his home. That was the place where he could just forget about the rest of the world. All he wanted to do was win. And I think that's a pretty rare quality to have, because a lot of tennis players, if they're not happy in life or they have issues outside, it's tough to concentrate when competing. Lleyton never had that problem."

Hewitt, with his drive and precision and precocity, was the first great rival of Federer's professional career: the first peer who consistently underscored his deficiencies. Both had foreseen the other's rise, through the eyes of their coaches but also through their own eyes, beginning with their fiery junior duel in Zurich.

Hewitt reached the sunlit summit first, yet he could sense that Federer was climbing up out of the mist in a hurry, and he said so in Shanghai, making it clear that he believed Federer would win a Grand Slam title.

Hewitt, only a few months older, already had two, and Federer was increasingly impatient. Too impatient, it seemed, as the 2003 season developed.

Federer was at his best in the Davis Cup with teammates to lift him and in regular, best-of-three-set tour events. He won titles in Marseille indoors, Dubai on outdoor hard courts, and Munich on clay before reaching the final in Rome, losing to Félix Mantilla. But when Federer returned to Paris and Roland Garros, seeded fifth and with justifiably big plans, he crumpled under Grand Slam pressure again.

Instead of making a run at becoming the first attacking player to win the French Open since Yannick Noah, he lost in the first round in straight sets 7–6 (6), 6–2, 7–6 (3) to Luis Horna of Peru on the main Philippe-Chatrier Court.

It was another deflating moment for Federer on one of the game's center stages, and it was his second straight opening-round defeat at Roland Garros after losing to Arazi in 2002.

Horna was a solid, hard-running clay court player and former French Open junior champion, but he was also ranked 88th in the world and had never won a main-draw Grand Slam singles match.

Federer, in reasonable form, would surely have prevailed. Instead, he looked trapped in the headlights: muddled about tactics, shanking backhands off the frame, and casting wounded looks at Lundgren in the stands.

He did reel off five straight games after losing the first three. But he could not close out the first set, missing a forehand on his lone set point at 6–5 in the tiebreaker. That gaffe summed up his afternoon as he finished with eighty-eight unforced errors in just three sets.

The headline in *L'Équipe*, the French sports newspaper, described it poetically: "Naufrage en eaux calmes" (Shipwreck in calm water).

Federer seemed oddly calm after the shipwreck, too.

"Maybe he should just shout or break a racket and get it all out," Lundgren said.

That was amusing advice considering how much effort had been expended to get Federer to quiet down and focus. But he was still struggling to get the balance just right.

"I definitely got too calm on court for a while," Federer told me many years later. "I realized that I needed some fire and some ice. When I was young, I didn't understand what having the right energy, the right intensity, was. It was like, what does that mean? Is it like a look thing? Is it like a walking-around thing? What is it? But it's that laser-focus, point-by-point mentality, because what happens when you are young is you start drifting off. That's the battle."

Federer did his best to describe the battle during our interview:

"When you're young, you're like, 'Oh, what are we doing for lunch? What are we doing after?'" he said. "Sometimes you are in the mood. Sometimes you are not, and the problem is when you are not, you start losing points like it's a waterfall. It's like 15–love, 30–love, 40–love, love–15, love–30, and then you are like, 'Oh my God, I have to focus, and it's too late.'"

Lundgren sensed the same struggle.

"Roger knew he was doing something wrong with screaming and shouting and being upset, showing it too much," he said. "The other players are not stupid. How are they going to beat you? Not by playing tennis. They beat you mentally, so he learned that. But then he got too mellow, so that was not good, either, and all of a sudden he found a way."

For Federer, there was nothing sudden about it. He felt it was a two-year process: one that began after Hamburg in 2001 and culminated in 2003 at Wimbledon just as a lot of the game's chattering classes were openly wondering whether Federer genuinely had a champion's mentality.

He had played sixteen major tournaments and had yet to get past the quarterfinals, losing in the first round on six occasions.

It was not just Hewitt who had taken the lead in their tennis generation. Marat Safin and Juan Carlos Ferrero, both twenty-three, were also Grand Slam champions (Ferrero had just won the French Open). Nalbandian, twenty-one, had reached a Wimbledon final. Roddick, twenty, had reached the semifinals of the 2003 Australian Open after saving match point and beating Younes el-Aynaoui in a character builder of a quarterfinal that stretched to 21–19 in the fifth set, then the longest in Grand Slam history. Roddick also had just beaten Andre Agassi on his way to the grass court title at Queen's Club before arriving at Wimbledon.

Federer was clearly a flashy shot maker, a crowd pleaser, and a well-liked colleague in the locker room, but he had to feel that he was losing ground even if he had just won the first of his many titles in Halle, Germany, on grass.

"People are so quick to build a narrative," Roddick told me. "So, when Roger didn't advance past the quarters of a Slam early, I feel like a certain narrative was building especially because he was so smooth, and it was easy, and you didn't see him grunt and sweat. It just looked different than the rest of us."

He was definitely quite a contrast with Roddick, who was all muscle, hustle, dripping sweat, nervous energy, and abrupt, full-cut power.

"I feel like everyone gets thrown into a bucket with a label," Roddick said. "If Roger would have had the same exact results but been five foot ten and played a little uglier, he wouldn't have been given the soft label. It's because he was that good, because he walked a certain way and carried himself a certain way, that soft was the easiest label. I think it was probably the laziest label that everyone would accept."

That is a player's perspective and an understandable one. The sports media are adept at quick analysis, not nearly so committed to the long view and giving players enough rhetorical runway to comfortably advance at their own pace. But labels are rarely without some foundation, and the question at this stage was legitimate:

Did Federer have the requisite grit?

Sampras certainly believed so. Already retired, though it was not yet official, he picked Federer to win Wimbledon in 2003. Sampras, after all, could relate to thriving at the All England Club after struggling in Paris. He had done it so often. As if to prove how tough a double it was, the year of Sampras's best result at the French Open—a semifinal run in 1996—was also the only year he failed to win Wimbledon between 1993 and 2000.

But Federer was fresh and much happier on grass at this stage despite having come to it late after learning the game on clay in Basel.

Displeased with some of the press coverage of his early exit in Paris, he kept the interviews to a strict minimum at the All England Club, and maximized his time at his rented home in Wimbledon village with Vavrinec and Lundgren.

"I was still just under the radar back then," he told me. "Not doing any press for me was very unusual, but I got to Wimbledon and I was just like, 'Okay, I just have to focus here. I cannot lose another first round here.' There was a lot of pressure involved because of all those situations."

He swept through his first two matches against Hyung-taik Lee and Stefan Koubek and then dropped a set in a victory over young American Mardy Fish.

But in the fourth round came trouble. As Federer warmed up against Feliciano López, another junior rival turned pro rival, he felt his lower back lock up like it had never locked up before. He called for the trainer at 1–1 in the first set and could not get a clear answer on the nature of the injury, which Lundgren later explained was a pinched nerve caused by Federer's back being thrown out of alignment.

"I gave myself two games to see how things would go," Federer said.

Unable to rip full-force shots or move normally, he would have been happy with a rain delay in those days before the Centre Court roof.

"I was looking up at the sky, hoping for a miracle, some dark clouds, something to save me," he said. "I changed my tactics. I waited for him to make errors, tried to pressure him on important shots, because I know that playing against an injured player is not easy."

López served for the first set at 5–4 and failed to convert, and

Federer, his back loosening up, went on to prevail 7–6 (5), 6–4, 6–4, rallying from a 0–3 deficit in the third set.

"I don't know how I won today," said Federer, who acknowledged that he had considered retiring for the first time in his pro career.

"Considering my draw, that would have been really infuriating," he said.

No former Grand Slam singles champions were left after all the upsets, which included the little-known Ivo Karlović's first-round stunner over Hewitt on Centre Court and the unseeded Mark Philippoussis's five-set defeat of Agassi in the fourth round.

Federer, at No. 4, was the highest seed remaining, but he was not a clear favorite. Roddick was an unmistakable threat, which he reaffirmed by dominating Jonas Björkman in straight sets in the quarterfinals, while Federer rolled past Sjeng Schalken, feeling much better after Wednesday's rain had given him an extra day to recuperate.

It would be Federer versus Roddick in the semifinals: a new-generation duel that would be their first of many at major tournaments and their first on grass.

Roddick was full of competitive fire and personality. He was a wise-cracking little brother who had grown up determined to keep pace with his older sibling John, who became a leading junior and all-American at the University of Georgia but could not break through on tour.

Andy was an underpowered baseline scrapper as a youngster but matured into a force of nature with an explosive serve and forehand and plenty of swagger. After his first-round loss at the French Open, he had made a surprise move: splitting with his longtime coach and mentor, the Florida-based Frenchman Tarik Benhabiles, and hiring Brad Gilbert, a motormouthed tactical wiz who had been ranked as high as No. 4 in the world before coauthoring the book *Winning Ugly* and coaching Agassi to greater heights.

Roddick and Gilbert decided that despite Roddick's intimidating serve, he would not play classic grass court tennis. Instead of serve-and-volley, he would try to pounce on attackable balls with his forehand and only then rush the net.

It worked until he ran into Federer, which could not have come as a shock to Roddick. He had lost all three of their previous matches, including a quarterfinal in Basel in 2002 when Federer hit one of the shots of his career (or anybody's career): a sliced retreating overhead near the back wall off a Roddick overhead that hooked past the stunned American at the net.

"I felt like he was playing video games while the rest of us were trying to play tennis," Roddick said of that moment.

Roddick tossed his racket playfully at the grinning Federer, then walked around the net to retrieve it. But the whole scene was serious foreshadowing: a solid Roddick effort trumped by a Federer stroke of genius followed by Roddick deflecting some, though not all, of the pain with his wit.

At Wimbledon, Roddick had cause for hope. This was his second Grand Slam semifinal and Federer's first. Roddick also had the benefit of counsel from Gilbert, who had coached Agassi to victories over Federer.

"Going into the match, I honestly felt like it was fifty-fifty or maybe even fifty-five–forty-five Roddick," Gilbert told me. "The way Andy was serving, I felt pretty good about where he was at. And nobody in the semis of Wimbledon that year had ever been in the semis of Wimbledon before."

Perhaps it would have turned out differently if Roddick had managed to convert the set point he had on his own serve at 6–5 in the first-set tiebreaker. Instead, he ran around his backhand and struck a straightforward midcourt forehand—one of his staple shots—into the top of the net.

Federer took the hint after that unforced error, winning the next two points and the set. He shrugged off a break point in the opening game of the second set with a perfectly weighted backhand drop volley that had so much spin it practically stopped after the bounce.

It was showtime.

"This is some of the prettiest tennis I've ever seen," said Mary Carillo, the veteran American analyst who was calling the match for NBC.

Gilbert referred ruefully to the end of the first-set tiebreaker and beginning of the second set as "those seven minutes."

"I'm sure Andy would tell you the same thing: He wishes he had those seven minutes back," Gilbert said.

But Gilbert acknowledged how far Federer had come since he had watched him play Agassi in Basel in 1998. "His backhand had dramatically improved, and his serve was so pinpoint accurate compared to what it was," Gilbert said. "He was leaping so much more off the ground on his serve. He made massive improvements on those two shots."

Federer was not quite playing classic grass court tennis himself, staying on the baseline after many of his second serves, content to trade groundstrokes with Roddick and wait to pounce. Many of his most memorable winners were passing shots, hit with equal precision and panache off both wings.

Roddick did his earnest best: even diving for a backhand volley in the second game of the second set, but Federer smoothly tracked it down and flicked a forehand winner. He was entering the zone, parrying Roddick's power with advanced swordplay, willing the ball where he wished. He remained deep in his own bubble with the exception of the smile he allowed himself after closing out the second set and a high-level rally by swatting a sharply angled forehand half-volley winner moving forward.

"Just ridiculous," said Roddick. "I don't know if anybody else can do that shot. It was almost like he was trying to do a trick shot out there. But it worked, and I just had to say, 'Too good.'"

Roddick was relegated to the role of delivering the paint to the artist. Federer would finish with 61 winners and just 12 unforced errors. Nearly twenty years later, Roddick sees no reason to view his 7–6 (6), 6–3, 6–3 defeat through a dark lens.

"I remember the missed forehand in the breaker because that could have changed it, but I think I played well and just got outplayed," Roddick said. "I don't know if this is good or bad, but for me it was easier to sleep if I felt I had at least done my part. It was very apparent what a natural fit his game was for grass, and the thing that doesn't get talked about enough is how he could mix things up on grass. He has won Wimbledon staying back 95 percent of the time. He has won it serving and volleying 80 percent of the time, so depending on the conditions, he was able to adjust."

That tactical variety does indeed set Federer apart from his role models. He did not—like Becker, Edberg, or Sampras—rely on essentially the same Wimbledon game plan year after year. With his wide range and comfort zone, he adapted to the opposition; to the racket and string technology; to the grass itself, which Wimbledon altered in the early 2000s, creating a firmer surface that produced a more reliable, slightly higher bounce that was more friendly to baseliners.

But this first of Federer's many Wimbledon victories still bore a strong resemblance to the tennis he had grown up watching from Wimbledon. Federer's opponent in the 2003 final was Philippoussis, a barrel-chested six-foot-four Australian who played pure serve-and-volley on grass but often did not have to volley that year because of all the aces he was smacking, including forty-six in five sets against Agassi.

Like Federer, Philippoussis had made his first major impression at age nineteen by upsetting Sampras at a Grand Slam tournament: defeating him in the third round of the 1996 Australian Open under a closed roof in straight sets. The son of a Greek father and an Italian mother, Philippoussis was nicknamed "Scud" because of the missiles that came off his racket, but he was much more than just a banger. His racket skills, including a one-handed backhand, were extraordinary. In my view, he is one of the most gifted players never to win a Grand Slam title.

He became a star in Australia the night he beat Sampras and ended up enjoying plenty of Australian nightlife in the years to come. Consistency was a problem. So were injuries. He reached the 1998 US Open final, losing to compatriot Patrick Rafter, but then in the quarterfinals of Wimbledon in 1999 he heard an ominous crack in his left knee when he was up a set on Sampras. He retired from the match and went on to have three knee surgeries, spending more than two months in a wheelchair in 2001. By Wimbledon 2003, he was back on track, if only temporarily, and was taking his career and his opportunities more seriously at age twenty-six.

He had the tools and talent to win Wimbledon, but Federer was entering a new dimension, capable of doing damage so quickly from so many areas of the court. The final followed a similar pattern to that of the semifinal against Roddick. Federer won a tight first-set tie-breaker and then took command for good early in the second set by breaking Philippoussis's serve for the first time with a series of brilliant passing shots.

In the third-set tiebreaker, he jumped out to a 6–1 lead, giving himself five championship points. His first Grand Slam title was close enough to let the mind start racing. He looked cool, but that was a facade. He had to fight back tears prior to his first championship point and had to deal with the dialogue in his head, which he could still recall in detail years later.

"I'm like, 'It's about to happen. I'm going to be Wimbledon champion,' and I was like, 'Oh no, just keep yourself together,'" he said in the documentary *Roger Federer: Spirit of a Champion*. "'Just make an error, just miss one ball please, Mark. Just miss it, okay, so I don't have to hit a winner.'"

Federer had hit so many winners in that Wimbledon fortnight and had not faced a single break point in the final, but he got his wish as Philippoussis, after saving two match points, struck a backhand return into the net on the third with Federer rushing to net. Another winner would not be required.

Federer took one more step forward and then crumpled to his knees, both arms up as he looked back toward Vavrinec, Lundgren, and physiotherapist Pavel Kovac in the player's box.

Potential had merged with achievement by the score of 7–6 (5), 6–2, 7–6 (3), and though Federer might have made it look remarkably easy to the international audience encountering his fluid game for the first time, he knew the truth. "When I'm winning everything seems so easy, and when I'm losing it seems like, 'Oh, this guy's not trying,'" Federer told us. "But I'm always trying, and I gave everything I had these last two weeks."

Those who knew Federer well could have no doubt about what was coming next: tears courtside in his chair and more tears during the awards ceremony.

"We all cry easily in our family," Lynette Federer once explained.

The British tabloids, unsurprisingly, did not miss the opportunity. "It's Roger Blubberer," read the headline in the *Daily Mirror.*

Federer, who finally made it to the Wimbledon champions dinner he had skipped in 1998, acknowledged after reviewing the press clippings that he could have done without quite so many "crying pictures."

"Maybe a few more with the trophy would have been good," he said.

There would be plenty more of those in the Wimbledons to come. The changing of the guard had taken two years, but it was now complete. Like Sampras, Federer had won his first Wimbledon at age twenty-one. A weight had been lifted, a number of weaknesses addressed, and he was ready to hit some serious heights.

Christian Marcolli, the Swiss psychologist who had counseled Federer in his teens, was watching from afar. Marcolli and Peter Carter had agreed that when (not if) Federer won his first Grand Slam title, they would each smoke a cigar. Sadly, poignantly, he went onto the balcony of his apartment in Baar, Switzerland, and smoked his alone.

"We had this fundamental conviction," Marcolli told me, choking up as he thought about Carter.

In Ecublens, the Christinet family, who had hosted Federer for two years, watched the broadcast on their couch in the company of reporters from Swiss national television. After Federer hoisted the trophy, the Christinets hoisted glasses of champagne. "When I see him in tears, that really touches me," said Cornélia Christinet, tearing up herself. "When he was here, he was a true fourteen-year-old boy, natural, spontaneous with a real joie de vivre. But for me, this changes nothing. He will always be the Roger who was with us."

Christophe Freyss, the disciplinarian French coach who had been so set on taming Federer's comportment in Ecublens, actually saw Federer play in person at the All England Club in 2003. "I got into Centre Court, not in the box, just in one little corner," he told me recently. "And I was sitting there in that magnificent place looking at him down on the grass and saying to myself, '*Mon dieu*, look how far he has come.'"

Freyss paused a moment before continuing: "And now I'm thinking about how far he went after that."

CHAPTER SEVEN

MELBOURNE

Very soon after Federer won Wimbledon in July 2003, Peter Smith opened his email and was surprised to see a message from the new champion himself.

It was about Peter Carter, Smith's longtime pupil and confidant.

"Roger said, 'Every time I play well, or I play a good shot I think of Carts upstairs. I look up and know Carts would be looking down on me from above, and that he'd be proud of me,'" Smith said. "Roger wanted to let me know, I think, that he credited Peter with where he was at, and he was committed to being the best player he could be from then on."

Nearly twenty years later, Smith still chokes up about that note. He was diagnosed with Parkinson's disease in 2011 and is no longer able to work or instruct at the same pace.

"It's very long-term, and I'm a long way down the track," Smith said.

But Smith savors his memories of Carter, which are still vivid, and knows how much Federer's success would have meant to their friend.

"Roger really made up his mind that he was going to be what Carts told him he could be: the best player on the planet, not just the most talented or most gifted player on the planet, but the best," Smith said.

The paradox was that because of Federer's new maturity and mission, Smith's most successful protégé, the hometown player he had helped develop into a precocious champion, would definitely lose his edge.

But Lleyton Hewitt, a born scrapper, was not about to surrender his era without a fight. When Federer and the Swiss Davis Cup team arrived in Melbourne for a semifinal in September 2003, Hewitt was not just prepared but inspired.

Hewitt had slipped from No. 1 to No. 7 in the rankings after failing to reach the semifinals of any Grand Slam tournament in 2003. He had lost in the first round of Wimbledon as defending champion to the low-profile, high-altitude Croatian Ivo Karlović, who stands six foot eleven. He had lost in the quarterfinals of the US Open to Juan Carlos Ferrero in part because of a hip problem.

But Hewitt was determined to salvage his season, and the Davis Cup was both his opportunity and his passion.

In Australia, the Davis Cup has long been more than a mere sports competition. It once played a role in nation building: demonstrating remote Australia's can-do spirit to a faraway world in the 1950s and 1960s with an evolving, seemingly inexhaustible supply of net-rushing talent under its obsessive and territorial captain, Harry Hopman—a former sportswriter, of all things.

In that period, the Davis Cup was still close in prestige to individual events like the Grand Slam tournaments, and from 1950 to 1967 the Australians won the Cup fifteen times, defeating the United States in the final on nine of those occasions.

Domination came easier then. The reigning champion did not need to start from scratch each season but instead received a bye to the final as the other nations played off during the season to determine a challenger.

The reigning champion also had the advantage of hosting the final, known as the "challenge round." Traveling from Europe or the United States to Australia in those years was draining enough, but the challengers then had to face great players like Frank Sedgman, Lew Hoad, Ken Rosewall, Rod Laver, Roy Emerson, or John Newcombe with roaring crowds behind them.

It was a stacked deck, and so it remained until 1981, when the challenge round was abolished and a sixteen-team, four-round World Group was established.

Though Australia's victories became rarer, the cultural value of the Davis Cup still ran deep. Federer understood this because of his conversations with Carter, who had daydreamed as a boy of playing in the Cup for Australia. He had to settle for being Switzerland's unofficial Davis Cup captain, albeit too briefly.

Carter introduced Federer to many of the former great Australian players and coaches who crossed their paths during Federer's early years. The Australians were usually extroverts who liked to tease and were particularly quick to puncture inflated egos. They were friendly off the court but ferocious competitors on it.

Federer, with his own ability to pivot between those two domains, could relate to all of that, and he also came to admire Australia's tennis legacy. Though he had been an indifferent student in his school years, Federer was drawn to the history of his chosen sport: a curiosity that only deepened as he proceeded to make so much tennis history himself.

"I asked a lot of questions, and I had a great bunch of guys around me when I came up on tour that educated me as well," Federer said in a background interview for the 2018 documentary *Strokes of Genius*. "They were like, 'Look, this is somebody who played semis at Wimbledon back in 1968 and this is somebody who won the doubles back in 1954.' And I'd be like, 'Oh wow! Please tell me about it!'"

Federer was intrigued by those who had helped tennis make the transition from the amateur era to the Open era in 1968, when professionals were allowed to compete at the major tournaments like Wimbledon. He knew that these trailblazers, who often earned little during their careers, had made it possible for him and other contemporary stars to make a fortune.

"I always felt like, well, you're going to be respectful to older people but even more so maybe to older tennis players, because those are my biggest inspirations and motivations when I'm playing tennis today," he said. "They did something very special that I could profit from even today. I wish that all the youngsters coming up on the tour will be super, super curious to find out everything about tennis. About the records of Arthur Ashe. Why Jimmy Connors? Why Martina Navratilova? Why Gabriela Sabatini? You name it. Just to know what's so interesting about these people because everybody has a super-interesting story, every single player. They don't have to be former world number ones."

This was classic conversational Federer: ebullient and rambling with a penchant for re-creating past dialogues, including internal dialogues.

But despite his wish, most of his tennis contemporaries were not nearly as curious about the greats of the past. Hewitt, like Federer, was an exception. Though he could be prickly and evasive with Australia's journalists, there was no questioning his enthusiasm for representing his nation.

At age five, he had watched on television as Australian star Pat Cash rallied from two sets down at Kooyong Stadium in Melbourne to beat Mikael Pernfors and Sweden in five sets in the 1986 Davis Cup final.

Hewitt could practically recall it point by point because he had kept a videotape of it.

"That's the match I always look back on," he once told me. "It was one of the greatest Davis Cup matches ever."

Becoming a professional athlete was not a hazy, distant goal in the Hewitt family. Hewitt's father, Glynn, and uncle Darryl played Australian rules football for a living. His mother, Cherilyn, was one of Australia's best at netball, a leading sport for women, and became a physical education teacher.

Hewitt played "Aussie Rules" and tennis until he was thirteen, when, at a similar age to Federer, he felt compelled to focus on one sport. Of modest size but stout spirit, Hewitt chose wisely. At age fifteen, he became the youngest man to qualify for the main singles draw of the Australian Open; like Federer in his midteens, he was asked to join his country's Davis Cup team as a hitting partner. The Australians called hitting partners "orange boys" because they had once been in charge of bringing the fruit to the Davis Cup players. Hewitt was an orange boy for the first-round match in 1997 against France at White City

Stadium in Sydney. John Newcombe was the Australian captain, Tony Roche the coach, and Patrick Rafter the key player as he rallied from two sets down, with Newcombe swearing and inspiring him on the changeovers, to defeat French star Cédric Pioline in another five-set thriller. Australia went on to win the round.

"I spent a great week just hanging around those guys who I looked up to and idolized at the time; you could not have asked for a better atmosphere," Hewitt said. "Newk told me that hopefully in the next three or four years I could be out there on the court."

It would not take nearly that long.

The following year, at age sixteen, Hewitt stunned the tennis community by upsetting Andre Agassi to win the ATP tournament in his home city of Adelaide.

The first person to call Smith after the victory was Peter Carter. In the past, he had phoned Smith to rib him, maintaining that Hewitt might be an impressive prospect but that Federer was better.

"This time Carts said, 'I just saw your boy play a bit. It looks like he might have gone ahead,'" Smith said with a laugh.

Hewitt and Federer had to scrap their plan of playing doubles together in the junior event at the Australian Open, because Hewitt's surprise victory in the Adelaide tournament earned him a wild card into the main draw of the Australian Open.

While Federer became the world's top junior, Hewitt became a full-time professional. In 1999, he broke into the top 25 in the ATP rankings and was a pillar of the Australian team that won the 1999 Davis Cup on the road in Nice against the French.

Hewitt at his peak was a relentless and quicksilver counterpuncher, and after reaching No. 1 in back-to-back years and winning Wimbledon and the US Open, he was on a mission to win the Davis Cup at home. But in order to host the final, the Australians first had to get past the rising Federer and the Swiss.

Both teams were intent on honoring Carter. John Fitzgerald, the Australian captain, was also from Adelaide, where Carter had trained and lived in his youth. The Australian and Swiss federations agreed to create the Peter Carter Memorial Trophy, which would be awarded to the winner whenever Australia and Switzerland played in the Davis Cup.

The teams also honored Carter's memory with a minute of silence before the opening day of singles matches in Melbourne Park, best known as the site of the Australian Open.

The Australians could have shipped in a temporary grass court for the semifinal, but that seemed foolhardy in light of Federer's performance at Wimbledon. Instead, the Australians chose the same hard court surface used for the Australian Open. Known as Rebound Ace, it was a rubberized, relatively high bouncing surface that could be easier on the body in some conditions but became more hazardous in extreme heat as footing became stickier.

But it was cool, even chilly, in September in Melbourne, and the opening match had to be played under Rod Laver Arena's closed roof because of rain. Hewitt defeated Michel Kratochvil in straight sets and Federer then did the same to Mark Philippoussis in a rematch of their Wimbledon final.

The following day, Federer and Rosset, Switzerland's playing captain, faced Wayne Arthurs and Todd Woodbridge, the great Australian doubles player who had long paired with Mark Woodforde before Woodforde retired.

The match was tense, and Arthurs and Woodbridge prevailed 4–6, 7–6 (5), 5–7, 6–4, 6–4, with Federer losing his serve in the fifth set at 3–3, double-faulting twice in the game.

Australia now had a 2–1 lead with Federer and Hewitt set to play the first of the two reverse singles matches on Sunday.

The sellout crowd in Rod Laver Arena included Kim Clijsters, the popular Belgian tennis star who was Hewitt's girlfriend at the time and considered somewhat an honorary Australian. Peter Carter's parents, Bob and Diana, also had made the journey from their home north of Adelaide.

The Australians needed just one more victory to win the semifinal, but it seemed highly unlikely that Hewitt could provide it as Federer gradually imposed his will and bigger game.

Federer was no poker face on this occasion. His hunger for success was evident, and after missing a forehand as he tried to close out the first set, he shouted "Fuck" repeatedly. Hewitt did the same after losing the next point. It was a brief flashback to their profanity-filled duel as teens in Zurich, but neither player would lose focus this time.

Federer won the first set 7–5 and the second 6–2, smacking winners on balance and off. He took a 5–3 lead in the third after breaking Hewitt with a forehand inside-out winner, clenching his fist and roaring at his teammates. He then served for the match.

At 30–all, he was just two points from victory.

"I mean, you would have bet your house on Roger at that stage," said Roger Rasheed, Hewitt's coach, who was sitting in the stands in Laver Arena with the Swiss fans shaking their cowbells and the Australian fans cheering on Hewitt without much conviction.

But on the next point, Hewitt hit a great, deep forehand return off a Federer first serve that landed on the back of the baseline. Federer, who wrongly thought the ball was going to land out, reacted late and flicked a backhand out of play. It was break point at 30–40, and Hewitt converted it with another deep return that Federer sliced into the net.

It was 5–4 now, and on the changeover, Rosset, the Swiss captain, was full of urgency. He squatted in front of the seated Federer, put his hand on Federer's leg, and peppered him with advice and encouragement in French.

It was to no avail. Hewitt held serve, despite Federer twice more getting within two points of victory, and the feisty Australian, practically lit from within, went on to win the tiebreaker to extend the match to a fourth set.

"It was important for Lleyton to get into a dogfight against the best players," Rasheed said. "Because once he felt like he was in that sort of Rocky Balboa fight, that put him in a different headspace that only he would understand. He would just start believing things would happen: 'I'll turn this around. I'm getting stronger again.' It was almost like Popeye having another can of spinach."

The Rocky comparisons were meaningful to Hewitt. He used to shout "C'mon, Balboa!" to himself during matches.

The fourth set was close: Hewitt broke Federer's serve to win it 7–5 with a reflex two-handed backhand volley with both men at net. But the fifth set was a rout as Federer faded physically (and emotionally) and Hewitt closed out the comeback and the semifinal victory 5–7, 2–6, 7–6 (4), 7–5, 6–2 with a precisely placed overhead.

"This beats the hell out of winning Wimbledon or the US Open," said Hewitt.

Federer kept his composure on court. In private, it was a different matter. Many factors were at work. He had become the leader of the Swiss Davis Cup team, using his clout to push out the captain Jakob Hlasek in 2001. Winning with Rosset and his friends was a major goal, one that had just been thwarted even if the Swiss would still likely have lost the semifinal with Philippoussis a heavy favorite in the final singles match, which was never played.

Above all, it was the memory of Carter that made the defeat so painful. Carter had long made Hewitt a reference point for Federer: the player he needed to become good enough to beat, the player who lacked his firepower and long-term potential. When Federer met with Carter's parents after the match, the emotions overwhelmed him.

"It was a very tough moment for Roger, similar to the funeral in Basel," Rosset said. "You cannot be indifferent when you see a guy whom you care about so much suffering like that. It breaks your heart, too."

Georges Deniau, the veteran French coach who had joined the Swiss team at Rosset's request, said that Federer sought refuge in the small room where the racket stringer had been working.

"I've rarely seen a man cry like that," Deniau told France's *Tennis Magazine*. "Nobody dared to bother him. I went in after a little while. He had his head in his hands."

Federer told me many years later that he still considered that match one of his "very toughest losses" but that it also helped him know, in his marrow, that he had the game to beat the leading players. He had dominated Hewitt, his rival in chief, for nearly three sets on the road. Yes, he had lacked the sangfroid to finish the task, but he was rising to a new level. He could sense it.

The surprise was that the Davis Cup did not cast a pall over the rest of his 2003 season, and that would become one of Federer's hallmarks through the years: the capacity to rebound quickly from disappointment, sometimes brutal disappointment.

"He bounces back really fast," Paul Annacone, one of his longtime coaches, told me. "Yes, he gets dejected, but by the end of the night or the next morning, he is bouncing back. I've never met anyone who does a better job of finding the balance between appreciating things when they win but still being able to move on when bad stuff happens."

In his next tournament after the Davis Cup defeat, Federer successfully defended his title indoors in Vienna. But though he faltered in the other European indoor events, in part because of a sore back, he saved his final flourish of the season for the Masters Cup, the year-end championships, which had moved from Shanghai to Houston for two years.

The elite eight-man tournament, once a fixture at Madison Square Garden in New York in the heydays of Jimmy Connors and John McEnroe, had not been held in the United States since 1989. The driving force behind the return was the owner of Houston's Westside Tennis Club: Jim McIngvale, an irrepressible, sometimes irascible furniture magnate nicknamed "Mattress Mack."

McIngvale was and remains one of those archetypal self-made American characters who dreamed big, worked hard, consumed and donated conspicuously, and spoke his mind as a matter of course, diplomacy be damned. He and his wife, Linda, were serious tennis fans, and though their club was a long way from Wimbledon and Roland Garros on the map, they did their best to bridge the gap by installing all four Grand Slam surfaces at their forty-six-court complex, including grass and red clay, both rarities in North America.

McIngvale spent roughly $7 million on the hosting rights for the Masters Cup, which some in the tennis world privately dubbed "the

Mattress Cup." He spent $20 million more on the new outdoor stadium and everything else.

It all had cost much more than he expected, and he was feeling understandably a bit edgy and proprietary. He took offense when Federer, in a news conference on the eve of the event, said he thought the 7,500-seat stadium was small for a tournament of this magnitude and pointed out that the playing surface had a slope and was uneven in places.

McIngvale confronted Federer in the locker room before his opening round-robin match with Agassi. ATP officials intervened to mediate, eager to preserve the pride and enthusiasm of one of the rare American businessmen ready to invest heavily in tennis.

Federer eventually apologized. McIngvale accepted and later said that Federer was "a good kid and a great player."

But the official transcript of Federer's comments on the stadium was expunged, Soviet-style, from the tournament website and is still quite a challenge to find today.

"I don't understand why people wrote that I was criticizing," Federer said later. "That was just my first impression. I can also talk differently when I arrive and say everything is great, you know. But that was just my feeling. If I can't say my feelings anymore, I don't come to press conferences anymore."

Nonetheless, it was an early lesson in the consequences of speaking too freely and a reminder that, with his increasing prominence, his comments would quickly be parsed and amplified, particularly if they created or revealed conflict.

He learned the lesson well, certainly too well from a journalistic perspective. He has given in excess of a thousand press conferences in multiple languages since then and controversy has been rare. He avoids politics, cultural rubbing points, and public score settling (at least without a racket in hand).

But the kerfuffle in Houston certainly did not hurt his performance in Houston. Quite the contrary. Instead, he broke down barriers.

He took to the court after his exchange with McIngvale and played boldly under pressure to beat Agassi for the first time, saving two match points in the final set before prevailing 6–7 (3), 6–3, 7–6 (7).

Federer now had a victory over Sampras and Agassi, tennis's two leading men in the 1990s, compatriots with contrasting styles and personalities but a similar attacking mind-set: Sampras in the forecourt; Agassi from the backcourt.

"It's just nice to beat such players one time in your career," Federer said afterward.

In his next round-robin match, he defeated another of his bêtes noires. Nalbandian, the rugged Argentine with a complete game and a two-handed backhand, had beaten Federer as a junior and in their first five professional matches, including the US Open quarterfinals earlier in 2003. But Federer overwhelmed Nalbandian this time 6–3, 6–0 largely from the baseline: a change in tactics from their past matches.

He then blew past reigning French Open champion Juan Carlos Ferrero 6–3, 6–1 to finish round-robin play undefeated and qualify for the semifinals against Andy Roddick.

McIngvale was not only waving the American flag. He wore shirts decorated with it and cheered unabashedly for Agassi and Roddick, whom he called "my boys."

Such jingoism from the man in charge did not delight the other six singles players in the field: all Europeans or South Americans. This was, after all, the Masters Cup, not the Davis Cup.

"It's a lack of respect," Nalbandian said.

But McIngvale was so far getting what he wanted: a full stadium for the night sessions, with both Roddick and Agassi into the final four.

Federer had other plans for the weekend, however, and was deep in the same sort of groove he had found at Wimbledon.

His first victim was Roddick, who had won his first major in 2003 as well, prevailing at the US Open after saving a match point against Nalbandian in the semifinals. Roddick arrived in Houston fresh off of hosting *Saturday Night Live* in New York and spoofing his American elders: Agassi and John McEnroe.

"My life has become this circus," he said.

In August, Federer had been one victory away from securing the No. 1 ranking when he faced Roddick in the semifinals of the Masters Series event in Montreal. Though Federer served for the match, he let the moment get to him and lost to Roddick for the first time (6–4, 3–6, 7–6 [3]).

"I remember thinking this is kind of what I needed, to win a tough one against him," Roddick told me. "But at that point and time you are thinking week to week as opposed to what the historical significance of this person might be. It was less about a matchup for me and more about I was playing great and executing well. When I lost to him in Basel or earlier, I felt he was probably the better player then, more developed, maybe two years further along. So I felt that Wimbledon and that match in Canada were the first time we were both vying to be the top player in the world or at least in that conversation."

Roddick would get to No. 1 first after winning in New York and then secured the year-end No. 1 ranking ahead of Federer in the round-robin phase in Houston.

But Federer beat him in straight sets in the semifinals 7–6 (2), 6–2 and overwhelmed Agassi 6–3, 6–0, 6–4 in the best-of-five-sets final. Agassi, one of the best returners in the game, did not manage to get even one break point against Federer's serve.

Agassi had not competed since the US Open, celebrating the birth of his and Steffi Graf's daughter, Jaz Elle. He might not have played in Houston at all if not for his loyalty to McIngvale. Agassi appreciated McIngvale's charitable endeavors, entrepreneurial spirit, and support of American tennis. In light of Agassi's lack of recent match play, a run to the final was a very good run. Darren Cahill, Agassi's coach, was certainly satisfied, but when he went to the locker room, he was surprised to see Agassi sitting with his head down and not lifting it.

"He didn't say anything," Cahill said. "I'd never seen him like this. Normally he can take a loss no problem, and he's over it in two or three minutes, but he had his head down for about twenty or thirty minutes."

Cahill finally approached him, placed his hand gently on his back, and told him how proud he was of the way he had competed in Houston and that he had just run into a hot player in Federer.

"Let's move on," Cahill said.

Agassi looked up and said, "Mate, our game has forever been changed. It will never be the same. This guy is just taking this game to a whole new level. We haven't seen this type of level before."

Cahill was stunned. "Andre is usually full of just confidence, no matter what," he said. "These great champions always think, 'Listen, if I get it together and play my best tennis, I can beat these guys.' This, I think, was the first time that a legend of the game that I've been around thought to himself, 'Jeez, I can't beat this guy if he plays like this.'"

Agassi, who was thirty-three at that stage, knew exactly what he was talking about. He would never beat Federer again, and that resounding victory in Houston would foreshadow some of the most dominant seasons in tennis history.

But first came a December surprise. At the end of a breakthrough season and with the top ranking in close range, Federer announced that he and Lundgren were splitting.

It seemed like a bolt from the blue. The Swiss press had just finished publishing stories on the special relationship between Federer and Lundgren in which Lundgren talked about the off-season program for December and their lofty goals. Even Robert Federer chimed in: "Peter is there for Roger around the clock."

But just as Federer had made a tough decision to travel on tour with Lundgren instead of Carter, Federer made another risky choice to change a winning team.

This was a pattern throughout his career. Federer, for all his conviviality and loyalty to boyhood friends like Yves Allegro and Marco Chiudinelli, was not too sentimental to break bonds when his inner voice was shouting that he needed change.

Despite the timing, he said it was not a decision that he had made abruptly but one he had been thinking about since the start of the 2003 season and more frequently in recent months.

"It was a long process," Federer said at a hastily arranged press conference in Geneva after the *Neue Zürcher Zeitung* broke the story of the split. "We are stopping at an all-time high for me, which also made the decision very difficult. But I am convinced this is the right next step."

Federer said he felt they had fallen into a routine.

"At the end of the season we both felt that it wasn't like it used to be," Federer said. "I let him know my decision last week. He was disappointed but he understood my arguments. We always signed one-year agreements. We've arrived at the end of a cycle."

Though some who know Lundgren and Federer have maintained that Vavrinec played a decisive role in the split, Federer has always rejected that theory.

"It's clear that there is internal discussion within the team about a decision like this," he said. "But the decision comes from me alone. I am the one who has to be satisfied. Nobody else."

Lundgren still sounds wistful about the way it ended but told me that the decision, while not mutual, was, in some ways, a relief. His girlfriend and two young children were living back in Sweden, where they were building a house. His contract with Federer was for forty weeks of work a year, much of it involving travel. He said he was approaching burnout without realizing it. He had been a successful tour player himself and then transitioned quickly into coaching.

"I basically felt that I didn't have a life myself, and that was nothing against Roger," he said. "When Roger called and said let's stop, I felt that I was done. Of course, I felt empty after what he said. For so many years we'd been working and spending so much time together and all of a sudden one day it's over. But I felt I had said everything I know, and it was time for him to hear another voice. That's really how I felt. When we split, it was almost like I was happy that he took that decision."

Lundgren took several months off, away from the circuit, before agreeing to coach one of Federer's rivals: former No. 1 Marat Safin, another phenomenal talent with composure issues.

Federer's elastic one-handed backhand in full flow in Madrid: eyes on the contact point. *(Courtesy of Ella Ling)*

Federer wins the boys' singles title at Wimbledon in 1998 at age sixteen. *(Photo by Mike Hewitt/ Getty Images)*

The new Wimbledon champion poses with Mirka Federer, Lynette Federer, coach Peter Lundgren, and physiotherapist Pavel Kovac in July 2003 at the All England Club. *(Photo by Thomas Coex/AFP via Getty Images)*

Federer and Nadal meet at the net with darkness falling after the 2008 Wimbledon final: one of the greatest tennis matches ever played. *(Courtesy of Ella Ling)*

Federer smashes a racket in frustration while playing Novak Djokovic in Miami in 2009, a rare relapse for a man who learned to control his frustration. *(Courtesy of Ella Ling)*

Nadal celebrates above the fold in the *New York Times*: rare air for a tennis match, but the 2008 Wimbledon men's final transcended the sport. *(Courtesy of the author)*

The tears flow as Federer finally wins the French Open in 2009. Former rival Andre Agassi presented him with the trophy at Roland Garros. *(Photo by Ryan Pierse/Getty Images)*

Federer's signature shot: the airborne inside-out forehand. *(Photo by Julian Finney/Getty Images)*

Switzerland wins its first Davis Cup. Left to right in 2014 in Lille: Michael Lammer, Marco Chiudinelli, Stan Wawrinka, Federer, and captain Severin Lüthi. *(Photo by Julian Finney/ Getty Images)*

"The lack of facial contortion when he hits the ball speaks volumes. Playing tennis is natural, effortless for him, an extension of his body and mind." *(Courtesy of Ella Ling)*

The on-court postvictory interview. Federer has given hundreds over the years. Here with Jim Courier at the 2017 Australian Open. *(Courtesy of Ella Ling)*

Comeback complete. The moment of victory at the 2017 Australian Open: Federer's most surprising Grand Slam title. *(Courtesy of Ella Ling)*

Djokovic, the most elastic man in tennis. *(Courtesy of Ella Ling)*

Federer and Nadal played doubles together for the first time at the 2017 Laver Cup in Prague. (They won.) *Photo by Clive Brunskill/ Getty Images for Laver Cup)*

Coach Ivan Ljubičić plays it cool while Federer trains in 2019 on Roger-Platz, the court named for him in Felsberg, Switzerland. *(Courtesy of the author)*

Federer on the clay between coaches Lüthi and Ljubičić as practice partner Dan Evans limbers up. *(Courtesy of the author)*

Club members with a view of the snowcapped Alps and a Federer training session at Tennisclub Felsberg. Nobody clapped until the end. *(Courtesy of the author)*

One of Federer's most painful defeats: the 2019 Wimbledon final. *(Photo by Matthias Hangst/Getty Images)*

Federer played long enough for his children to watch him at work. The twins at Wimbledon in the front row with Pierre Paganini, Mirka Federer, Lynette Federer, and Severin Lüthi. *(Courtesy of Ella Ling)*

Federer and Nadal get into the spirit of the 2019 Laver Cup. *(Photo by Julian Finney/Getty Images for Laver Cup)*

Federer and comedian Trevor Noah celebrate at the exhibition in Cape Town that drew a record tennis crowd of 51,954 in 2020, just before the pandemic closed borders and stadiums worldwide. *(Photo by Ashley Vlotman/Gallo Images/ Getty Images)*

There are more powerful serves, but Federer's trademark is precision under pressure. *(Courtesy of Ella Ling)*

Federer prepared for the 2004 season in Biel/Bienne with fitness trainer Pierre Paganini and then traveled to Australia with Vavrinec, physiotherapist Pavel Kovac, and Federer's close friend Reto Staubli, a former Swiss tennis champion who had been part of the 2003 Wimbledon celebration.

Federer had no official coach at this stage: highly unusual for a great young player who could have met the salary demands of any coach of his choosing. But Federer was in no hurry to replace Lundgren, and Staubli, eleven years older, agreed to use some vacation time from his job at a Swiss bank to provide informal counsel and serve as a hitting partner. He also booked practice courts and scouted some of Federer's upcoming opponents.

Staubli might not have been a coach in name, but in 2004 he would certainly do a lot of the work typically associated with a coach, although he avoided giving Federer technical advice on his strokes or technique.

Federer's plan was to avoid full-bore competition until the Australian Open began. In 2003, he had played more than ninety singles matches—a big number at tour level—and he knew, through Paganini and his own instincts, that it was better to build up to the Open more slowly.

He played hard court exhibitions in Hong Kong and at Kooyong Lawn Tennis Club in Melbourne, losing to Agassi in their unofficial match. But Federer seemed relaxed, no longer a great talent lacking great achievements. When the Australian Open began, he was ready, sweeping through his first three rounds without surrendering more than four games in a set.

That set up a fourth-round rematch with Hewitt in the same stadium where Federer had cracked on court and off four months earlier. This time, it was Hewitt who took the early lead, winning the opening set as Federer struggled to produce depth with his groundstrokes and his usual precision with his serve. But with Hewitt serving at 2–3 in the second set and a 40–15 lead, Hewitt double-faulted and on his next first serve was called for a foot fault that nullified an ace. Rattled by the line umpire's call, Hewitt lost the point and eventually his serve.

A match can turn on so little in tennis, a game of momentum. Federer put his foot on the accelerator pedal and left it there, winning eight of the next nine games despite the interruption caused by the fireworks that began to explode near Rod Laver Arena midway through the lopsided third set.

It was Australia Day, a national holiday, but it did not feel much like a celebration of Australian tennis as Federer rolled to a commanding lead before the match tightened again. But in the fourth set Federer broke Hewitt's serve at 2–2—a break that included one of the points of Federer's career as he scrambled to the corners, lobbed on the full stretch, then read the direction of Hewitt's overhead perfectly and stabbed a forehand winner on the run.

Rasheed was openmouthed in the player's box after that one, and he was not alone. But Hewitt would get one more chance with Federer serving for the victory, just as he had served for it in September.

After a double fault early in the game, Federer missed a routine backhand slice at deuce to give the Australian a break point.

"For sure the memories of Davis Cup surfaced there," Federer said. "He wins that game, and the crowd gets into it. Who knows?"

But Federer came up with a sharply angled first serve that forced Hewitt far off the boundaries of the court. The Australian shouted as he was hitting the return, almost as if he was already aware that it was going to land just wide. Break point saved, and though Hewitt gave it his utmost—diving on the next point and rolling like a goalkeeper after landing on the hard court—he could not stop Federer from finishing the match the same way Hewitt had finished in the Davis Cup: with an overhead winner.

"I'm very, very happy to have taken my revenge," Federer said of his 4–6, 6–3, 6–0, 6–4 victory. "I had so many things swirling through my brain, but there was no way I wanted to relive that nightmare."

The result was one more big hint that the players who once had

Federer's number were rapidly losing their ability to keep pace with his new math. Down went Nalbandian in four sets in the quarterfinals. Down went Ferrero in straights sets in the semifinals, guaranteeing that Federer would ascend to No. 1 in the rankings after the tournament for the first time.

"Number one in the world is something that comes naturally when you win big tournaments," said Federer, who was most interested in the big tournament at hand.

The last obstacle to an Australian Open title was Safin, the first player of Federer's age-group to become a Grand Slam champion. Just seventeen months older, he broke through by beating Sampras in the 2000 US Open final with a performance that was, on balance, more extraordinary than Federer's defeat of Sampras at Wimbledon less than a year later.

Federer overcame Sampras in a fifth set that could have swung either way. Safin, then twenty years old, obliterated Sampras 6–4, 6–3, 6–3, making Sampras look like yesterday's champion as he struggled to keep pace with Safin's roundhouse punches and counterpunches.

A few weeks later, Safin reached No. 1, even though that achievement was not properly recognized because the ATP Tour was experimenting in 2000 with a new approach called "the Race." It emphasized the season-long points race over the traditional rolling fifty-two-week ranking system that had been in place since 1973.

This marketing experiment did not last long, and Safin was soon on the list of No. 1s where he belonged. He is, in many ways, the most instructive comparison with Federer, even though Nadal and Djokovic would eventually take up most of that air and space.

Though he hit his backhand with two hands, not one, Safin had many of the same ingredients as his Swiss peer: world-class athleticism, phenomenal ball-striking talent, effective volleys, and easy, elastic power as well as a mastery of spin.

Federer was more fluid and surely a step faster, but Safin, three inches taller at six foot four, could still run like a deer when fit. Ruggedly handsome, he also had undeniable swagger and sex appeal. He walked like a lumberjack happy to head to the forest, and though his job satisfaction fluctuated wildly, you could not take your eyes off him as he patrolled the court, shoulders rolling and gold chains swaying as he prepared to smash an ace or some equipment (who could know?).

Federer might have been the guy you wanted your daughter to date. Safin was more likely the guy your daughter wanted to date.

Safin had arguably more charisma off the court with his spontaneity, natural wit, and inability to provide a canned answer. He, too, spoke three languages: Russian, Spanish, and colorful if imperfect English. He had a different sort of charisma on court with his expressiveness, quick-to-boil temper, and penchant for producing winners (and errors) from unexpected places.

That last sentence once would have applied to Federer, of course: Both men share the dubious honor of having been fined for lack of effort in a pro tournament. But while the Swiss learned to suppress and channel his tennis demons, Safin never got the balance right for long.

"I get bored too quickly," he once confessed. "And angry too quickly, too."

Many a racket paid the price, and unlike Federer, Safin also struggled with significant injuries throughout his professional career, partly because he played through the pain for the money.

It is hard not to wonder what might have been if he, in his teens, had met a fitness guru like Paganini, spent some quality time with a performance psychologist like Marcolli, or found a life partner like Vavrinec who understood and supported all that was required to remain a tennis champion and had no problem speaking her truth to power.

Safin was a genuinely cutting-edge talent, and I am convinced that he, Federer, and Nadal could have run roughshod over the 2000s together in the sort of three-way rivalry that later became all the rage.

But it was not to be. While Federer came remarkably close to maximizing his abilities and optimizing his chances, Safin undeniably did not.

That did not make him less interesting, just less successful, even if he ended up in the International Tennis Hall of Fame, the first Russian to receive that honor and three years ahead of his Davis Cup teammate Yevgeny Kafelnikov.

"The higher I went, the more I started to be heavy in my head," he told me in 2021 on a Zoom call from Moscow during the coronavirus pandemic. "I had sometimes the sparks of wow, this is really pleasant, but most of the time it was heavy, heavy, heavy pressure. I felt this all the time, and I got burned out."

Safin was born in Moscow in 1980. His parents are Tatars: Muslims and descendants of the Turkic people who ruled central Asia centuries ago.

Both were tennis players. His mother, Rauza Islanova, was at one stage the second-ranked women's player in the Soviet Union and would likely have been a touring professional in a different era. Instead, she became a tennis coach at the Spartak Tennis Club, one of the leading sports clubs in Moscow. Safin's father, Misha, was the manager of Spartak, and though Safin wanted to be a soccer star, he became a tennis star by default and grew up on the same courts as two other future stars: Anastasia Myskina and Anna Kournikova, both of whom Safin's mother coached in their youth.

She also coached her own children: Marat and his much younger sister, Dinara, who also would reach No. 1 in the world. No other brother and sister have reached the top spot in singles. Clearly, Islanova knew what she was doing, and when her beloved and gifted son was twelve, she and Marat agreed that he should leave the country to find a better and more weather-friendly outdoor training environment.

He traveled to Florida to Nick Bollettieri's academy. Bollettieri remembers having to make a difficult decision whether to give a scholarship to Safin or the slightly older Marcelo Ríos. He chose Ríos, a Chilean who also reached No. 1, albeit with much less charm than Safin. "That's the kind of choice you never want to have to make," Bollettieri told me.

Rebuffed, Safin returned to Moscow and soon left for Spain, another top destination for ambitious Russian tennis players. He was thirteen and saw his parents and younger sister only twice a year for two weeks at a time. He never lived at home with them in Russia again, although his mother and sister did eventually join him in Valencia. Though he cheerfully says, "What doesn't kill us makes us stronger," he also conceded that the early separation impacted his emotional growth and stability.

"When you are alone at a young age, you have a lot of things that happen in your life and you have nowhere to express them and understand them," Safin told me. "You hold them inside of you, and you don't know what to do with them. You end up carrying them."

After four years in Spain working with coach Rafael Mensua in Valencia, he announced himself to the tennis world by defeating Andre Agassi and defending champion Gustavo "Guga" Kuerten in the 1998 French Open.

In form and on task, Safin was nearly impossible to resist, and he was not quite in peak form at the 2004 Australian Open as he came back from the torn ligaments in his left wrist that had spoiled his 2003 season, sending him tumbling down the rankings to No. 86.

But he arrived healthy, if unseeded, in Melbourne and fought his way through a series of marathon matches, including back-to-back five-setters against Roddick in the quarterfinals and Agassi in the semifinals.

It was quite a contrast with Federer, who had not been pushed to five sets by anyone in Melbourne. Safin's accumulated fatigue certainly was a concern, but he had had two days of rest to Federer's one ahead of the final.

"It's good to see him back," Federer said. "We're all happy, but we're scared at the same time."

Federer and Safin had long been friendly. At the ATP event in Copenhagen in February 2000, they went out on the town together. Safin was twenty years old, Federer was eighteen, and Safin said they were refused entry to a nightclub because nobody recognized them or believed that they were in the semifinals of the singles.

"That's really funny to think about now," Safin said.

They even won the doubles title together in Gstaad in 2001. "He's a very sensitive guy, I would say very perceptive and emotional," Safin said of Federer.

But they were now about to play for a Grand Slam title, and the baseline pace was torrid from the start in their final, neither player eager to give ground, and both lunging into the corners to retrieve the other's bolts. They traded blows and service breaks before Federer prevailed in the first-set tiebreaker. As a frontrunner, Federer has had his wobbles, but he methodically drained the suspense if not the appeal from this final. The points, many won or lost at net, were routinely eye-catching. Federer's forehand was the dominant stroke, and though a weary Safin yelled "I'm fine!" to the crowd at one stage early in the third set, that was nothing but bravado. Federer closed out his 7–6 (3), 6–4, 6–2 victory and, after a moment's hesitation, dropped to his knees and raised both arms to the sky.

There would be no "Roger Blubberer" headlines for his second major title. Equanimity was the rule this time, and what it reflected, in part, was a player who now expected such achievement. But Federer certainly had his poignant moments. He thought about Peter Carter and what it would have meant to have him be part of a victory in the tournament that was closest to Carter's roots. Carter had been convinced that Federer would be "the best player the world has ever seen" and had said as much to Peter Smith's son Brett many years earlier when he had introduced him to Federer.

Federer was not nearly there yet, but he was ranked No. 1, and with his second major title, he put an end to a streak of eight Grand Slam tournaments won by eight different men. Federer's rise meant the end of parity.

"My goal is to stay number one for as long as I can," he said.

He strengthened his hold on the top spot throughout 2004: reaching eleven singles finals and winning all of them. He won on the three primary surfaces: seven times on hard courts, twice on clay, and twice on grass. He won on four continents: Australia, Asia, North America, and Europe. He compiled a 74-6 overall record.

There were some disappointments, beginning with a surprising 6–3, 6–3 defeat in the third round of the Miami Open to a promising but then-little-known Spanish teenager named Rafael Nadal.

Switzerland lost to the French in the Davis Cup quarterfinals in April despite Federer's two singles victories, over Nicolas Escudé and Arnaud Clément. Federer faltered again at Roland Garros, losing a match in straight sets in the third round to three-time French Open champion Gustavo Kuerten, who was still working his way through hip problems. Above all, through Federer's lens, there was another medal-free visit to the Olympics where he and Yves Allegro lost in the second round of doubles, and Federer was upset in the third round of singles by a young Czech with startlingly effortless power: Tomáš Berdych.

But the season was much more joyride than letdown, and the joy was greatest at the Australian Open, Wimbledon, and the US Open. At Wimbledon, Federer rumbled through the draw, dropping 6–0 sets on Alex Bogdanovic in the first round, Alejandro Falla in the second round, and Hewitt in the quarterfinals on his way to a 6–1, 6–7 (1), 6–0, 6–4 victory. After beating Frenchman Sebastien Grosjean in straight sets in a match that required two days to complete because of rain, Federer earned a Wimbledon rematch with Andy Roddick, this time in the final.

Roddick was having another glittering grass court season. He had decided not to shave until he lost, and he arrived at the final looking scruffy indeed after defending his title at Queen's Club and dropping just one set at Wimbledon.

Roddick and his coach, Brad Gilbert, were determined not to give Federer the time and space to wave his tennis wand. The idea was to use Roddick's brutish power to full effect to shorten the points, often from the baseline, and for much of the match the plan worked.

Sitting courtside, you could sense Federer's surprise and Roddick's determination. Roddick started the match like a bull who had just been released into the arena.

"I think you have to be tough with Roger; there's no doubt," Roddick explained. "I wasn't wanting to get in rallies, where he could kind of do his thing, you know, come up with spectacular stuff."

Roddick broke his serve in the third game to take a quick lead and then maintained that edge after a brief rain delay and won the first set.

"I got surprised," Federer conceded. "Even though everybody knows his power."

Federer responded by taking a 4–0 lead in the second set, but Roddick rumbled back to 4–4 only to lose the set when Federer broke his serve for the third time with a forehand winner.

Roddick did not crumble. He took a 4–2 lead in the third set, but the players then had to flee the court again because of more rain. This time, after consulting with Staubli and Vavrinec in the clubhouse, Federer returned with new, more aggressive tactics. He began serving and volleying more often: chipping and charging and attacking the net.

It was the right move, and he broke back to win the third set in a tiebreaker.

"Most people would have been like, 'Oh shit, Roddick is kind of rolling me today,' but he stayed the course and switched it up," Roddick said. "You kind of realized his tennis IQ at that point."

Federer still had to save six break points on his serve at 2–3 in the fourth set, but that would be the final set as Federer closed out his second Wimbledon title 4–6, 7–5, 7–6 (3), 6–4.

"I threw the kitchen sink at him, but he went to the bathroom and got his tub," Roddick said, memorably, on court.

I recently asked Roddick if he really did think he had thrown everything at Federer on that intermittently soggy afternoon, or was that just a good line.

"Both, you know," he said. "But there's only so much I can do. What's the one advantage I have over him? It's being able to pound it and go through someone. It's not as if I'm gonna make the adjustment to get cute and hit chips to him, because that's gonna end terribly, you know? So I could have made adjustments, but the way I was playing was the way that I had to play. I had to execute a very risky game plan very well for a long time against Roger."

I asked Roddick if he had ever played that well and lost.

He thought for a long while before responding, atypical of him with his fast-twitch wit. When he answered, he answered softly.

"A couple times it's happened," he said. "They've just all been against Roger."

He laughed, more wistful than amused. "I haven't lost to anyone else playing that well," he added.

But Roddick, who would suffer so much disappointment because of the cruel beauty of Federer's tennis, still feels that the 2004 Wimbledon final was an opportunity that slipped away rather than a match that Federer was destined to win.

Gilbert agrees. "I'll put that in the top three or four matches in my career as a coach of taking the loss really hard," he said. "I mean, God, he had chances. Andy was thumping the ball that match, and normally he struggled with Fed's serve but he broke his serve four times. It was high-level, high-intensity, but I felt like that match was there for Andy to win it. But I do think when Fed won, that took him instantly to another level. That was the first time he was a back-to-back champ at a Grand Slam event, and then he was well on his way to the greatness. Until that point, I felt like there was very little separation."

So, what would big separation look like in the months and years ahead?

Gilbert, one of the game's best tacticians, noticed Federer's serve improving, getting even more precise and difficult to read. He noticed his returning become more consistent even though his return position was tight to the baseline rather than deeper in the court like some of his rivals. "He just got so many returns into play from there, like an Andre," Gilbert said, referring to Agassi. "But Fed didn't crush it. He just poked so many back in play."

Floating deep returns into play would not have worked in the serve-and-volley era when net rushers would have knocked such returns away for winners, but fewer men were serving and volleying at this stage, including Federer. It was a matter of reading the trends and adjusting.

But the area where Federer really excelled, in Gilbert's opinion, was his ability to be lethal on his own service games by pouncing on the return, most often with his forehand. Because of his quickness, he was able to use that forehand in parts of the court where many others could not have managed it.

"By 2005, 2006, he was the greatest I had ever seen at just hitting the spot with his serve and then on the next ball, he could just hurt you everywhere," Gilbert said. "That, for me, is what dramatically improved, that ability to get so many free one-two points. That took him into a whole other stratosphere, and that's what gave Roddick more problems than anything."

Federer explained to me that the midcourt forehand was, in a sense, a contemporary version of serve-and-volley. "Before, it was about being at net, but today it's when you get that midcourt ball after the serve, you'd better take advantage of it; otherwise, you will pay the price," he said.

I asked Roddick to describe what it *felt* like to face Federer at this stage and beyond, how it differed from playing other greats of the game.

Roddick did not mention the forehand first. He talked about Federer's backhand chip.

"It felt like it was almost rotating backwards by the time it got to you, so unless you actually made great contact with it, it would kind of go dead on you," Roddick explained. "It was a different type of chip. You couldn't just kind of meet it front on. There was some work to do. Tim Henman would stick his chip, and it was hard. Same with Pete. It came through firm. Roger's could come in slow and then would just, like, check in a weird way, and you couldn't really go after it."

Then Roddick mentioned Federer's serve, still the most underappreciated element of his game, even deep into his career.

"It would go 122 without sounding like it was going 122," Roddick said, referring to miles per hour. "It wouldn't just pop off the racket. It felt like it was soft and got there quick, if that makes sense."

Did he have any grasp of how the physics of that worked?

"I'm not a scientist," Roddick answered. "I was too busy trying to problem-solve."

Agassi calls Federer one of the greatest "target servers," with his formidable ability to hit corners and lines, even on big points.

Many players talk about the late dip in Federer's topspin forehand as it approaches the baseline: not quite "the cliffhanger" of his youth but in that same vein. What surprised Roddick was that Federer was able to get that extreme, delayed-impact topspin without apparently extreme measures.

"Other guys are on their back foot; Rafa finishes with his racket behind his ear," Roddick said, referring to Nadal. "Normally it would tend to be a pronounced action to get that kind of result, whereas Roger would do it, and it wouldn't have to be extreme to get the ball to react that way."

On the returns, what Roddick admired but also resented was Federer's body control. "I could throw one down at 140 that took a lot of effort, and he was able to get neutral with about six inches of swing, just by meeting it," Roddick said.

It was a case of Federer's processing speed again making the difference.

"It's saying something when you're serving 140, and the guy's not in a rush," Roddick said. "You don't do that without having complete control of your hands. If I serve 140 against most people, they're making an exaggerated movement. They're getting their body out of the way. He was in complete control even if he was uncomfortable. So that was probably more annoying to me than a lot of other things."

For Roddick, that extreme body control was a big part of the explanation for Federer's longevity on tour.

"Just think of all those wasted extra movements the rest of us make throughout our careers that he's not making," Roddick said. "That's saving a lot of mileage and a lot of stress. The racket is like an extension of his hand, and that's kind of what it felt like when you were facing him."

The self-contained, new-model Federer also gave an opponent like Roddick very little to feed off. He was not easy to read and certainly not in your face.

"Well, he doesn't give you anything to hate, which is kind of annoying," Roddick said, laughing hard. "You know, Lleyton and I would butt heads, and you'd kind of have this atmosphere where you were like, 'Screw that guy!' You kind of want to have that chip on your shoulder. Maybe you need it against certain people, and I can certainly find it against most. I had a hard time doing it against Pete and Andre, because they were heroes of mine. Against Roger, he's not going to give you a sideways look, or he's not going to stare you down before a match or fist-pump you at the wrong time. He just doesn't give you anything, which is foreign with someone who is kind of in your way as far as your profession goes.

"It probably helped him a ton. In a decade full of guys where all we wanted was a reason to dive in, he wouldn't go into the gutter with you. You couldn't really turn it into a street fight."

Ultimately, this was a dovetail fit for someone like Federer, who much prefers consensus to conflict and who, perhaps in a nod to his Swiss side, likes his schedule to run as smoothly as a downhiller's skis on even terrain. He is certainly image conscious, which was one of the incentives for his behavioral change. Now that he had learned to manage his emotions, there would be no more background noise, no more static. His work could speak for itself, and it was often magnificent.

It could also be devastating. Hewitt experienced the full effect in the 2004 US Open final as Federer humiliated him 6–0, 7–6 (3), 6–0 in just one hour and fifty-one minutes.

Such a score line beggared belief against a hardwired fighter like Hewitt, a player who had once dominated their rivalry and who was resurgent and riding a sixteen-match winning streak coming into the final. Hewitt had not dropped a set in the tournament, but Federer reeled off the first set in just eighteen minutes, hitting a forehand winner on the opening point and an ace on his opening serve. Hewitt, seemingly all too aware of which way the wind was blowing, did not help his cause by double-faulting twice on break points.

He pushed back in the second set, in which Federer began making actual errors and failed to serve it out at 5–4. But the Swiss dominated the tiebreaker, and in the third set, he resumed his flirtation with the perfect tennis match that he had often mused about as a youngster.

Backcourt. Forecourt. Serve. Return. Offense. Defense. No matter the sector, he controlled it. Tennis routs can be painful to watch, as excruciating as a child's nervy piano recital. There is no place for an outmatched opponent to hide on that big, open-air rectangle, no substitute allowed, but at least Federer routed Hewitt in style.

"Too good, mate," Hewitt said as he crossed to the other side of the net to congratulate his onetime Wimbledon doubles partner, now the winner of three Grand Slam titles in one season and a global star.

"I don't think I've ever seen a guy play that well in my life," Hewitt said later.

The numbers on the stat sheet were not all ethereal. Federer put only 56 percent of his first serves in play. His winner-to-unforced-error count—40 to 26—was excellent but hardly unheard of. And yet the impression left by the first and final sets was extraordinary. No man had won two sets at love in a US Open final since Richard Sears in 1884.

Alan Schwartz, the baritone-voiced president of the United States Tennis Association, took the microphone at the awards ceremony and spoke to the crowd.

"For those of you who wonder what it is to be in the zone, you saw it today," he said before turning to Federer. "Roger, you are living proof that this game is easy. You made it look easy. I never saw anyone do it as smoothly."

The new US Open champion smiled, but such comments, ones Federer had already heard so often at age twenty-three, were both flattering and diminishing. His game was beguiling, no doubt, but the polish also made it too tempting to ignore how much had been required of Federer to make it look so easy.

Sampras, nearly as fluid a mover, faced a similar dynamic during his career. "Just because it looks easy doesn't mean it's not hard," Sampras told me. "It might look like Roger and I are not trying or we're not that into it. We're just very efficient: our movement and our games and our strokes. It's like one swing of the racket, one forehand, one serve, and boom, it's done, while most other players are grinding, grinding, grinding."

The misconception has troubled Federer even if he understands its source.

"I think the problem of playing effortless tennis was a big one early on in my career, because somebody's going to look at you and go, 'Okay, very talented,'" Federer said in the *Strokes of Genius* background session. "When I lost, everybody would tell me, 'Why don't you try harder?' And when you win, it's like, 'Ohhh my God. What a beautiful game!'"

Federer sensed there was "no middle ground" in the analysis. He knew, no matter how nonchalant and loose-limbed he might appear, that he was pushing himself. Virtuoso performances became his trademark, but he has often taken more pride later in his career from the matches where he hits quite a few wrong notes and has to pound on the keys before finding a way to get through.

"Those are maybe the most satisfying wins for me today, because I couldn't always show my fight and my grit, which I do believe is also a big quality of mine," he said. "Otherwise, I wouldn't have won over one thousand matches in my career, but it was always a two-edged sword. I feel like that was quite complicated for most of my career."

Many a tennis player would, of course, love to face such a "problem." Federer has seldom lacked for positive feedback, and making it look easy was also intimidating to all those straining so visibly to keep pace.

Players like Roddick, with his shirt grabbing, cap tugging, and brusque movements. Players like Hewitt, who packed on more than ten pounds of muscle working with Roger Rasheed in an attempt to add power to his game.

At the start of 2004, Hewitt led his head-to-head series with Federer 7-2. After six straight defeats, including two more at the Masters Cup in Houston, where Federer defended his title, Hewitt finished the year trailing 7-8.

Hewitt simply did not have the weapons to hurt him. Federer was able to beat Hewitt at his own game from the baseline. When Federer did choose to push forward, he could do it from a position of strength, and he possessed the racket skills and anticipation to deal with one of the great strengths of Hewitt's game: his passing shots.

Federer won thirty-one of thirty-five points at net in the US Open final, which might have been the only stat of the day that genuinely was otherworldly.

Just what was Hewitt to do?

Peter Smith remembers sitting near him once at a tournament and realizing that Hewitt was talking to himself.

"I don't even remember where it was," Smith said. "We were sitting on a wall somewhere, and I hear Lleyton mumbling, and then I realize he's saying, 'He's too quick.' And so I said to him, 'Who's too quick?' And Lleyton said, 'Roger's too quick.'

"And at that stage everyone in the world thought Lleyton was the fastest thing that had ever moved on a tennis court," Smith said. "But he looked up at me and said, 'He's that quick. No one knows it, but he's that quick.'"

These haunted looks—Agassi's in the Houston locker room, Hewitt's on the wall—were testimony to what Federer represented.

Sampras captured the zeitgeist in a comment to *Sports Illustrated* before the start of the 2005 season: "There's no one who can play with him," he said. "For the next four or five years his competition will be the record books."

Though Federer had won four majors, the focus was already on Sampras's record of fourteen. As he returned to Melbourne to defend his Australian Open title, there was also serious talk about the first Grand Slam for a man since 1969, when Rod Laver won all four of the major tournaments in the same year.

The odds are always against a Grand Slam, but it did not seem far-fetched for Federer. He, unlike Sampras, was a consistent winner on clay. He had the all-surface skills and edge over the opposition to dream that dream. He also had a new coach: Tony Roche, the reserved and lantern-jawed Australian born in Wagga Wagga who in his playing days had won the French Open—now the only major title that Federer lacked.

Roche was a part-time consultant without a formal contract, not a full-time coach, but he was widely admired for his technical and tactical expertise and had coached former No. 1s Ivan Lendl and Patrick Rafter.

Federer's decision to bring him into his small, tightly knit team, which included Vavrinec and his parents, was a signal that he was not afraid to change even after an extraordinary 2004 season.

To launch 2005, he swept through five matches at the ATP event in Doha, winning the title on his way to Melbourne, where he demolished five more opponents without dropping a set.

Andre Agassi, now thirty-four and seeded 8th, had spent the off-season making another push to remain relevant at the top of the game. He had lost thirteen pounds, about six kilograms, in an attempt to get quicker and take some pressure off his fragile hip. A four-time Australian Open champion, he had returned to Melbourne with renewed optimism and energy, accompanied by his wife, Steffi Graf, and their two young children.

Federer trounced him 6–3, 6–4, 6–4 in the quarterfinals.

"I would suggest," Agassi said, "that his next opponents don't look to me for advice."

Federer's next opponent, Safin, was now in position to get expert counsel. He had hired a new coach of his own in April 2004: Peter Lundgren.

After being so close with Federer, Lundgren was well aware of what Federer thought of Safin's game. He knew that Federer's sensitive side would emerge against such players in a way that it no longer did against the hoi polloi.

"There are a few players he doesn't like to play, and you can see it on his face," Lundgren said. "It's like I can see from his expression that he's under pressure now."

Federer and Safin had played for the first time with Lundgren in Safin's corner at the World Tour Finals in Houston. Federer won that semifinal in straight sets—6–3, 7–6 (18)—but had to navigate an epic, thirty-eight-point tiebreaker before closing it out on his eighth match point.

"It was difficult to be there, a strange feeling," Lundgren told me in Houston of coaching against Federer. "But I think Marat's shown that he can compete with the best player in the world, so for next year, we are going to try to improve a few things and hopefully he can beat Roger a few times."

It was the longest tiebreaker in a significant men's match at that stage. John McEnroe's and Björn Borg's much more famous tiebreaker in the fourth set of the 1980 Wimbledon final extended to 18–16.

What was remarkable about both marathon tiebreakers was the quality of play under pressure: more about winners than errors.

"We were pushing each other to the limits," Federer said.

But in the end, Safin's double fault at 18–18—his first of the set—had been critical.

"I was probably going for too much, because I knew I have Roger Federer on the other side, so I had to do something extra," Safin said.

Federer was clearly in his head, a turbulent place to begin with, but before the rematch in Melbourne, Lundgren wanted to make it unmistakably clear that Safin was in Federer's head, too.

When they sat down to discuss the match, Lundgren asked Safin what his expectations were.

"I hope I get a few games," Safin said.

Lundgren asked him again, heard the same answer, and then raised the tone.

"Let me tell you something," Lundgren said. "Since I coached Roger, I can tell you that one of the few guys that he respects is you."

Then Lundgren left.

"That's the only thing I said. I didn't talk about tactics or anything else," Lundgren told me. "Marat looked at me for a couple of seconds, and he didn't say a word, and I knew he took it the right way."

What happened next was one of the great tennis matches of any era: a titanic prime-time-to-late-night tussle brimming with power, inspiration, and resilience that had both men, not just Safin, shouting with the tension of it all.

Safin, by his standards, kept his emotions in check. "I knew if I go crazy, I'm done," he said.

It is rare to see Federer sweat. As the match extended and gathered narrative arc, he even began to look slightly disheveled: his long hair matted and slightly out of place, the front zipper on his drenched blue shirt sometimes askew.

It was as if Federer and Safin had picked up where they had left off in that Houston tiebreaker, and for those of us who were there in Rod Laver Arena well past midnight, it will go on our short lists of matches to savor.

"I've seen a lot of tennis; that was in my top ten for sure, top five even," Lundgren said.

Every set was tight. Many points were short and explosive, but the best was strength against strength: Federer's pure forehand against Safin's pure two-handed backhand; Federer's feathery touch at the net against Safin's perfectly weighted passing shots.

Best to have been there to truly understand, but to watch it again after all these years is no letdown. This was a match full of peaks and few valleys, and Federer, despite all of Safin's clear commitment, was the first to get a match point.

It came in the fourth-set tiebreaker with Federer serving at 6–5. Federer tried a surprise attack by serving and volleying on his second serve. Safin ripped a backhand return crosscourt. Federer lunged for the backhand volley and then lunged high again to parry the next passing shot, hitting an absolutely exquisite backhand drop shot from a position that few could have managed. The ball died in the forecourt, but Safin hunted it down and audaciously flicked a lob over Federer's head.

The Swiss retreated and with just a bit of time did something atypical. Instead of making a hard shot look easy, he made a straightforward shot more complicated. He attempted to strike the ball between his legs instead of running past the ball and taking a fuller cut. Federer's "tweener" struck the net, and he threw his head back and howled in the general direction of the moon.

"A guy with stone hands is not going to make that shot in a thousand years, but Roger is probably going to make it," Safin told me. "I just put myself on top of the net and closed my eyes, and he missed it by nothing."

Safin had new life on his twenty-fifth birthday and used it well, winning the next two points to force a fifth set. After more than three hours they were even, and hardly anybody in the arena was leaving.

"Something clicked in my head after he missed the shot between his legs, and it told me that this is my window," Safin said, rolling a cigarette as he looked back. "I was like, 'This is the chance. This is the chaaaaaance.' I knew from there that I was going to win. I think it was the first time in my life I had faith in me."

Federer was showing signs of wear. He was already playing with a blister on the bottom of his left foot. After the fourth set, he received treatment on his right index finger because of some nerve impingement.

But the fifth set was still worth everybody's wait as both combatants strained to deliver the knockout blow.

Federer saved Safin's first two match points when the Russian served at 5–3. It would be another half an hour before they could arrive at a conclusion.

Lundgren, watching from Safin's player's box, was giving a running commentary on the match to Safin's agent, Gerard Tsobanian. "He knew when Roger would hit certain shots, when he'd take risks," Tsobanian said. "He knew, when he faced break point, where he'd serve."

Federer saved another match point at 4–5, 30–40 with a volley after a scrambling exchange. Safin saved a break point at 6–6 when Federer mishit a forehand on the move.

Federer then saved two more match points at 6–7 and one more at 7–8.

Safin, in a different time and headspace, would not have kept it together, but on his seventh match point, he took a chance and went for a backhand down the line from an extended position. Surprised, Federer lunged right and fell but still put the ball in play before losing his grip on his racket.

After more than four hours, this magnificent semifinal was truly there for the taking. Safin slapped a forehand into the open space with Federer watching from his knees as the ball bounced twice.

Safin did not pump his fist, rip his shirt, or roar like a lumberjack who had just felled a redwood. Instead, he waved both arms, as if to say, "Good riddance!" and then leaned on the net to wait for Federer to rise, collect his belongings, and shake hands.

"It was too much to carry, that match," Safin said. "I just wanted it done, done, done."

The score line was 5–7, 6–4, 5–7, 7–6 (6), 9–7, but it is best to commit other things to memory: like the gasps of the crowd in the midst of so many rallies; like the racket Federer threw late in the fourth set, his new age veneer developing cracks under Safin's pressure; like the sight of Federer barefoot and hobbling with his head bowed as he walked down a corridor inside Laver Arena shortly after his defeat.

Even diminished, it had taken a supreme effort to stop his momentum. Meanwhile, back on court, Safin was giving a postmatch interview to Jim Courier, the retired two-time Australian Open champion. Despite the late hour, the arena was still packed, and though it was no longer officially Safin's birthday, the crowd serenaded him nonetheless.

Safin would go on to beat Hewitt in the final and win his second major title. Rather than a harbinger of grand victories to come, it would be his last.

"I got wrapped up with my internal conflicts, completely wrapped up and completely confused with my life and my career," Safin told me.

More injuries did not help. He retired at age twenty-nine.

But the 2005 Australian Open was definitely a sign of things to come for Federer. He was the world's best tennis player, no doubt, but he was also beginning to inspire greatness in others. And as he and Safin dueled on a warm Australian summer night, his rivals and future rivals were watching closely from afar.

CHAPTER EIGHT

———◦———

PALMA DE MALLORCA, Spain

It was one of the strangest tennis matches in history, and seven thousand spectators were in sold-out Palma Arena to watch Roger Federer and Rafael Nadal play it.

"If we had fifteen thousand seats available, we could have sold them just as fast," the event director, Alberto Tous, said.

The temporary indoor court was covered with two tarpaulins when the fans arrived on May 2, 2007. As the festivities began, the tarps were slowly pulled back to reveal the gimmick: On one side of the net was red clay; on the other was freshly laid grass.

The concept was the wild brainchild of Argentine advertising executive Pablo del Campo. Nadal had won seventy-two consecutive matches on clay and back-to-back French Opens; Federer had won forty-eight straight on grass and four straight Wimbledons. The idea in Palma was to have them face each other on their best surfaces at the same time.

It was outside-the-box thinking, I will give it that. Dubbed the "Battle of Surfaces," it was above all an indicator of just how much interest there was in watching Federer and Nadal play on anything at this stage.

Their rivalry had taken over tennis, and the surprise to me at the time was that Federer and Nadal actually agreed to interrupt their spring season and risk injury for an exhibition on unsure footing (granted it was for 400,000 euros apiece).

But Mallorca, the Spanish island in the Mediterranean, was Nadal's home, and the two young stars were both with the same apparel sponsor, Nike, and the same management agency, IMG. Del Campo, who had been trying to convince Federer to embrace the idea since 2005, finally succeeded.

Fever dream or not, it was happening.

"It's a bit crazy and people might say, 'Why then? It's bad timing,'" Federer said before arriving. "But we also enjoy playing tennis for fun for a change. It doesn't always need to be crazy serious out on the match courts."

There is no arguing with that. Tennis exhibitions are often hit-and-chuckle affairs, awash in trick shots and banter, but it quickly became clear that this was not exhibition tennis as usual. Federer and Nadal, clearly struggling to take each other lightly, lunged for passing shots and stuck by many of the same patterns they used in their matches that counted.

Only the concept was a lark, and it required them to change shoes at each change of ends in order to adjust to the shift in surface. Grass court shoes, with their knobby soles, do not work well on clay, and Federer confessed that even after switching to clay court shoes, he still sometimes forgot to slide.

Federer and Nadal were lucky there was grass at all. A worm infestation and the lack of natural light had made the first batch of indoor grass unplayable, so on the eve of the match, organizers had to scramble and cart in blocks of putting-green turf from a local golf course.

The bounces were, as you might expect, less than ideal, including the bounce on match point in the third-set tiebreaker where Federer almost whiffed a forehand as Nadal closed out his 7–5, 4–6, 7–6 (12–10) victory.

Watching a replay today, the hybrid court looks as odd now as it did then: a two-tone contrast that makes it seem like you are watching a split screen instead of a single match. Though a rematch was scheduled for the same location the following year, the experiment has yet to be repeated.

The name Battle of Surfaces was a nod to Battle of the Sexes, the 1973 zeitgeist match in the Houston Astrodome that was won by

Wimbledon women's champion Billie Jean King over self-styled male chauvinist Bobby Riggs. In absolute terms, the Battle of the Sexes was certainly a weirder occasion, with the fifty-five-year-old Riggs entering the court in a rickshaw pulled by female models and the twenty-nine-year-old King entering Cleopatra-style on a litter festooned with flowers and carried by bare-chested male porters.

But at least King and Riggs played on the same surface on both sides of the net.

"I have to admit it was a strange one," Nadal said, fluttering his lips when we talked about it in 2020. "It was actually quite difficult for both of us, but I had fun, honestly. And it's something that's going to stay in our memories for the rest of our lives. We won't do that again."

They have made lots of memories together.

Nadal, a forehand-whipping, *vamos*-shouting prodigy, was coached from the beginning in Mallorca by his uncle, Toni Nadal.

Like Federer, who was a ball boy at the ATP event in Basel, Nadal had early exposure to the elite. From 1998 to 2002, a clay court ATP event was held on the island. The winners included future Grand Slam champions Juan Carlos Ferrero, Marat Safin, and Gastón Gaudio.

Nadal and his family attended the tournament, and in 2000, when Nadal was fourteen, his excellent junior results earned him the honor of carrying the Spanish flag during the opening ceremony of the Davis Cup final in Barcelona's Palau Sant Jordi. Dark hair clipped short, he stood, a bit self-consciously, next to Spanish stars Àlex Corretja, Albert Costa, and Ferrero on the indoor clay as the anthems were played. Who could have known then that Nadal would turn out to be the biggest Spanish tennis star of them all?

At that stage, Spain was by far the strongest traditional tennis nation not to have won the Davis Cup, founded in 1900. It was an emotional and raucous three days as Spain ended a century-long wait, with Ferrero defeating Lleyton Hewitt in four sets in the decisive match in front of a sellout crowd of 14,500.

Juan Carlos, then the Spanish king, watched from the front row. Nadal took it all in, too, and seventeen months later he won his first tour-level match after getting a wild card into the Mallorca Open: upsetting Ramón Delgado, a Paraguayan ranked in the top 100.

Nadal was just fifteen, and it was not the first time he had ambushed an older visitor on his home island. A year earlier, Australian star Pat Cash had come to Mallorca for an exhibition match with German star Boris Becker at the Santa Ponsa Country Club.

When the aging Becker had to withdraw with an injury shortly before the match, Cash felt that the show must go on and agreed to play the island's most promising youngster so that the paying customers would have some tennis to watch. Cash, then thirty-six, had naturally never heard of Nadal and could not have imagined what sort of fourteen-year-old he was about to face or, perhaps it is more accurate to say, experience.

"Nadal came bounding out like this was his big chance, and the crowd immediately responded to the exuberance of youth," Cash wrote in the *Times* of London. "If you think Lleyton Hewitt is pumped up on court, you should have seen Nadal. Fist pumps, posturing, shouted celebrations. If I heard the yell '*Vamos*' once, I heard it 100 times."

Cash won the first set; Nadal took the second and then won the decisive match tiebreak to claim victory.

"There he was at the net, diving to make seemingly impossible volleys and bouncing up to brandish yet another celebratory fist," Cash remembered. "Part of me thought he was disrespectful, but once I got over my initial anger at being beaten by a child, I realized I had just encountered a talent that could win tennis's greatest prizes. The next day I phoned several of my sponsors and told them to invest in this boy. I'm sure they now regret their hesitancy."

Some sponsors did not require a phone call. Nike already had signed Nadal at age twelve.

"The sweet spot for us was eleven, twelve, thirteen," said Mike Nakajima, a former director of tennis at Nike. "We signed Maria Sharapova at eleven, and she could say six words in English, and the first thing she tells me is, 'I don't like your socks.'"

Rafael's English was not much better, but he was more polite.

The first Nadal I covered as a sportswriter was actually not Rafael. It was his paternal uncle Miguel Ángel, a rugged central defender on Spain's national soccer team in the 1994 World Cup in the United States.

Rafael was eight years old at that stage, loved soccer almost as much as his uncle, and sometimes attended his club games with FC Barcelona even if he was a Real Madrid fan like his father, Sebastián. It is not difficult to see from where Rafael's desire to be a professional athlete emerged. One look at Miguel Ángel, an imposing figure, also helps you understand where Rafael got his own solid build. When Miguel Ángel did not retire until age thirty-eight, that should have been a clue that his nephew was going to have staying power, no matter how much pain he had to endure.

The Nadals go back generations in Mallorca. Their fief is Manacor: a cozy and attractive inland town that had fewer than forty thousand inhabitants during Nadal's childhood. Nadal lived with his parents, grandparents, and extended family in a five-story apartment building in the town's main square overlooking the eighteenth-century church and with easy access to Manacor's tennis club and its red clay courts. Manacor lies a few kilometers from Porto Cristo, a fishing village and resort where the Nadals, an affluent family with numerous business interests, owned another property right on the ocean that they also shared.

It was an idyllic childhood setting, further proof that champions do not need to emerge from hardship. Rafael grew up shuttling between Manacor and Porto Cristo and between soccer and tennis, which Toni, another of his paternal uncles, introduced him to at age three.

Soccer held sway until Nadal was twelve. He was a fast left wing who could score and score some more, often with his head, but by then he was also the Spanish and European junior tennis champion in his age-group. His father, Sebastián, felt it was time for a choice.

Like Federer at the same age, Nadal based the decision on his clear potential for tennis success, his preference for having full ownership of his results in an individual sport, and in the most remarkable parallel with Federer, on a new soccer coach who had benched him for a game after he had missed a practice because of tennis commitments.

"If not for that coach, I might have been a soccer player instead," Nadal said.

On such turning points does a great rivalry depend.

Like Federer, Nadal also started spending his weeknights away from his close-knit family in his midteens. Because of the lack of quality practice partners in Manacor, he needed to train frequently at a regional training center in Palma, the island's largest city, about fifty-five kilometers to the west. To cut down on the commute Nadal started attending the same boarding school his father and uncle Toni had attended, but he was homesick and eventually returned to Manacor full-time.

As with Federer, academics were not Nadal's passion. I once asked him what his favorite subject was in school, and he thought for a moment and answered, "Sports."

Well aware of his exceptional prospects, Spanish tennis officials on the mainland tried to convince the Nadals to send their son across the Balearic Sea to Barcelona, the hub of the sport in Spain.

That was the path followed by the best player to emerge from Mallorca: Carlos Moyá, who was tall, self-contained, and preposterously handsome (and was actually the first Mallorcan tennis star to wear a sleeveless shirt on tour).

Moyá, long hair flapping and forehand firing, won the French Open in 1998, receiving the trophy from Pelé on the eve of the World Cup in France. Moyá briefly reached No. 1 the following year and was a close-range reminder to Nadal that tennis greatness was not a pipe dream. They first hit together when Nadal was twelve and began training regularly together when Nadal was fourteen. That was a magnanimous gesture by Moyá and a huge boost for Nadal. How many talented young teens can practice with an active Grand Slam champion on a regular basis?

The Nadal family was convinced that it was better for Nadal's well-being that his game be developed in Mallorca, even if it cost them financial support from the Spanish federation.

"His father just felt it was the best decision for Rafael to stay home, surrounded by his family with people to back him up," Toni told me. "When you're young and you leave home, the tennis can go well, but as a person, it doesn't always go well. We had problems at times with the training, finding the same level of players as Rafael, but with hard work we managed it."

They already had received some counsel from Jofre Porta, a national coach based in Palma. Toni made big changes: switching Rafael from a double-handed forehand to a single-handed forehand at age nine because he and Porta both knew that players who hit with two hands off both sides were rarities in men's tennis. None had reached No. 1, although Monica Seles had managed it in the women's game.

At the same stage, Rafael also began playing his forehand with his left hand even though he ate, wrote, shot baskets, and played golf with his right hand. Rafael had a stronger left foot in soccer. Being left-handed, as any regular tennis player knows, is often an advantage because of the novelty and reverse effects and the ability it provides to hit sliced serves in the ad court, pulling an opponent wide and opening up attacking options.

Toni noticed that when his nephew hit two-handed groundstrokes, he had the most power and success from the left side.

"It just seemed like his more natural side," Toni told me. "That side needed to be the forehand."

Ultimately, the choice was Rafael's, and on such turning points does a great rivalry also depend. Nadal as a right-hander would surely have been a potential champion as well with his talent, character, and in-the-moment mentality. But he would not have posed such a tactical conundrum for Federer, who could have used his most reliable weapons—the inside-out forehand and short crosscourt backhand chip—much more effectively.

The downside to the decision was that Nadal had pain in his left shoulder, discomfort he alleviated by developing his trademark forehand style of following through above his head after whipping through the ball with tremendous racket-head speed.

Porta and the other coaches dubbed that signature forehand "the Nadalada," a term that never went mainstream, which is a pity.

I met the Nadals for the first time in 2003 at Wimbledon, when Rafael made his Grand Slam debut at seventeen. I had yet to see him play in person or even on-screen. This was before streaming, before YouTube, Twitter, and Instagram. Many matches were not widely broadcast. The general public's scrutinization of rising tennis talent did not start so early then. More scrutiny might have helped my evaluation: In the first article I wrote about Nadal in 2002 for the *International Herald Tribune* after his win over Delgado, I mentioned that Nadal, like young French prospect Richard Gasquet, had a fine *one-handed* backhand (journalism is a perpetually humbling experience).

But it was still reassuring to sit in the stands on an outside court at the All England Club and watch him dash about the grass with evident glee in his second-round match against Lee Childs, an overmatched British wild card. Reports in the Spanish press of Nadal's potential were clearly not exaggerated.

From a distance, he looked like a full-grown man. It was only up close that you realized he was so young. His angular features did not yet seem fully defined. His cheeks were chubby. Shaving was clearly optional.

What was most noticeable then is the same thing that is most striking now: his relentlessly focused and positive approach to competition. Disappointment might have flashed across his face, even entered his thoughts, but it was out of there in an instant, ejected to emphasize the challenge and the point directly in front of him.

Federer had spent years training himself to manage his mind and, above all, his expectations. Nadal seemed to have the knack from the start: no sports psychologists, no smashed rackets.

"Never," Nadal said. "If I had thrown a racket, my uncle would have kicked me off the court right away."

Nadal did not just embrace the moment. He gave it a bear hug and lifted it off the ground with its heels kicking, and he was true to that spirit when he faced Federer in a night match in the third round of the Miami tournament in March 2004.

Though it is often labeled their first meeting, it was actually their second. Nadal and Tommy Robredo had beaten Federer and his friend Yves Allegro 5–7, 6–4, 6–3 in doubles the week before in Indian Wells in the round of 16.

But Federer had yet to experience Nadal in full, whipping up trouble and covering the court all on his own.

All those who might have thought that Nadal would be intimidated should have consulted the score of his first tour match against Moyá the year before: Nadal beat him 7–5, 6–4 in Hamburg.

Not even beloved and benevolent boyhood role models were safe in the face of Nadal's drive and talent. But contrary to the perception today, Federer was not Nadal's longtime idol. The gap in their ages was significant—nearly five years—but Federer had only recently emerged from the pack of talented players near the top of men's tennis. As Nadal grew up, Federer was hardly the clear player to beat. This was not at all like Federer facing Sampras at Wimbledon or Naomi Osaka later facing Serena Williams at the US Open.

Federer was newly but firmly entrenched at No. 1. He had just won titles at the Australian Open, Dubai, and Indian Wells, and had won fifty-five of sixty-two sets coming into the Miami match. He was feeling ill, although not too ill to take the court, and had worked his way through a tough three-setter the night before against Nikolay Davydenko.

"Is there a realistic chance of Nadal beating Federer today?" asked John Barrett, the venerable British commentator and former player who was working the match for television.

With Nadal preparing to serve at 1–2 in the first set, Barrett's broadcast partner, Doug Adler, answered in the negative and said, "The last thing you want to do is lose to a seventeen-year-old coming up."

Barrett agreed and said, "I think if Federer is in the mood, then I think it will be..."

He stopped midsentence as Nadal tossed the ball into the air. What ensued was the first point that showed Federer the true depth of the challenge. He hit a slice deep into what was supposed to be Nadal's backhand corner. Nadal was quick enough to run around it and rip a forehand. Federer smacked a backhand into the other corner that he could have rightly expected to be a winner. Nadal sprinted across the backcourt in a flash and ripped another forehand at full stretch to keep the rally alive before winning it with a flurry of punches disguised as passing shots.

It was a mind-bending preview of so many Federer-Nadal rallies in the years to come. Barrett wisely never bothered to finish his thought about how unrealistic the chances were of an upset.

Even then, Nadal already was, in some respects, the Nadal we know. He was obsessing over the precise positioning of his water bottles on changeovers and, yes, already picking at the back of his shorts. But some tics had yet to appear, like the compulsive preservice touching of his shoulders, nose, and ears.

His pace between points was deliberate but not quite so ponderous. In general, he got on with it, and he got on with it brilliantly as Federer struggled to adjust to his heavy spin, power, and energy.

Federer was far from his best, missing routine forehands and misplaying volleys, but that was also because of Nadal's pressure.

Shots that finished off others did not finish off Nadal, with his speed and ability to produce probing responses from what looked like vulnerable positions. His passing shots were next-level; Federer failed to win a point in his first six forays to the net.

The youngster was not entirely immune to the occasion: On his first break points, his returns were shaky. But he adjusted quickly, a sign of his clarity of thought under duress. As the match continued, he often dictated terms from the backcourt, even when Federer moved closer to the baseline and cranked up the cadence. Nadal put 81 percent of his first serves in play and did not face a single break point, not even when he cold-bloodedly served for the upset, attacking the net on the final point after breaking down Federer's backhand (another preview of matches to come).

Final score: 6–3, 6–3 Nadal, in just sixty-nine minutes.

"One wonders just what the future holds for this astonishingly talented left-hander from Mallorca," Barrett said.

Watching him dismantle Federer with gusto in Miami, it was clear that he was already a champion. It was just a matter of when he would be healthy enough to make it official.

It would not happen in 2004. He missed the heart of the clay court season and Wimbledon with a stress fracture in his left foot. In what felt rather like a lottery, the French Open winner turned out to be Gastón Gaudio, a one-Slam wonder from Argentina who saved two match points against his favored compatriot Guillermo Coria in an emotional journey of a final that seemed to knock the stuffing out of both men's careers.

For me, any lingering doubts about Nadal's potential and poise under pressure were erased for good later that year when he faced Andy Roddick at the 2004 Davis Cup final in Seville, Spain.

The final was played in front of 27,200 spectators—then a record crowd for an official tennis match—and it was chilly enough in early December to see your breath on occasion in the outdoor stadium.

Nadal was supposed to play only doubles, but his captains were no fools. They knew what they had and decided to risk internal dissension for the national good: naming Nadal as a replacement for the slumping Ferrero in one of the opening-day singles matches.

Roddick, a tennis patriot who loved Davis Cup to the detriment of his regular tour results, was inspired. But Nadal was transcendent, winning 6–7 (6), 6–2, 7–6 (6), 6–2.

I was living in Seville at the time and wrote this from the stands (in a sweater and scarf):

"The tennis world is full of youngsters who look terrific from the baseline in practice, but what makes for greatness is an ability to embrace the big occasion. Despite Spain's well-deserved reputation for embracing life with exuberance, its top players have generally been self-contained characters on court: Sergi Bruguera, Àlex Corretja, Albert Costa, Moyá and Ferrero. But Nadal wears his emotions on his sleeve, which would be a much more appropriate metaphor if he had not played today in a sleeveless shirt. There are fist pumps, scissors kicks and howling, airborne delight.

"To sum up, he brings the crowd in—Jimmy Connors or Lleyton Hewitt style—which might not be the way to avoid running out of steam over the course of a long season or the way to endear himself to his peers but is certainly a way to endear himself to the Spanish. By the end of today's swashbuckling recital, they were thoroughly under his spell."

He was still ranked just 51st, but that could not and did not last. He broke out with eleven titles in 2005, including the French Open in his debut at age nineteen. By July he had climbed to No. 2 in the rankings.

Federer held him off, just barely, in a five-set Miami final in April, rallying to win after losing the first two sets and trailing 1–4 in the third.

The intensity of the combat was enough to make Federer briefly lose his cool, as he had against Safin at the Australian Open a few months before. After fighting back in the third set, Federer failed to convert a break point at 4–4, and when Nadal held his serve, Federer flung his racket to the court.

"I was missing one opportunity after the other; I really felt like I'm climbing uphill all the time," Federer said. "I just had enough. So I threw it hard. Maybe it did me good, and I kind of woke up maybe. Who knows?"

Nadal smartly took the rare display as a compliment, and he would often be attuned to the changes in the Federer microclimate in the years to come.

"Of course it's surprising to see Federer throwing his racket," he said. "But it makes you think you're closer to victory."

Nadal *was* getting closer: He was within two points of the title when he took a 5–3 lead in the third-set tiebreaker. But Federer rose up just in time, sweeping the next four points to take the set and then showing more staying power to win: 2–6, 6–7 (4), 7–6 (5), 6–3, 6–1.

"For me this was a big match, because I know what a great player he will be one day," Federer said.

He did not have to wait long. Two months later on clay in Paris, Federer could not find a way back, losing to Nadal in four sets on Nadal's nineteenth birthday in the semifinals in their first Grand Slam match. Two days later, Nadal defeated Mariano Puerta in the final to join the likes of Björn Borg, Mats Wilander, Boris Becker, Michael Chang, and Pete Sampras, all Grand Slam men's singles champion in their teens.

The title in hand, Nadal cried for the first time after a victory (the parallels with Federer have their limits).

"He's going to become a legend," Puerta said.

Players who become good enough to win a major are all remarkable, all worthy of your attention. Think of the millions who pick up a tennis racket. The odds of getting to the top of the pyramid are absurdly long. But the prodigies, for better or worse, hold a particular appeal. There is a whiff of destiny to their success, a fascination with their ability to skip the usual steps on the ladder and with how high their head start might allow them to climb.

Spanish tennis had produced plenty of stars since Manolo Santana won four majors in the 1960s. But Nadal was its first superstar: a genuine prodigy who was an irresistible combination of can-do charisma and old-school values like humility and family. It certainly did not hurt that he was good-looking. Tennis still had elitist overtones in Spain, evoking private clubs and class distinctions, but Nadal *vamos*ed full force into the mainstream.

Interest was not restricted to Spain: My story on his French Open victory and the celebration that followed was on the front page of the *New York Times*.

English was a challenge for Nadal at this stage, but my Spanish was functional, if hardly a melodic marvel, after years of living in Seville. We did an interview near midnight as he feted his breakthrough victory at the Café de l'Homme, a restaurant on the Trocadéro esplanade with a view of the Eiffel Tower. It was a surprisingly sedate celebration, but as we would learn through the years, the Nadals were intent on keeping big victories in perspective, even underplaying them.

The new champion was surrounded by family and friends. He wore a dark suit and conservative tie: quite a contrast with the white capri-style pants and fluorescent green sleeveless shirt he had worn throughout the tournament.

"I hope all this won't change me," he said. "I would like to stay the same as I've always been. I hope that I will pull it off, and I believe I will be able to pull it off."

It certainly helped to be Miguel Ángel's nephew. The Nadal family had been dealing with celebrity worship for decades and was much better equipped than most families to draw a line between the private and the public spheres.

⇒◇⇐

I had discussed Nadal with Federer for the first time shortly before the 2005 French Open when he gave me an interview for the *New York Times* and *International Herald Tribune* in the penthouse suite of the Hôtel de Crillon: his princely redoubt with a sweeping view of the Place de la Concorde and the Assemblée Nationale.

Life was already very good for Federer, who was deep into his second year at No. 1, and also very good for Vavrinec. At this stage Federer had no full-time agent and had split with IMG. His parents were helping manage many of his business affairs, and Vavrinec, who had stopped her tennis career because of chronic foot problems, was his personal assistant and media liaison as well as his girlfriend.

It was a line-blurring role, one they were still working through. As we talked, she tried on designer clothes for a planned magazine photo shoot. She interrupted us intermittently to get Federer's opinion on her latest casual-chic option. He gave her his full attention, answered yea, nay, or "not bad," and then politely resumed the interview with: "You were saying?"

"Nadal, I was saying Nadal."

"Quite impressive, isn't it?" Federer said. "He's already bigger than me, and he's five years younger. Imagine how he looks in five years! It is good for tennis that you've got these different types of guys and players, but at eighteen, nineteen, I was nothing like that."

"Well, it certainly keeps you from getting complacent," I said.

"I think it's also good he's a lefty," Federer said. "We don't have many great ones anymore."

He talked about the retirements of Thomas Muster, Goran Ivanišević, Petr Korda, and Marcelo Ríos, all great left-handers. He could have mentioned his own coach: Tony Roche, a left-hander as well.

"We are short of them," Federer said. "I think it's nice to have him, because it also changes the dimensions of the court, the way you play. The spins come the other way, so that's going to be interesting, too. That puts in a totally different game plan."

It was an intriguing response on several levels, not least because Federer has long had a tendency to speak about Nadal as if he were a natural phenomenon, like a king tide or a tropical storm ("Quite impressive, isn't it?").

But what struck me that day, when Vavrinec was not transporting us off topic with another peasant-inspired blouse, was how Federer was already very much in guardian-of-the-game mode. This youngster was emerging, ready to beat them all to a pulp (respectfully), and Federer viewed it as good for the sport that he provided stylistic variety. Perhaps it was his way of detaching himself from the direct impact that Nadal might have on him and his livelihood, but I am convinced it was also due to genuine curiosity. Federer watches a lot of tennis, including a lot of replays of his own matches.

"I mean, we haven't seen Marat or Lleyton or Andy or Coria play lefties anymore," he said. "We've only seen them playing righties."

I thought at the time that it was too bad that the Nadals, for whom leftiness was a choice, were not listening in, because they certainly would have found it all amusing...and reaffirming.

Federer also made it clear that he knew what he and everybody else was up against.

"I could see quite a while ago that he was going to arrive," he said of Nadal. "It was just a matter of when. After the Spanish team picked him for the Davis Cup final last year, I thought, 'Good luck, Andy!'"

But for the rest of 2005 at least, Nadal did not venture far into Federer's domains. They did not play again that year. After the French Open, Nadal won five more titles, all at tournaments Federer skipped, but lost early at Wimbledon and the US Open.

Federer won both of those majors, beating Roddick in straight sets at the All England Club and Agassi in four sets in New York.

Agassi, the oldest men's Grand Slam singles finalist since Ken

Rosewall in 1974, was remarkably competitive in defeat at age thirty-five. But he was unbeatable in the interview room when it came to putting Federer's tennis virtues in perspective.

Agassi before the final: "The challenge is really simple. Most people have weaknesses and most people only have one great shot. Federer doesn't have weaknesses and has a few great shots. So that equates to a problem."

Agassi after the final: "Pete was great. I mean no question. But there was a place to get to with Pete. You knew what you had to do. If you could do it, it could be on your terms. There's no such place like that with Roger. I think he's the best I've played against."

The numbers at this juncture were dizzying. Federer was now 6-0 in Grand Slam singles finals and had won twenty-three tournament finals in a row. Until then, the Open-era men's record had been twelve, jointly held by Björn Borg and John McEnroe. Federer's victories had come on all the major surfaces: sixteen on hard court, four on grass, and three on clay.

We met the day after the US Open final at a sports bar in Times Square as part of his postvictory media tour. He was more subdued than usual after going to bed at 3:00 a.m. He seemed more satisfied than elated as he took a seat in an overstuffed chair and stretched out his legs. There is a feline quality to Federer's movement on and off court, and I wrote in the *Times* that he reminded me of "a well-groomed and contented cat."

I mentioned his twenty-three-final winning streak. "That's the one I'm really proud of," he said. "I wasn't really famous for consistency when I came along, so I turned that around and that makes me feel really good about myself, to know that when it really matters, I can find a way to be always on top of my game and pull it off every single time, even though I know that streak might end very quickly."

Interest was already snowballing in how long it might take him to smash Sampras's record of fourteen Grand Slam singles titles, which no longer looked impregnable just two years after Sampras's retirement became official.

"I don't like just to look at the Slams as the only thing that matters,"

Federer said. "For me, it means the other tournaments, when I'm competing against the best players or playing in front of thousands of people, don't really matter. I have thirty-two titles, and six of them are Grand Slams, so you see the majority are other tournaments."

It was a point well worth making. In a crowded media landscape, only the gaudiest numbers rise above the fray. The Grand Slam count was the shiniest at this stage but not a dependable historical reference, considering that an all-time great like Borg played the Australian Open just once and even a more enduring talent like Jimmy Connors, whose career spanned twenty years, played it just twice.

Comparing across eras was tricky, sometimes pointless, and even Agassi had skipped the Australian Open for the first eight years of his pro career and missed it twice more since then because of injury. But that had perhaps kept Agassi fresh deep into his thirties.

"I'm not surprised that Andre wants to keep going, even at thirty-five," Federer told me. "As long as he's not playing with pain, and he's happy to play a few tournaments a year, why shouldn't he?"

For anyone searching for hints about Federer's own long-range plans, that was a big one. He had been watching Agassi closely, but he would soon be watching Nadal much more closely.

——◦◦——

The Spaniard was indeed the real deal, but he was forced off the tour again in late 2005 and early 2006 when his left foot problem returned. His usual doctors were mystified, and a specialist in Spain told him that it was a rare congenital problem with a small bone, the navicular, and that he might not play competitive tennis again. Nadal was devastated but his father was doggedly optimistic, and they were finally able to find a way to diminish the stress on the bone with custom insoles and shoes, designed on a trip to Nike in Oregon. It was not a definitive solution. Nadal's condition, known as Müller-Weiss syndrome, continued to trouble him, even late into his career.

But he was able to resume his march to the top but with the new understanding that tennis careers were ephemeral. He was already playing each point as if it were his last, but now he had the feeling that it could actually be true.

After missing the 2006 Australian Open, he returned to the tour with a vengeance, beating Federer on a hard court in the final in Dubai, which by then was already Federer's second home and warm-weather training base.

This was the year they became archrivals. They played six times in total, the most they would face each other in any season. Nadal won four of the matches: three on clay. All but one of those 2006 duels was in a final, and one of them was an ultramarathon: a five-set test of grit at the Italian Open won by Nadal in five hours and five minutes by the long-form score of 6–7 (0), 7–6 (5), 6–4, 2–6, 7–6 (5).

Even after all these years, I still consider that match their second best in pure tennis terms, and it was surely their edgiest, with Federer accusing Toni Nadal of illegally coaching Rafael from the player's box.

Nadal rallied from 1–4 in the final set and saved two champion-ship points in his final service game as Federer made two unforced errors with his signature shot, the forehand. Those gaffes and the ones that followed in the tiebreaker made it unmistakably clear just how far Nadal had worked his way into Federer's head.

Against others, Federer let it flow. Against Nadal, he pressed. Federer was still No. 1, still a serial champion at Wimbledon and the US Open, the two highest-profile tournaments in the world. But Nadal had redefined Federer, making him vulnerable.

That might seem an exaggeration, considering that Federer won three of the four major singles titles in 2006 and 2007 and remained atop the rankings for a record 237 consecutive weeks. But even during those high-achieving seasons, it was difficult to shake the image of Nadal beating him again and again on clay, of Federer's chin and con-fidence dropping as the pattern repeated.

If he had lost those same matches to a mix of different players, it would have had a lesser impact. But that he lost them to the same man, five years his junior, only magnified the effect and the public interest.

Federer's moment to roam free, unfettered and comfortably ahead of the chase pack, was briefer than many remember: one full season in 2004 (and that's if you don't count the loss in Miami) and most of another season in 2005. But the rivalry that quickly developed with Nadal—and not in Federer's favor—also humanized him in a manner that, it seems to me, contributed to his enduring popularity. His smooth, creative game was hypnotic, even to the layman, which no doubt helped. His good manners and remarkably fan-friendly approach were factors. So was his spartan approach to playing through pain, which was partly a form of respect to the fans. But Federer was also not a true tennis ogre for more than a season or two.

It was harder for fans to grow weary of Federer winning titles, big or small, when Nadal had reminded them that winning was not a given.

"For the public to relate to someone the way they relate to Roger, I think they have to feel someone is vulnerable," Andy Roddick told me. "Look at the way the public viewed Andre when he was brash, young, and had the pirate look versus after he had gone through some personal, terrible things and come out the other side. I think people want to be able to relate to someone. So when Roger can't fix something at work, people can think maybe he's like the rest of us in a very small way. And he's not going to give us a reason. He's not insecure enough to have to defend himself."

Martina Navratilova thinks his nationality helped, too. "I mean, he's from Switzerland, you know; he's neutral," she said. "He doesn't threaten anybody."

Swiss nationality was not enough to turn Martina Hingis into a universally beloved figure, however. Navratilova, who won Wimbledon nine times in singles, was an irresistible force for a stretch: winning six straight major titles in the 1980s. She was rarely a crowd favorite, often crushing the suspense out of matches in her prime.

"I was always picking people apart at the net and was faster and stronger, and so they felt sorry for my opponent," Navratilova said. "With Roger, nobody ever feels sorry for the opponent. They're just admiring his tennis instead of worrying about the other guy he's picking apart who can't win a game."

But picking apart Nadal was a task that Federer could rarely accomplish. Even Federer's safest haven, the grass of the All England Club, soon became a danger zone.

Nadal was no mere clay court specialist, even if it took the rest of us a while to figure that out. Toni had focused hard on encouraging all-court skills in Nadal's youth, requesting that he rush the net against lesser players even if it meant that he might lose to them.

Though his big forehand windup and unintimidating serve were not the ideal fast-court tools, he possessed the requisite punching power, athleticism, and mentality. Nadal was not afraid to take a chance, as anyone who heard him test out his rudimentary English in front of large audiences could confirm and admire.

As a professional player, Toni's lack of a weapon had been his failing. He wanted his nephew to be better armed.

"I was a defensive player and not all that successful, so the idea was for Rafael to be an aggressive player," Toni Nadal told me. "As it turns out, that style of game also fits his personality."

He is actually a bundle of contradictions. In Nadal's 2011 autobiography, *Rafa*, his mother, Ana Maria, talks about how he had persistent anxiety about something bad happening to his family. He reminded his mother to drive slowly on the way to Palma and to extinguish the fire in the fireplace at night, even calling from a restaurant to make sure it had been done.

Unlike many other Spanish men's players, Nadal had grown up with Wimbledon squarely in his sights. Toni emphasized its importance from an early age even if Roland Garros was the title that Spanish stars like Sergi Bruguera, Alberto Costa, and Moyá were winning. By age fourteen, Rafael was talking openly about wanting to win at the All England Club. Santana, after all, had proved it could be done by a Spanish man in 1966. Before Nadal's debut, Feliciano López, a left-hander five years older than Nadal, already had reached the fourth round at Wimbledon twice with his elegant, attacking game and crisply chipped backhand.

"Spanish players are starting to get good results on these kinds of surfaces," Nadal told me at his first Wimbledon. "You can see that especially from the young players coming up that have the interest to play on these surfaces and develop their games, and I think that's good for tennis."

It helped Nadal that Wimbledon no longer rewarded only the big server and net rusher. The bounce was truer and slightly higher now, which allowed baseliners to put more returns in play and do more damage with passing shots. The polyester strings and modern racket technology also helped the baseliner's cause and to homogenize play at the four major tournaments and beyond.

Nadal versus Federer on grass bore little resemblance to Sampras versus Ivanišević on grass. Nadal versus Federer at Wimbledon, stylistically, was not far from Nadal versus Federer at the Australian Open: lots of baseline exchanges, occasional forays to the net, and first-strike tennis when a ball landed too short or floated too high.

In 2006, Nadal reached his first Wimbledon final and pushed Federer to four sets and was frankly happy just to be there, even if Federer looked as relieved as he did delighted by his fourth straight Wimbledon victory.

But by 2007, when Nadal returned to the final, the Spaniard's expectations had changed.

It was a unique year at Wimbledon. The superstructure above Centre Court had been dismantled to facilitate the upcoming installation of a retractable roof. Centre Court, the Globe Theatre of tennis, was—for one summer only—more like the Rose Bowl: open to the sky and even the sunshine, which was abundant for the final.

It came down to a fifth set and Nadal had Federer pinned at 15–40 on his serve in the third game and again in the fifth. Both times, Federer escaped his grip with help from Nadal, who missed makeable returns on two of the four break points and anxiously missed a forehand wide on another.

Federer then broke Nadal's serve to 4–2 with an inspired inside-in forehand winner to unlock a tight rally. The momentum had shifted for good, and Federer finished off his toughest major final yet with an overhead and dropped to the grass as if he had been struck by a flying object, covering his face with both hands.

He was already in tears as he landed, and though Nadal held it together, he was soon sobbing as he sat in a shower stall with the water running, despondent over his tentative play in the fifth set.

Federer had matched Borg's modern-era men's record with his fifth Wimbledon in a row, something Federer had stopped Sampras short of achieving.

Borg, the equanimous Swede, was sitting in the front row of the Royal Box for Federer's latest triumph, his fair-haired mane gone gray. Nadal had been compared to Borg much more often with his heavy topspin, two-handed backhand, and killer instinct. But Federer knew Borg and found inspiration in his presence.

"Very fitting," Federer said. "To see him waiting there was great."

I found it intriguing that Borg had suppressed his emotions and burned out while Federer had suppressed his and played on (and on) with passion.

He was certainly dressed for tennis history: taking part in the awards ceremony in a white jacket and long white sweatpants that echoed the trousers of yore (no matter that Federer had slipped the pants on backward by mistake).

Trophy back in hand, he spoke with Sue Barker of the BBC on court and was asked about Nadal. "I'm happy for every one I get now before he takes them all," Federer said. "He's improving so much."

It was the eleventh Grand Slam title for Federer and he would run his total to twelve by winning another US Open two months later, but Federer was increasingly accepting of being viewed as part of a pair.

"In the beginning, I didn't want a rival," he said.

———◇———

Federer and Nadal were a great stylistic contrast in some respects, a contrast that Nike carefully cultivated, just as it had with Sampras and Agassi in the 1990s.

Federer was elegance, acquired cool, and effortless power; Nadal was exuberance, innate fire, and flexed biceps. Federer was smooth and classical; Nadal was rugged and avant-garde. Federer was tradition; Nadal was youth.

Their pregame approach was also worlds apart. James Blake, the American who was No. 4 in the world in 2006, beat Nadal in the semifinals in Indian Wells that year and then lost to Federer in the final.

"It was so funny to me, the differences in dynamic in the locker room," Blake told me. "Both those guys are great people, but before the match, Rafa's got his big Bose headphones on and he's running up and down the locker room, doing the sprints, taping his fingers. He's like a caged animal. And then the next day I'm playing Roger, and we're talking about his house back in Switzerland, and he's just bought some land and it's about what he and Mirka are gonna do. And it was honestly like we were sitting at a coffee shop as calm as can be."

And yet both men, not just Nadal, were remarkable at flipping the switch when it came time for combat, of transforming themselves into steely-eyed champions. It was simply that Federer waited until later in the process to make the shift. Nadal's transformation came in the locker room, Federer's on court.

"I think people discredit what a killer Roger really is," Blake said. "Because he is so relaxed before the match and he's saying, 'Oh yeah, come out and see the Swiss countryside, it's beautiful blah blah blah,' and then he goes out and kicks my ass. He still has that absolute fighter's mentality, that attitude of 'I'm *gonna* win.' But he doesn't go about it the way people might associate with, like, the Rocky Balboa thing."

Nadal, with his prebattle rituals and kangaroo jumps in the stadium tunnel, projected *warrior* to his peers, and it was intimidating. Federer was more 007, every bit as deadly but able to neutralize the threat without you seeing him sweat and just in time for cocktails.

But there were also strong commonalities, both broad-brush and granular.

They were sensitive and empathetic and raised by their families to believe that manners matter: to shake the hand firmly, to make the eye contact, to notice the effort and the favor. Federer's motto was: "It's nice to be important but more important to be nice." Nadal and his family subscribed to: "You are not special because of who you are but because of what you do."

Both were soccer fanatics who could have been professionals, and though both happily finished formal schooling at sixteen, they were curious about the wider world that they were now roaming in pursuit of tennis glory. Both were close to their parents but had relied heavily in their youth on a former tennis pro whose own career aspirations had fallen short. Even their choice in fitness trainer was similar. Both Pierre Paganini for Federer and Joan Forcades for Nadal were deep thinkers who preferred to work unconventionally in the shadows instead of traveling the circuit.

Paganini and Forcades, a part-time schoolteacher from Mallorca, realized that traditional preparation was not ideal for their clients: eschewing the training run and the weight lifting to focus instead on movement that related directly to the percussive stop-start rhythm of tennis.

"I don't think Roger has gone for a run in twenty years," said Yves Allegro late in Federer's career.

Both Federer and Nadal were also, on a more fundamental level, anchored in a culture with egalitarian values that tempered their sense of self-importance and also allowed them to live without being hassled or hounded: Federer in Switzerland, Nadal in the clan cocoon in Mallorca.

The language barrier between them was real for quite some time, but as Nadal's English slowly improved (Federer's Spanish never did) they realized—like a photo developing in a darkroom—that they shared more than they could have imagined.

"We know the respect we have for each other," Federer told me more than a decade ago. "I see it in his eyes, and he sees it in my eyes. We know what we feel for each other."

It is not a close friendship by either man's definition of that term, but it is something special.

"'Friendship' is a strong word," Nadal said to me in our most recent interview. "But I think I have a very good relationship with Roger with lots of respect and lots of confidence in each other. We confide in the other, and that's the most important. I cannot compare Federer with some friend of mine from Mallorca who has been a friend of mine for my whole life, but I think both Roger and I appreciate all the things we have experienced together."

Federer had seen Nadal grow in confidence off the court (on the court had never been a problem).

"We like seeing each other and also chatting together and making sure that tennis moves forward the right way," Federer said. "I remember Rafa when he was younger, and he was so shy, and he was looking up to me and he said, 'Whatever Roger wants, I'm happy with that.' And then he grew into a much stronger character, you know, and we still had a good time."

Both have an old-school streak, a perception that face-to-face relations and traditions are worth preserving and that their sport should not force too much change upon itself.

"In the end, I think that's true about us," Nadal told me. "We've had many conversations, and I think we have many opinions that are very similar in many ways, our way to understand sport and our life in sport."

Both have increasingly used analytics to some degree at their coaches' behest, but both prefer to free their minds and let their instincts reign under pressure.

"Roger, for example, is not a big fan of stats in tennis," Nadal said. "Neither am I. He likes and respects the history of sport and respects the stories of champions, like I do. I think we share many things in the end. And I believe we've come to understand each other more with the years."

Among their mutual understandings: Their rivalry was very good for business.

That would have been true even without 2008. They dueled memorably many times outside of that year, but 2008 was what bound them together for good in the collective consciousness.

It was a two-step sequence: anticlimax on the clay; splendor on the grass.

The letdown came in the French Open final, their third straight final at Roland Garros. The buzz before the match was more like a roar. I can still close my eyes and see Larry Ellison, the American billionaire software mogul, taking his seat a few minutes before the final. Ellison, an avid recreational player, was one of the world's wealthiest men, capable of buying a Hawaiian island (he purchased Lanai) or of dropping hundreds of millions of dollars in pursuit of yachting's increasingly peripheral America's Cup. But on that Sunday afternoon in Paris, Ellison's expression said that he would not want to be anywhere else on the planet than in that seat, ready to watch the latest and perhaps greatest duel between Federer and Nadal.

In just one hour and forty-eight minutes it was over, and it took that long only because Nadal plays his service games at such a measured pace.

The final score of 6–1, 6–3, 6–0 was the most lopsided result in a Grand Slam men's singles final since John McEnroe allowed Jimmy Connors only four games in the 1984 Wimbledon final.

Nadal broke Federer's serve in the opening game. He soon went on a streak of winning twenty-two of twenty-five points.

Federer, being Federer, tried to reshuffle the deck. He stayed back and rallied, but Nadal was too quick, too opportunistic, and too relentlessly precise, making just seven unforced errors in the match. Federer tried to attack the net, only to risk whiplash as the passing shots zipped by.

The deck was stacked, and by the end Federer was only slightly more embarrassed, it seemed, than Nadal. When Federer's last forehand approach sailed long, Nadal, so often knocked off his feet by the emotions of winning Roland Garros, did nothing more than raise both arms, smile, and shuffle to the net for the handshake.

"First of all, I don't prepare my celebrations; I do them as I feel them," Nadal said. "In the other years I won in four sets, they were closer than this one. This time, there were no moments of maximum tension. And considering my relationship with Roger, it seemed like the right way to go about it."

It was a frank, reasonable answer: a Nadal trademark. But he was as surprised as everybody else by the rout.

They had played just a few weeks before on clay in Hamburg, with

Nadal fighting off a Federer comeback to win in three close sets. But in Hamburg the bounce is lower and conditions generally heavier. In Paris, Nadal had shifted into a clay court gear that Federer did not possess, and became the first man since Borg to win the French Open without dropping a set.

Borg, back in the front row for the final, had a very different view of the Federer-Nadal rivalry than he had experienced at Wimbledon the year before. Or perhaps it was more accurate to call it the Nadal-Federer rivalry: Nadal now led the series 11-6 and had won nine of their ten matches on clay.

"I definitely think he's improved," Federer said. "He's much better on defense, much better on offense. When you really cannot play your game and he can play exactly what he wants from the baseline, well, you end up with scores like this sometimes. It's tough for the opponent, obviously."

So tough that you had to wonder what the fallout would be for Federer for the rest of 2008 as they left clay behind.

"Look, I've beaten Rafa 6-love in a set; I've beaten him in finals before; I've beaten him quite comfortably on previous occasions," Federer said. "That didn't really give me the edge on clay against him, you know."

It had been, for multiple reasons, a difficult stretch. In March, I broke the story that Federer was recovering from mononucleosis. I broke it only because Federer, in the age before social media, decided that speaking to me and the *Times* was the best way to spread the word and help put his recent struggles in perspective.

He had played just two tournaments in 2008, losing both. Novak Djokovic had beaten him in straight sets in the semifinals of the Australian Open; then, at just twenty years old, he went on to win his first Grand Slam title.

"I've created a monster, so I know I need to always win every tournament," Federer said, sensing the consternation in his postdefeat press conference. "But semis is still, you know, pretty good."

Federer then lost to another twenty-year-old, Andy Murray, in the first round in Dubai after taking a five-week break from competition.

During that break, he had tests done in Switzerland and Dubai after falling ill for the third time in six weeks. The doctors told him he had contracted mononucleosis, most likely in December 2007. Mononucleosis can produce symptoms similar to the flu and lingering, debilitating fatigue. Physicians often recommend that patients avoid intense physical activity because of the risk of rupturing the spleen.

Mario Ančić, the talented Croatian, had been forced to miss the first six months of the 2007 season, bedridden for more than two months because of mononucleosis. He ultimately ended his career because of it. Robin Söderling, another Federer rival, retired because of it in the 2010s.

"There was a soccer player in my home club in Switzerland who was out for two years," Federer said when we spoke by phone. "You hear two years and you hear six months. So I was like, 'Oh my God.'"

Federer said he had received medical clearance to resume training shortly before the Dubai event.

"I finally have the green light and finally I can give 100 percent in practice again, because it wasn't fun sort of being there sort of halfway," he said. "I didn't enjoy that too much. But again, it was interesting, and you've got to go through those moments as well. I know that. Through a career, a long career maybe as number one, you have to go through injuries and sicknesses."

He said that he had not wanted to mention the illness publicly for fear of detracting from Murray's and Djokovic's victories and seemed sheepish that he was mentioning it at all.

But he felt he needed to disclose the situation before resuming play in Indian Wells. If the chattering classes and his fellow players were going to question his level of play, at least they should have the whole picture.

His dominance, in his view, was far from over.

"I don't think it's fair to assess it this way," he said. "For me, it was only a matter of time before the younger guys were going to come up. Now that they're here, they're good and everything, but I'm still number one in the world. I think they are doing well. But I think it would be very premature, almost a little bit rude toward me because of everything I've already done over the last few years. I think it's not fair if you just say, 'The guy has lost two matches, played two tournaments and didn't win both, and it's over for him.'"

—⊃⊂—

From the start of his career, Federer was particularly good at reading the room. His antennae picked up negativity in the gallery at almost the same speed he could flick a half volley in midcourt, and he frequently tried to head off uncomfortable lines of questioning before they developed.

But 2008 was an unprecedented challenge in spin control. Federer brought in José Higueras, the much-respected Spanish coach, to help him during the clay court season, beginning in Estoril. Higueras, a former Spanish star who now lived on a ranch in Palm Springs, California, had been instrumental in Michael Chang and Jim Courier winning the French Open. That was still the only major that Federer lacked.

"Roger wasn't in the best of shape, because the body I think takes about eighteen months to get rid of the mono completely," Higueras told me. "I met him in Estoril, and I lost my bags, so I didn't have any. After dinner, he said, 'Hey José, come to my room.' And so I went to his room and we ended up watching matches until one in the morning. What really impressed me about him is how interested he was about everything, asking you about everything. He knew the juniors, and he knew everybody, and that was pretty refreshing to me, to be honest."

Higueras convinced a skeptical Federer to start using a forehand drop shot on clay as a change of pace. Federer, a quick study, won Estoril. But all of Higueras's clay court savvy could not help Federer against the onslaught in the Roland Garros final.

"Rafa was at the peak of his game, and obviously for Roger it was always a tough match on clay, not only tennis-wise but mentally also, and once he started going down, he just couldn't make it work," Higueras said.

Higueras, who was working only certain weeks with Federer, had planned to head to Spain to see family, but shortly after the final, he got a message from Federer's agent, Tony Godsick, saying that Federer would like Higueras to join him for Halle, the grass court event in Germany the following week.

"I already had my flights, but I thought, 'Jeez, after this beating I can't say no,'" Higueras said. "So we went to Zurich for a couple of days and then went to Halle and we went out on the practice court and it was like he had just won the French Open for the fifth time in a row, you know, the joy of hitting balls and playing the game. It put me in a good mood, to be honest, and that is something that either he learned from somebody or he was born with it, because the ability to shake off a loss like that and not carry it with you for a while is pretty impressive. I think it's something he's done consistently through his career."

Federer won Halle without dropping a set to regain some momentum, but the reality was that when Wimbledon arrived, Estoril and Halle were his only two titles of 2008. Both were lower-tier events. That was cause for alarm, and Nadal was only getting stronger after beating Roddick and Djokovic to win at Queen's Club against a better grass court field than Halle's.

"Nadal was just a wrecking ball," Brad Gilbert said.

Federer took the hint once Wimbledon began, lifting his level and sweeping into the final without losing a set. Nadal dropped only one.

The rematch was set.

"It certainly is a dream final for everyone," Federer said.

The dreamy elements were indeed in place.

It was tennis's most compelling matchup on the most atmospheric and historic court in the sport. Federer was trying to break Borg's modern-day men's record by winning his sixth straight Wimbledon. Nadal was trying to win his first and become the first man since Borg to complete the elusive French Open–Wimbledon double.

"I think the public perception is feeling like it's sort of Nadal's destiny to win here after such a close final last year and really dominating Roger in Paris," Darren Cahill told me before the final. "But I just love the way Roger has stepped up his game since Paris. I think his form in this Wimbledon has been his best in 2008, and I think he is taking as good a form going into a final here that I've seen from him going into any final here. I think his serve is right on song again. He's placing it in the box beautifully, hitting closer to the line with lots of aces. And what I also like, quite honestly, is the quickness of step and lightness of foot in his movement. He's got the sharpness back in his game."

Another straight-set rout seemed out of the question, but Nadal was newly determined as he prepared for his third straight Wimbledon final against Federer. Yes, he needed a painkilling shot in the sole of his troublesome left foot shortly before the final, but that was unfortunately not all that unusual. He did not feel he was the favorite this time, but for a change, he did not feel like the underdog.

It was an open match in his view, and perhaps Nadal's conviction that it would be open was one of the many factors that made it just that.

He won the first two sets, rallying from 1–4 in the second, and though Federer started taking more chances on his return games and attacking the net more frequently, Nadal came close to taking command of the third set as well. At 3–3, Federer fell behind 0–40 on his serve before escaping. With Federer leading 5–4, rain interrupted play for more than an hour.

Federer, again operating without a formal coach in Higueras's absence, received a pep talk from Vavrinec as soon as he left the court. According to Jon Wertheim in his book *Strokes of Genius* about the 2008 final, Vavrinec reminded her boyfriend that he, not Nadal, was the five-time champion. But Federer said later that he had no recollection of this.

"She wouldn't say that, I don't think, to be quite honest," he said in an interview with the *Sunday Times*.

Little more than an hour later, Federer returned to the grass with new energy, winning the tiebreaker and forcing a fourth set. The final was about to take flight in earnest, and though Federer was in the ascendancy, Nadal rose to stay with him.

It was best to have been there, of course. Wimbledon should be on all of our lists: more crowded and less clubby than one imagines, but ultimately true to its reputation. The palette and acoustics of Centre

Court alone merit the visit, the way sounds meld and rumble through the space, distilling the collective disposition.

The tennis is better in person, too, allowing you to grasp, truly grasp, just how much spin is on Nadal's and Federer's forehands, how quickly they can close on a drop shot from the baseline, and above all how percussive the shot making can be when both are trying to break the other down.

Television has yet to find a way to communicate all that, but well over a decade later, none of us can be at the 2008 final, and to travel back in time and click Play at any moment in the match's final two hours is to feel the drama. It is there in the intense concentration of the combatants, the sharp and immediate reactions of the crowd.

It was a quick-shifting mood, which is what a mutual tennis masterwork requires, and the mood in the Nadal camp was buoyant after he took a 5–2 lead in the fourth-set tiebreaker. He was two points from the championship with two points on his own serve to come.

Had he learned how to finish off Federer at Wimbledon? It seemed not: He double-faulted as his tentative second serve hit the net cord. He then left a ball short in the court for Federer to attack and missed a backhand pass he had made thousands of times against lesser opponents.

His lead was only 5–4 now, and then it was gone altogether after Federer won two points on his serve. Nadal survived a set point and a long rally and then earned his first championship point at 7–6. Federer did not tarry, nailing a first serve wide that Nadal returned long with his forehand. It was 7–7: time for Nadal to hit a running forehand pass winner down the line. That might have been the shot of the match if Federer had not slapped a backhand passing shot winner down the line to end the next exchange and save a second championship point.

After those top-this-top-that displays of precision under pressure, it was 8–8, and when Federer won the next two points, it was, happily, time for a fifth set.

It is more of a pure pleasure to write about it here and now than it was then. The rain delay meant that we already were pushing against our European newspaper deadlines. The bittersweet reality of a fifth set meant that push had come to shove.

I spent the remainder of the match frantically shifting my eyes from the tennis to my laptop screen and wishing I could simply savor the tennis.

In time-crunch cases like this, we prepare what are called switch ledes: two versions of a story, one for each possible champion. One of my ledes had Federer extending his reign in the fading light; the other had Nadal ending it in the fading light. It would take more than an hour to find out which lede needed to be deleted.

The last rain delay came at 2–2 with Federer serving at deuce. When play resumed after nearly half an hour, Federer slammed back-to-back aces to hold.

He looked ready to win, and he later earned a break point with Nadal serving at 3–4, 30–40. Nadal saved it by ripping a forehand and then smacking an overhead winner off a short defensive lob.

He looked ready to win, too.

"Roger! Rafa! Roger! Rafa!" The Centre Court crowd could not reach consensus.

Federer got within two points of victory with Nadal serving at 4–5, 30–30, but Nadal played boldly again to hold.

The numbers on the scoreboard seemed forever pulled into alignment: 5–5. 6–5. 6–6. 7–6. 7–7.

What was hard to grasp for those watching from afar was how genuinely dark it was getting. Television cameras amplify the available light. Conditions were approaching unplayable, with automatic flashbulbs going off in the stands as some of the fifteen thousand spectators continued to record the moment.

Who could blame them? The climax, however difficult to make out in the shadows, was worth the wait. Federer saved three break points in the next game with Vavrinec leaning back in her seat and closing her eyes at one stage, drained from watching her man on a tightrope. But Federer could not save a fourth break point, missing a forehand approach shot just long.

"I almost couldn't see who I was playing," Federer said.

It was still Nadal, who would serve for the championship at 8–7 with new balls, and in light of the light (it was past 9:00 p.m.), Nadal presumably needed to win this game if he did not want to endure a fitful night in his rented Wimbledon home waiting to resume the final on Monday.

It would have been a pity to chop up the conclusion of this tennis epic. Even Federer understood that, although he had no intention of helping Nadal to the finish line. This was the last year of this kind of pressure at Wimbledon. The superstructure for the retractable roof was now in place over Centre Court. By 2009, the roof and accompanying lights would be operational. No matter the weather, finals would be sure to start and finish on the same day.

But this was still 2008—Nadal's year on so many levels. Federer saved a third championship point at 40–30 with one of his best and firmest backhand returns of the match, but Nadal remained impassive and won the next point with a first serve that Federer could not handle.

Championship point number four. Nadal, hair matted against his neck, went through his routine, put one more first serve into play, then hit a frankly uninspired and conservative backhand on his next shot that landed short.

Federer moved forward to pounce with the shot that had been most instrumental in his winning five straight Wimbledons: his forehand.

This one hit the net, and Nadal hit the deck, sliding onto his back on the dirt that had once been grass.

Wimbledon had a new champion, and men's tennis had a new dynamic: 6–4, 6–4, 6–7 (5), 6–7 (8), 9–7.

Federer looked the way you would imagine the loser of such a match might look: downcast, withdrawn, wounded.

"Probably my hardest loss, by far," he said later, his eyes red. "I mean, it's not much harder than this right now."

Nadal looked fittingly fulfilled: climbing into the player's box to embrace his family and team. It was reminiscent of Pat Cash's climb when he won Wimbledon in 1987, but Nadal added his own 2008 twist by walking across the commentary cabin roofs to the Royal Box to greet Spanish Crown Prince Felipe and Princess Letizia.

"It's the best victory of his career; mentally he's never been as strong," said Toni Nadal. "Not even at the French Open."

But Federer believes the rout in the 2008 French Open final is one of the factors that led to Nadal having the confidence and strength to take Federer's Wimbledon crown. Federer also complained about the visibility and the decision to play on.

"It would have been brutal for fans, for media, for us, for everybody to come back tomorrow, but what are you going to do?" Federer said. "It's rough on me now, obviously, to lose the biggest tournament in the world over maybe a bit of light."

Still, it was every bit as dark for Nadal, and he managed to serve out the championship.

"I think I've already proved that I'm not just a clay court player," Nadal said. "But to win is very special to me. Of the four Grand Slams, it's the most traditional. It's really *the* tournament."

———◦⊃⊂◦———

Greatest match of all time? Do we truly have to decide? Borg's five-set victory over McEnroe in the 1980 Wimbledon final really should not be dismissed. It, too, was lefty versus righty, and a greater contrast in character and style with much more net play than baseline play, which will always be quintessential Wimbledon for my generation and those that preceded ours.

McEnroe called Nadal and Federer's duel "the best match I've ever seen." But McEnroe was clearly too busy playing in that 1980 final to be able to judge its comparative merits. McEnroe saved seven championship points, four more than Federer: five of them in the tiebreaker, which he won 18–16 to force a fifth set. Though many of the service games in the fifth were lopsided, it did end with a cocksure backhand passing shot winner from Borg while Federer and Nadal's duel finished, unfittingly, with an edgy error.

For staying power and titanic mental strength, Djokovic's nearly six-hour victory over Nadal in the 2012 Australian Open also deserves some love. For unrelenting emotion and sentimental payoff, I have a soft spot for Goran Ivanišević's five-set victory over Patrick Rafter in the 2001 Wimbledon final on a People's Monday, when the hoi polloi got to experience Centre Court. But I know that is the heart, not the head, talking.

What seems clear is that the greatest match cannot be played in isolation. It needs an extended buildup and a killer backstory, and then it needs, of course, to be a suspenseful, smack-yourself-in-the-forehead spectacle that expands the conception of what humans can do with a racket in hand.

Take your pick if you must. I would go with Borg-McEnroe if you boxed me in, but this is all out-of-the-arena chatter. A match like the 1980 Wimbledon final or 2008 Wimbledon final is also about what happens next.

To watch Borg and McEnroe share a laugh and a knowing look more than forty years after their duel is a reflection of the bond it formed between them. Their rivalry was just beginning in 1980, but it did not have long to run with Borg walking away from the sport the following year after McEnroe solved the riddle of Borg in the Wimbledon and US Open finals. In all, they played over a span of just four seasons.

Federer versus Nadal endured long enough to become deeply embedded in the landscape, an institution. Their 2008 duel was much closer to the start than the finish on their competitive timeline. But as empaths, Nadal and Federer could sense how much that match deep into the twilight touched others and how much it touched them both, too. It will, I suspect, give them occasion to come together long into the future, just as they did in the winter of 2016 when Federer made another trip to Mallorca for an event that was nowhere near as surreal as the Battle of Surfaces.

Both he and Nadal were recovering from injuries, and Nadal, after considerable effort and investment, was formally opening his tennis academy in Manacor. He needed Federer's star power, and so Federer hopped on a plane in Switzerland and joined him for the day.

They sat side by side on the stage, deeply connected, just as they were that evening at the All England Club when the flashes illuminated their faces as Nadal proudly held the gold trophy and Federer glumly held the silver plate.

CHAPTER NINE

PARIS

It was less than an hour after the 2008 French Open final in which the great Roger Federer had been crushed like the red brick that is used to make the Roland Garros clay.

Did he still truly believe that he could win this tournament one day?

"Yes," Federer answered at his somber, postdrubbing news conference.

"Are you sure?" said the same reporter, unconvinced.

"Are you happy that I tell you no?" Federer replied, getting testy, which is rare. "In that case, no. You pick the answer. I'm telling you yes."

Skepticism was certainly warranted. Federer had won just four games in three sets against Rafael Nadal: looking a bit like a man with a bow and arrow trying to hold off a laser-guided missile. He had played three straight French Open finals against Nadal and had become less competitive each year.

But it was also possible to see the future through Federer's eyes. He was, without doubt at that stage, the second-best clay court player in the world, capable of beating everyone regularly on the surface except Nadal.

Novak Djokovic was rising fast and already a Grand Slam champion but not yet at the summit of his art on clay. Stan Wawrinka had only just entered the top 10. Clay court masters Juan Carlos Ferrero and Guillermo Coria had faded. Gustavo Kuerten had announced his retirement.

From Federer's perspective, it was one man, just one, who was blocking his path to completing his collection of Grand Slam singles titles. Why shouldn't Federer believe he could solve the riddle at Roland Garros, just as he had solved the riddles of Lleyton Hewitt and his own temperament early in his career?

"Well, I mean he's tough to beat but he's not impossible to beat; that's a big difference," Federer said of Nadal.

Clay was Federer's original surface. He learned the game on it in Basel: playing outdoors in the warmer months and then indoors under the big, heated bubbles that were inflated over the courts at clubs like Old Boys.

"It's very common in Switzerland to have indoor clay in the bubble so the club can still keep running through the winter," Federer told me. "I also played some on carpet or surfaces like that, but most of it has been clay my whole time as a junior."

North American–style hard courts are rare in Switzerland. Clay rules, and it has advantages for all ages. Because of the added friction when the ball strikes the ground, the game is slower, which encourages point construction and the development of a full range of shots, including the drop shot. On faster, less gritty surfaces, one swing of the racket can resolve the conflict. On clay, more patience is usually required, and through the years, I have come to prefer watching tennis on clay: for the movement, for the tactics, and, on a purely aesthetic level, for the way the shadows extend across the red clay in the late afternoon in Rome or Paris.

Patrick McEnroe, the former director of player development at the United States Tennis Association, believed that one explanation for the dearth of topflight American men's tennis players in the 2010s was that the Europeans had a developmental advantage growing up on clay. He maintained that too many young Americans were adept at striking the ball but not at playing the game itself. Clay was perhaps the best classroom, blunting raw power and encouraging point construction, and it had other advantages.

Perhaps one of the many reasons Federer was able to thrive on tour for more than twenty years was that he did not grind down his body as a youngster by playing most of his tennis on hard courts. Clay is generally easier on the joints, but it has not always been easy on Federer's ego.

In his first tour-level match in 1998, he was defeated by Lucas Arnold Ker in Gstaad on clay and then kept losing on it.

"I lost my first eleven matches, which was tough," Federer told me many years later, the precise number still locked in memory. "There were a lot of close ones, but eleven is eleven. It was quite a thing."

One of those early losses on clay came at the 1999 French Open in Federer's Grand Slam debut. He was facing Patrick Rafter, the charismatic, net-rushing Australian who had won back-to-back US Opens in 1997 and 1998. Rafter was a natural fast-court player but understood how to slide and attack on clay because, like Australian greats Rod Laver and Roy Emerson, he had grown up playing in sunny Queensland on courts made of "ant bed": crushed dirt from termite hills.

"It's very slippery; you slide a lot," Rafter said. "It's the closest thing to clay we have back in Queensland."

Rafter had reached the semifinals of the French Open in 1997 and the final of the Italian Open on clay just a few days before arriving at Roland Garros. Federer, who had never met Rafter, was seventeen and fortunate to have a main-draw wild card, usually reserved for promising young French players. But Federer's agent with IMG at the time, Régis Brunet, was a well-connected former French player, and Federer had finished as the world's No. 1 junior in 1998, even if he had lost in the first round of singles and doubles in the French Open junior tournament.

Because Rafter was a star and seeded third, the match was played on the second-biggest venue: the Suzanne Lenglen Court with its capacity of ten thousand.

It is an elegant, modern arena with terrific sight lines and great press seats directly behind the baseline: still the best place to watch a tennis match to understand the big picture and avoid twisting your neck to follow the ball. I was one of the thousands in the stands, and probably one of the few who had come to see Federer instead of Rafter. As a tennis writer, you always need to be on the lookout for the next big thing, and two agents I knew well had mentioned Federer as a candidate. What intrigued me most was that the agents I spoke with were not working with Federer, so they had no incentive to build him up. They just knew he was special.

Wild cards can be a major factor in a young player's rise, allowing them to skip or shorten the usual slog through the satellite circuit or qualifying rounds by quickly earning significant points and exposure, which is important to potential sponsors. Players from the Grand Slam nations—Australia, Britain, France, and the United States—have the biggest advantage because they can get early access to the majors. But despite being Swiss, Federer received numerous wild cards in his early years: more than ten at tour level, including one for Wimbledon in 1999 after winning the boys' title. In Paris, he was hoping to capitalize on the opportunity to lift his ranking. At that time, an outsider who defeated a highly ranked player received bonus points on top of the regular points that came with winning a match.

"It would have been double bonus points if I beat Rafter in a Slam," Federer said. "So instead of forty-five points, I would have made ninety. Obviously, I was never going to beat him, but you still start dreaming and go, like, 'What if? Could you imagine what that would do to my ranking?' Before the match you are just going through it all in your head."

Federer's elegance did not leap out at you at that stage. He had yet to make the acquaintance of *Vogue* editor in chief Anna Wintour. He wore baggy tennis clothes and a ball cap that he often had on backward. He rushed between points as if he were impatient for resolution; overeager to smack the next winner. There was still a looseness in his game then, certain patterns where he still seemed unclear on how to get his mind and body organized. But his shot making was undeniably flashy, his service motion fluid, and his power impressive for seventeen. When he came out swinging and won the first set, I was feeling rather good about being in the right place at the right time: an eternal journalistic quest. But that was unfortunately the end of Federer's shock upset bid. He won only five games from there as Rafter finished him off 5–7, 6–3, 6–0, 6–2.

"I think I was always a big match player, a big court player against top guys, but I knew it was going to be tough for me against Rafter with his kick serve and my one-handed backhand," Federer told me. "After the first set, he got the hang of how I played, and he, like, sliced and diced me. I was still missing some tools that I needed to get out of those rallies, and Pat was a veteran. He knew what he was doing."

And yet Rafter was impressed, and not just because the affable Rafter was being affable.

"Oh, he's very talented," Rafter said. "You know, he can do everything. He's got a good serve. He can volley. He slaps some returns. He's dangerous off that. Got quite a good forehand and a good backhand. He's very young. He's got to start working hard. I think if he can work hard and have some really good commitment, he'll be an excellent player."

Rafter's early analysis held up astonishingly well over the years, but Roland Garros remained a challenging environment for Federer despite his fluent French and early exposure to red clay. He reached the fourth round in 2000 and the quarterfinals in 2001, both excellent results at that stage of his development. But in 2002 he lost in the first round to Hicham Arazi of Morocco; and in 2003, when Federer already had broken into the top 5, he was upset in the first round by Luis Horna of Peru.

Both the Arazi and Horna defeats were in straight sets. Federer explained that he found it difficult to orient himself on the main Philippe Chatrier Court because of its vast expanse, with more space than usual available for players to move outside the lines.

"I really struggled with the size," Federer told me. "I just felt in my vision it made me a little bit unsure sometimes."

Above all, it seemed he was struggling with the pressure. In 2004, he lost in the third round 6–4, 6–4, 6–4 to Kuerten: a misleading result if you focus on Kuerten's three French Open titles and affinity for clay. Kuerten, diminished by chronic hip pain, was well past his prime by 2004 and seeded only No. 28.

Federer was No. 1 and held the Wimbledon and Australian Open titles. "I should have beaten him, but again somehow it didn't work," Federer said.

With that in mind, Federer decided to come to Paris early in 2005 and spend as much time as possible practicing on the center court in an attempt to get genuinely comfortable. When I interviewed him shortly before the tournament began, he was full of confidence and full of rebuttals when I brought up all the great attacking players who won the other three majors but never won in Paris. The list included Boris Becker, Stefan Edberg, and Pete Sampras. Federer for now was part of their club.

"It is really tough to serve and volley your way to a French Open win," Federer said.

"Pete did often try to stay back," I said.

"Yeah, but he was born for coming to the net more often because of his big serve and his technique off the baseline was very flat," Federer said. "And he was also playing with that little racket."

Federer was referring to the Wilson Pro Staff with the eighty-five-square-inch head that Sampras never abandoned—a decision he now regrets. Federer beat Sampras with the same racket in 2001 but switched to a slightly bigger version in 2002 to give himself more margin for error.

"I'm not saying with another racket Pete would have won the French, but it would have helped," Federer said. "Mine is a 90, and I feel like I stay back much, much more. You cannot compare me, especially to McEnroe. But Edberg, Becker, Sampras, they all came to the net so much more often. They almost had to try to get there; otherwise, they would lose. If you could keep them at the baseline, you were the better man, where I feel like if I'm at the baseline, I'm the better man."

What I always have liked about interviewing Federer is that he strives to give you straight answers even if he might sound arrogant. He knows that risk exists, but he prefers to remain "natural," to use his word, because it keeps the process simpler and allows him to avoid contradictions and explanations down the road.

He was genuinely convinced he had a better shot than his role models at Roland Garros, and in comparative terms, he had a point. McEnroe was no doubt at his best at net and used very little topspin. Edberg's forehand was a liability in extended rallies. Becker's movement was not at Federer's level on any surface (unless Boris was diving on the grass). Sampras's was not at his level on clay, and Sampras also suffered from a congenital blood disorder, thalassemia, that could affect his stamina in the long, grueling matches that often developed on clay.

"Wimbledon will always stay number one in my heart, that's clear, because of the emotions I had there, and because of my idols," Federer said. "They all won over there, but I am aware that if I can win the French, what it does to my spot in history. So for this reason, I think this will always have a very special place for me in terms of how I prepare for it, because I will only get another seven to ten to maybe fifteen maximum chances."

"Fifteen?!" I sputtered.

Federer was then twenty-three. Fifteen more French Opens was a whole lot of long-term thinking.

Federer laughed. "Hey, if you look at Andre, you almost have to go there," he said of Agassi, who would reach the US Open final later that year at age thirty-five. "Look, I like the challenge. On clay, I have many tough opponents, more than on other surfaces, and I think for this reason, I even work harder on this surface. It's just a pity, a good pity, that I play so well on all surfaces, so it doesn't allow me to have the best preparation for clay or have enough hours on clay or enough tournaments."

In retrospect Federer missed a big opportunity in 2004, which was the last year before Nadal descended on Roland Garros. Nadal's arrival in 2005 changed the equation, foiling everyone's plans. What Michael Phelps was to pool water, Nadal was to red clay.

"After 2004, I started to play much better," Federer told me much later in his career. "And I made my semis and my finals, but then the problem is that Rafa came alive, and Rafa was Rafa, and it was very difficult."

Federer made Nadal sound more like a Norse deity with a magic hammer than a Mallorcan mortal with a Babolat racket. But who could blame him? There was no human frailty in Nadal's French Open record. By 2009, he had won four straight titles and compiled a 45-0 record in all best-of-five-set clay court matches, including Davis Cup and Masters Series finals.

"It's hard to think that's possible," said American player Sam Querrey, one of Nadal's many clay court victims. "Because I took a set off him on clay last year in Davis Cup, and I'm not a clay court wizard. I think most people would have thought by now he would have gotten tired or someone just would have had an unbelievable day and he would have had an off day. But he just seems to pull it out."

There were, however, reasons for concern for Nadal in 2009, two of which were known only to his inner circle.

For the moment, the general public knew only that Federer had defeated him in the final in Madrid on clay one week before the start of the French Open. But that seemed understandable because of the quick conditions in Madrid, which is 2,100 feet above sea level, and, above all, because Nadal had been required to struggle for more than four hours in the semifinals against Djokovic the night before facing Federer.

What was not public knowledge was that Nadal had tendinitis in his knees and that his parents, Sebastián and Ana Maria, had separated.

Sebastián had informed his son in February on the plane on the way back from the Australian Open, where Nadal had won the title for the first time by defeating Federer.

Nadal, in the midst of the most fulfilling phase of his young career, was stunned by his father's news. Nadal said in his 2011 autobiography, *Rafa*, that he did not speak to his father for the rest of the trip home as he absorbed the shock. He described it movingly with the help of John Carlin, the British-born journalist who worked for *El País* in Spain.

My parents were the pillar of my life and that pillar had crumbled. The continuity I so valued in my life had been cut in half, and the emotional order I depend on had been dealt a shocking blow. Another family with grown-up children (I was twenty-two and my sister, eighteen) might have taken a marital separation more in its stride. But this was not possible in a family as close and united as ours, where there had been no conflict visible, where all we had ever seen was harmony and good cheer. Assimilating the news that my parents had been going through such a crisis after nearly thirty years of marriage was heartbreaking. My family had always been the holy, untouchable core of my life, my center of stability and a living album of my wonderful childhood memories. Suddenly, and utterly without warning, the happy family portrait had cracked. I suffered on behalf of my father, my mother, and my sister, who were all having a terrible time. But everybody was affected: my uncles and aunt, my grandparents, my nephews and nieces. Our whole world was destabilized, and contact between members of the family became, for the first time that I had been aware of, awkward and unnatural; no one knew at first how to react. Returning back home had always been a joy; now it became uncomfortable and strange.

Nadal still lived with his parents, which was not unusual for someone his age in Mallorca. But being on the road was no escape, as he explained in an interview the following year after the split had become public. "Many times I suffered from a distance because I was away from home and did not know how things were," he said. "You don't know if what they are telling you is the reality, if things are good or bad."

Nadal was in a funk, but as he rightly points out, his parents' separation did not prevent him from winning four more tournaments between February and the start of Roland Garros.

In practical terms, the bigger problem was his body, above all his knees, which had been bothering him since the Miami Open in March, where he lost in the quarterfinals to a towering emerging talent, the Argentine Juan Martin del Potro, in a third-set tiebreaker.

But in a grueling, repetitive sport where being able to perform at 100 percent is far too rare, Nadal has played through serious pain more than most. His significant early injuries were one of the reasons, along with his hard-charging style and unorthodox forehand technique, that many of us who followed the sport closely were convinced that he would not be able to thrive on tour past his twenties.

"He started to win so early that maybe he will retire at twenty-six like Borg," said Sebastien Grosjean, one of the leading French players.

We were all wrong. Nadal's drive to compete was even stronger than his left arm (or was that his right arm?), and in 2009 he took a short break after the Madrid final and decided that he would try to defend his title(s) at Roland Garros.

Federer arrived from Madrid with momentum after ending Nadal's thirty-three-match winning streak on clay, but also with scar tissue from earlier in the season.

The biggest damage was done in Melbourne, the city that had brought him so much joy and pain in recent years. Federer reached the 2009 Australian Open final despite a sore back and then had the advantage of one more day of rest than Nadal. The Australian Open, at that stage, was the only Grand Slam tournament to play the men's singles semifinals on different days. Federer won his against Andy Roddick in straight sets on a Thursday night. Nadal won his against fellow Spaniard Fernando Verdasco late on a Friday night, and it required a supreme effort.

At five hours and fourteen minutes, it was the longest recorded match in the tournament's history, but it was also a high-quality duel: full of all-court play, winners on the move, and clutch-serving even if it ended unfittingly on a double fault. Nadal and Verdasco thoroughly deserved the standing ovation they received from the crowd that had stayed past 1:00 a.m., transfixed.

Standing was not quite so easy for Nadal, and he had to recover in less than forty-eight hours to face Federer for the first time since the 2008 Wimbledon final. There were ice baths, ice massages, and protein supplements. Nadal and his team did what they could, and Toni Nadal delivered one of his best locker room speeches, citing Barack Obama, the recently inaugurated American president, whose mantra was "Yes, we can!"

Nadal told me he repeated those lines to himself on every changeover, and as demoralizing as it was for Federer to realize, Nadal, even far from fresh, was the superior tennis player. He beat Federer again in five sets in a match that would have earned more glowing reviews if it had not come directly after their transcendent Wimbledon final.

This 7–5, 3–6, 7–6 (3), 3–6, 6–2 victory required Nadal to rally in the opening set and to fight off all six break points he faced in the third set. But the fifth set was short on suspense, as Nadal broke Federer early to take the lead and held it firmly.

"Perhaps I should not have been out there in the fifth set at all," Federer said. "I should have won the first set and the third. The rest of the story, we all know it."

The defeat prevented him from tying Sampras's men's record of fourteen Grand Slam singles titles, but missing the record was less problematic than losing another important match to Nadal.

Federer choked up as he received the runner-up's trophy from Rod Laver, a champion who symbolized all the Australian values that Peter Carter and Tony Roche had talked about with Federer. Shortly after Federer started his speech and thanked the crowd, he began to cry in earnest.

"God, it's killing me," he said, and though the crowd shouted its support, he was unable to continue and stepped away from the microphone.

Federer's comment was, in his view, misinterpreted. It was the giving of the speech that was "killing" him, not losing the final. But there was no doubt he was distraught.

Nadal now had a 13-6 lead in their series and a 5-2 edge in Grand Slam finals (2-2 outside Roland Garros). The Battle of Surfaces concept no longer worked: Nadal had encroached on Federer's side of the net.

In a more benighted time and place, Federer's postmatch breakdown in Melbourne would have been viewed less charitably. It is hard to imagine any of the Australian tennis greats who were in attendance at the ceremony losing their composure to that degree after a loss.

Such a display would have been considered "unmanly" in the heydays of Laver, Ken Rosewall, and John Newcombe. But Federer, so often moved to tears in both victory and defeat, had expanded the emotional range of the men's champion. He had cried in 2006 on the same court in a different context when he had received the champion's trophy from Laver after beating the surprise finalist Marcos Baghdatis.

"Those were tears of relief," he said.

And yet Federer, so open with his feelings, was still embarrassed at monopolizing the attention at the moment of Nadal's triumph.

"I didn't want people to feel sorry for me in Australia," he told me later. "I didn't want people to feel sorry for me in Wimbledon, either. It's not the way it's supposed to be. It's supposed to be a celebration of tennis, of a happy moment, of being happy for the guy who won. Sure, you can be disappointed, but it shouldn't override the whole thing that just happened."

Nadal handled the situation with remarkable class and sensitivity. With Federer unable to continue his speech, Nadal was brought forward ahead of schedule, but after receiving his trophy, he detoured to Federer's side, put his left arm around his neck, and moved his head close to Federer's to console him.

Federer returned to the microphone at Nadal's urging. "I'll try again," Federer said. "I don't want to have the last word; this guy deserves it. So Rafa, congrats. You played incredible. You deserve it, man. You played another fantastic final so all the best for the season."

Federer then thanked "the legends" for coming out and started to lose his composure again, but he quickly wrapped up and left the stage to his rival.

"Well, good evening, everybody," Nadal said before turning to face Federer. "Well, first of all, Rog, sorry for today."

The crowd laughed.

"I really know how you feel right now," Nadal continued. "It's really tough. But remember you are a great champion. You are one of the best of the history. You're going to improve the fourteen of Sampras for sure."

I have been following tennis since the early 1970s and cannot recall another psychological dynamic quite like this. Nadal clearly had taken command of the rivalry and the sport, even if Federer had won his fifth straight US Open in 2008, but Nadal was insistent on maintaining his rival high on a pedestal, at least when the ball was out of play.

Frankly, it seemed disingenuous: an odd new form of wishful thinking. When a group of us met with Nadal the next day at a Melbourne hotel, we pushed him on it.

"Right now, Roger has fifty-six titles or something like this and I have thirty-two; it's a lot different," he said. "He has thirteen Grand Slams. I have six. He has fourteen Masters Series. I have twelve. That is the only place we are close.

"No discussion; no discussion," he repeated.

Perhaps I am a little slow on the uptake, but what became completely clear to me that day for the first time was that Nadal was fixated on process: He was much more about the thrill of the hunt than the satisfaction of the kill. So many champions are searching for release, from the pressure, the expectations, the challenge at hand.

Nadal was different. To revel in surpassing Federer was not the point. The meaning was in playing each point.

"I love the competition, not only in tennis," he told us. "I love the competition in all aspects of life. When I compete, I love to be there and fight for the win."

He paused a moment, his telltale left eyebrow arching.

"Maybe," he said, "I like more fighting to win than to win."

Nadal is still far too young to be thinking about a tombstone, but some distant day that sentence should be on it.

I am not quite sure what belongs on Federer's. His leitmotif is more challenging to discern. Like Nadal, Borg, and most great tennis players, he hated to lose at anything as a youngster, kicking over Monopoly boards or their equivalent. But he could not have played on tour across four decades without enjoying the experience as well as the achievements.

"I am actually not so much of a box ticker, to be honest," he once told me after he already had, from an outsider's perspective, ticked quite a few boxes.

Federer seems to be at his most fulfilled as the centerpiece of harmony: the focus of attention that he can gallantly deflect while remaining the focus of attention. He is quite good at being adored, but he is also adaptable: a sign of self-confidence and emotional intelligence. He has ultimately adjusted to a tennis world in which he is not the alpha male, but I have always felt he was nostalgic for his days at the undeniable core of it all.

"Roger Federer is beauty; that's what he brings," Jim Courier told me. "Rafa is grit, and I've heard about Rafa saying, 'I know if I can make a match with Roger into a fight, if it becomes a real fight and a scrap and a war, I know I will win because I am more comfortable in that environment than he is.' I think there is something to that. Roger plays a game that is incredibly beautiful and incredibly easy to watch and for him seemingly incredibly easy to play, and he's said it himself, he misses those years when he didn't have a rival, when it was so easy for him. He misses that friction-free world, which is what he was living in the mid-2000s on everything but clay, and he's had a lot of friction since."

But Nadal thrives on friction. Courier likes to say he "runs on doubt," and he does seem to be at his most fulfilled when the goal is visible but still out of reach and the sweat is dripping off the bridge of his nose.

"I think as we've come to see with Rafa, that's just who he is, he operates out of a humble zone," Courier said. "And that's what keeps him grounded and motivated. He feels he has to prove it every day and none of what he has done ultimately matters today. He's not someone who verbalizes how confident he is in the way that Roger does, sometimes to the point where Roger says things where it comes off as incredibly arrogant, but for Roger it's just matter-of-fact."

Santiago Segurola, longtime sports editor of Spain's *El País* newspaper, has called Nadal "a man from a Mediterranean island who is actually a Calvinist in shorts."

That gets at the crux of it, even if you need to be careful not to stretch the Puritan comparisons too far: Nadal does wear a watch worth $1 million and recently bought an eighty-foot yacht for about $6 million.

To interview Nadal or Federer at their tournament hotel is a reminder that you cannot afford their tournament hotel. And they can sometimes be oblivious to how the 99 percent live: Federer once helpfully suggested to a middle-class underling that they purchase a Rolex watch. But amid the trappings, of which there are plenty, there is also an untouched quality to both men, which is a tribute to their bedrock values and to the fact that tennis does not allow a champion to coast. Every match is a fresh chance to stumble. There might be some first-round byes for the stars and all the courtesy cars a man could desire, but there are no substitutions. The awareness of that sharpens the mind, quickens the step, and staves off ennui and existential dread if you truly enjoy the feeling of ball meeting string bed day after day after day.

Federer and Nadal do truly seem to enjoy it, and they have proved it by enduring with the help of each other's excellence.

Federer inspired Nadal to improve his backhand, both his two-handed drive and his one-handed slice, shore up his serve, and move closer to the baseline during rallies to find a way to shorten points. Nadal inspired Federer to upgrade his net game, rip his backhand with more authority, and even seek out new coaching voices.

Severin Lüthi, a friend since the days in Ecublens and now the Swiss Davis Cup captain, had become a fixture in Federer's team, but Higueras had gone back to work for the United States Tennis Association at the end of 2008. Federer had long been interested in hiring Darren Cahill, the clever and articulate Australian who had done such good work with Hewitt and Agassi and had been ahead of the curve in tennis by analyzing video to break down opponents' patterns.

"As great as Roger is, it's always good to have another pair of eyes," Higueras told me.

"People ask me sometimes, 'What can you possibly tell Roger? He knows everything already,'" Lüthi once said to me. "But I realized over the years, he wants to hear it again, even if it's a small thing like stay lower to the ball. Because he says sometimes I also forget things or I just don't realize."

Cahill, who had resigned as Australia's Davis Cup captain, reached out to Federer in 2009, and once Federer's back pain had eased, they decided to meet in Dubai in March for a twelve-day test session. Like many, I expected it to be an excellent fit and was surprised in mid-March when Federer's agent, Tony Godsick, telephoned to inform me that Federer and Cahill would *not* be working together going forward.

To me, their partnership had seemed like destiny, particularly with Cahill's close connection to Peter Carter. Even Federer's mother, Lynette, had talked to Cahill years earlier about making it happen whenever Agassi retired.

"I got a glimpse into his life, the way he trains, his professionalism," Cahill told me about the time in Dubai. "Everything about him is a coach's dream, no question about it."

But Federer was not quite ready to commit as the trial neared an end, and Cahill had connections with ESPN and the Adidas player development program that he was concerned about preserving. He also was surprised by the underlying uneasiness he was feeling.

"Roger reminds me of Peter every single day, just looking at him," Cahill said. "So just being around that brings back great memories, but also brings back tough memories for me.

"I don't really know how to explain it, but I felt like, am I doing it for the right reasons? Would Peter be upset with me for doing it? I found some things going through my head about whether this was the right thing to do and whether I was the right person for Roger. It never totally sat completely right with me because Roger was Peter's boy. To me he was always Peter's boy. That's not the reason I said we shouldn't work together, but I'm just trying to explain to you deep down in my stomach how I was feeling."

As a result, Federer was without a high-profile coach when he arrived at Roland Garros, but at this stage Lüthi surely deserved more credit for his contributions. For me, Lüthi always looked like he had just risen from a midafternoon nap with his sleepy gaze and unruly hair. He also had never made it as a tour-level player. But Günter Bresnik, one of the game's most experienced coaches, maintained that appearances were misleading.

"Lüthi is the most underestimated coach on the tour," Bresnik told me. "He is also very modest, low-key, never wants to be in front, but he is there all the time. He did a really good job in a difficult period. I would say technically he is not the best coach. He is not someone who would develop a player, teaching strokes, but being around and understanding what a player needs, when to be pushed, when to be left by himself, finding the right moment to say something, he is one of the best in the world definitely."

Bresnik has the insight of someone who speaks with Lüthi in German and can understand how he communicates with Federer, with whom Lüthi speaks primarily Swiss German.

The spring of 2009 was eventful on and off the court. On court, Federer lost in March in the semifinals of the Miami Open to Djokovic, breaking another racket in anger during the defeat. Off court, Federer and Vavrinec were married on April 11 in Basel, with Vavrinec several months pregnant. The newlyweds postponed the honeymoon until later in the year.

The clay court season beckoned, and Federer had a shaky start at the French Open. He dodged big trouble in the second round against

Jose Acasuso, a free-swinging Argentine, before winning 7–6 (8), 5–7, 7–6 (2), 6–2. Federer had to save four set points in the opening set, rallying from a 3–6 deficit in the tiebreaker. He had to save another set point in the third set after being down two breaks of serve.

Federer needed four more sets to defeat Paul-Henri Mathieu of France in the third round on Saturday, but the next day, an off day for Federer, a shock wave reverberated through Roland Garros when Robin Söderling did what no man had done before: defeat Nadal in a best-of-five-set match on clay.

Söderling was a huge-hitting Swede with a lupine gaze and a haircut worthy of a medieval blacksmith. He was an established threat. He was seeded 23rd and in the previous round had just defeated David Ferrer, another Spanish star who never surrendered a point without a fight.

But Söderling's victory over Nadal, in light of Nadal's stature and thirty-one-match French Open winning streak, was still one of the biggest upsets in tennis history. It was all the more stunning because of the match Söderling and Nadal had played in Rome earlier in May.

Nadal had won 6–1, 6–0.

But this time the Mallorcan failed to generate consistent depth with his groundstrokes and returns, allowing Söderling the space to take big, confident cuts at his forehand and two-handed backhand from inside the court. Instead of letting Nadal's topspin push him back, the six-foot-four Söderling stepped confidently into the court and swung freely, depriving Nadal of time to get organized. The Swede, well coached by former world No. 2 Magnus Norman, was also able to win twenty-seven of thirty-five points at the net, a remarkable strike rate against a player of Nadal's defensive skills. But those skills were not as sharp as usual, in part for those reasons that only his inner circle understood.

"His game didn't surprise me," Nadal said. "I was more surprised by mine."

There was certainly no sympathy from the French crowd. Eager for regime change, it roared for Söderling, chanting "Ro-bin" repeatedly until he finished off his 6–2, 6–7 (2), 6–4, 7–6 (2) victory.

Nadal and his uncle Toni were hurt by the crowd reaction.

"I felt all the stadium against me," Nadal told me years later, still wounded. "So that's something that is difficult to understand when it is a place that I love a lot, and I love the French people. I love Paris probably more than any other city in the world."

But Roland Garros crowds have long embraced the underdog, and everyone was an underdog against Nadal.

"I tried to think, 'Don't think!'" Söderling said.

There is a T-shirt in that mantra, and Federer was soon trying to adopt the same philosophy. He no longer needed to solve the riddle of Nadal on Paris clay. Söderling had done it for him, and with Djokovic already out after a third-round loss to Philipp Kohlschreiber, there was no ignoring the obvious.

This was *the* opportunity for Federer to win the French Open.

Nadal, still his cheerleader in chief, made it clear that he supported him before heading home to celebrate his birthday in Mallorca for a change instead of in Paris.

"It would be good for him to complete his Grand Slam," Nadal said. "Federer had the bad luck to lose three finals and one semifinal here, but I think that if there is someone who deserves it, it's really him."

Deserving it and winning it are different matters, however. Andy Murray certainly "deserved" to win the Australian Open after reaching five finals there but never managed it. This was a new kind of pressure for Federer, well accustomed to being a big favorite but not accustomed to becoming a big favorite out of the blue.

"Tonight's sleep will be different for Roger, that's for sure," said Fabrice Santoro, the French veteran.

His waking hours were different, too.

"Just knowing and feeling that tension in the team," Federer told me. "All of a sudden, it was like everything was saying, 'Oh my God. This could be your chance.'"

The day after Söderling's earthquake of an upset, Federer took the court against Tommy Haas, the dangerous German who had helped spoil Federer's Olympic debut in 2000. This time, Haas looked intent on spoiling Federer's Nadal-free moment.

Federer started well, sweeping through his first six service games without dropping a point, but after losing the first-set tiebreaker he began to unravel, looking edgier by the unforced error.

Haas won the second set, too, and then with Federer serving at 3–4 in the third, Federer missed two forehands in a row that he would normally make, giving Haas a break point at 30–40.

The crowd seemed subdued. The applause before he served the next point was far from thunderous. Federer missed his first serve down the T but kicked the second serve to Haas's backhand. The German hit a looping crosscourt return, and Federer, who was leaning to that corner, did what he has done thousands of times under duress: run around his backhand to position himself to hit a leaping forehand from just behind the doubles alley.

That signature shot had been far from reliable on this breezy, sunny afternoon, but Federer jumped and struck and delivered an inside-out winner at a sharp angle.

Break point saved and, as it would turn out, tournament saved.

"Brute courage," said Frew McMillan, the Eurosport commentator.

"Honestly, I made it and said voilà!" Federer explained later.

Something had shifted within him, and though Federer did not show much emotion after his fateful forehand, he did shout triumphantly after winning each of the next two points to hold serve. It was 4–4, and the crowd was well into it now, roaring for Federer's winners and also for Haas's double fault and badly botched forehand volley that cost him his serve in the very next game.

Federer was on his way to a much happier place, allowing Haas just two more games as he closed out a 6–7 (4), 5–7, 6–4, 6–0, 6–2 victory.

He and Haas would become very close friends in the coming years, which says a lot about Haas's capacity to forgive. This was a match that neither man would forget.

Federer beat another dangerous player, Gaël Monfils, in the quarter-finals, getting nearly as much crowd support as the elastic Frenchman. Federer has never been one to camp out in his hotel no matter how nice his hotel (this one was the five-star Park Hyatt Paris-Vendôme).

He prefers to enjoy the cities where he works, and he was getting plenty of positive feedback as he and Mirka patrolled Paris.

"When I walk on the streets or drive in the transportation, or I go for dinner, everybody is like, 'This is your year. You've got to do it!'" Federer said. "They're screaming from their scooters and out of the car. They even get out at the red lights and want me to sign an autograph or take a picture."

But red lights were flashing again on court during his semifinal with Juan Martin del Potro, a six-foot-six, twenty-year-old Argentine on the rise with a flat forehand powerful enough to generate seismic activity. As he clubbed winners and dictated play on the clay, del Potro's sleeveless shirt was surely triggering some painful Nadal flashbacks for the Swiss.

Federer trailed two sets to one before rallying to force a fifth set. He and del Potro traded early breaks before Federer got back in front again after del Potro double-faulted into the tape to lose his serve at 3–3. Though Federer could not convert his first match point at 5–3, he converted his second with a cocksure forehand winner straight off the bounce.

"I don't think I was necessarily the better player," Federer said. "It was just my experience that got me through: being in so many Slam semis and him never being in any."

As Federer waited for del Potro to arrive for the handshake, he leaned heavily on the net, head down for a moment. The stress of the chase was palpable, but if Vavrinec, seven months pregnant, could handle it, he could, too.

"I'm doing great," she told me cheerfully after her husband's latest escape in what, with Mirka, amounted to an in-depth interview at this stage.

All that stood between Federer and the career Grand Slam was Söderling, who had demonstrated that his great performance against Nadal was no fluke by defeating two more higher seeds.

In the quarterfinals, he overwhelmed No. 10 Nikolay Davydenko in straight sets. In the semifinals, he held off No. 12 Fernando González in five.

"It's been hard, but not as hard as I thought it would be," Söderling said. "I had maybe the biggest challenge in tennis right now to beat Nadal here on clay in Paris. I felt like I wasn't finished with the tournament. I was still in the tournament, so even though I played a great match, I wanted more. I still feel that way."

In a normal year, a breakthrough run like Söderling's would have been the main talking point at Roland Garros, but not this time. The full focus was Federer, who was simultaneously chasing Sampras's Grand Slam record and trying to do what Sampras never managed by winning "the French."

Success would put Federer in the running to be considered the greatest player of all time, but it was clear that this was a debate that could never have an undisputed champion.

"Too much has changed to really compare [eras]," Brad Gilbert said.

The modern game of tennis has a long history even if you don't go all the way back to the indoor version of the game, now known as "real tennis," that was first played in the royal courts of Europe in the Middle Ages. Wimbledon was first played in 1877, and its early champions had to win only one match to defend their title: the so-called Challenge Round.

Until 1968, only amateur players were eligible for the Grand Slam tournaments and Davis Cup, which was a major event. American Bill Tilden, the greatest men's player of the 1920s, was not even eligible to play the French Championships until 1925, when it became open to non-French players. He often missed Wimbledon and never traveled to the Australian Championships, which would have required an even longer steamship journey than the one to Wimbledon.

Comparing Tilden's ten Grand Slam singles titles to Sampras's fourteen was clearly not a fair comparison. After World War Two, the best amateur men's players frequently turned professional early in their careers and took part in barnstorming tours, often organized by American star Jack Kramer. Players like Kramer, Pancho Gonzalez, Lew Hoad, Rosewall, and Laver missed many years of Grand Slam play, and they rarely tallied their total number of majors anyway. It was not the coin of their realm, although Laver was certainly feted for completing a true Grand Slam in 1962 by winning all four majors in the same calendar year.

Laver completed a second Grand Slam in 1969, a year after tennis had become open to professionals, and he finished with eleven majors. "That wasn't a number we talked about," Laver told me.

You certainly wonder how many more Laver might have won if he had been eligible from 1963 to 1967. But then you also have to take into account that Laver would have faced stiffer competition up until 1962 at the majors if all the best players in the world—men like Hoad, Rosewall, and Gonzalez—had been eligible.

The debate over the greatest ever in men's tennis is, as you can see, unresolvable, and even restricting it to the Open era does not settle it. Björn Borg, Jimmy Connors, John McEnroe, and other stars of the 1970s and 1980s often skipped the Australian Open, which was the most distant and least prestigious of the majors at that stage. Connors, Borg, and their generation did not consider the Grand Slam count to be their sport's defining statistic. If they knew what they know now, they might have made a few more trips to Australia.

"Now the Grand Slams have taken over," Connors said on the podcast *Match Point Canada*. "I played the Australian Open twice. I missed six or seven years of the French Open at the height of my career, so basically, I made my name and my reputation off of two tournaments: the US Open and Wimbledon.

"It took me twenty years to play maybe fifty Grand Slam tournaments. These guys are doing four a year, so listen, it's all about what's going on now. That is the way it is in all sports."

But at least comparing Federer's total to Sampras's total was a fair comparison. They both had competed in a period when all the majors were considered worth the journey by both the players and their sponsors, who often built bonus clauses into contracts that were linked to Grand Slam participation and success.

Federer would eventually play in sixty-five straight Grand Slam tournaments. And though Sampras's chances of winning the French Open were essentially zero in the latter phase of his career, he still made an appearance every year until 2002, his final season.

Despite his friendship with Federer, Sampras was not in the stands for the 2009 final, but Agassi, Sampras's longtime archrival, did make the journey from his home in Las Vegas at the French organizers' invitation.

He, too, had won his lone French Open after a long wait and against an unexpected opponent (Andrei Medvedev in 1999). Medvedev was a square-shouldered and reflective Ukrainian—almost as good an interview as Agassi—who had dropped to No. 100 in the world in the rankings at that stage. Agassi won the title only after rallying from a two-set deficit.

Federer would require nothing so dramatic. He had the confidence of knowing that he had beaten Söderling in all nine of their previous matches and had just bested him on clay in Madrid. He had the full approval of the crowd, which gave Federer a standing ovation as he walked on court just behind Söderling.

But there were still some strange twists. With Federer up a set and Söderling serving at 1–2, an intruder ran down a staircase in the lower section of the stands and leaped over the barrier and onto Federer's half of the court. He approached Federer, brandished a banner, and tried to force a hat onto Federer's head.

"It definitely felt uncomfortable once he came close to me," Federer said.

Fortunately, the intruder, a serial publicity seeker, had no intention of doing bodily harm, but it took far too long for a security guard to reach the intruder, tackle him, and escort him off the clay.

Söderling went on to hold serve, with Federer looking shaky for the first time in the final.

"It definitely threw me out of my rhythm a little bit," Federer said. "One game later, I thought that maybe I should have sat down and taken a minute or two to kind of reflect on what just happened: 'Was that real or what?'"

But this was the day that Federer would banish his French Open ghosts for good, even if it was not much of a day for a tennis match. There was a swirling wind, and for most of the last two sets, there was persistent rain that ranged from barely perceptible to something closer to a downpour.

Tournament director Gilbert Ysern considered halting the final. But the forecast for later in the afternoon was unpromising and the forecast for Monday was for heavy rain. Ysern knew they needed to finish the match as expeditiously as possible. Federer did his part: playing a brilliant second-set tiebreaker, hitting aces on all four of his serves, and then breaking Söderling's serve in the opening game of the third set.

When it came time to serve for the match at 5–4, his heart was pounding in his chest, as it had against Philippoussis at Wimbledon in 2003. Federer showed signs of cracking and had to save a break point at 30–40. But he won the next point with a rare foray to the net and then, with fans shouting during his windup on match point, he put a first serve into play that Söderling returned into the net. Federer pitched forward onto his knees on the damp clay, his hands cradling his face.

His Grand Slam collection was complete at age twenty-seven.

"This could be my biggest victory, the one that takes off the most pressure," he said after the 6–1, 7–6 (1), 6–4 win. "Now, for the rest of my career, I can play relaxed and never hear again that I never won the French Open."

At least the second part of that sentence proved true. The rest of Federer's career would last far too long for him to stay relaxed in the face of every challenge. But he was certainly a man fulfilled in the Paris drizzle and only the sixth man at that time to win all four majors. The others: Don Budge, Fred Perry, Roy Emerson, Laver, and Agassi, who was, fittingly, the man to present Federer with the cup.

"There seemed to be a form of destiny involved," Agassi told us in the players' lounge. "A lot of people say it's better to be lucky than good. I'd rather be Roger than lucky. The guy has earned his place in the game and earned this title. Winning here was just something that would have been a bit of a crime if he never did. He's been the second-best clay courter for five years running, and if it weren't for one kid from Mallorca he would have won a handful of these things."

Federer certainly had paid his dues, and though it no doubt would have been more symbolic if he had beaten Nadal for the title, he had been presented with an opportunity and seized it.

"I mean, it would be great to beat Rafa at the French, but it's not something I feel my career necessarily needs," Federer told me later. "Some might think that's what form it should take, but then again I've never played Rafa in all my US Open finals. It happens as it happens. You just can't make up the draws. You have to beat who is on the other side of the court. Don't get me wrong, it would be amazing, but I really don't know if it would be any more special."

The French Open victory, for him, belongs in his top three, along with Wimbledon in 2003 and the Australian Open that came so unexpectedly in 2017.

"Roland Garros, I had to come to love it," Federer told me. "I had to come to—how do you say it?—embrace it.

"It didn't come like, 'Hey, French Open, this is it!'" he said, snapping his fingers. "That was always going to be Wimbledon. I remember seeing Becker, Edberg, and Sampras all holding up that trophy, and all three of those guys didn't do that at the French."

The long wait for Roland Garros—ten years after his debut against Rafter—deepened the meaning.

"I had won the other Slams by '04," Federer said. "I think waiting for it so much longer made it so special. I think the fans felt that. I felt that, and that's why I see Paris as growing into the man and growing into the person. The French really challenged me, and I had to work so hard for it in '09. It was such a huge mental win for me: the unbelievably close matches against Tommy Haas and DelPo. Even Monfils was tough and then Söderling in the rain. It challenged me on many levels knowing that Rafa had been knocked out, because when is that ever going to happen again? So when I look at the French, I see it as a challenge I came to grips with, and I see it as a lot of mixed good emotions."

Nearly one year after the victory, we met again in Paris. He had been back to Roland Garros to train indoors in the late autumn, the leaves gone, the normally packed passageways as empty as Chatrier stadium.

"You should take the time for these moments, because they are nice," he said. "Just sit in the stands somewhere, right? Look down and reflect."

He told me that his memory works like a slideshow, with one image giving way to the next. "Me on the knees in disbelief," he said. "The racket dropping right next to me. The orange clay, so vibrant and vivid. Holding the trophy up and kissing it. Tearing up during the anthem. Those are the moments I see most right now."

But the moment that choked him up as he described it a year later had come after the ceremony and the adrenaline rush.

His father, Robert, had fallen ill and been unable to attend the final in person. Federer went to his hotel room while his mother and Mirka waited by the open door.

"He was very sick, and he was in bed with his blanket up to here," Federer said, pointing at his chin. "I was like, 'Hey, how are you doing?' And he was like, 'Ohhh, so bad.' And so I showed him the trophy and said, 'Look! We did it!' That was a very strong feeling."

They had come a long way, father and son, since the time Robert had obliged his temperamental son to find his own way home from the clay courts in Basel.

"We chatted tennis sometimes," said Paul Annacone of Robert Federer. "And Robbie would say stuff once in a while like, 'Ah Roger, hit the bloody backhand. Don't chip that thing.' He would say it to Roger, too, and they would laugh and elbow each other, and Roger would put his dad in a headlock. It was just so loving, so endearing."

Later in the evening, Federer returned to his own Paris hotel room, trophy still in hand. Normally, the French Open organizers do not allow it off the grounds. The champions receive only a smaller replica. But Federer, after lobbying, had been granted an exception for one night.

"They said, 'We only have one, so you better make sure you don't lose it or it doesn't get stolen,'" Federer said.

After all those years and all those losses to Nadal, he was taking no more chances. He placed the trophy on his bedside table.

"I slept next to the Coupe des Mousquetaires," he said with a laugh.

When he opened his eyes the next morning, it was still there. No, he had not been dreaming.

CHAPTER TEN

———◦◦———

LOS ANGELES

A fulfilled and relaxed Federer turned out to be a particularly dangerous Federer, and so on very short notice, Pete Sampras boarded a plane in Los Angeles with his wife, Bridgette, and arrived in London the morning of the 2009 Wimbledon final.

For the moment, Sampras and Federer were tied for the men's record for Grand Slam singles titles with fourteen apiece. But Sampras suspected they would not remain tied much longer, with Federer merrily surfing the wave of his breakthrough French Open victory and about to play Andy Roddick for the Wimbledon title.

Sampras had received the invitation on Friday from the All England Club. He was in the air on Saturday.

"It was one of those things I think you just do for the sake of the sport," Sampras told me. "It was my respect for the record, my respect for Roger. I think everything just combined into the fact that I hopped on a plane and just felt it was the right thing to do."

Sampras had not returned to Wimbledon since 2002, when he had crashed out in the second round in five sets against the little-known George Bastl. That poignant upset came on the old No. 2 court known as "the Graveyard" because of the effect it often had on the fortunes of seeded players.

Sampras, struggling with his game, had read a letter of support from his wife during the changeovers, and though the seven-time champion insisted after the defeat that he was not going to finish his

Wimbledon career on such a downbeat note, he did indeed finish his
Wimbledon career on such a downbeat note.

Bastl, Federer's Davis Cup teammate, was a Swiss ranked 145th and
had made it into the tournament only as a lucky loser: a player who
loses in the qualifying rounds but is still awarded a spot in the main
draw because of a late withdrawal.

"That's really not how I wanted it to end for me at Wimbledon: on
Court 2," Sampras told me years later, still unhappy at being booked
into the Wimbledon equivalent of Off Broadway but above all disappointed in his performance.

In 2009, the Graveyard court was about to be demolished and
replaced: part of Wimbledon's long-running modernization that can
sometimes feel like busywork at the expense of charm and tradition.

Other big changes since Sampras's days of dominance were already
complete, none more significant or symbolic than the new thousand-
ton Centre Court roof with translucent panels that, even when
retracted, sometimes cast a shadow over the Royal Box.

No doubt it altered the atmosphere of the most atmospheric court
in tennis, but after more than a century of rain delays, Wimbledon
now had a reliable—and very expensive—backup plan. Which of
course meant that there would be no rain at all during the tournament's first week.

The tennis gods have a sense of humor.

"This is the first time ever at Wimbledon somebody is waiting for
rain," said Ian Ritchie, the club's chief executive.

Sampras and Federer had become friends since Sampras's retirement. They played a series of three exhibition matches in Asia in
November 2007 and another match in New York in March 2008 that
drew nearly twenty thousand fans to Madison Square Garden.

Traveling together in Asia created a bond.

"Pete was one of my heroes," Federer told me. "I wanted to have
those experiences while I was still active and not just do something
like that when I'm retired. I think there's a big difference doing it earlier in your career."

It was a lucrative tour, but it also fit with Federer's interest in developing meaningful relationships with the players he had admired in his youth. He would later hire Stefan Edberg as his coach.

Sampras, then thirty-six, had hesitated before agreeing to the trip. He was happy off the road in Los Angeles, content with being present day to day for his wife and two young sons, Christian and Ryan. He was playing much more golf than tennis and knew he would need to resume regular training in order to make the tour with Federer entertaining and competitive.

"I didn't really know Roger that well, and then we traveled all through Asia, flew together, had dinners together, and really got to know each other and had some pretty good matches," Sampras told me. "Roger's a bit of a prankster. He has that goofy side, and I was retired, so I was a lot more relaxed and easygoing."

Federer came with Vavrinec. Sampras came with his brother Gus, who is also his manager. During his years on tour, Sampras struggled to separate his professional and personal spheres and said he doubted he would have done such an exhibition circuit during his heyday with a tennis elder like John McEnroe.

"I'm not sure I would have, but Roger was open and willing to do it," Sampras said. "We hung out. We shot the shit, just talking tennis, talking sport, talking just like two guys getting to know each other, and ever since then, we've kept in contact through technology and texting."

They are different personalities: Sampras a monolingual introvert; Federer a polyglot extrovert.

But Sampras is much more open and animated one-on-one, and the two champions discovered they had more in common than their single-handed backhands, running forehands, unreadable serves, and affinity for Wimbledon.

Both were the sons of strong-willed immigrant mothers, and both in tragic fashion had lost a trusted coach who was also a close friend.

Peter Carter died at thirty-seven in South Africa. Tim Gullikson, who guided Sampras to No. 1 and six major singles titles, died at forty-four in 1996 from inoperable brain cancer. I knew Tim and his identical twin brother, Tom. Born in Wisconsin and raised to treat others with respect, they were two of the best people in tennis, and I remember speaking with Tim in Europe in 1994 after he had blacked out and fallen in his hotel room while traveling with Sampras. Tim had cuts and bruises on his face but made light of the situation, not yet aware of the severity of his condition, which was initially misdiagnosed.

At the 1995 Australian Open, Sampras ended up in tears on court during a quarterfinal against Jim Courier after Gullikson had collapsed again and been forced to return home for treatment. Gullikson never was able to resume traveling with Sampras on the circuit, coaching him from afar for as long as he was able.

Both Sampras and Federer had to work through their grief on tour at a young age, and each found inspiration in his mentor's memory. Both also eventually worked with coaches José Higueras and Paul Annacone and appreciated discretion from their employees and friends.

During their travels and discussions, Sampras was struck, above all, by Federer's openness to new experiences and his enthusiasm for some aspects of the tennis circuit that had sapped Sampras's will to continue (he played his last tour match at age thirty-one).

"Roger loves the travel," Sampras said. "He loves the new cities, the new people, just a different personality, so much less anxiety than someone like me. When I traveled, it was always work and work and stressing and stressing. I carried the weight of number one and winning majors, and it definitely hit me harder in some ways."

Sampras remembers feeling happiest at the end of a major tournament, not simply because he was close to another prestigious title but because the locker room was nearly empty.

In that silence, he found his peace and his reward.

"The last few days of Wimbledon were my best days because there was nobody around," Sampras said. "It was like, I've earned this, to not have to change in front of thirty guys."

Social interaction drained Sampras's fuel tank—not a problem for Federer, with his booming voice and ability to joke, chat, and then flip the switch when it came time to walk on court.

"Roger can put his guard down and let people in," Sampras said. "I'd walk into a locker room, and I'm going to my locker and staying away. Roger comes in, and he's more personable and saying hi to everyone. He's just basically nicer."

Sampras struggled to manage his relationships with his rivals, particularly those he considered friends like Jim Courier. Federer developed strong connections with his peers, served multiple terms on the ATP Player Council, and eventually created the Laver Cup, a team tennis event that allowed him to spend even more time with his rivals and even lose to some of them.

"The generation that I grew up watching—McEnroe, Lendl, Connors—there was a genuine dislike for each other," Sampras said. "In our generation it wasn't a dislike, just more of a distance with me, Andre, Jim, Michael [Chang], and [Boris] Becker. I just couldn't separate the two worlds. Jim and I were good friends. We did cross the line with going to dinner together, playing doubles together, traveling together. And when I started to play Jim early on, it just was uncomfortable, like I was playing my brother although not quite to that extreme. It just made me think twice, like I almost felt bad for him when I beat him, and I didn't like that feeling where it was something that was going to maybe get in my head the night before the match or during the match, like 'He's a good guy.'"

For Sampras, who ended up with an ulcer at one stage, the tour felt more like a rock-filled harbor that needed to be navigated with care than a home away from home.

"When I look back at my career, that's why I kind of was aloof and separate from a lot of my opponents," Sampras said. "Just because I didn't want to go there. I didn't want to know them off the court too well. I just liked to keep it black-and-white. That was just better for my personality. I know how Roger has a great relationship with Rafa and they talk all the time. For me, when you are in the heat of the battle, something about that other person would get in my brain, and it just wouldn't work for me."

Still, by 2009 it was hard to argue that Nadal had not set up camp in Federer's head despite all of Federer's ability to compartmentalize. But the camper was nowhere to be found at this Wimbledon. Nadal was unable to defend his title because of the knee tendinitis that had also contributed to scuttling his French Open title defense.

Nadal's absence was a respite for Federer and another opening, but it was a letdown for all those hoping for a rematch of the smash hit 2008 Wimbledon final that had elevated the sport worldwide.

Federer, who rested and celebrated at home in Switzerland after winning Roland Garros, arrived at the All England Club without having played a grass court match since that demoralizing loss to Nadal in 2008.

Clearly, the defeat had not broken his spirit. Nor had the loss of the No. 1 ranking or his teary speech after losing to Nadal at the Australian Open in January.

Federer played pretty, but he was also resilient, capable of absorbing mighty blows to his ego and rebounding.

Consider what had happened in his next Grand Slam tournament after the 2008 Wimbledon defeat: He won a fifth straight US Open title after taking strength and solace from the feedback he received from fans.

Their collective take was, "Sorry you lost at Wimbledon, Roger, but what a match!"

It slowly dawned on Federer that the 2008 final had torn down some of the fencing between the Rafa and Roger camps, at least for a little while. The match had touched many people, perhaps more deeply than the result. There was the contrast in styles, the sportsmanship, the dramatic finish.

"You name it," Federer said in a background interview for *Strokes of Genius*. "It was only later when I realized the magnitude of the match. In the moment itself, I went back, cried in the locker room, cried when

I left the site. I still remember vividly when I walked out through the Millennium Building. I was like, 'Oh my God, this is the worst day of my life. And you can tell me how much you want that this was a great match. I don't care. I lost. I would rather have lost in straight sets. Then it would have just been so simple rather than going through this emotional roller coaster.'"

But by the time the 2008 US Open arrived, he could see the forest and the trees. Dejection gave way to quiet satisfaction. It would no doubt have been nice to have won one of the greatest matches ever played, but at least his sport was the winner, too.

The French Open victory was further confirmation that Federer had recovered his mojo. Annacone compared it to Sampras's 2002 US Open victory, which came little more than two months after the upset loss to Bastl at Wimbledon.

"I remember it with Pete," Annacone told me. "There were a lot of months there where it was: 'What's wrong? Step slow. You got married. You did this. You did that.' I knew Pete wasn't done. I think the greatest players tend to rise to challenges, and that's what Roger has accomplished."

He also had gotten lucky with Söderling's upset of Nadal, but Federer still had needed to navigate the five-setters against Haas and del Potro and find a way to win the arguments with the voice in his own head.

Returning to Wimbledon felt like coming home, and after Roland Garros he was brimming with the *bien-être* of a champion who knew that the biggest questions about his career had at last been answered convincingly.

In Nadal's absence, he played the opening match on Centre Court: an honor usually reserved for the defending men's champion. Federer made quick work of Yen-hsun Lu on the fresh grass, winning in straight sets.

That set the tone for Federer's no-nonsense march to the final, which included a semifinal victory over Haas, who had let Federer off the mat at Roland Garros. The turning point in Paris had been the Federer inside-out forehand that had saved a break point late in the third set.

"It's in the past; it's done," Haas said. "But being a friend of his and knowing how much it meant to him winning the French Open, I'm happy he made that shot."

Haas was less delighted that he was unable to secure a single break point against Federer at Wimbledon, but it was that sort of tournament for the Swiss, who was serving as well as he ever had. His early-season back problems, related to disk impingement, were behind him, at least for now.

"I was in pain, clearly," Federer told me. "It's always the same. You jump with your right leg, and you land with your left. So obviously your back doesn't like that, and you do that for ten years or more, it's not going to be great."

For Federer, a key moment had come in Rome in May, shortly before Roland Garros, when he made it clear to Lüthi and his team that he needed to push his limits in a practice session on the clay.

"Something completely extreme," Federer said. "I told them, 'You have to chase me around the court, put the ball even outside the doubles court, doesn't matter. I have to chase down every ball, knowing that I can slide, stretch my back, go down low, just get the ball back no matter how I play it, just get it back. I have to be able to hit those; otherwise, I don't know deep down if my back is really holding up.' Because I was scared sometimes."

Federer's serve had suffered from those doubts as well.

"That's why my serve let me down in Australia this year against Nadal in the fifth set, because I was scared it was not going to hold up," he explained. "It was subconscious. I was scared without wanting to be, and I just needed to put in some serious and specific practice, a lot of serves in a row knowing that my back can handle it. After that, it all came together."

But there was still one match to go at Wimbledon against a familiar opponent whose serve was also the barometer of his confidence and power game. Roddick was resurgent and more mobile after losing fifteen pounds at the request of his new coach, Larry Stefanki, a quotable and confident American who was known for making quick impacts on leading players.

"Larry came in the first day and told me I was too big to play tennis," Roddick told me. "There was no room for me to be offended if we're trying to make me a better tennis player."

Both Federer and Roddick were newlyweds, and both had been married in April: Federer to Vavrinec and Roddick to the model and actress Brooklyn Decker.

They were both in the right form and frame of mind to win Wimbledon, and Roddick had navigated the tougher draw, defeating Lleyton Hewitt in the quarterfinals and Andy Murray in the semifinals.

It was the third Wimbledon final for Roddick and an impressive return to form after his second-round defeat the previous year. Roddick, with his gift for metaphor, came up with a novel way of describing his 2008 experience at Wimbledon.

"When you've seen the Rolling Stones from the front row, and then all of a sudden you're like, you know, seven or eight rows back and there's a really tall guy in front of you waving his hands and screaming, you can't see much," Roddick said. "It's not going to be as good as the other shows."

So what row was he in this year?

"Getting closer," Roddick said. "I can see what Mick Jagger is wearing now."

That sparked uproarious laughter. But the stakes were serious in this final for Roddick and deeply personal. He had once been ahead of Federer's curve, reaching No. 1 before the Swiss, but he had since been thoroughly eclipsed despite all of his earnest effort.

"I've never been bitter about anything," Roddick said before the final. "I've been disappointed. I've been sad. My worst day is a lot of people's dream. I've always kind of had a sense of perspective about that, and I think that's helped a little bit."

With Stefanki behind him, he had rebuilt his confidence at age twenty-six and adopted a more judicious approach to using his big weapons.

"I like his chances," Stefanki told me. "Especially if he is calm and relaxed and believes in his style, which means he doesn't always have to do it with brute strength."

But there was no escaping the math entirely ahead of the final. Federer had an 18-2 career record against Roddick for a reason and was 7-0 against him in Grand Slam tournaments.

With Federer back in full flow, it seemed clear what would be required for Roddick to dam up the works.

"Probably the match of his life," said Patrick McEnroe, the US Davis Cup captain.

Roddick, though routinely hilarious, can also be flippant and caustic. He can be so quick not to suffer fools that he misidentifies the fools, and while Federer was poetry in motion, Roddick's game was pugilistic prose: abrupt movement, big cuts, and perspiration, so much perspiration, dripping from the shirt, the shorts, the cap.

"I don't know how he does that, by the way," said Federer, who rarely let anyone see him sweat.

But I must confess that I had come to admire Roddick: for his ability to put his thoughts and emotions so quickly into clever words (no writer's block for Roddick), but above all for his ability to keep striving even as the suspicion that he had been born in the wrong tennis era loomed ever larger.

True to himself, he gave it his best in the final, taking the first set 7–5 as he surprised Federer with his improved two-handed backhand and well-timed attacks.

Roddick was poised to win the second set as well, serving and competing ferociously to take a 6–2 lead in the tiebreaker. He needed just one more point to put himself in a commanding position in the final.

"A two-set lead with his serve, it didn't look good," Federer told me.

But Federer saved all four set points. The one that sticks in the memory is the last, which came with Roddick serving at 6–5. He hit a second serve. Federer chipped a backhand return low and crosscourt, a shot that had been giving Roddick and others fits for years. But Roddick had a clearer tactic now and quicker feet, so he moved in and ripped a forehand into Federer's forehand corner and rushed the net.

Federer hit a forehand passing shot back up the line that stayed high, so high that Roddick thought about letting it go but ultimately decided against it. But that meant his high backhand volley was out of sync and landed well wide of the open court. It was 6–6. And two points later, it was one set apiece.

"I just choked on the decision-making," Roddick said of the errant volley when we spoke in 2020. "There was a little bit of a gust of wind, and it looked like it was blowing back in. They always tell you to play it if you're not sure, and I unfortunately played it as if I was unsure. But I put less stock in that than anyone else."

That was because he had rewatched the tiebreaker by chance several years later while riding a stationary bike at a gym. The set point that seemed just as critical to him was the first at 6–2.

Roddick had smacked a forehand on the run that landed near Federer's feet on the baseline. Federer half volleyed the powerful shot, casually flicking a backhand winner crosscourt. It was a relaxed stroke that only a man feeling at peace with the pressure could have managed.

"To me it's amazing that what gets focused on is me missing what was actually a tough volley—it was high and away and he was actually back in the court—as opposed to the shot he came up with to save set point," Roddick said. "Because the volley is the only thing that gets mentioned, I actually had forgotten about that shot until I watched it back. I can't believe he pulled that off."

Federer won the third-set tiebreaker despite seeing his 5–1 lead shrink to 6–5. But on the set point, he put a strong first serve into play and then pounced on the short return with his forehand to go up two sets to one.

Roddick then won the fourth, and for the second straight year, the men's final would come down to a fifth set that stretched into overtime.

With no rain delays this time, Federer and Roddick had plenty of daylight to work with, and they used it. On and on, they held serve—beyond expectation, beyond logic.

Sampras, who had arrived in the Royal Box after the third game of the match and been greeted from the court by Federer, had not slept on the red-eye flight from Los Angeles.

"Listen, the whole thing was a bit of a blur," Sampras said. "Just the adrenaline of being back there brought up a lot of emotions for me. There were a lot of different things going on in my head: him breaking this record, just being back on that court. It was a whirlwind, eerie, surreal feeling for about five hours."

Even for those who were not jet-lagging, the games in that fifth set ran together as the aces and service winners piled up. Federer looked over at one stage at his wife, Mirka, now eight months pregnant, and felt a flash of concern for her.

"I was a bit worried," he said. "I thought to myself, 'Ooh la-la, this is a very long, tough match even if a lot of the rallies are pretty short.'"

But there seemed no way to shorten the spectacle. At 8–8 Federer fell behind 15–40 on his serve and saved the first break point with a well-placed serve and the second with a forehand swing volley.

Roddick could not have known—and would not have wanted to know—but those would be his last break points of the final. He was in the precarious position of serving second and therefore having to hold to extend the match.

A year later at Wimbledon, another big American server, John Isner, and Frenchman Nicolas Mahut would stupefy the sports world as Isner prevailed 70–68 in the fifth set of a first-round match that required three days to complete.

But in 2009, Roddick and Federer were the ones breaking new ground. Their fifth set was by far the longest in a Grand Slam single final in terms of games played, and as it played out and on, Federer told himself that after the 2008 final he was due to get lucky.

The opening came with Roddick serving at 14–15. He had held serve thirty-seven straight times, but the American looked a touch weary. His footwork and timing were less precise, his groundstrokes starting to misfire. Federer pushed him to deuce twice and finally earned a break point, which was also a championship point.

Roddick missed the first serve and made the second, but then mishit a forehand on the fifth stroke of the rally to end this epic final after four hours and eighteen minutes.

Federer celebrated by jumping instead of dropping to the ground: a form of respect for an opponent he knew well and liked. He did not want to make Roddick wait for the handshake after a defeat as tough as this one.

"Sports or tennis is cruel sometimes; we know it," Federer said. "I went through some five-setters in Grand Slam finals, too, and ended up losing. It's hard."

Federer sounded like he was talking about ancient tennis history as opposed to the two five-set losses to Nadal in the last twelve months. But Federer's rebound had been so quick and profound that it was as if he were back in the pre-Rafaelite era, ticking off consecutive majors with Nadal out of the frame.

He was now past Sampras, the player who had popularized the Grand Slam record as he successfully chased Roy Emerson's mark of twelve.

"Sorry, Pete, I tried to hold him off," Roddick said during the ceremony.

It might actually have been the match of Roddick's life. He played and served with such precision and conviction, but it still had not been quite good enough.

"I feel bad for Andy, I really do," Sampras said. "This was his chance. He came up short, but Roger, the great ones at the end, he just had a little bit more."

Sampras's syntax did not quite scan—it had been a long afternoon—but the compliment was clear. The margin in this final had been as thin as a blade of grass, but Federer's body of work was something much more imposing.

Sampras had required 12 years and 52 appearances to win 14 majors. Federer had needed just 6 years and 41 appearances to win 15.

In the final, Federer had served a career-high fifty aces to Roddick's twenty-seven and maintained a remarkably even keel.

There were not even any tears on the grass.

"No, not this time," Federer told me. "It was a little bit emotional later maybe when I saw my whole team again, Mirka and the group. But on the court, it wasn't a day for tears. I think it was more one of those moments where I was feeling like, 'I did it!' Kind of an energetic, crazy moment. Because when I saw the footage again, I was like, 'Oh my God. I'm jumping like a boy who can't believe he won.'"

Even years later, Federer still sounded relieved when we looked back. "This is one of those matches you don't even want to watch the end anymore," he said. "It really felt just like a coin toss."

But Roddick, as it turned out, could not even win a coin toss against Federer at Wimbledon, and the public felt his pain, even many of those who had spent the day cheering for Federer.

As Federer made his latest victory lap in Centre Court with the trophy, Roddick sat in his chair dejected only to hear a few voices turn into a thunderous chant: "Roddick! Roddick! Roddick!"

"An amazing feeling," Roddick told me. "Probably one of the coolest moments I've had in my career."

The support did not stop there. As he walked around New York City with his wife in the days after the final, everyone from baristas to construction workers on the job expressed their condolences.

"I literally wasn't going more than half a block without someone coming up and talking about the match," Roddick said. "That was a first for me, and these weren't tennis fans. They were people who had just got involved in the match somehow, so that was cool. I got a lot of notes and messages from a lot of my idols and people I look up to. I've never had that sort of reaction in my career."

For Roddick there was a clear before and after Wimbledon 2009. The coin toss of a final had made him an unambiguously sympathetic figure.

"I actually don't think my relationship with tennis would be as good as far as the way people think about me in retrospect had it not been for losing that match," Roddick said. "I feel that was my last day of being polarizing as a tennis player. If I'd won that, maybe it would have gone the other way."

Roddick talks about "the Starbucks moment."

"Where, you know, eleven years later you're in a Starbucks and that match is what people remember," he said. "Even with winning the US Open and everything else, that's forever going to be the thing that is remembered more. And I was also kind of a pawn in the historical significance game with Roger and Pete, and I think all of that added to this heightened sense that I was the other guy between those two that day. And Pete? Pete doesn't fly anywhere. He obviously was coming to watch the king get crowned, and I was just trying to be the guy who shot Bambi."

Roddick just missed and has no hard feelings today, but he did have hard feelings at one stage. A couple of months later, Federer was deep into another fifth set at the US Open final against Juan Martin del Potro and double-faulted twice to lose his serve and eventually the match.

"I think I might have actually said 'Fuck you, Roger' when I was watching that match," Roddick said with a laugh. "I love Juan Martin. So I was really happy for Juan Martin but simultaneously I was pissed because Roger actually kind of choked a little bit. 'Choke' is a strong word because it gets overused, but it was nervy. He kind of just gave away the fifth set, so I think I was more pissed at him that day than I was at any other point in my career."

Roddick's career would last only three more years, and he never made it past the quarterfinals at a Grand Slam tournament again before retiring in 2012.

He had been dealt a difficult hand—following the great American generation of Sampras, Agassi, Courier, and Chang—and had played it to the best of his ability.

They had won a combined twenty-seven major singles titles. He won just one, which is still one more than any other American man since 2003. Roddick's career looks better with each passing year, even if that also reflects how far American men's tennis has tumbled.

"I kind of always believe in Andy," Federer told me late in Roddick's career. "I think he once even thanked me for sticking by him, same as I did with Lleyton when people were writing Lleyton off. I think that is why we have great respect between each other in our generation, because we all came through together and we know how good we are and we know how hard it is to stay at the top. I think it's nice that we stick up for each other, because it's just not as simple as it seems. We've got a knockout system every single day. It's not like soccer. You can leave on Sunday, it's 1-all, and you're all going to sleep okay because nobody lost. With us, it's black or white. There's no place to hide, and on top of that there's the grind of what we do, eleven months a year."

But the grind clearly did not have the same effect on each of them. While Roddick retired at thirty, Federer played on (and on), even into the 2020s.

And while Federer is a member for life at the All England Club, Roddick had to cope with what might have been when he returned in 2015 to do television commentary for the BBC.

He had struggled to process the loss before then, sometimes waking up and feeling as if he had been "punched in the stomach." But returning to the club for the first time since retirement was another level of reminder.

"I didn't realize the pain of it until then," he said. "It wasn't a woe-is-me thing. It was just that I wanted to walk through that gate as a Wimbledon champion, to walk around that place being part of the fraternity."

Wimbledon, with its focus on tradition and protocol, puts particular emphasis on its links with the past. Roddick, fraternity brother or not, is part of its history as a three-time finalist, in the same group with Hall of Famers like Ivan Lendl, Ken Rosewall, and Patrick Rafter who could never change their luck at Wimbledon.

Sampras and Federer were in a higher category of their own: the two most successful men's players of the Open era at the All England Club. That is one more bond between them, even if they dominated with very different playing styles.

For years, Sampras remained curious and a bit mystified by that contrast, and after Annacone became Federer's coach, he organized an evening in Los Angeles shortly before the Indian Wells tournament in March 2011.

Sampras and Federer, a major NBA fan, attended a Los Angeles Lakers game together and met Kobe Bryant, who was a major tennis fan and informal adviser to players like Maria Sharapova and Novak Djokovic before his tragic death in a helicopter crash in 2020.

Sampras, Federer, Annacone, and their wives later met for dinner in a private room at a restaurant in Beverly Hills. Sampras had been peppering Annacone with questions about the state of play on tour and wanted to understand in detail how Federer had beaten him in the fourth round of Wimbledon in 2001 with a classic serve-and-volley game but had then gone on to win his Wimbledon titles largely from the baseline.

"Roger at that point already had a million majors but he's still a little kid, still kind of looks up to Pete and still looks up to the legends, he just does," Annacone said. "Pete is not open with a lot of people but in an intimate setting like that, he's great. And so we all sat down, and I literally just listened and Pete was like, 'All right, dude, what the eff is going on with tennis?' And Roger's like, 'What do you mean?' And Pete's like, 'No one's coming in at Wimbledon anymore. How does that happen? How is that working?'

"And Roger thinks about it for a second and then basically explains the evolution of one era into the next for Pete, and this goes on for a couple of hours. If I'd been a journalist then, I would have sneakily recorded everything."

What Federer explained was that when nearly everyone served and volleyed on grass, staying back was the wrong choice because it would have meant hitting too many passing shots. But as equipment and playing styles changed, Federer realized that he had an edge over the field from the baseline, too, just as he did on hard courts and even on clay against players not named Nadal.

The new grass court template was not serve-and-volley, it was serve-and-rip-the-forehand-as-soon-as-possible-and-then-if-necessary-volley. That is still attacking tennis, just a different form of it.

But there are those who disagree with Federer's conclusion.

"I think Roger abandoned serve-and-volley because he bought into the idea that everybody was abandoning it," said Craig O'Shannessy, a tennis analytics pioneer who has worked with Djokovic, Kevin Anderson, and others. "But when you look at the win percentages, they've always been positive. Whether they are serving and volleying at Wimbledon 30 percent or 6 percent of the time, the win percentage is still in the 65 to 70 percent range. Obviously, Roger has won eight titles there and done extremely well, but abandoning serving and volleying at Wimbledon is statistically not a good thing to do."

Tennis is a perpetual search for the right poison and the antidote to that poison. It is often a cyclical process, which means that serve-and-volley may have its day again at Wimbledon if enough would-be champions start young enough and hone the skill under great pressure.

But until then, Federer's results speak for themselves, as do Sampras's. They were the best of their time on grass with very different philosophies. Each respects the other's skill and commitment.

It was a long flight back to Los Angeles the day after the 2009 final, but Sampras was glad to have made the whirlwind journey, even if he arrived home without his record.

"I never could have imagined," he said, "that it would only take seven years for someone to beat fourteen."

Sampras was in for more surprises in the years to come.

CHAPTER ELEVEN

FEUSISBERG, Switzerland

"Welcome to Switzerland!" said Roger Federer, spreading his arms in the direction of Lake Zurich and sounding proud and proprietary.

Federer was back on top of the tennis mountain, and he seemed to be on top of the world as well when I visited him on August 7, 2009.

I had come from France in a hurry for an interview because he was returning to competition earlier than expected. At his suggestion, we met near his apartment for brunch on the wide terrace of the Panorama Resort and Spa, named for its killer view from on high of Lake Zurich.

"I live just down there," he said, pointing toward the lake and the affluent town of Wollerau. "Nice and quiet. Drive five minutes, and you have the cows. I like it."

It was a gorgeous late morning—sun-kissed, crystalline light, a hint of a breeze—and to this day, I cannot recall seeing Federer in a better mood outside of winning a match point at a major.

This interview, for a change, was not specifically about his tennis. It was about becoming a father. Mirka had given birth two weeks earlier in Zurich, on July 23, to identical twin girls: Charlene and Myla.

"It must be an amazing thing to look at yourself without looking in the mirror," Federer said of his daughters. "They are going to be playing tricks on us like crazy."

With reliable Swiss timing, the Federers had become parents in the narrow gap between Wimbledon, where Federer won his record fifteenth Grand Slam singles title, and the US Open, where he was soon to chase his sixth straight singles title.

"We didn't completely just aim for a certain window, so for it to happen during this period of time, we got lucky," Federer said. "I was scared. You know how it is. After week twenty-five, you never know when a baby can come, so at the beginning of the French Open, I was thinking that we have to get through two Grand Slams."

There was further discussion at Wimbledon about what to do if Mirka went into labor.

"Mirka said, 'Well, you go play the match and you come back. You can't just run away from the match, it's impossible,'" Federer explained.

But neither Roger nor Mirka ended up missing so much as a round, although they did cut it close. Federer won Wimbledon on July 5, and a little more than a week later, at her doctors' request, Mirka checked into the Privatklinik Bethanien, one of the top hospitals in Zurich, well ahead of her due date. Federer joined her, sleeping in the same room for nine days before the twins were delivered by cesarean section and then for another ten days afterward.

"It felt like the third Grand Slam in a row with Paris, Wimbledon, and the hospital," Roger said.

They had found out Mirka was pregnant in early January at a tournament in Doha, Qatar.

"I was pretty, like, shocked in a good way," he said. "My head was spinning, and I was making jokes to Mirka: 'Be careful! Don't lift that! You should be lying down!' And she was like, 'Stop it! Don't talk to me like I'm so pregnant!'"

Two weeks later they found out about the twins during her first checkup in Melbourne at the Australian Open. Roger's head was spinning anew.

"I was like, 'Oh my God! This is the best thing ever!'" he said.

He went out the next day and defeated the young and dangerous Juan Martin del Potro 6–3, 6–0, 6–0 in the quarterfinals.

"The twins gave me wings, right?" Federer said. "It was like, okay, seems like it's not affecting me if Mirka goes to a screening or anything. That was a good start. It gave me confidence."

After his loss to Nadal in the final, the Federers waited until March to announce Mirka's pregnancy, and their physician told them it was wisest not to mention twins right away. Roger later learned that his maternal grandmother also had been a twin but that her sibling had died during childbirth. It was indeed best to be cautious.

"You just never know what can happen," Roger said. "But the next thing you know, I'm seven months through the year and at the end, nobody's really asking me questions about if it's twins or not. And then I said, 'All right, I'll just play along until the very, very end.'"

That meant talking about "the baby" during his news conferences, and he had gotten so deeply into the habit that he sometimes mentioned "the baby" during our interview, too.

"I had to really battle myself," he said. "I had a couple where I said, 'We're really excited to have some babies,' and I was thinking, 'Is that already giving it away?'"

Federer, aware that I was the father of three daughters, asked about my family.

"I'm surrounded by women, and now you are, too," I said.

"How is that? Is that good?" he asked.

"Well, it brings out your sensitive side, which I'm not sure you need," I said.

Federer laughed hard. "Exactly!" he said.

It had long been clear that Federer had a love of the game and the tour that was well beyond the norm, but this was the first time I realized it was beyond the norm even for a tennis champion.

Many new fathers have returned to the court soon after the birth of their children, including Andre Agassi, but Federer seemed particularly eager to take the whole family on the road right away and then stay on the road. Mirka and the twins had checked out of the hospital in Zurich only on Tuesday. It was now Friday, and Myla and Charlene already had Swiss passports and, in a few hours, would board their first plane.

"I was obviously only going to do this if everything was safe and good," Roger said. "Mirka went through a check yesterday. The babies have been at the hospital for ten days, and everything is perfect. So we're doing it. Big family. Big trip. On the bandwagon. Here we go again. I'm really excited to see how we're going to manage it."

As an American married to a Parisian and covering sports globally, I had experienced plenty of long-haul journeys with very young children. Much as I cherished my daughters' company, "excited" was not the first word that sprang to mind at the thought of loading the gear, dealing with disrupted sleep, and managing the dread that our neighbors in economy class were feeling at the sight of babies on the red-eye.

The Federers would not be traveling in economy, however. Though they had taken commercial flights many times across the Atlantic as a couple, they had opted for a private jet for their first family outing and were headed for Montreal. They were taking a nurse on the road with them.

"That's a big help, but Mirka is really hands-on," Federer said. "Mirka doesn't mind getting up in the night, doesn't mind feeding the babies at whatever time, changing the nappies. For her, if she can't do it, it's like she's missing out on something."

The original plan had been to return to the tour the week after Montreal in Cincinnati, but Mirka had made it clear she was open to moving up the timetable if there were no medical issues. They decided on Montreal on Thursday: just one day before departure, which is why I had needed to hustle to get to Switzerland before takeoff.

"Every day Mirka was like, 'Are we going? Are we going?'" Federer said. "She was ready."

If anyone wonders how Federer played on with great success for more than a decade after becoming a family man, much of the explanation is in that short paragraph.

"She's a rock," Federer said. It's a word he's often used to describe his wife. "So strong, and maybe that's from tennis as well. Her mind is very strong and also the way she's handling everything now since the births. It's what I expected from Mirka, because she's such a wonderful person, but for her to prove it to me and show it to me, what a great mother she will be and is now, it's great."

As so often with Federer in English, the terms and tenses don't quite flow like his tennis flows, but what a precise transcription of his words frequently fails to capture is his warmth and positive energy. His body language is open: no folded arms across his chest. His eyes, despite being deep-set, are full of impending mirth. His tone is merrily conspiratorial, and if he rambles a bit, it is—astonishingly after so much winning and luxurious living—out of an eagerness to please: to provide you with all the content you require to capture this moment, however you may choose to capture it.

There would be plenty of obstacles on court for him in the years to come, including the continued excellence of Nadal and the rise, fall, and renaissance of Djokovic. But Mirka was no impediment to excellence behind the scenes. She supported Federer's playing career wholeheartedly, embraced the peripatetic life with gusto, and displayed executive-suite organizational acumen.

"I think Roger owes 50 percent of his career to Mirka, because she manages an incredible number of things," said Marc Rosset, who has known them since before they started dating. "If you are an elite athlete and you are married with an actress and she says that's great, you practice or go to this tournament but maybe we should do this or that instead, that is perhaps why your career stops more quickly."

Mirka, no trophy wife, certainly understood what her husband required to keep winning trophies. The daughter of an immigrant jeweler, she also enjoyed the goodies that tennis greatness provided: the highest-end homes and possessions, the five-star travel, the easy contact with other prominent people, including Anna Wintour, the *Vogue* magazine editor who was a major tennis fan and became an informal adviser.

"I think Anna had a huge influence on both Mirka and Roger," said Max Eisenbud, the IMG vice president who has long represented Maria Sharapova.

"I did make the mistake once of asking Mirka's help to plan my honeymoon," said Justin Gimelstob, a former ATP Tour player and board member. "She came up with the best honeymoon places: every concierge, every hotel, every outing, the sequencing, everything was great. What I realized when I got the bill was that I took the honeymoon of a twenty-time Grand Slam champion and my career-high ranking was 63."

But Mirka, unlike the supportive partners of most other tennis legends, understood the professional game on a granular level. She had been a top 100 player: an Olympian and Fed Cup team member. If not for her chronic, career-ending foot problem, she surely would have soared higher.

Though it is hard to imagine now, friends tried to talk the nineteen-year-old Federer out of starting to date the twenty-two-year-old Mirka after the 2000 Olympics. The friends could sense that with Mirka, who was more mature and polished than Federer at that stage, the relationship could get serious quickly.

"We all kind of said, 'Roger, no, no, no. You're too young. Just stay free a little bit longer,' but he went against our advice," Sven Groeneveld told me. "And obviously he made the right choice."

Mirka was Federer's serious girlfriend before he became a full-blown tennis star, long before he won his first Wimbledon. Federer appreciated that and trusted in that.

"I got together with her when I had zero titles, and we kind of went through all of this together, and now we have a family," Federer told me. "It's pretty incredible."

He also liked that she understood and played the game at a high level.

"I never started dating a tennis player because of that," Federer told me. "But in my situation, I think it really does help, because she knows in some ways what it takes, and she did it on a level that was still very good but not at my level. She already put in a massive amount of hours herself. So when I tell her, 'Look, I need to go to practice,' she's the first to say, 'I know, I know you need it, and you need only maybe 20 percent of what I needed.'"

Yves Allegro, Federer's friend and former doubles partner, remains close with both Roger and Mirka. He saw a quick change in Roger after they started dating.

"At that age, a woman is already a little ahead of the guys, and she was three years older," Allegro told me. "Roger started to dress a little bit differently, started to be a little more mature. I think Mirka, she understood tennis because at that point she was still a player herself. For his stability, it was perfect. She's a key player in his career, definitely, and she was also a huge support when Peter Carter died."

Bill Ryan was Federer's agent when he and Mirka began dating. "She was clearly the boss once they got together," Ryan said. "You could see he was smitten with her."

Mirka remained part of Federer's tennis brain trust for years, even after veteran coaches like Tony Roche, José Higueras, and Paul Annacone joined the team.

"I don't ever remember her going, 'Paul, Paul, why can't you get Roger to do this or that?'" Annacone said. "It was never that way at all. But the bigger the occasion, the more likely she would be to ask a question or two."

Annacone flashed back to the eve of the 2011 French Open semifinal against Djokovic, who had won forty-three straight singles matches before Federer stopped the streak with one of his finest performances.

"I remember being together with all of us the night before, and Mirka going, 'All right, guys, what do you think?'" Annacone said. "And then us having a conversation just about tactics."

When Annacone came to Zurich in 2010 for what was essentially a trial run, he had dinners with Roger and Mirka together. Annacone already knew Mirka socially through his former employer Tim Henman and through Federer's agent, Tony Godsick.

"Mirka was really direct," Annacone said. "She was asking questions, saying, 'This is where Roger has had issues strategically, what is your philosophy about this stuff?' It was really information gathering. I never felt I was under the gun, and Roger was the same way. I never felt oppressed by it and never felt it was out-of-bounds, and the more I got to be around them, the more I respected and appreciated their relationship and roles. Because Roger clearly loves her unconditionally, and she's strong, and she's smart, and she knows tennis and she knows life. She also is relentlessly protective of those she loves, her husband and her family, and, by the way, the people who work in that group."

Others who know the Federers note that Mirka can play the bad cop to Roger's good cop, that her straightforward approach and capacity for confrontation can allow him to preserve the role he prefers.

"Roger likes to keep it smooth, no conflict, but she can be tough and make it tough," said one former player who spoke anonymously to avoid damaging his relationship with the couple. "She has a lot of influence on Roger, his tennis, and his schedule. I would have struggled with that. It would not have been good for my marriage."

But Roger and Mirka were accustomed to mixing business with their relationship.

In January 2002, they played in the Hopman Cup together for Switzerland, both with long dark ponytails and white Nike headbands. They failed to keep from blushing and giggling when they were interviewed on court by former Australian great Fred Stolle, who kept alluding to their relationship (and struggling to pronounce Mirka's full name).

It is all the more poignant to watch that moment now, because Mirka's playing career was almost over.

"At Hopman Cup, I remember she cried before playing against Arantxa Sanchez Vicario, and I was like, 'Why are you crying?'" Federer told me. "And she said, 'You don't understand. I have so much pain in my foot. I can barely run, and I have to go out and play a match.' And I told her, 'Well, then don't play,' but she said, 'Of course I'm going to play, but it hurts so much.' I never had it quite like this. I mean, I was close to it, and I went on court, but this thing with Mirka was I guess a different animal, because shortly after that she did retire."

She lost in the opening round of qualifying at the Australian Open and in Indian Wells and Miami. But the pain was constant, and she stopped for several months before deciding on surgery on her heel. During her recovery period in the autumn of 2002, Roger asked if she could help book a hotel for him. Gradually, she took on more and more of the travel planning for Roger and Peter Lundgren, who was then his coach.

Doctors eventually told Mirka that the operation had been a

mistake, but she could no longer move at the level needed to compete on the tour. She was just twenty-four years old.

"I tried so hard to come back, and I wanted so much to come back, but there was nothing more I could do," Mirka said in Paris in the spring of 2005, when she was still experiencing foot pain after her retirement.

By then she was traveling with Roger and coordinating his sponsorship and media commitments. This was the period when Roger split with IMG and relied on his parents, Mirka, and a Swiss legal adviser to help him manage his burgeoning affairs.

"I think in a way her career continued with me, especially the first few years," Federer told me in 2016. "I think that was good for her that my career just took off as she retired, because she was full on into the next thing. She couldn't even think, 'Oh God, my foot hurts so bad, and my heel is killing me, and I can probably never play again.' And the foot is still not good even today, so I guess she did take the right decision rather than rehabbing for three straight years."

When he broke through to win Wimbledon in 2003, Mirka was thrust into the role of managing the avalanche of interview and appearance requests.

"There was this big boom, and everybody wanted so much from us," Roger told me. "To be caught off guard, it was interesting."

He imitated Mirka's voice: "'Ohhh, my phone doesn't stop ringing! It's crazy. I don't know what to do.'"

He then reverted to his own voice: "And I'm like, 'Just switch it off, I want to have time with youuu,'" he said, dragging out the last vowel pleadingly.

He imitated Mirka's voice again: "And she's like, 'I can't do that.'"

Federer recounts this dialogue in English, but he and Mirka communicate in Swiss German even though both are multilingual (Mirka also speaks English and Slovakian). Whatever the language, work-life balance was indeed a rubbing point in those early years.

"In the beginning, sometimes we had issues where I think that and she thinks this, and we're like, 'Okay, let's not fight,'" Federer told me in 2005. "At least if we fight about it and we forget about it after, then we can cuddle each other. By now, it's no problem, but that first title at Wimbledon, you go through those times where she's so exhausted and is maybe irritated a little bit, like I am. We still can never quite end the workday. Sometimes early morning she looks at her emails or has to make one more phone call, and I'm like, 'Hmmm,' but it's no problem."

After December 2003, when Federer surprisingly split with Lundgren, Mirka's influence and role continued to grow.

"Mirka's the one who really tied up all the loose ends for Federer," said Paul Dorochenko, the French physiotherapist and osteopath who worked with them both in their youth. "I honestly think when they split with Lundgren it was more her decision than his. She's really not very nice, rather cold in fact. But she did a lot of good for Federer, because she took care of everything, and the only thing Roger had to do was play tennis. She did all the things behind the scenes, and there were more and more of those."

Opinion in tennis is more divided about Mirka than it is about Roger, but perhaps that is because she guards the family bubble so diligently and communicates, by design, so little with the outside world, unless you count all her raised eyebrows, clenched fists of encouragement, and exhales of exasperation in the player's box, where she has chewed more gum through the years than a first-base coach.

"I just really like her, and I have a lot of respect for her," said Andy Roddick, Federer's longtime rival.

Maria Sharapova told me that when she won Wimbledon by surprise at age seventeen, she shared a table at the champions dinner with Mirka and Roger, who had just won his second straight men's title.

"When I got up to get the trophy next to him at the ball, I remember Mirka telling me that my dress was crooked, and I was like, 'Oh my God, I don't want my dress crooked when I'm standing next to Roger Federer!'" Sharapova told me. "So I was like, 'Thank you so much, Mirka.' I was so clueless."

Marc Rosset, the Swiss star who was once a mentor to Federer, points out that Mirka had the largely thankless task of being the media gatekeeper in the early years.

"Mirka was someone who was much criticized in the beginning because the Swiss press was not happy because they felt they had to go through her to get to Roger," Rosset said. "But before criticizing someone, you should walk in their shoes. She had that tough role. She was the public relations manager and all that, and of course she did everything so that Roger could have the most normal situation and concentrate on tennis. She protected her man, which is normal. In the beginning, there were many complaints, but honestly I have nothing nasty to say about her. She did what she thought was best for him, and if Roger accepts that and is content with that it's not for us to criticize."

Groeneveld believes Mirka had a clear vision for Federer.

"She knew what had to be done," he said. "She was the one when it came down to making a decision with Peter Lundgren, when that came to an end, she played a role in that of course. The coaching decisions, those are tough for Roger. He's so loyal to his people. It's hard for him to let go of somebody."

Federer has long maintained that though he certainly consulted with Mirka about the split with Lundgren, it was ultimately his decision: one that Lundgren told me came at the right time for him, too, even if it was painful.

For much of 2004, Federer had no formal coach, and he did not rejoin forces with IMG until late 2005. Ron Yu, who became Federer's regular stringer, remembers that when he went to Federer's Hamburg hotel in 2004 for their first long conversation, Mirka was part of the meeting. Godsick eventually took over the public relations duties, relieving Mirka of having to say no most of the time to the press. But she remained deeply involved in Federer's career.

"Obviously when we didn't have any kids and especially in the times when I didn't have a coach or management, actually, we were having breakfast, lunch, dinner almost alone at the table every single day," Federer told me not long after Myla and Charlene were born. "So you can imagine we had so much time to talk about everything, which was a very interesting time in our lives. Today, we are sitting six to eight at a table. It's overflowing almost, so it's changed a lot, and so we need to really be very specific and precise in how we want to have some alone time."

Federer conceded that his tennis game remains a topic with Mirka during "alone time."

"I know she likes that, too," he said with a grin. "I like to have tennis conversations with her because I know she has seen me practice and play matches more than anybody out there, and this is where sometimes I pick her brain a bit."

It would, of course, be ideal to get Mirka's perspective on all of this, but she and Roger decided in the mid-2000s that she would stop giving interviews, part of an increasingly muscular effort to preserve their private life.

Their small-scale wedding on April 11, 2009, in Basel was such a well-kept secret that even some members of the Swiss Davis Cup team did not know it was happening. In all my interviews with Federer, he has been genuinely testy only once. That was in 2012 when I mentioned his family's home near Lenzerheide in the Swiss Alps.

"Don't write where I live," he snapped. "I don't like that."

The location later became public knowledge, but Federer, a global figure with a deserved reputation for amiability, had a growing desire to establish clear boundaries. That meant that Mirka, once his press attaché, would no longer speak to the press. If there were questions about the couple, Federer would field them.

That was certainly a loss to our understanding of the big picture. Tennis spouses are generally not as central to the story as Mirka. She would have had plenty to illuminate and perhaps debunk, including reports of her pre-Roger romance with a member of Dubai's royal family. But above all, it would be fascinating to hear her thoughts on her husband's career. She has played a decisive role in making him the best version of himself on court and in building his brand.

"I am not his coach, it's enough to give him some advice," she told the French sports publication *L'Équipe* in 2005 in one of her final interviews. "Roger loves talking tennis. I know the game and the tactics. Because he is intelligent, he acts like a filter: He keeps only the best information. It's perhaps what connects us so strongly, that we both come from the same world, the tennis world. I am never going to take him shopping the night before a Grand Slam final."

The journey has not always been smooth. The Roger Federer perfume, in which they both invested, was a flop, but it did leave them with a version of the "RF" monogram that was later modified and used with much more success by Nike and now Uniqlo.

"The RF hat was the number one hat we've sold, and Nike makes a lot of hats, and tennis is a very small business for Nike," said Mike Nakajima, who spent thirty years with the company. "Mirka has a lot more say in what Roger wears than what Roger does. She was a lot more, I would say, vocal about what Roger likes and doesn't like, what color looks good on Roger and what color doesn't look good. But you know what? We have a better half for a reason. Sometimes Roger may not have been vocal enough to say, 'I really don't like what you guys did here,' and I think in that sense, Mirka took that on."

She has taken on plenty more through the years, including a second set of twins (remarkably, Federer's sister, Diana, also has twins). Mirka and Roger's sons, Leo and Lenny, who are fraternal, not identical twins, were born on May 6, 2014, leaving just enough time for Roger to make it to the Italian Open and French Open. The logistics of it all have sometimes been daunting, but Mirka's goal was to turn the road into a home, even booking the occasional camper van.

Money helps smooth out the bumps, no doubt. There have been a lot of private-plane rides and a rotating cast of nannies. "We have a few just to make sure they don't overwork and that we have a good vibe," Federer told me.

When it came time for formal schooling for Charlene and Myla, the Federers hired an accredited teacher to travel with the family for kindergarten and primary school, with the girls studying in hotel rooms or other spaces converted into classrooms.

"It seems like the right thing to do, so we can all stay together,"

Federer told me in 2015. "I wasn't sure if that was what I really wanted for the kids at the beginning, but I must say it keeps us together. The girls enjoy it, and I love being with my family, and so does Mirka. She loves being with me, so we get to see each other every single day, basically, and I think that's more important than being apart from each other and them going to normal school at the moment. But things can change very quickly."

Federer would be off the road for extended periods in 2016 and again in 2020 because of knee surgeries and the coronavirus pandemic. (He also skipped the clay court seasons in 2017 and 2018.)

"Kids get used to everything, but the girls were asking, 'When are we leaving again?'" Federer told me of his six-month layoff in 2016. "Because they were happy to get back on the road. It was like, 'When are we going next time to Australia? Or when are we going next time to New York?' And I'm like, 'Not for a little while.'"

But the family has continued to globe-trot together, and at this stage both the Federers and their children have friends in most of the places where they trot.

"In the twenty years I've been on tour now, I've got to know a lot of people; in every city we know somebody, and we are always happy to catch up with them," Federer told me. "And that's why our life on the tour does feel kind of like a home."

Annacone struggles to recall an event during his years coaching Federer when there were not "at least three to four different couples or friends" on-site to spend time with the Federers.

"They had dinners, and they spent some days together and they would hang out and chat and go for walks and do things couples do together," Annacone said. "And that separation for Roger was fuel for him to keep doing tennis at a high level."

Annacone, after his experience with the more insular Sampras, was concerned Federer might be drained from all the socializing. He talked about those concerns with Godsick, Lüthi, and ultimately Federer.

"Roger was like, 'I don't think I'm at that stage yet where I'm aging enough where I feel like it loses any part of my fuel,'" Annacone said. "Suffice to say I've never seen Roger lose a match because of it, never sat there and gone, 'Wow, that's because he had friends visiting.' He's incredibly efficient with his processes, his emotional processes, his practicing. Everything he does seems to have a recharging effect on him. The social interaction, all the other stuff, it's like it regenerates him more than draining the fuel tank."

His daughters have even offered him some advice during practice sessions.

"Once they told me I should play on the lines," Federer explained at the 2016 Australian Open. "They think that's a good thing. I was like, 'Okay, I'll try that.'"

They also suggested he sneakily look in one direction and hit the ball in the other.

"I said, 'Okay, I'll try that, too. It's not as easy as you think it is, but I'll try,'" he said.

Federer frequently makes the point that travel is not tough on his children because it is all they have ever known. "It's on us that it's tough," he said of himself and Mirka, "because we worry. For the kids, it's easy actually because we make sure it's as easy as possible for them."

He was not the first men's star of his generation to travel with family in tow. Lleyton Hewitt and his wife, Bec, did it with their daughter Mia, born in 2005, and son, Cruz, born in 2008. They eventually became a family of five when daughter Ava was born in 2010. Hewitt, who retired from singles in 2016, often played on the show courts with Cruz, who also got to hit with Federer and Nadal. Hewitt's example certainly made the family plan seem all the more possible to Federer.

"They're going to have lifelong memories out there with me," Hewitt said. "Probably pushed me to play that little bit longer to enjoy it so they could get something out of it as well."

But Hewitt's last great season was 2005. Federer continued to win big as he juggled a large family and grand tennis ambitions.

"I wouldn't be able to do it," Roddick told me. "I was a stress ball without family obligations and all that. I needed to have tennis, and now I need to have family and business. I wouldn't have been able to intertwine all of them."

In 2017, Roddick asked Federer about the challenges, and Federer responded that it was particularly fun some weeks when he and his family all shared the same room, as they had one year at the Western & Southern Open in Cincinnati.

Roddick was flabbergasted.

"I was like, '*What* do you mean, you all stayed in the same room? Like a bunch of rooms connected?' And Roger's like, 'No, we all had a big room,' and I'm like, 'See. That's the stuff no one else does or can do without losing their minds. That's not a real thing to stay in a room with four kids and a wife and win a Masters Series event.'"

But Federer thrives on compartmentalizing. Taking his mind off the tennis while taking his children to a museum in Paris or a park in Melbourne helps him to fully focus when it comes time to perform on court. "Before a night match, everyone else is in their room, trying to get rest with every machine hooked up to them, making sure they're ready, eating perfect, and Roger is out there in Central Park with the kids," said John Tobias, a leading tennis agent. "I think that relaxed approach really benefits his tennis. Other people are wound so tight because they think about it all day long, so when the moment comes they struggle." Returning to his family also helps him move on more quickly after a defeat—already one of his strengths before he and Mirka had children.

"He has happiness to fall back on," Chris Evert told me. "I just adore the fact that they travel everywhere with him, like a traveling show. The whole family is so tight. I really admire that, and I think Roger is a really good person. He's got a good heart, and that's hard to find when you're in a tough, tough sport. It's hard to find the gentleness."

Annacone remembers Wimbledon in 2011, where Federer lost to Jo-Wilfried Tsonga in the quarterfinals after blowing a two-set lead for the first time in his career in a Grand Slam singles match. It was, on the surface at least, a devastating moment.

"I was thinking, what am I going to say afterwards, how do I figure out the speech?" Annacone told me. "So, he does all his press, and we jump in the car and go back to his house, which is a thirty-second ride at Wimbledon, and he literally puts his bags down as we walk in the door and gets down on his hands and knees and in thirty seconds he's on the floor with the twins, Myla and Charlene, and they are laughing and giggling and rolling around."

After Federer rose, Annacone suggested they take a walk for their postmatch debrief. Annacone asked Federer what thought process allowed him to shake off a tough defeat and share an apparently carefree moment so quickly with his children.

This, according to Annacone, was Federer's answer: "Look, I've won a lot of titles, and I've lost a lot, and I just really feel that that stuff balances out. I can give you some instances where I have won titles where I shouldn't have, and I can give you some instances where I lost some at big moments. More times than not I'm going to win those, but what drives me is just understanding that it happens, and that it does balance out."

As if to underscore the point, Federer won Wimbledon again the following year, his first major singles title since the 2010 Australian Open.

Pierre-Hugues Herbert, the French player, once said that traveling with his own family brought him a sense of "lightness" on and off the court. Federer would agree, but in a sense he and Mirka have simply incorporated their children into their long-standing approach to travel.

Federer actually had a fear of flying as a youth. "I used to get very sick on the plane," he said. But he soon conquered that, and early in his professional career he and Mirka chose not to stay in the official hotels with most of the other players and their coaches.

"I see them enough at the courts; I just want to get away and get more privacy, I guess," Federer told me in 2005. "We also try to stay in hotels that are very central, so we get a good look at the city and don't only see the hotel room and the courts."

In Paris that year, he was excited to visit the Louvre for the first time, and so it went in many of the world's major cities.

"These are little things you start doing over the years to get away from the sport and do something different," he said. "Because tennis is a big focus, but there is also something else in life, the private side with my girlfriend and my family. I want to keep that intact as well, because I can only play good tennis when I'm happy."

Federer's priority, even back then, was to keep himself fresh physically and mentally: to be smart about scheduling and training loads but also to be smart about how much he put himself in the spotlight and in group settings. He is an extrovert, though not quite as much of a social animal as Pete Sampras might suspect when he sees Federer small-talking and fist-bumping his way through the locker room or the player restaurant.

Federer conserves his energy, or perhaps it would be more accurate to say that he conserves his enthusiasm, so that when he inevitably finds himself in such public settings he can meet and greet them in high spirits.

There are lessons here for many of us. Federer and I talked about this again much later in his career.

"As much as I take things very serious, I am very laid-back, so I can really let go very quickly," he said in 2019. "I truly believe this is a secret for a lot of the players and for the young guys is to be able, when you leave the site, to say: 'Okay, I'm going to leave it behind. I still know I'm a professional tennis player, but I'm relaxing. I'm doing it my way, whatever helps me decompress.'"

Federer stopped speaking for a moment and showed me his clenched left fist.

"Because if you are constantly like this," he said, looking at his fist, "that's when you burn out."

"So, you've never had even a bit of burnout?" I asked.

He thought for a good thirty seconds before answering.

"If I do feel burnout coming on, what I've tried to do is break it down to the absolute minimum, and that's practice, matches, and family," he said. "All that goes without saying, but maybe then you do less press, less autographs, less stuff in the public eye. I will practice off-site because I need to quickly gather myself, gather my energy for the main purpose, which is the match. I had a process of three months once where I asked the tour to help me out a little bit because I was just tired from the constant everyday grind of being in front of the media. That's where I felt it the most, but that was a short period of time. It started with Indian Wells and Miami and went all the way through the clay court season."

He is not quite sure if the year was 2012 or 2013, but it was most likely 2012 because he did not play Miami in 2013.

"I think it probably had something to do with Myla and Charlene as well, because I was full in with the kids," he said. "Today, when I think back to 2010 and 2011, all I remember is the moments away from the tennis, not my on-court performances, because I was a father, you know, and so happy it was that way, but '10 and '11 was a blur. You could ask me, 'How did you play at the French in '10?' I couldn't tell you. 'How did you do in Melbourne in '11?' I couldn't tell you. In '12 things start coming back, because I won Wimbledon and all that, but maybe during this time I was just tired from also taking care of the kids and really just getting a hang with Mirka of how we were going to do this."

I covered the Paris Indoor tournament in November 2011 and remember Federer telling us he had not gotten much sleep before the final against Jo-Wilfried Tsonga.

One of his twin daughters had woken him and Mirka up at 4:00 a.m.

"Mirka told me, 'All right, we're taking her in our bed,'" Federer said. "I didn't even argue. I took her in the bed. You especially don't want to have an argument at four in the morning."

Federer beat Tsonga to win the title, and though traveling with his young children certainly impacted his sleep, he is someone who seems to be able to thrive and compete without too much of it.

"I get a call in California," Annacone said. "And I'll talk to him and I'll be like, 'Isn't it quarter to three in the morning in Dubai right now?' And he'll be like, 'Yeah.' And I'll be like, 'Okay, what are you doing?' And he goes, 'Nothing. I was just going through emails.' So I actually think late night is his therapy time. That's his alone time, that's his me time, and I don't mean this in a mean way, but he doesn't need to be Paul's player, or Mirka's husband, or Myla's and Charlene's dad, or Roger Federer the icon."

Annacone said that during his years coaching Federer, he was initially concerned by his sleep patterns.

"I was concerned a lot early in our relationship because I didn't understand it," he said. "I had to talk to Severin a lot about it. I talked a lot to Tony about it and Mirka. I'm not saying he didn't ever sleep. I just hadn't been around someone that had the flexibility in the approach that he does to so many things. At Wimbledon, he has different houses all the time, doesn't have superstitions, he doesn't always need to practice in the same place or have one favorite meal. This is in that same vein. But I was always amazed at how little sleep he needed to be energetic and optimistic."

The French have a fine expression that applies to Federer: *"Joindre l'utile à l'agréable,"* which translates loosely as combining business with pleasure but is actually broader in scope, encompassing the tasks of daily life. If you're going to empty the dishwasher or stack the wood, find a way to make it novel and amusing.

This has been a key element in Federer's career longevity. Too much routine can kill the joy; too much constant focus can grind you down. Pierre Paganini, his intuitive fitness trainer, certainly understood this, but so did Mirka, who had learned through painful experience.

"Early on when I became number one, we decided with Pierre that less is more," Federer told me in 2011. "We have to take care of the body, because Mirka's body went first because she maybe overpracticed. So I think she could also give me some advice, some knowhow. Her body is still fragile today when she goes and does sports. Mine isn't, and it's incredible because I've done so much more than she has. So, I guess it's a bit of luck, too, and smartness because of the people that have surrounded me. And this is where it's definitely been so helpful to be with her for sure."

Mirka helped him with both the big picture and the details.

"Like don't train six or seven hours and don't get treatment," he said. "She went all out all the time and then bang! Or she'd explain to me how to manage a blister, which might sound like a silly thing but these all add up. She was just very caring for me because she did learn it the hard way."

Federer's luck has changed in recent years. His back has been a long-term concern, but it is his knees that have truly betrayed him. He underwent his first surgery of any kind in 2016 after injuring his left knee in Melbourne when twisting while running a bath for his children. He underwent two surgeries on his right knee in 2020 and then, perhaps most disappointingly, another more elaborate knee surgery in August 2021 that cut his latest comeback short.

But Federer has long had excellent timing, and not just on his groundstrokes. If there was any season to miss almost in its entirety, 2020 was it.

As for many of us, the pandemic gave him time in one place with his family: a big chunk of it in Valbella at the mountain retreat that he and Mirka had built as a vacation home but that eventually became their primary residence instead of the lakeside house in Wollerau.

"I think it has been quite lucky for my children and for us to find that tranquility away from all the hustle and bustle," he told me in 2019 before the pandemic.

Mirka and the children ski regularly (Roger is now waiting for retirement). Leo and Lenny have been more interested in playing tennis than Charlene and Myla and have shown considerable promise, but Roger, raised without undue pressure from his parents, is very wary about projecting.

He knows what kind of odds he had to beat to even make it on tour, much less become one of the most successful players of all time. There will be no golden-child or golden-twin predictions of greatness. But like his parents, he does have expectations.

"What I want for them for sports is that they actually enjoy it, so I'm trying to explain to them how fun it is, how fun it's supposed to be, and what they can learn," he said. "But you do feel like my parents did, which is, 'Okay, I've invested time now. I've brought my children to tennis practice or soccer practice or skiing lessons, whatever it is, and then when they come back and I hear they were terrible, I just get a little bit frustrated. Because I've taken the time to bring them there and watch them and they're really not putting in the best effort.' This is what drained my parents so much. It's like, 'I'm just not going to bring you anymore and, by the way, it cost us quite a lot of money to bring you there as well. So I'd rather you just be at home reading a book or go play against the wall for free and do it yourself. But don't waste the coaches' time.' That was the message from my parents, and I feel like Mirka and me, we are very similar in that respect. All we're asking for is just put in a good effort."

Ideally, parents set the example. Showing tends to work better than telling in the behavior department. Federer, an overwrought athlete in his youth, is not expecting model behavior.

But he has done what he can to show the twins what effort means, and that includes enduring: competing and thriving long enough for each of his children to have a memory of him on Centre Court at Wimbledon or on the practice courts at the US Open.

That was Mirka's long-declared dream, perhaps in part because she thought it might be motivation for her husband.

It is a dauntingly ephemeral thing: sports greatness. But Federer over a twenty-year span has made it seem more reliable and durable with ample help from his coaches, his trainers, his therapists, his friends, his agent, and, above all, it seems clear, from his wife.

"I don't think she wants me to play for her now," Federer told me. "I don't think that's part of her thing anymore. In the beginning, I think it was a great help for her to see it that way. And afterwards, we just had a blast on the tour all by ourselves just trying to cope with everything, and then with the kids it was so fresh and amazing and inspiring and happy."

As it turns out, his optimism was warranted on that sunlit morning in August 2009 with Lake Zurich shimmering in the distance. Big family. Big trip. On the bandwagon. They did make it work. He did play on with his children in tow, longer than even he or Mirka would have imagined.

CHAPTER TWELVE

NEW YORK

"The greatest shot I ever hit in my life," said Roger Federer at the 2009 US Open.

You could argue that he has been paying for it ever since.

The shot was struck against Novak Djokovic very near the end of their semifinal. Federer was up two sets to love with Djokovic serving to stay in the match at 5–6, 0–30. Moving forward, Djokovic hit a drop shot. Federer chased it down. Djokovic countered with a lob volley that forced Federer to reverse course and sprint back toward the baseline. With the ball perilously close to bouncing a second time, Federer smacked it between his legs with his back to the net, sending the ball crosscourt past the stunned Djokovic for a winner.

It was 0–40, and though Federer cracked a forehand return winner on the next point to close out his fortieth straight victory at the US Open, the only shot anyone wanted to talk about was that "tweener."

There are harder things to do in tennis: Try hitting a drop shot return off a huge serve or an angled backhand overhead off a deep lob (or beating Nadal on clay).

But a tweener, which was rarer in 2009, is pure showtime: tennis's version of a no-look pass for a dunk. In a flick of the wrist, it turns a deeply defensive position into an attack. Though it often misfires and is often the wrong choice of shot, Federer's worked to perfection, unlike the tweener he had tried back in the day on match point against Safin in Australia.

"The way I was able to hit it with pace and accuracy, it's something that happens so, so rarely," Federer said.

The exquisitely timed winner seemed a reflection of Federer's deep and contented groove after his victories at the French Open and Wimbledon and the birth of the twins. It was also the latest proof of his ability to rise above in New York, particularly against Djokovic, whom he had now defeated in three consecutive US Opens, including the 2007 final.

"I get the feeling he plays more relaxed," Djokovic said. "Because now he became a father and got married and broke all the records. He just gets on the court, and he wants to play his best and win more. That's what makes him even more dangerous. I mean, that shot that he hit, you saw the reaction of the crowd; what can I explain?"

How could anyone have guessed at that giddy Federer-esque high point that his US Open winning streak was about to give way to a long-running series of confounding defeats? Or that, over the next decade and beyond, he would never beat Djokovic again in New York or in any best-of-five-set match on a hard court?

Of the many twists in Federer's great career, this was one of the most surprising. I certainly did not see it coming as I wrote my latest piece for the *New York Times* on that Sunday night in the US Open press room full of clattering keyboards and deadline stress.

Juan Martin del Potro's 6–2, 6–2, 6–2 destruction of Nadal in the day's other semifinal did give me some pause, but Nadal was playing with a torn abdominal muscle and battling through an injury-filled year. Federer had won all six of his previous matches with the twenty-year-old del Potro, a six-foot-six intimidator with a gentle disposition and ferocious, flat groundstrokes. He was nicknamed "the Tower of Tandil" after his hometown in Argentina. While it was true that del Potro had just pushed Federer to five sets on clay at the French Open, Federer had overwhelmed del Potro at the Australian Open earlier in the year. The quick, lower-bouncing surface in New York seemed an ideal spot for Federer to cause del Potro more pain with his skidding slice.

"In spite of how well del Potro played on Sunday, Federer is a heavy favorite," I wrote.

The early-evening final was on Monday due to rain's impact on the schedule earlier in the tournament, and the final turned into a five-set slugfest full of forehand winners and shouts from the rowdy Open crowd that sometimes disrupted the players' service motions.

Federer had his chances to take command but surprisingly faltered. He failed to serve out the second set and failed to bring his best to the fourth-set tiebreaker, double-faulting on the opening point. He even failed to keep his cool, getting surly with American chair umpire Jake Garner late in the third set when del Potro was slow to challenge a line call.

Federer, a tennis traditionalist at heart, was opposed to the introduction of electronic line calling in 2006. He was still chafing at the imposition three years later and always seemed to use the system as if he were dragging his monogrammed sneakers. Perhaps that explains why a man with great court vision challenged incorrectly so often.

"Come on!" Federer said as he took his seat. "I wasn't allowed to challenge, like, after two seconds, the guy takes, like, ten every time. How do you allow that stuff to happen? Do you have any rules in there or what?"

Federer had a point on the late challenges, but Garner tried to calm him.

"Stop showing me the hand, okay?" Federer snapped. "Don't tell me to be quiet, okay? When I want to talk, I talk all right. I don't give a shit what he said. I just say he's waiting too long."

This was not the *comme il faut* Federer to whom viewers had grown accustomed. This was a flashback to a testier time, and a sign that he sensed danger, as he had when he cracked his racket against Djokovic in Miami earlier in the season.

Del Potro, whose career would be sadly diminished by major wrist and knee injuries, did not miss this opportunity: taking Federer's topspin on the rise and finding openings with startling ease as he served and rumbled to a 3–6, 7–6 (5), 4–6, 7–6 (4), 6–2 upset. Those who think Federer always has overwhelming crowd support did not attend this final. It was a big house divided, and del Potro looked a lot cooler at crunch time in his first Grand Slam final than Federer in his twenty-first.

Rewatching the exchange with Garner made me think of an observation made by Paul Dorochenko, Federer's long-ago fitness trainer.

"The Federer we see on court today is a manufactured product, a manufactured product of Nike's marketing that represents the values we want to give tennis: the gentleman and all that," he told me. "But deep inside, Federer was never a gentleman. He's a fighter. When he extends the hand with a smile to Nadal, I'm not at all convinced."

It is a minority view, but a provocative one. Are we, after all, the sum of our actions or the sum of our thoughts, suppressed or expressed?

The 2009 US Open final felt like an unguarded moment for Federer. But then it was worth noting only because Federer's behavior on and off the court has been so exemplary for so many years. That restraint was in line with two of his childhood heroes—Sampras and Stefan Edberg—but still striking when you consider some of the champions who preceded him: Jimmy Connors, John McEnroe, and even early-career, pre-philosopher Agassi, who had a foul mouth and a wavering commitment to the truth, and had once spit in the direction of an umpire.

But of all the Grand Slam tournaments, the US Open is the one that can reliably fray your nerves. It is the last of the four and comes near the end of a long season full of jet lag and jostling for position. The players, like the fans, have to navigate Manhattan and Queens traffic to reach the site. It is an end-of-summer happening, full of cocktails, tennis fanatics, Hamptons tans, and late-night hollering. As vast as the grounds have become, the push and pull of the public can still make it feel oppressive.

Federer, raised in a more peaceful place, had long thrived amid the din. He had learned to love Manhattan, regularly shifting hotels year to year to get a different feel for the city.

I interviewed him in his suite at the Peninsula in Midtown on the

Friday before the 2006 US Open. The room was a spotless tribute to Mirka's influence, with eleven freshly strung rackets aligned in a row on the hearth, their grips all resting against the brick at the same angle.

"Mirka helps me out, you know," Federer said. "I like it tidy anyway. I used to be so untidy. There was a time when I didn't want it to be tidy."

"Now, maybe it's nice to have a little order in a disorderly world," I suggested.

"Exactly," Federer said. "Especially here where I'm going to be for hopefully three weeks or so."

Not that he was camping out in his hotel.

"In the beginning, everybody says it's such a hassle," he said. "All they do is talk about what a long ride it is out to the tournament, and the site is so big, and it's New York and the traffic and everything. But I've started to look at these tournaments from a different view. What else do they have to offer off the court? I know how it is around the grounds, but you can't measure a tournament just for around the grounds. You also have to see what the city can do, and this is an incredible city. It never gets boring, always something to do, the best restaurants, they have great shopping. It's just a great buzz.

"The times are past where I want to watch TV and go to the site and hang out with the guys," he said. "I'm kind of in the stage now where I want to see more of where I'm going and understand more of the history about the country. Before it was very, very different, because you're sucked in where you want to do well, you're the next great thing, and you want to fulfill this, and you are under pressure, and all you think about is tennis all day long. That's changed, obviously. In the last three years, especially since I became number one, you have a different perspective on tennis, and to me, it's helped me. I'm a more balanced guy. I don't feel like I'm under pressure anymore, even though the pressure is high, and it makes it much more enjoyable to play."

He certainly had found his five consecutive US Open finals enjoyable, without even being pushed to a fifth set as he defeated, in order,

Lleyton Hewitt, Andre Agassi, Andy Roddick, Djokovic, and Andy Murray.

But del Potro stopped him short of a sixth straight title in 2009, just as Nadal had stopped him short of a sixth straight Wimbledon.

"Five was great," Federer said in New York. "Six would have been a dream, too. Can't have them all.

"This one I think is easy to get over, just because I've had the most amazing summer," Federer continued, looking like he meant it.

It was without doubt a missed opportunity, however: one that Federer, at his finest, would not have squandered. But surely, with his affinity for fast courts, there was always next year at Flushing Meadows, and in 2010 Federer did indeed find himself back in striking range: deep in another fifth set in another semifinal against Djokovic with two match points on the Serb's serve at 4–5, 15–40.

Djokovic could not make a first serve but still managed to win both points: hitting a fearless forehand swing volley winner to get to 30–40 and a nearly-as-bold forehand winner to get to deuce.

Federer could certainly have been more daring on the second match point, but Djokovic beat him to the bravado, then held serve and broke Federer in the next game.

Serving for the match, Djokovic fought off a break point with another big forehand that Federer could not handle. It was deuce again, and two points later Djokovic, not Federer, was in the final.

"It was just one of those matches you will always remember," Djokovic told Mary Joe Fernández, the insightful CBS analyst who, in the conflicted world of tennis, did the interview despite being married to Federer's agent, Tony Godsick. "To be honest, I was just closing my eyes and hitting the forehand as fast as I can on the match point, so if it goes in, it goes in; if it goes out, another loss to Federer in the US Open."

Flash forward one year to the same court and same semifinal round in 2011. By now Djokovic, tennis's third man, had become the main man: reeling off titles on all surfaces and rising to No. 1 for the first time in July after winning his first Wimbledon.

Federer had played the spoiler in Paris: stopping Djokovic's forty-three-match winning streak by beating him in the semifinals of the French Open. Now, Federer had Djokovic back on the ropes in New York.

It was a grinding, draining match. Federer won the first two sets. Djokovic fought back to win the next two, but in the fifth set, Federer took the lead and served for a place in the final at 5–3.

At 40–15, Federer once again had two match points, with the pro-Federer crowd of twenty-three thousand roaring its support inside the steep-sided bowl of Arthur Ashe Stadium. A lesser competitor would have crumpled, but, as in 2010, Djokovic did not. He walked with a strut and then nodded his head and pursed his lips as he settled into position to return. Some interpreted that as resignation, an acknowledgment of Federer's superiority. That was not how it looked to me.

Federer sliced the serve wide. Djokovic lunged right and took a full and ferocious cut with his forehand just behind the doubles alley and hit a winner crosscourt that was so crisply struck that Federer barely moved.

Djokovic milked the moment, raising both arms to the crowd as he walked slowly to his towel, earning some cheers and jeers: a preview of how fans would respond to just about everything he would do in tennis in the decade to come. He then settled in with a smile to return on the second match point, as if to say, "Come what may, you will not defeat my spirit."

Federer, grim-faced, hit a good serve to Djokovic's body that Djokovic parried with his backhand. The return landed fairly deep, though not too deep. Federer moved around it to hit an inside-out forehand, but his bread-and-butter shot glanced off the net cord and failed to cross.

For the second straight year, Djokovic had saved two match points, this time on Federer's serve, and Federer, visibly rattled, would soon lose his serve on a double fault.

The next three games, which were also the last three games, felt rather like you were intruding on someone's private grief.

It was brutal for Federer but reaffirming for Djokovic, who celebrated after the handshake by clenching his entire body and delivering a primal scream at full flex to his team in the player's box. But Djokovic was soon back in an eerily familiar place: in front of the microphone with Mary Joe Fernández after a great escape.

"Very similar situation," Djokovic said. "I was hitting the forehand as hard as I can, and you know you're gambling. If it's out, you lost. If it's in, you maybe have a chance, so I was lucky today."

It was not quite a replay, however. This time, Djokovic danced on court at Fernández's request after getting the crowd to dance along with him.

It was all a great deal more festive than Federer's postmatch news conference, which was one of the lower-water marks of a career usually spent on the high ground.

"I didn't hit the best serve," he said of the first match point. "But it's just the way he returns that. It's just not a guy who believes much anymore in winning, and then to lose against someone like that, it's very disappointing, because you feel like he was mentally out of it already. And he just gets the lucky shot in and off you go."

He was asked if the forehand winner was a function of luck or confidence.

"Confidence? Are you kidding me? I mean, please," Federer said, rubbing his face with his hands. "Look, some players grow up and play like that. I remember losing junior matches. Just being down 5–2 in the third, and they all just start slapping shots. It all goes in for some reason, because that's kind of the way they grew up playing when they were down. I never played that way. I believe in [a] hardwork's-gonna-pay-off kinda thing, because early on maybe I didn't always work at my hardest. So, for me, this is very hard to understand how can you play a shot like that on match point. But look, maybe he's been doing it for twenty years, so for him it was very normal. You've got to ask him."

The 2011 US Open felt like *another* unguarded moment for Federer, even if there were some who agreed with him.

"Novak was tanking on that; he'd given up," Jim Courier said. "And he got the benefit of a winner when he was angry, and that's not the right way to play, and Roger takes offense at that. I'm not saying it wasn't sour grapes. I mean, Novak has the right to hit that shot. There's no rule book that says you're not allowed to do that. It's just if that were the right play, Novak would do it every time, because he's a math guy, Novak. He plays percentage tennis. That was the antithesis of that. Roger knows that. Novak knows that, and it irritates Roger."

Federer's bitter riff might have landed differently if Djokovic had not been the dominant force in men's tennis. The Serb's 2011 record was 63-2 at this stage, and he was about to win his third major of the year, beating Nadal in the final in four sets.

To suggest that Djokovic's deep reservoir of confidence had played no role in coming up with the goods under pressure seemed, to me, a lot less charitable than Djokovic's self-deprecating on-court interview.

Federer, usually clear-eyed in defeat, sounded like a sore loser, and it is worth underscoring that Djokovic did not have to swing away, eyes wide open or tightly closed, on the second match point. Federer missed his forehand before Djokovic got another chance to defy the odds.

But that Federer error was not the shot that lived on in memory, not the shot that loomed larger as Djokovic went on to break up the Federer-Nadal duopoly with help from Murray and stake his own claim to being the most successful player of the Open era. Courier simply calls it "the Return."

"When you are match points down in the fifth set after four hours of play, and you hit that forehand winner, you must be a little amazed under the circumstances that you hit that shot," Djokovic said. "You definitely don't expect yourself to come up with it. It's all mental, I think, in the end. It's all mental to be able to handle the pressure well, to be able to step in and take the chances that are presented."

Djokovic, from my point of view, is the most fascinating of the men who have hoarded the loot in this golden era in tennis. He is a bespoke, bristle-haired blend of generosity and bellicosity who seems as committed to raking his inner Zen garden as he is to ripping his own tennis shirt in two after converting match point.

The dualities and complexities can make him a tough riddle for a journalist to solve, and even if you think you have nailed it, his supporters online and elsewhere are lightning-quick to remind you that their man is misunderstood in the Western media. He is also a moving target, restlessly trying to change not only his game but himself. But the change needs to come from within. Best of luck budging him if he does not agree, as he made clear during the coronavirus pandemic by refusing to be vaccinated even after being deported from Australia in January 2022 on the eve of the Australian Open.

He had arrived in Melbourne to defend his title believing that he had been given a medical exemption from the country's vaccination requirement because he had recently contracted the coronavirus. But federal immigration officials revoked his travel visa shortly after arrival and detained him, holding him in a hotel normally used for asylum seekers and refugees while Djokovic appealed the decision (and his case became ever more a global talking point).

Though his visa was briefly reinstated, he was eventually deported on the grounds that his presence risked promoting anti-vaccine sentiment in Australia, a country that had some of the world's strictest protocols and longest lockdowns during the pandemic. But Djokovic, despite the international furor, did not back down, telling the BBC several weeks later that he was prepared to miss future tournaments and a chance at becoming the greatest men's player in history rather than accept being vaccinated. At the time, according to the men's tour, he was the only player ranked in the top 100 in singles who had not received the coronavirus vaccine.

"The principles of decision-making on my body are more important than any title or anything else," Djokovic said. "I'm trying to be in tune with my body as much as I possibly can."

Djokovic emphasized that he was not an anti-vaccine advocate and had received vaccines in his youth. Rather, he was in favor of personal choice, but the Australian fiasco and his outlier stance made him even more of a polarizing figure. Some saw him as a man of principle, prepared to pay a price for going against the grain. Others saw him as a misguided and entitled star, misusing his bully pulpit by spreading the wrong message on vaccination and global health by his example.

What is irrefutable is that he had a more traumatic childhood than Federer or Nadal. Djokovic did not come from a comfortably middle-class family or a stable European country. He grew up in Serbia in the midst of Yugoslavia's violent breakup, seeking refuge in bomb shelters between practice sessions when he was eleven and twelve years old as NATO planes attacked Belgrade between March and June 1999: a time that Serbs often refer to as "the seventy-eight days of shame."

"What doesn't kill you makes you stronger, so this is kind of the motto that Serbian people live on," Djokovic once told me. "We remember all these things and we will never forget, because it's just very strong inside of you and very deep inside of you. It's traumatic experiences, and so definitely you do have bad memories about it. We heard the alarm noise about planes coming to bomb us every single day a minimum of three times for two and a half months, huge noise in the city all the time, all the time. So in my case, when I hear a big noise even now, I get a little traumatized."

That must be difficult considering his choice of profession, where the roars of a crowd are part of the soundscape (unless a global pandemic forces the stands to remain empty). Like Federer and Nadal, Djokovic could easily have been pulled to another sport. His father, Srdjan, and his uncle Goran were competitive ski racers in the former Yugoslavia. Djokovic started skiing at age three in the Serbian mountain resort of Kopaonik, where his family ran several small seasonal businesses, including a pizzeria and art gallery, on the ground floor of a shopping complex.

"Of course, we thought Novak would be a skier because we were skiers," Goran Djokovic told me.

If not for Peter Carter in Basel, Federer might have chosen soccer. If not for Uncle Toni in Manacor, Nadal might have done the same.

Djokovic's tennis muse was a charismatic and cerebral woman in her fifties: Jelena Genčić, a former national team handball player for Yugoslavia with pale blue eyes and the sort of silken, well-measured voice that gives goose bumps to pupils (and visiting sportswriters). Genčić already had coached two future Grand Slam champions in their youth: Monica Seles and Goran Ivanišević. But Djokovic knew nothing of this at age six when he walked across the street in the summer of 1993 to the three hard courts that, in one of those coincidences that change many lives, had been built next to his family's restaurant.

Genčić was giving a tennis clinic.

"It was the first day of my first year in Kopaonik," Genčić told me when I traveled to Serbia for the *New York Times* and *International Herald Tribune* in November 2010. "And he was just standing outside the tennis courts and watching all morning, and I said: 'Hey little boy, do you like it? Do you know what this is?'"

At Genčić's invitation, Djokovic returned in the afternoon to take part himself with a neatly organized bag of equipment. He already had started to play and watched plenty of professional tournaments on satellite television, but this, in the truest sense, was where his against-the-odds tennis journey began: at the right place and right time with the right mentor.

"One racket, towel, bottle with water, one banana, a dry extra T-shirt, wrist band, and the cap," Genčić said. "I said: 'Okay, who prepared your bag? Your mother?' And oh, he was very angry. He said, 'No, *I* am playing tennis.'"

What struck her from the start was his sensitivity and how carefully he listened.

"Every word," she remembered. "A very good boy. Very intelligent. I'd say, 'Did you understand me?' And he would say, 'Yes, but please, tell me again.' He wanted to be so sure."

On the third day, Genčić reached out to Djokovic's parents, Srdjan and Dijana, and told them they had a *zlatno dete*: a golden child.

"I said the same thing about Monica Seles when she was eight," she said. "After three or four times with Monica, I told her father, Karolj, that she would be the best in the world."

Genčić, who had no children of her own, worked with Djokovic intensively for six years in Kopaonik and the Serbian capital of Belgrade and continued to advise him beyond that.

"She taught me everything," Djokovic told me. "I think it is the most important part of your tennis career, between six or seven and twelve. That is when you learn how to play tennis, when you need to learn good technique and when you need a great coach."

There are too few female coaches at the elite level of professional tennis. This needs to change, but it is important to note that Djokovic is not the only men's No. 1 to be instructed at a formative stage by a woman. Jimmy Connors, Marat Safin, and Andy Murray were all coached early and well by their mothers.

Genčić worked on every aspect of Djokovic's game and nudged him to the conclusion that a two-handed backhand was a better fit for his talents than the one-handed drive used by his idol Pete Sampras.

Genčić was rightly convinced that the future of tennis involved taking the ball early off the bounce, and Djokovic had to react and move very quickly when he played in Kopaonik, where conditions are fast with its base elevation of nearly six thousand feet.

Seles already had changed the women's game, becoming the first player able to stay tight to the baseline and attack off both wings with her powerful and often sharply angled two-handed groundstrokes.

Agassi was playing a similarly relentless style on the men's tour, and Genčić insisted that Djokovic also learn how to handle and produce pace without retreating. She emphasized net play, even though Djokovic would make his reputation on tour as a defensive wizard with phenomenal returns.

"In the early days, he played very good volleys," she said.

She also stressed the importance of stretching, advice that clearly made an impact as anyone would know who has watched Djokovic slide into a near split as he chases an opponent's shot into the corner.

"Novak was not too strong a boy," Genčić told me. "You know how he is now elastic and flexible? Do you know why? It's because I didn't want to work too hard with him."

Genčić showed me her racket, a battered Prince that no longer had a butt cap on its grip.

"This is the heaviest thing he had to handle," she said. "We only worked on his legs, his quickness, only fitness on the court, not in the weight room. We stretched and did special movements for tennis, to be flexible, to be agile, and to be fast with the legs. And now he's excellent, excellent, excellent."

If anything defines Djokovic's game to a wider audience, it is his elasticity on the move. Everything else is so solid and compact that it is easy to underappreciate.

"Novak is boringly amazing," said Brad Stine, the veteran American coach who has worked with Jim Courier, Kevin Anderson, and others.

But no other men's player could routinely contort himself like Djokovic.

"There was some sliding before Novak, but we never saw anybody that could recover from the sliding like he can and play attacking shots," said Ivanišević, the 2001 Wimbledon champion who later became Djokovic's co-coach with Marián Vajda.

Djokovic's flexibility is a talent, but it also comes from lifelong habits. Watch him between matches at a tournament, and he is always twisting his own body into some extreme position or hanging by his fingers from a doorframe.

In an interview with the *Times* of London, Djokovic's wife, Jelena, was once asked what their life was really like away from the tennis tour.

"That's easy to answer," Jelena said. "Life is about stretching. I always find him on the floor, legs all over the place."

That cracked Djokovic up, and Genčić, who died in 2013 at age seventy-six, surely would have liked that answer, too.

"She taught me and convinced me," Djokovic told me once at Wimbledon, "that if I stayed flexible, not only will I be able to move well around the court and be able to recover well after the matches, but also I'll be able to have a long career."

Todd Martin, the former American star who once coached

Djokovic, saw him work daily with his support team, including physiotherapist Miljan Amanović.

"Novak wakes up, and it's like before he has his orange juice in the morning, he puts his leg on top of Miljan's shoulder and they basically hug," Martin told me. "He stretches the hamstring before he does anything, and I'm telling you, he does it dead cold."

Coaching was Genčić's avocation, not her livelihood. She was a journalist by profession, working as an editor on arts programs for Yugoslavian and then Serbian national television. She introduced Djokovic to higher culture: Russian poetry and classical music, including Tchaikovsky's *1812 Overture*.

"I could see he thought it was wonderful," Genčić said. "I explained to him, 'When you play a match, Novak, and this is very important, when you play a match and suddenly you feel not very good, remember this music, remember how much adrenaline you have in your stomach and your body. Let this music push you to play stronger and stronger.'"

The Djokovic family had no background in tennis, but they certainly knew about Seles, an ethnic Hungarian from the Serbian city of Novi Sad who already had won eight Grand Slam singles titles and risen to No. 1 in the world after immigrating to the United States with her family.

Seles had also earned millions of dollars, and with Yugoslavia in crisis, the golden child's talent seemed worth a serious investment of time and money.

The problem was finding the money.

"I have to say that Srdjan and his wife, they were not crying, they were thinking," Genčić told me.

They borrowed from friends and poured their own meager resources into the family project. It helped that Genčić did not charge for lessons, and as president of the tennis club at Partizan Belgrade, she also arranged for Djokovic to have free equipment, including Prince rackets. But he needed international competition to progress, and funds were terribly scarce.

"Srdjan was pushing like crazy," Goran Djokovic said of his older brother. "Sometimes people don't like him, but he has the energy of a bull. It was not good times. There were sanctions, and the war was starting. It was not an easy time for Serbia, for Yugoslavia, but all the money we had we invested in Novak. He had to be the one in front of the family who had to have everything he needed: the new racket, the good food, and everything. Of course, we can live very easily if he didn't play tennis, but we had vision.

"We didn't want bad vibrations, only good energy," Goran added. "But of course people were talking sometimes, saying, 'This family is crazy, who do they think they are? How can they even think Novak will be something?'"

In 2019, when I visited Djokovic in Monte Carlo, where he now lives in luxury with Jelena and his two young children, he told me about one of the moments that shaped him during his boyhood.

His father gathered the family, including Djokovic's two younger brothers, in their rented Belgrade apartment and slammed a 10-deutsche-mark bill on the kitchen table.

Djokovic slammed his own hand on the table as he told the story.

"Ten deutsche marks was like ten dollars, and my father said, 'This is all we have,'" Djokovic said. "And he said that more than ever we have to stick together and go through this together and figure out the way. That was a very powerful and very impactful moment in my growth, my life, all of our lives."

When Djokovic was twelve, Genčić realized he had to leave Serbia to find sufficient competition and progress. She contacted an old friend, Nikola "Niki" Pilić, a former Yugoslavian star from Croatia who had reached the 1973 French Open final and whose dispute with his national federation led to the men's boycott of Wimbledon later that year.

Pilić now ran a tennis academy in Germany near Munich. Genčić convinced him to take Djokovic despite the academy's policy of not accepting players under age fourteen.

Djokovic traveled with his uncle Goran to Munich. With the restrictions in Serbia, they had to cross the border, leave their car at the airport in Skopje, now the capital of North Macedonia, and fly to Germany. But his uncle soon returned to Serbia, leaving Djokovic for three months in a place where he did not speak the language.

When he left home at fourteen, Federer, at least, could take the train home to Basel on weekends.

"Everything affects your mentality, your psychological strength," Djokovic told me. "I was already by myself for three months when I was twelve and a half, so I had to be responsible. I had to be brave enough to be by myself and push hard, and that's what I did. I learned how to be independent."

Djokovic would spend several years based at Pilić's academy, part of a wave of phenomenal Serbian players who had to leave their country to break through, including future women's No. 1s Ana Ivanovic and Jelena Jankovic.

"Novak really matured very early," said Ivan Ljubičić, the Croatian star who later trained with Djokovic under Italian coach Riccardo Piatti. "Novak knows what he wants. He knows how to get it, and it's nice to have this, but all these top guys—Rafa, Roger—have that. Either you struggle big-time and kind of get lost or are forced to learn fast, and they did."

But Djokovic lacked a similar safety net to the stars who would turn out to be his rivals. More than Federer or Nadal, he *needed* to make it after all his family had sacrificed, and though Genčić had predicted that Djokovic would be in the top five by age seventeen, it took a bit longer.

"We missed by two years, because we didn't have the money to achieve all that I wanted," she told me.

He did make his Grand Slam debut at seventeen, qualifying at the 2005 Australian Open and facing Marat Safin in the first round in Rod Laver Arena.

Safin won 6–0, 6–2, 6–1 and went on to win the title.

"I was [No.] four in the world, and the guy just passed the qualies, so what do you expect?" Safin told me. "I was playing well. I was coming to win the tournament. He was coming to see what happened. But look how it turned out for him, so he should pay for a couple of dinners for me!"

Djokovic, despite a stubborn streak, is a quick study, and though Federer gets deserved credit for being multilingual, Djokovic is a higher level of polyglot. He speaks four languages fluently (Serbian, German, Italian, and English) and others proficiently (French, Spanish, and even some Russian).

He learned pro tennis quickly, too. By the end of 2005, he was in the top 100. By the end of 2006, he was in the top 20, and by the end of 2007 he was No. 3 behind Federer and Nadal, both of whom he beat to win the ATP Masters 1000 event in Montreal, Canada.

He was twenty years old and about to become a Grand Slam champion, winning the 2008 Australian Open after defeating Federer again, this time in straight sets in the semifinals.

"The King is dead, long live the King," Djokovic's mother proclaimed.

That was premature, as it turned out. Federer, diminished by mononucleosis at that stage, would return to the top in 2009. Nadal had a resurgent 2010.

Djokovic did not reach No. 1 until he won Wimbledon in 2011, defeating Nadal in the final.

"For four years it was Roger, Rafa, Rafa, Roger," Dijana said. "Now it's Novak, Novak, Novak, Novak."

She had a point by then. Her son would go 4-1 against Federer in 2011 and 6-0 against Nadal (on three different surfaces, including clay). But it was hard to imagine Lynette Federer thinking, much less saying, a similar thing about her son in his days of dominance. The Djokovic clan was decidedly more confrontational, an approach that often did their son no favors in the image-making game.

Dijana was practically a UN peacekeeper compared with her husband. Srdjan once said of Federer that he was "perhaps still the best tennis player in history but as a man he's the opposite" and later mocked him for continuing to play with his fortieth birthday approaching.

"Since both Nadal and Novak are breathing down his neck, he simply cannot accept the fact that they will be better than him," Srdjan told the Serbian outlet Sport Klub. "Go, man, raise children, do something else, go ski, do something."

Clearly Srdjan did not forget or forgive Federer for telling him and others in Djokovic's box to keep quiet during the Monte Carlo Open in 2008.

If all this seems petty, that is because it is petty, and Federer has not responded in kind. But the Djokovics' combativeness also comes from parental protectiveness: the fierce belief that their son deserves more respect, like their beleaguered country.

For the Djokovics, who are Orthodox Christians, there is a big hint of the divine in Novak's rise.

Though Robert Federer has certainly worn plenty of RF caps, he has never worn a T-shirt bearing his beloved son's likeness in the stands, as Srdjan and Dijana did when Djokovic faced Federer at the 2010 US Open. Later that year, when I visited Srdjan's office in Belgrade, I spotted a religious painting on the wall of the late patriarch Pavle, head of the Serbian Orthodox church, with Novak's glowing face painted below, making him, literally, a sports icon.

"In the worst moment for the Serbian people he was sent by God to show that we are a normal people and not murderers and savages," Srdjan said of Novak in a 2021 interview in Serbia.

Novak long felt the frustration of being reflexively viewed as an outcast because he was Serbian. He mentioned this often in our early interviews, but his exploration in 2006 of representing Britain instead of Serbia was driven by economics and the desire to get more support. Ultimately, he decided against it.

"I never had the professional conditions to succeed and develop as a professional player *in* my country," he explained to me, referring to his need to train in Munich and elsewhere.

"So that's why there were options to go somewhere else and just try to help myself and my family so we can live better," he said. "But I think we made a great decision, and we stayed like this. It's much different if you stay with your people, your religion. For me, when you come back home it feels much different. It feels like you belong there."

Though based in the tiny tax haven of Monaco, he has come to embody the embattled Serbian nation and is a much feistier ambassador than Federer, the world's most recognizable Swiss.

Serbia became an international pariah during Yugoslavia's implosion under leader Slobodan Milošević. The country's size and clout shrank steadily.

It became landlocked when Montenegro, a region where the Djokovic family had roots, declared independence. Kosovo also broke away, and Kosovo is where Srdjan and his siblings were born.

"A Serbian from Montenegro born in Kosovo, that is a special kind of temperament," Genčić told me. "The Djokovics are very strong people."

The NATO bombings in 1999 that had such an impact on Djokovic were the response to a Serbian crackdown on Albanian separatists in Kosovo, where the vast majority of the population is ethnic Albanian.

The breakaway province declared formal independence in 2008 with the support of Western powers like the United States and Germany, but Serbia and scores of other nations continue not to recognize it as a sovereign state.

The issue remains deeply sensitive to the Djokovics, and Novak has expressed his opposition to Kosovo's independence.

"I've read the history books, and I remember what I've been taught," Djokovic once told me. "It's part of my country and part of my family."

Such open involvement in politics is another difference with Federer, who is, in some respects, a natural politician. He has an ability to both read the room and connect with the room and to make his interlocutor feel as if they are at the center of his universe, be it a tournament director or a courtesy car driver.

Federer wears his privilege lightly and has carefully avoided political commentary throughout his career. He has restricted his lobbying to inside-tennis issues such as his recent support for a potential merger of the men's and women's tours and his long-standing opposition to in-match coaching.

In that sense, he is a champion whose discretion was better suited to the early twenty-first century than to the 2020s, where it is fast becoming the norm for athletes to use their platforms to weigh in on everything from racism to sexism to climate change. Federer has faced some criticism and small-scale protests from activists who have called out Credit Suisse, one of his sponsors, for its ties to investments in fossil fuels. The protesters used the hashtag #RogerWakeUpNow on social media, with one of their posts being shared by prominent climate activist Greta Thunberg.

Federer released a statement in response in early 2020:

As the father of four young children and a fervent supporter of universal education, I have a great deal of respect and admiration for the youth climate movement, and I am grateful to young climate activists for pushing us all to examine our behaviours and act on innovative solutions. We owe it to them and ourselves to listen. I appreciate reminders of my responsibility as a private individual, as an athlete and as an entrepreneur, and I'm committed to using this privileged position to dialogue on important issues with my sponsors.

Sponsors once shied away from athlete advocacy, but now they often celebrate it, as they did with Naomi Osaka in 2020 after she won the US Open while protesting racial injustice and police violence.

Djokovic, long a more outspoken figure than Federer, was perhaps ahead of the curve, although his views on the coronavirus vaccination, which he long resisted expressing publicly, certainly did not broaden his fan base.

In the piece I wrote after interviewing Djokovic in 2019, I categorized Nadal as the fighter, Federer as the pleaser, and Djokovic as the searcher. He is restless, constantly looking for better methods and fresh influences, and that no doubt helped him break down the formidable barriers to entry into the top tier of men's tennis.

"Federer and Nadal have inspired me to get the best out of myself and my tennis," he once told me.

When Federer emerged, the best players of the previous generation—Agassi and Sampras—were aging or in decline. But Djokovic arrived in the midst of Federer's and Nadal's prime times. He became their rival and often their better: holding a career edge over both players, including an even bigger edge in the Grand Slam matches, which, more than ever, define players' reputations and legacies.

"When I play Rafa, I feel it's on my racket more; if I want to shorten the point, I can do that," Federer once told me. "Against Novak, it's different. He hits so hard and flat and deep into the court, so you can't just say, 'Okay, I'm going to go for broke,' because he actually hand-cuffs you. So you have to be willing to go for tougher rallies."

Djokovic has certainly ruined plenty of Federer's afternoons and evenings: beating him in the Wimbledon finals of 2014, 2015, and, most painfully, 2019 after Federer held—strange but true—two more match points.

Federer versus Nadal has been the contemporary rivalry that attracted the most attention inside and outside tennis, but Djokovic versus Nadal has been the most contested, with Djokovic versus Federer close behind.

From my perspective, the Djokovic-Federer duels have an edge that the other Big Three rivalries lack. Federer and Nadal have, after all, become friends and ATP allies. Federer and Djokovic remain coworkers who want the same promotion. There have never been shouts or shoves in the locker room. It is simply a feeling that comes through when you watch them square off across the net, and it is perhaps that underlying tension that makes Federer press when he needs a point rather than letting the inspiration flow.

Nadal was certainly more deferential to Federer in his early years, even as he was beating him regularly. Djokovic pushed the envelope, doing great impressions of other players' styles that pleased the crowd but amused his rivals much less. He also earned an early reputa-tion among his peers for gamesmanship, with frequent injury time-outs and off-court breaks that, justly or not, were often perceived as attempts to break his opponents' rhythm.

To be fair to Djokovic, his breathing problems were real, and he underwent multiple surgeries for a deviated septum before changing to a gluten-free diet in 2011. He solved his endurance issues long ago and has also been one of the players who most frequently applaud their opponents' brilliant shots. But he and Federer, despite regular contact off the court through the ATP Player Council, have never been genuinely close.

"I think for Roger there's more baggage with Novak than there is with Rafa," Paul Annacone told me. "I honestly haven't talked to Roger ever about that, really. He's never said to me that Novak is a jerk, but maybe that's the thing, though; maybe that little extra tension makes Roger actually want it too much against Novak."

If Federer chooses to attack it is a fine contrast in style: Federer's underrated serve versus Djokovic's peerless returns; Federer's volleys versus Djokovic's precision passing shots; Federer's drop shots in the forecourt versus Djokovic's speed.

Unlike Nadal, Djokovic is a right-hander without extreme topspin. He cannot consistently get the ball high to Federer's one-handed backhand. If both stay on the baseline, it is strength against strength: Federer's inside-out forehand against Djokovic's elastic backhand, Federer's variety against Djokovic's mobility. Neither likes to give ground, and both can maintain phenomenal timing off the short bounce, which means the court must feel cramped to both of them.

"I think Novak is the only guy who can stay with Roger toe-to-toe from the backcourt on any surface," Pete Sampras told me. "He can take Roger's punches because he moves so well, and if Novak gets those shots back, Roger can panic a little bit, and say, 'Well, what do I do now?'"

Facing Djokovic can feel like playing against the wall or something more contemporary. Take it from Ivanišević, who coached against Djokovic before he coached Djokovic.

"When Novak is at his best, it's like playing a video game where you can't fucking win," Ivanišević told me. "Everything comes back. You know, like in *The Terminator* where that liquid guy keeps getting killed and coming back again and again. You can't win points, so it's hard to know what to tell a player to do. Just play, I guess. Just play and pray."

Federer has had his moments against Djokovic since that tweener in New York. The French Open semifinal victory in 2011 was, for me, one of the finest performances of his career: a razor-sharp recital of attacking baseline tennis on clay that began at full throttle with a seventy-minute opening set won by Federer in a tiebreaker.

It was fast-twitch tennis—*L'Équipe* called it "ping-pong tennis"— on what was supposed to be the game's slowest surface, but the tournament was not so slow that year with a new Babolat ball and dry conditions throughout the event. Federer and Djokovic kept taking time away from each other and still finding ways to beat the clock. I watched much of it from courtside, and it was the sport at its finest: precise, bold, resourceful, acrobatic, and intense.

With the Roland Garros crowd urging him on, Federer varied spins with his backhand, rarely missed the target with his forehand, and hit clutch serves by the bunch, including the ace that finished off the match in the fourth-set tiebreaker at 9:38 p.m. with darkness falling.

"I just hoped it was going to end that night because otherwise it would have been a crapshoot the next day," Federer told me. "I felt really good on the court and actually really calm."

If he had maintained that level and mood, he would likely have beaten Nadal in the final, too. Nadal, the king of clay, was shaky on his throne that year. But Federer's revolt fell short again as he lost in four sets after losing the first set despite a 5–2 lead.

"I thought Roger should have won the French that year," Annacone told me. "Other than the shock of having match points in the semis of the US Open against Novak, that loss was the most painful for me as a coach, because I felt I didn't do a good enough job getting Roger to believe before that final. I felt Rafa was vulnerable at that point."

Federer's brilliant victory over Djokovic in the 2012 Wimbledon semifinals did not lead to disappointment, however. Federer followed up by beating Andy Murray to win his seventeenth Grand Slam singles title, watching with empathy as Murray cried during the awards ceremony.

But for the rest of the decade, Federer failed to beat Djokovic at a major. Federer's eight victories during that span all came in best-of-three-set matches, two of them in round-robin play at the ATP Finals.

They would face off just once more at the US Open. That was in the 2015 final, where it was louder and clearer than ever that Federer was the crowd darling.

"More or less anywhere I play against Roger, it's the same," Djokovic said. "So it's just like that. I have to accept it. I have to work and earn a majority of the support maybe one day."

That comment was made after the Wimbledon final earlier in the summer that Djokovic won in four sets: a sign of what was to come in New York.

Nadal had faded that year. Djokovic was the clear No. 1, Federer the clear No. 2. Djokovic was the new market leader when it came to major-to-major consistency, but at that stage he had just one US Open title to Federer's five.

Federer had won twenty-eight straight sets coming into the final and truly believed in his chances. Djokovic prepared by watching *300* on the eve of the final, the graphically violent tale of outnumbered Spartan warriors fighting ferociously if fruitlessly against great odds.

Gerard Butler, the film's star, was a friend and in Novak's box for the final. Djokovic fared better than the Spartans, but he, too, was outnumbered with a well-lubricated New York crowd cheering his missed first serves and unforced errors with gusto and chanting "Roger" as if Federer were an all-American champion instead of a Swiss neutral.

Federer was remarkable at age thirty-four, but Djokovic was, again, better at twenty-eight.

I once asked Djokovic how playing Federer was different from playing his other main rivals like Nadal and Murray.

"Roger is the most unpredictable of all of them; he has so much talent and can play any shot," Djokovic said. "I think the worst thing for any tennis player or any athlete to deal with is unpredictability, not knowing what is coming next. That is what Roger possesses, that variety in his game, and so that is what plays with your mind. What is coming next?"

Djokovic talked about Federer's so-called "SABR" (Sneak Attack by Roger), in which he moved unusually close to the service box to hit a half-volley return.

"Will he do his SABR thing?" Djokovic said. "Will he come to net? Will he stay back? Will he chip it? Will he hit it? It keeps you guessing all the time, and that is why it's so tough to play Roger."

Federer did shuffle his cards, attacking the net regularly this time as he channeled the counsel of his co-coach Stefan Edberg, who had come on board after Federer's amicable split with Annacone in late 2013. But Djokovic had become the game's supreme shock absorber and a fine shape-shifter as well. The tactics that work in the first set against him are probably not going to work in the fourth. He, too, could be unpredictable.

Federer's last opportunities to force a fifth set came when he had three break points as Djokovic served for the title at 5–4. But Djokovic saved all three and, crucially, saved nineteen of the twenty-three break points he faced that night.

"You have to find the right dose of risk," Federer said. "Sometimes I did it well and other times not as well."

Djokovic's 6–4, 5–7, 6–4, 6–4 victory put him in double digits with ten Grand Slam singles titles and left Federer, the all-time men's leader, stuck at seventeen.

The result also tied Djokovic's and Federer's head-to-head series at 21-21 before Djokovic took the lead, most likely for good, in the years ahead.

Federer was left with regrets but also the memory of all those chants and cheers far from home.

"It's definitely one of the reasons I keep playing: these goose-bump moments," Federer said. "It's a great consolation for me to receive this kind of support in a country that is a long way from Switzerland and is one of the countries that is the most powerful in sports in general. They love winners here."

Djokovic certainly had grounds for disagreement, and the next morning when we met for a postvictory interview, he explained one of his coping mechanisms.

"What I was actually doing was trying to play a mind game with myself," he said as we rode in a van through the streets of Midtown. "They would scream, 'Roger!' and I would imagine they were screaming, 'Novak!'"

That was quite a confession—poignant and, in the literal sense of the term, pathetic. But Djokovic seemed resigned for now to his lot: a great champion beloved in Serbia but not necessarily beyond.

"I go through a lot of emotions on the court, like anybody else," Djokovic said. "I just think, over the time, I've managed to learn how to use the experience and how to handle and cope with this pressure in tough moments. But I also think a lot comes from my character and from the fact that I grew up in circumstances which were not very ordinary and maybe not the circumstances that most of the guys grew up in. They have shaped me and my character, and those memories give me that bit of strength that I use in occasions like the one last night."

Djokovic's voice was hoarse, his hedgehog hair a bit out of place. He had scrapes on his right wrist and arm from a fall he had taken early in the final. But we were out of the van now and walking quickly in Central Park, heading toward a photo shoot. Djokovic, who usually stayed in New Jersey during the Open at his friend Gordon Uehling's estate, had decided to stay in a Manhattan hotel with his family this year.

"One of my close friends said, which I think is right, that this city has so much energy going on that if you stay in the city for a certain amount of time, it gives you a lot of energy," Djokovic said. "But if you stay for too long, it can take your energy."

I asked him if the city had given him the energy he needed to prevail this year.

"It did, but I feel like from today, it's starting to take it away," he said. "So I need to slowly go back home."

We were approaching our destination, and I had time for one more question. So I asked him: What would it take for a Grand Slam crowd to support him the way it had supported Federer in New York?

Djokovic considered that for a moment and then answered at length. He is more a man of paragraphs than a man of sentences.

"Honestly, I think, first of all, it's about enduring," he said. "True tennis fans respect somebody that shows commitment to the sport—not just shows results, but shows his passion for tennis and respects them, the tournaments, the opponents, and the sport in general. I think it's also about what you represent. Are you respecting the true life's values, and are you a man of conscience that plays tennis but also gives back?

"I think the whole package is important. That's what I try to do. It's how I've been brought up, and I hope the crowd recognizes that. But in the circumstances, when I'm playing against Roger at this point, I cannot expect something else."

Djokovic shook hands and said farewell.

"To your stage," I said, pointing to the rocks overlooking Wollman Rink.

Djokovic stepped up, the Midtown skyline behind him and a phalanx of photographers in front of him. The US Open trophy was soon back in his hands and still out of Federer's.

CHAPTER THIRTEEN

LILLE, France

The 2014 Davis Cup final was forty-eight hours away and Roger Federer, for a change, looked much older than his years as he gingerly hit tennis balls on the indoor clay.

He did not slide on the gritty red surface that had been installed in Pierre Mauroy Stadium. He did not bend low for volleys and certainly did not lunge into the corners during his brief and halting Wednesday practice session.

Switzerland's long-awaited, first-ever Davis Cup title was in reach, and Federer was racing the clock at half speed, trying to recover from a back injury before play began on Friday against the French.

His teammates were counting on him, and they were much more than teammates. The four-man Swiss squad included Marco Chiudinelli, Federer's boyhood friend from Basel; and Michael Lammer, his friend and former housemate in Biel. The team captain was Severin Lüthi, Federer's longtime personal coach and confidant, who traveled with him year-round and knew his game better than anyone by this stage.

There was also Stan Wawrinka, the powerful Swiss star whom Federer had mentored and who had bloomed relatively late into one of the finest players in the world, winning his first Grand Slam title at the Australian Open earlier in the season at age twenty-eight.

Federer has spent most of his long career chasing individual honors, prioritizing his schedule and his needs. Winning the Davis Cup, still the most prestigious team event in the sport, was certainly one of

Federer's personal goals: a chance to fill one of the last gaps on his tennis résumé. But the week in France was above all about the collective interest, about finishing off a task they all had started long ago.

"I know I'll never have as cool a team as this one," Federer told me.

He had played in the Davis Cup before he played in any of the Grand Slam tournaments, before he played in Monte Carlo, Rome, Indian Wells, or most of the other more prestigious tour events.

He was just seventeen when he made his Davis Cup debut at home against Italy in April 1999 on a quick indoor court in Neuchâtel. With a backward cap covering his bleached-blond hair, Federer played with precocious aplomb, no sure thing in the early days. In the first best-of-five-set match of his career, he defeated Italian veteran Davide Sanguinetti 6–4, 6–7 (3), 6–4, 6–4.

"I thought I would have a hard time with Roger on court," the former Swiss captain Claudio Mezzadri recalled as we watched Federer practice for the final in France. "Roger had no experience in best-of-five or Davis Cup or with a large crowd, and I was very surprised because he was just cool and relaxed and played a beautiful match. As the captain, I really only had to say a few words to him. And when he came off the court, he was telling me all the feelings he experienced: 'This is what it's like to hear three thousand or four thousand people cheering,' things like that. It was like he was recording it all in his mind and then playing it back for me."

Switzerland went on to beat Italy and then lost to Belgium in the quarterfinals in April as Federer was beaten in both of his singles matches. He lost the first in five sets to Christophe Van Garsse, a talented player who never made a big impact on tour but was often inspired in the Davis Cup. He lost the decisive match in four sets to Xavier Malisse.

Those were emotional defeats, but Federer now understood firsthand the power of the Davis Cup: how it magnified each match and allowed a journeyman like Van Garsse to suddenly take center stage.

Federer played every round for Switzerland in his youth and even led an open revolt in 2001 against Jakob Hlasek, then the Swiss captain, that made it clear Federer was not shy about leveraging his newfound star power. But when Federer became entrenched at the top of the game, he began skipping the opening round of the Davis Cup to manage his schedule.

Without him, Switzerland was unable to prevail and progress.

Federer routinely reemerged in September after the US Open to play in the relegation round and attempt to save Switzerland from being sent down to the Davis Cup's equivalent of the second division. It usually worked, although the Swiss did get relegated twice.

Still, it was a strange and unsatisfying state of affairs. Federer was playing the Davis Cup nearly every year, but not when it mattered most.

"It's been hard for me not to do it," he told me in 2010. "I wish just once in these last six years we would have won the first round without me, and I had a chance to step in again in the quarters or something. But it never happened, so it's been unfortunate. But I think the day will come that I'll want to play with the guys because they are all best friends of mine. For me it's heartbreaking to take that decision, but I can't chase all my dreams at once, so some have to wait."

Even when he did fully commit, it still went awry. In 2012, the Swiss hosted the United States at full strength on indoor clay in Fribourg in the first round. On the opening day, Mardy Fish upset Wawrinka by winning 9–7 in the fifth set, and John Isner upset Federer in four sets.

Federer, who usually treated the sensitive Wawrinka with great care, was in a straight-talking mood and chose to criticize Wawrinka's performance against Fish rather than focus on his own defeat.

"Above all, it's too bad that Stan could not put pressure on them by beating Fish the first day," he said. "It was really close and that could have changed everything. Because after that, against Isner, we knew that anything could happen."

In Federer's view, Wawrinka "did not play very well," and he struck a similar tone after they lost the doubles together. "I played a good doubles; Stan was not bad but was often in trouble on his serve," Federer said.

It was Federer's undiplomatic side on display. He might have been correct, but he was certainly not the ideal messenger. When we spoke later in the season, he made it clear that he regretted it.

"Some press conferences you can't go and say exactly what you think just because it just doesn't work; it's not good for everyone," he said. "I said Stan unfortunately didn't play his best, and the next thing it's 'Federer criticizes Stan.' I was like, 'Come on. Are you serious?' I lost two matches, and he lost, okay, two matches, but I'm the number one on the team. It's my mistake, not his. So, you kind of learn, and you're like, instead of saying, 'Hmmm, he didn't play so great,' you just say, you know, 'I played like shit.'"

Federer chuckled at that and shook his head, but there was not much Swiss laughter in Fribourg as the Americans won 5–0.

"Everything was set up and then suddenly we lost in the first round, so that was quite a big letdown," Lammer told me. "That really reminded us how difficult the road was."

Federer skipped the Davis Cup altogether in 2013, and Wawrinka, Chiudinelli, and Lammer kept Switzerland in the World Group without him by beating Ecuador in Neuchâtel.

"The feeling was 'Let's save it again' because everybody still had the dream to hold the trophy," Lammer said. "Everybody knew Roger's situation. It was not like, 'Come on, you have to do this!' He had so many goals. It was difficult for him to make those choices. I think everybody knew he wanted to play, but we didn't want to put pressure, not at all."

By 2014, Federer was ready to try again, even if he did not make that clear until the last minute, deciding to travel to Serbia for Switzerland's first-round match in February after indicating that he likely would not play.

That seemed a wise approach: underpromise, then overdeliver. He and Wawrinka arrived together in Novi Sad, where former women's No. 1 Monica Seles grew up, and led the Swiss to victory.

But Serbia's biggest star was not there to resist them. Novak Djokovic decided to skip the round, underscoring the challenges facing the Davis Cup. The top players did not commit consistently, and too many great opportunities and matchups were missed. In this golden era for men's tennis, defined by great and long-running rivalries, the rivals hardly played at all in the Davis Cup, which was certainly one of the reasons the venerable event continued to lose traction.

Federer and Nadal never played each other in the Cup before it changed format in 2019. Federer and Djokovic faced off just once, and that was in 2006 before Djokovic became a full-blown threat.

All of the major players would win the trophy at least once, including Andy Murray with Britain. They just did not have to beat each other to do it.

The stars all recognized the Cup's history and its importance in building interest for tennis in their countries. Nadal and Djokovic had used their victories as springboards to greater individual success: Djokovic's 2010 title run with Serbia had set the table for his feast of a 2011 season. But with the Davis Cup's four rounds spaced out throughout the year, all the leading players were also convinced that committing to the full schedule each year was too much of a drain.

"Especially if you see the amount of tennis we play in all those other places from January to November," Federer told me. "I always said if you play a Davis Cup tie it's probably going to cost you a Masters 1000."

They pushed for changes, and Federer, a longtime president of the ATP Player Council, ultimately lost patience with the president of the International Tennis Federation, Francesco Ricci Bitti, who ran the Davis Cup. Federer once angrily dressed him down in a meeting at Wimbledon, extraordinary for a champion who so rarely got angry.

"Roger chewed him out in front of all of us about Davis Cup: what they had done, the lack of listening, pretending to listen, not changing," said Justin Gimelstob, an ATP board member at the time. "Roger called him on all of it. It was a master class."

Ricci Bitti, a cosmopolitan Italian, did approve some minor changes during his tenure, but with Davis Cup revenue vital to the International Tennis Federation, he refused to consider abandoning the annual model or even granting the finalists a first-round bye the following year.

The result of all this tension was ambivalence. Federer cared about the event, perhaps more deeply than he would have liked, but he also felt burdened by it.

The 2014 season was his chance to finally shed the weight. Winning the Davis Cup with one great player was daunting, usually requiring that player to win both best-of-five-set singles matches and a doubles match in each round over three days. But with two great players, the odds improved significantly, and by 2014, Wawrinka was undeniably a great player, too.

When the Swiss arrived in France, Federer was ranked No. 2 in the world and Wawrinka No. 4. But the question was not simply whether Federer could heal in time for the final; it was whether Federer and Wawrinka could heal their relationship.

It had taken some lumps the week before in the World Tour Finals in London when they played in the semifinals. Federer saved four match points before winning 4–6, 7–5, 7–6 (6). Federer aggravated his chronic back problems late in the match and ended up defaulting from the final against Djokovic the following day.

"I really don't understand how it happened," Federer told me. "A step here or there. Maybe the back was tired or the body, or it was those tense moments in the breaker. It was really unlucky."

But there was another problem. Mirka Federer had been watching and cheering from courtside during the semifinal, and late in the third set, Wawrinka had expressed displeasure with her making noise between the first and second serves. Mirka responded by calling him a "crybaby."

"Did you hear what she said?" Wawrinka said to Federer and chair umpire Cédric Mourier.

Wawrinka also complained to Mourier.

"She did the same thing at Wimbledon," he said, referring to Federer's quarterfinal victory earlier in the year. "Every time I'm on her side of the court, she shouts just before I serve."

The exchange would have made waves at any stage given Federer's prominence and pristine reputation, but it happened in London, a global media hotspot, with Federer and Wawrinka about to team up in pursuit of the Davis Cup. Cédric Mourier, the French chair umpire, even broke protocol by giving an interview about the incident to a French news outlet.

"It just flared up big-time," Federer told me later. "And then I saw Stan, and I saw Mirka, and I was in the middle of it, and I didn't even see what happened. It was just a heat-of-the-moment thing, and it blew over superfast and rightfully so because Mirka is only there to support me and not to distract him, and I think he knows that, too."

Federer and Wawrinka talked at length in a private room at the O2 Arena after the match. Lüthi, who has also advised Wawrinka over the years, was part of the discussion.

They succeeded in finding common ground.

"The last thing Mirka wants is to be, like, angry with my opponent," Federer said. "She's never done that in fifteen years and is not going to start now, especially against Stan."

But six years later when Wawrinka was asked to identify the biggest regret of his career, he said that it was "by far" the loss to Federer in London. He made no mention of Mirka's heckling.

"It was the semifinal of the Masters, the most prestigious tournament after the Grand Slams, which only brings together the best eight players in the world," he told the Swiss magazine *L'Illustré*. "I let my chance slip away. That was really, really tough. The night after, I hardly slept. I mulled it over a lot and talked with people close to me to work through it. What saved me was that I had to come together with the Swiss team for the Davis Cup final."

On Sunday, he caught the Eurostar train with Lüthi and the Swiss team's latest recruit: David Macpherson, the longtime coach of the American doubles stars Bob and Mike Bryan.

Lüthi and Macpherson were friendly, and Lüthi had sought some advice during the World Tour Finals about the upcoming Davis Cup doubles match against the French. Mike Bryan was involved, too.

"We were giving Sevi ideas, and Mikey just quipped, 'Why don't you take Mac to Lille?'" Macpherson told me. "I don't know if he was really being serious, but Sevi was like, 'Uh, is that possible?' And I said, 'Well, of course, if Roger would want that, how could I say no to that?'"

Federer liked the plan. He and Wawrinka had won the 2008 Olympic gold medal in doubles together in Beijing—a highlight of both their careers—but had lost their last four Davis Cup matches together. Something was missing.

Because of his back injury, Federer traveled to Lille after the rest of the Swiss team. But there was no sign of trouble between Wawrinka and Federer upon arrival. "We just looked at each other with a smile that said everything," Wawrinka said. "The chapter was closed."

"There was no tension in the room," Macpherson said. "It was just a nice little family team atmosphere."

After the first team dinner, Macpherson accepted Federer's invitation to his room to talk over the doubles.

"Just the two of us, and I reckon we were probably in his room ninety minutes," Macpherson said. "I was amazed at how thorough he was about wanting to delve into doubles and what he could do better as a doubles player. He's a student of the game, and this, for one of the few times in his career, was a very important doubles match. You could tell he didn't want to leave any stone unturned."

Macpherson later put together notes and video clips on their potential French opponents and compiled highlights of Federer's and Wawrinka's gold-medal run in Beijing, including their victory over the Bryans in the semifinals. He included footage of Federer's and Wawrinka's recent struggles.

Every night, Macpherson would meet with the team to spend twenty minutes talking about doubles. It was detailed advice, but the main conclusions were that Wawrinka needed to hit through his backhand returns instead of chipping and that the net player needed to be much more active and aggressive during Federer's and Wawrinka's service games.

All of this would have been in vain if Federer had been unable to play. Some were encouraging him to take a painkilling injection. When would he get another chance to win the Davis Cup?

"I was not far off," he told me. "I was just praying I didn't have to take it, and in the end I didn't have to, which I was very relieved about."

At that stage, Federer had never had surgery, never taken a cortisone shot.

"I believe you need to let your body heal and rest," he told me. "I'm too scared anyway of all medication and shots."

But getting on the court did not mean Federer would thrive on the court. The French players were well behind second-ranked Federer and fourth-ranked Wawrinka in the rankings at that stage, but Gaël Monfils, Jo-Wilfried Tsonga, and Richard Gasquet all had been in the top 10 quite recently. Amusingly, all of the players on the French team were domiciled in Switzerland for tax reasons, which led to jokes about this being an all-Swiss Davis Cup final.

Unlike Federer and Wawrinka, the French had been able to train on clay for weeks specifically for the final. They also had a big home court advantage with a sellout crowd each day in Lille.

I have been attending Davis Cup matches since the 1980s. I have covered everything from star-filled finals to the lowest rung on the ladder: a Group Four Euro/African zone match in Gaborone, Botswana, involving nations as disparate as Iceland, Sudan, and Madagascar, none of whose players had a single ATP point.

"For me it's too late for Wimbledon but at least I got one of my dreams," said Harivony Andrianafetra, a twenty-seven-year-old from Madagascar, when we spoke in Gaborone in 1997.

Some of my best experiences as a sportswriter have come at the Davis Cup; some of the loudest, too.

At the highest level, the atmosphere under the old format was similar to a World Cup soccer match except that a day of Davis Cup singles could last more than eight hours, leaving the players and spectators drained.

There was 1991 in Lyon, where the French surprised Pete Sampras, Andre Agassi, and the Americans and celebrated by dancing in a conga line behind their charismatic captain, Yannick Noah. There was 1995 in Moscow, where Sampras produced one of the great and most undervalued achievements of his career to beat the Russians on his worst surface (clay) and practically on his own. There was 2008 in Mar del Plata, Argentina, where a Spanish team lacking the injured Nadal upset David Nalbandian, Juan Martin del Potro, and the Argentines on the road.

And there was 2014 in the suburbs of Lille, where the crowd of 27,432 on opening day for France versus Switzerland set a new record for an officially sanctioned tennis match, just ahead of the 27,200 who watched each day as Nadal and Spain won the Davis Cup in 2004 in Seville.

Wawrinka did not give the French fans much to celebrate in the first singles duel, defeating Tsonga 6–1, 3–6, 6–3, 6–2. But in the second singles, Monfils cranked up his game and the volume, outclassing Federer 6–1, 6–4, 6–3 with one of his finest, most focused performances.

That made it 1-1 with three matches remaining: the doubles on Saturday and the reverse singles on Sunday. The question was whether Federer could or should play the doubles after his performance against Monfils. Lammer and Chiudinelli were ready and had worked with Macpherson all week, but both lacked experience under this kind of pressure and were ranked well below any of the French players.

Federer answered the question himself shortly after coming off court after losing to Monfils.

"I'm ready to go," he announced to Lüthi and Macpherson after consulting with Wawrinka.

"It was quite inspiring to hear that," Macpherson said. "Roger's confidence was not shaken in any way."

Though Monfils had clearly bothered Federer, the back had not. He was reassured and optimistic even after a straight-set loss. "As the match went on, I just started to loosen up," Federer said. "I guess I needed to hit thirty big serves. I needed to slide. I needed to be on defense. I needed to play offensive tennis, get information quickly."

He and Wawrinka came out the next day and played aggressively and brilliantly, defeating Gasquet and Julien Benneteau 6–3, 7–5, 6–4. It was a flashback to the Olympic performance in Beijing and an indication that they were indeed on the same wavelength despite all the static in London.

It has surely been a challenge for Wawrinka to make his way in tennis in Federer's shadow. It was akin to Andy Roddick following Sampras, Agassi, and Courier in the United States except that Federer, being Swiss, was a big fish in a very small pond.

But Wawrinka, who was sixteen when he first practiced with Federer, has long been quick to acknowledge that he benefited from Federer's example, encouragement, and even his scouting reports on opponents in the early years.

Federer, despite his comments in Fribourg, has been supportive of Wawrinka, who is four years younger and arrived on tour when Federer already was No. 1. Perhaps most important, Federer agreed to share the services of Pierre Paganini, his highly valued fitness trainer, with Wawrinka.

"Roger was like a big brother for me on the tour," Wawrinka told *L'Illustré*.

Wawrinka was asked what Federer's most precious advice had been.

"The importance of living in the moment," Wawrinka said. "For twenty years, he's had to deal with the daily demands of the press, the fans, the travel, the tournaments, and training. His days are ultra-full, and yet he remains amazingly calm. Even when he has to do something that he enjoys less, he does it to the max, better than anyone. Over the years, I've also tried to get closer to that."

It helps that Federer knows himself well and commits only when prepared to give his utmost. He said no to the Davis Cup many times. But in 2014 he had signed on for the full experience, and though his back was not cooperating, he gritted his teeth in Lille, just as he has so often around the world. From his debut on tour through the 2020 season, he never once retired from a match, which might be his most mind-boggling tennis achievement. "That should be regarded in the same breath as Cal Ripken Jr.," Andy Roddick said, referring to Major League Baseball's iron man. "In tennis, that's almost an impossibility. Nobody would take never retiring in a match over winning a Grand Slam, but I don't think anyone will do that again over a twenty-year career. And it's not like he hasn't gotten hurt during matches."

The Swiss needed just one more victory on Sunday, and Federer provided it in style against Gasquet, doing all the things he could not on Wednesday: sliding, bending low, and most certainly lunging into the corners.

"It's incredible how he gathered strength through the weekend," said Arnaud Clément, the French captain.

Federer held serve at love to close out the 6–4, 6–2, 6–2 victory, his last stroke a beautifully measured backhand drop shot winner. Before it had bounced twice, he was on his knees and pitching forward onto the clay, his shoulders heaving with emotion. He rose quickly and was met by Lüthi and his teammates, and they shared a communal embrace.

"On Monday or Tuesday, I never would have thought I could play three matches in three days," Federer said.

The Davis Cup was founded in 1900. It had taken the Swiss more than a century to join the list of champions.

"That was the goal when I was seventeen, and it took so long to do it," Federer told me. "Maybe the joy was even bigger because of that. I think you could see that."

A night of revelry awaited the Swiss: champagne for all and a few celebratory cigarettes for Wawrinka. There would be a heroes' welcome in Switzerland on Monday after a quick flight home on a private jet.

But first Federer had a last request in the locker room for his boyhood friends Lammer and Chiudinelli.

With the Cup finally secure and the adrenaline fading, his back was stiffening again.

"Roger was like, 'Please, can you take off my socks for me? Because I'm really dead, and I cannot bend anymore,'" Lammer said. "He put so much effort into that week. This is something people forget a lot. He always looks so smooth, so relaxed, but he knows how to suffer, to go through the pain, and not show it."

CHAPTER FOURTEEN

DUBAI

Roger Federer never played an official match on Court No. 1 at the Madinat Jumeirah tennis club. No tickets were sold to watch him at work there, but it is one of the courts where he logged the most hours through the years. It is a low-wattage place amid the bright lights of Dubai; the court where he often trained during breaks from the tour and the court where in November and December 2016, he prepared with the zeal of a younger man for his first full-blown comeback.

"I'm still hungry," Federer told me from Dubai shortly before catching a plane to Perth, Australia. "And now I'm refreshed and rejuvenated."

To reach the club, you come through the main entrance of the Jumeirah Al Qasr hotel, passing the equestrian-themed fountain and imposing gilded statues of horses that are positioned on the front lawn. In architecture if not much else, Dubai is Vegas on the Persian Gulf (gambling and alcohol consumption are officially banned here).

You walk through the soaring, ornate lobby with its potted palms and neo-Arabian facades and await a golf cart and driver, who transports you over bridges and canals, past peacocks and brightly painted sculptures of camels, until you reach a stucco clubhouse that is modest in scale compared to all the pharaonic structures nearby.

You alight, breeze past the club's front desk, and take a seat on a long wooden bench overlooking a blue Plexipave hard court where, in February, teaching pro Marko Radovanovic was gamely giving a group lesson to three schoolchildren of disparate skill and motivation.

The children seemed unaware that they were on sacred tennis ground.

"This is Federer's court, the only court he trains on here," Radovanovic explained between drills. "He has been coming for fifteen years."

Other luminaries also come to practice outdoors in Dubai's mild winter climate, including Novak Djokovic a few weeks earlier. But no modern tennis superstar has spent as much time in Dubai as Federer, who first played in the city's ATP event in 2002 and first won the title in 2003. He later bought a lavish penthouse apartment in the Dubai Marina in a skyscraper called "Le Rêve," which in French means "the Dream." It has gardens designed by Australian landscape architect Andrew Pfeiffer, a fitness center designed by Federer, and a concierge service that allows residents to book a Ferrari, a helicopter, or a private jet with "the press of a button." There are panoramic views of the gulf, the man-made Palm Jumeirah archipelago and the Burj Al Arab, the soaring, sail-shaped hotel where Federer and Andre Agassi once traded strokes on the helipad to promote the Dubai tournament and then very carefully peeked over the edge at the thousand-foot drop.

Radovanovic, a gregarious Serbian who grew up in Belgrade in the times of trouble, still holds dear the memory of teaching tennis to Federer's twin daughters.

In thanks, Federer signed a "Roger Federer 2016 calendar" for Radovanovic with a personalized New Year's message that is now on display in Belgrade.

"My mother stole that and put that on the wall of her house," Radovanovic said with a laugh. "We're all very proud. I have only the best memories of Roger playing there and of coaching his kids, who were very nice and cute. It was like a dream come true for any tennis coach."

But 2016 did not turn out to be a dreamy year for Federer. The day after losing in the semifinals of the Australian Open to Djokovic, he was running a bath for his daughters at their Melbourne hotel when, he said, he heard a click in his left knee as he twisted.

The click turned out to be a torn meniscus, and Federer underwent the first surgery of his career: not a bad run for a thirty-four-year-old in his eighteenth professional season. He had the arthroscopic procedure in Switzerland on February 3, just six days after the Djokovic match.

His fitness trainer, Pierre Paganini, who had worked so diligently and creatively to keep Federer free of injury, became emotional when we discussed Federer's rehabilitation.

"Rog worked with his physical therapist for two weeks and when we started the fitness training, at the beginning, he had to, for example, jog five meters and then walk backwards," Paganini said. "It was like he was learning to walk again. You can be the most positive person in the world and there are still moments where you wonder, 'Is he really going to be able to play high-level tennis again?'"

Federer surprised Paganini and himself by returning to the tour quickly—less than two months later—for the Miami Open.

"I'm just really, really pleased," he said at a news conference ahead of the tournament. "I didn't expect myself to be back here, to be quite honest, after the surgery."

The process, like much of what Federer does publicly, seemed remarkably smooth. But in this case, appearances were misleading. Federer withdrew before his opening match with a stomach virus and when he returned to the tour in earnest, it was on clay in Monte Carlo in mid-April. He lost in the quarterfinals to Frenchman Jo-Wilfried Tsonga and traveled to Madrid, where he had to withdraw on-site again after reaggravating his back issues during practice.

He lost in the third round of the Italian Open to young Austrian Dominic Thiem, a defeat that looks better now given Thiem's subsequent success than it looked in Rome as Federer visibly struggled to move without constraint.

With the heart of the season upon him, he was in trouble, but he had usually found a way to play through such trouble, managing his back and other pains.

He and his team traveled to Paris, still committed to his playing the French Open. They checked into their hotel, and Federer and Paganini went to the empty ballroom to do their fitness work before heading to Roland Garros.

"I was running around, and I finally just stopped and said to Pierre, 'What are we doing here?'" Federer told me. "And Pierre was like, 'What's happening? Is it your knee?' And I said, 'My knee feels like it weighs a hundred kilos. My back is not 100 percent. Why am I doing this? Why am I playing Paris?'"

They stopped the fitness work and talked for close to an hour. Federer later expressed his doubts to the rest of his team: physiotherapist Daniel Troxler and coaches Severin Lüthi and Ivan Ljubičić, Federer's friend and former rival who had joined the group in December, replacing Stefan Edberg.

Federer decided to try a practice on the red clay at Roland Garros, and he ended up on Court 1, the circular show court known as "the bullring."

"I was okay, but I was just never even close to 100 percent," Federer told me. "And this is when we said, 'You know what? Let's call it a day and just get ready for the grass.' I tried, you know, I really tried."

His withdrawal stopped his record streak of consecutive Grand Slam tournament singles appearances at sixty-five, a record that has since been broken by Feliciano López. But the streak never had much meaning for Federer. What mattered most to him was having a chance at winning, not participating.

It still hurt to miss Paris. Even today Federer sounds slightly sheepish, as if he should have found a way to avoid such an outcome. It is not easy for a world-class planner to surrender his plan. The trouble was that grass would offer no refuge in 2016.

"Maybe I could have, should have, taken more time after the Australian Open once I had surgery," he said.

He went to Halle, where he had won three straight titles and eight titles in all, and was upset in the semifinals by German teenager Alexander Zverev. Federer proceeded to Wimbledon, where he won four rounds in straight sets and then had to rally from two sets down to defeat Marin Čilić in a good news–bad news quarterfinal. The good news for Federer was that he had the staying power and the nerve to fight off three match points. The bad news was that he was clearly vulnerable.

The next round confirmed it as Federer faced Milos Raonic, an analytical Canadian with a brutal serve and a superstar-sized entourage that included new coaching consultant John McEnroe. Raonic had made significant progress, improving his agility and net game. But for me and for many others who watched that semifinal, what sticks in our memories are not the twenty-three aces that Raonic hit or the eight break points that Federer failed to convert or the two consecutive double faults he made to help hand Raonic the fourth set.

What many of us remember is the rally early in the fifth set with Federer serving at 1–2 and deuce. Raonic hit a low backhand chip down the line that landed short. Federer closed in and flicked a forehand half volley crosscourt that Raonic aggressively moved forward to meet with his own forehand.

But as Federer hustled laterally to try to prolong the rally, his left leg gave way, and he fell hard. Strangest of all for the Baryshnikov of tennis, he fell awkwardly and landed on his chest, racket skidding across Centre Court.

I remember a collective gasp in the Wimbledon press area, normally a seen-it-all sort of place. But this was new and, with sportswriters hardwired to sniff out symbolism, it seemed to be imbued with deeper meaning: Federer no longer was nimble enough to hold off the years or younger rivals.

He spent a moment lying facedown on the grass, then picked himself up and walked to his chair, calling for the trainer, which was nearly as rare as that ungainly tumble. This, after all, was a man who had never defaulted during a tour-level match. He returned to the court, lost his serve, and lost the fifth set 6–3.

The defeat was particularly poignant for Ljubičić, who was in part responsible, having helped shape Raonic into a better player when he coached him from 2013 to 2015. But Ljubičić, like so many of us watching that afternoon, knew that Federer was far from his peak.

I took an end-of-the era approach to my column in the *New York Times*:

Federer, a remarkable champion and ambassador, has clearly earned the right to play on as long as he pleases without much carping from the chattering classes, even if an 18th Grand Slam singles title now looks increasingly unlikely. Tennis, like life, is a cyclical matter. Seven-time Wimbledon champions fall, and new contenders rise to challenge the status quo. But in light of all the Grand Slam frustration and ambition that the 29-year-old Murray still harbors in his prime, it seems a good bet that Raonic's toughest task at this year's Wimbledon lies ahead of him, not behind him.

At least I got the last part of the column right. Raonic went on to lose the final to Andy Murray, who was in the midst of his greatest season and would win a second gold medal in singles at the Rio Olympics a few weeks later.

But there would be no Olympics for Federer, no fresh chance at the last big-ticket singles title he was missing. For the first time in his career, he stopped his season after Wimbledon. The fall against Raonic had sent him a signal, too.

"I never lose my balance like this, and I kind of tripped in a funny way," he told me. "I don't know if it was partly the muscles not being strong enough or whatever happened. It was very odd, and the problem was I fell on my left knee again, and that's why I was really scared after that. But I was down break points. Even fit, I would have maybe lost that match, so it's not an excuse there. But it was definitely an awkward fall. How many times did I fall down in my career? So rarely, and especially in a moment like this: you know, the semis of a Grand Slam."

He decided to rest and restrengthen his body and knee with the focus on 2017: a six-month hiatus that was by far the longest of his career at that stage. It was ultimately a straightforward call.

"This year I played one tournament where I was basically in top shape," he told me, referring to the Australian Open. "I don't think it cost me the rest of the season by playing the grass. I just think the knee and the body needed a break, and taking six months off, I could take the time the body and knee required to heal. Now I can look back and say: 'Look, if now it doesn't go well, I did everything I possibly could. There are no regrets.'"

The break was, in a sense, a preview of retirement.

"I did get that taste," Federer told me. "All of a sudden, I could be organized and say, 'Okay, we're going to be four weeks at home in a row in the same place. Who do you want to go for dinner with, Mirka? Or who shall we catch up with?'"

But real retirement was not a serious consideration, even if Federer had been fielding questions about it for more than seven years now, ever since he'd completed the career Grand Slam at the French Open in 2009.

He had, on occasion, tested the waters with Mirka.

"If I would ask her if I had one of my down moments, 'Really? Do we still need to be doing this?' she'd be like, 'You decide, but I think it's totally worth it. Look how well you are playing, and I can tell when you are playing good or bad,'" Federer said. "She's super honest, and she's always been of the opinion that as long as I play I can always achieve great things. So, it's nice to hear that from your wife."

Mirka also was quick to put his injury in perspective as someone whose own career was stopped by a chronic foot problem.

"She's like, 'Look at your little injury,'" Federer said, raising pitch to imitate her voice. "'Your little knee thing. That's nothing. Look at other guys, what they have, or look at what I had. That's bad. So you'll be fine. Trust me. The only thing we have to worry about is that you played maybe fourteen hundred matches in your career. That's the only problem we might run into, but this knee thing, come on, man, this is peanuts.' So that's how she talked to me."

Federer found this both amusing and reassuring, but he still put his long break to good use: decompressing in Switzerland but still following the tour. "I was surprised by how many times I caught myself checking live scores," he told me, laughing.

He moved his family to Dubai in November. It was a journey they had made many times: a quick shift to warmer climes and a radically different culture. Despite the fact that Dubai had an indoor ski resort, it is hard to imagine more disparate locales than a Swiss Alpine village with its chalets and cobblestones and a booming Gulf State metropolis with its skyscrapers and flat-desert grid plan. But the transition was not a big shift in one respect. Federer was still able to live a relatively peaceful, untrammeled life.

"That's important to me, and one of the things that Switzerland and Dubai have in common," he told me.

After playing in the Dubai tournament in 2002 and 2003, he returned to the city for vacation in July 2004 directly after winning Wimbledon for the second time and Gstaad for the first. Dubai in July is scorching, but Federer, weary after his rise to the top of the game, wanted to spend a few days in the heat and on the beach. He was so worn out that even walking to the water from the deck chair was an effort, and he called Paganini and joked that he was never going back to work.

He took some extra time before flying to North America, where he went on to win his first Canadian Open and first US Open, crushing Lleyton Hewitt in one of his most dominant performances.

Clearly Dubai had a rejuvenating effect, and he returned in October that year to train covertly with Tony Roche, the Australian whom Federer would eventually hire as a part-time coach. Dubai had the right climate and the right relaxed vibe, but it also was in the right place: a bridge between Europe and Asia with abundant flight connections and ever more amenities.

Federer would help set a trend as more athletes and entertainers began basing themselves in Dubai. Many were lured by the lack of income tax, but Federer chose to remain domiciled in Switzerland, which has certainly contributed to his enduring popularity at home. "He's actually a very rich guy, and usually people are very negative about that here, and they are not with him," said Margaret Oertig-Davidson, a university lecturer in Switzerland and author of *The New Beyond Chocolate: Understanding Swiss Culture.* "He's just cracked it somehow, and I think it's because he's still ordinary, or he's seen that way, at least. He seems to have held on to his Swissness, and people are proud to be associated with that."

Lucas Pouille, the young French star, was one of the tennis players who made the move to Dubai for fiscal reasons, and in December 2016, he was Federer's regular training partner at the Madinat club.

Federer often brought in young, promising players for practice weeks: a way to keep up-to-date with rising talent and feed off their enthusiasm while giving them the precious opportunity to absorb and improve, just as he had been given that chance by Marc Rosset when he was a teenager.

Mackenzie McDonald, a speedy American who won the NCAA singles and doubles titles at UCLA, was one of those who had come to Dubai at Federer's invitation.

"When you grow up watching that guy, and he's still top in the world and you get to be around him and learn from him, that's pretty cool," McDonald told me. "He's got a Plan A, Plan B, Plan C, all the way down the alphabet. If one thing is not working, he's got other tools, and you can see how well developed he is as an athlete. His hands are a joke. His legs are superstrong. His build is ideal for the game, but he turns it into a chess match. It made me realize I need to be less one-dimensional and add more things to my game. I'm a fast guy but feel I can become even faster if I move more efficiently like him. I wouldn't say there's any secret sauce, but I think he works extremely intelligently. I think he knows time management and knows what hours to put in where at this stage."

For McDonald, today's players often lack Federer's full body control and clean technique.

"You watch kids go out today and hit a ball, and they are off balance and just swinging," he said. "Bodies are being thrown around, but you can see that he had the right development and right coaches telling him to do the right things more so than not, and he's showing that everything he's done has paid off."

With the 2017 season fast approaching, Federer, a late convert to social media, decided to broadcast one of his practices with Pouille on Periscope to reconnect with his fans after his long break from competition. It was a rare thirty-seven-minute-and-four-second window into Federer's methods, including the short-burst, high-intensity interval drills with Paganini that are full of variety, like their dual juggling act with tennis balls to train his hand-eye coordination on the move.

"It's never routine," observed Emmanuel Planque, Pouille's coach, in an interview with Sophie Dorgan of *L'Équipe*. "There's always something new. His staff is always trying to surprise him and give him different looks. They keep him stimulated and on his toes. Severin takes a break and Ivan arrives. They alternate. To improve a player like that, you've got to surprise him. I feel their strategy is very good."

Federer, miked up for his own cameras, proved to be a fine emcee as he cracked jokes and delivered tips, explaining that service rhythm was the first thing to go during an extended break. He spoke in French with Paganini, Swiss German with Lüthi, English with Ljubičić, and French and English with Pouille as they sat courtside during a break and discussed the upcoming Hopman Cup, the mixed-team event in Perth, Australia, that Federer had chosen for his comeback event and had not played since 2002.

"Last time I played with Mirka, my wife," he said to Pouille. "And sixteen years ago I played with Hingis, and this year, or next year, I'm playing with Belinda Bencic. God, time flies."

But as the Periscope session made clear, Federer's enthusiasm remained intact.

"He was like a twelve-year-old kid," Planque said of the time spent with Federer that winter. "He was joking around during the warm-ups, imitating Stefan Edberg and Bernard Tomic. He would shout out of the blue. I loved it. We are lucky to have been able to share all this with him. It's precious, and in terms of technique, he's still the gold standard. It's like a continuing education for me; a coaching clinic each time. I have the master right there in front of me. I watch, and it's inspiring. I took 150 pages of notes."

What was also clear to Planque was that Federer was in rare form again, not merely fresh in the head and the legs after his long break but improved.

"He's progressed a lot technically on the backhand side, particularly on the return," Planque said. "He's changed his way of returning. He's more in front, more compact. He's more aggressive with a shorter approach to the ball. He has improved his control.

"It's all rather troubling," joked Planque, who kept having to explain to Pouille that he should not get discouraged by losing so many of his practice sets by lopsided margins to Federer.

"I really thought Roger was in a great place with his game," Planque said.

As it turned out, Planque knew exactly what he was talking about, and Federer's coaches were also optimistic. Lüthi, an even-keeled sort not given to brash predictions, twice told Federer that he thought he was playing well enough to win the Australian Open.

Ljubičić had stopped his tennis career at age thirty-three, worn down by injuries and the realization that he no longer wanted to spend so much time apart from his family.

"When you realize that 80 or 90 percent of the time during a workout is actually dealing with pain and trying to get exercises that would limit the pain rather than make you better, then it's not really fun anymore," Ljubičić told me when he retired in April 2012. "Playing tennis matches is the easiest part of all. It's just getting ready and practicing and traveling obviously now with two kids. It's not easy. I don't want to travel by myself. So I just felt that's it. It's not worth it anymore."

Yet here was Federer as eager as ever to be back on the road at age thirty-five: globe-trotting with his wife, four children, and support staff.

"We want to have him as long as possible," Ljubičić told me. "He's a treasure, so you don't want to burn him out."

Ljubičić cuts quite a figure at six foot four with his clean-shaven head and his baritone voice, and like many who were directly impacted by the violent breakup of Yugoslavia, he has had quite a journey. Born in Banja Luka, an inland city in present-day Bosnia and Herzegovina, he had to flee in May 1992 at age thirteen with his mother and older brother because of the rising tension in the city. With Banja Luka controlled by Serbians, there was increasing hostility toward ethnic Croatians like the Ljubičićs.

After a circuitous route that took them through Hungary and Slovenia, they ended up refugees in newly independent Croatia after crossing the border on foot.

Ljubičić, already a promising junior player, made the journey with two tennis rackets but without his father, Marko, who stayed in Banja Luka and was unable to contact his family for several months. They eventually reunited in Croatia, but Ivan was soon back on the move: leaving for Italy in 1993 to pursue a tennis career as part of a small group of young players from the former Yugoslavia.

He was fourteen, the same age that Federer was when he left Basel for Ecublens.

"Officially, my professional tennis career started in 1998, but I feel it started back in 1993," Ljubičić said. "That's when I left home, when my parents made it clear to me that tennis is what you do, that tennis is going to be your life because that's basically your only chance."

It was a daunting period, but through the years Ljubičić has come to appreciate the clarity that came with it.

"Looking back now I consider myself lucky, because in a way I was without a choice, and that is probably why I succeeded," he told me. "It's easy when you don't have a choice in a way. You see what you have to do, and you can focus 100 percent on that. If you have choices, and you make one, you are still, in the back of your mind, sometimes probably thinking maybe I should have done something differently. In the situation I found myself in back in the early 1990s, I had no other options. I have to admit I'm amazed that guys like Roger and Rafa had so many options and managed to focus on one thing and do it so well."

Ljubičić also had the good fortune to connect at age seventeen with Italian coach Riccardo Piatti, a fine builder of tennis strokes and tennis minds. Piatti coached Ljubičić for free in the early years.

"He said, 'Until you get into the top 100 I don't want a penny from you,'" Ljubičić said. "So that was great because I could focus on practicing with one of the best coaches in the world without thinking too much about economics."

Ljubičić would rise as high as No. 3 in 2006, the same year he reached the French Open semifinals. He also led Croatia to the 2005 Davis Cup title, celebrating with more than one hundred thousand fans in the Croatian capital of Zagreb. He remained with Piatti until he retired, sometimes sharing Piatti's time with other players like Frenchman Richard Gasquet or Djokovic. The Djokovic arrangement was politically symbolic: a Serbian and a Croat working closely together.

"I think knowing yourself is very important in tennis," Ljubičić said. "That was something about Novak that struck me immediately when I met him when he was seventeen or eighteen. He already knew exactly what he wanted, what he needed, and also what he *didn't* want or *didn't* need. He was great at that already from a young age, and that's what makes great champions. For me, it took me a little longer. I was twenty-four or twenty-five when I realized what kind of workout I needed, what kind of people I needed around me. That is also a kind of talent."

Ljubičić met Federer when Federer was just sixteen at a satellite tournament in Switzerland. "Sometimes you just click, and we clicked," Ljubičić said. "That's how friendships work. They just come along."

They were frequent dinner companions and frequent practice partners. Having sat in on a couple of their training sessions, I can confirm that they were not always entirely on task.

"Our practices were maybe not to be filmed and shown to kids," Ljubičić said with a laugh. "But we enjoyed it, so for us, that was important."

Federer, in the relaxed atmosphere of a practice session, can be even more fun to watch than when he is swooping around the court when it counts. He is more animated and tries some outrageous shots: acutely angled sliced backhands off balls bouncing high above his head, full-cut forehand half volleys on the baseline, flicks from unlikely places and positions. The extraordinary SABR ("Sneak Attack by Roger") in which he moved in quickly to return a serve straight off the bounce was, at first, an improvisational practice move.

"You definitely can feel like a spectator sometimes even when you are on the other side of the net," Ljubičić said.

Ljubičić won only three of the sixteen singles matches he played on the main tour against Federer. They never faced each other in a Grand Slam tournament, but Federer did win all four of their tour finals, including the Miami Open final in 2006.

Ljubičić was a frequent defender of Federer, and in 2011, when Federer had not won a major title in a year, Ljubičić guaranteed me in an interview that he would win more.

That proved correct when Federer won Wimbledon again in 2012, but by the start of 2017 Federer had yet to win another. He had come close—losing three finals, all to Djokovic—and was still a factor at the top of the men's game. But he was no longer in a lead role. He had not won the World Tour Finals, the game's fifth most prestigious men's tournament, since 2011; and in the four seasons between 2013 and 2016, he had won just three Masters 1000 titles compared to Djokovic's seventeen.

Ljubičić still believed in Federer's chances. It was one of the reasons he had agreed to work with his friend. Unlike the significantly older Edberg, Ljubičić had the advantage of having faced many of Federer's potential opponents and of having scouted the others when he was working with Raonic.

Federer's decision to hire Ljubičić was also another indicator of how much he valued long-term connections.

Lüthi met Federer when he was eleven. Ljubičić has known Federer since his teens.

The Croat is a natural and exuberant communicator who answers questions confidently and at length, a different personality than the more reserved Edberg. Which made it all the more surprising that Ljubičić stopped speaking publicly after joining Federer's team. It was not a directive from his new employer but a desire to internalize and take no risks of muddling his message to Federer.

He told me he was enjoying the new approach, much as we journalists were not.

"I prefer to keep quiet and let Roger talk, both with his racket and his mouth," he told me. "I know it's weird for me not to talk about tennis to anyone other than Roger, but it's worth it."

It was an intriguing moment in men's tennis: an inflection point, as it turned out. But that was far from clear as the players decamped to Melbourne.

Djokovic had continued to reign supreme until midway through the 2016 season, winning his first French Open and becoming the first man since Rod Laver in 1969 to hold all four major singles titles. It was the next-best thing to a true Grand Slam, which requires winning all four in the same calendar year. But that, too, seemed well within Djokovic's reach, with his multisurface skills and ability to embrace great pressure. Instead, he went into a slow and unexpected tailspin. American Sam Querrey upset him in the third round of Wimbledon. Stan Wawrinka rallied to beat him in the US Open final: the third time Wawrinka had defeated Djokovic en route to a Grand Slam title.

Djokovic did not win another tour event the rest of the year and even got passed by Murray in the final match for the year-end No. 1 ranking as Murray beat him to win the World Tour Finals in London.

Federer, who watches a lot of tennis when he is on tour, was still following it all closely from afar.

"It required something extraordinary, and Murray was able to deliver that, and that is where I take my hat off," Federer told me from Dubai. "The guy just won everything at the end of the year, and it's not easy for anyone because indoors I feel like the margins are slimmer. I feel Novak was the player of the year for six months, and Andy the last six months."

I asked Federer about Djokovic's surprising fade.

"Maybe it's only human and understandable that Novak had a letdown, because he achieved everything he wanted to," Federer said, referring to the French Open victory. "You have to maybe reinvent yourself or whatever you have to do. But it's nice to see that maybe it doesn't always come so easy for everybody for so long. And I think it actually creates a great story for next year. Andy's a great story. Novak's a great story. Rafa obviously is always going to be a good story. Me coming back is hopefully going to be a nice story, too. I think the beginning of the year, especially the Australian summer, is going to be epic."

Nadal also had cut his 2016 season short: stopping in October to heal a wrist injury that had troubled him for much of the season and had forced him to withdraw after two rounds at the French Open.

During his break, Nadal decided to bring on Carlos Moyá, his long-time friend and boyhood mentor, as an assistant coach for the 2017 season. Nadal also opened his eponymous tennis academy in Manacor and invited Federer to join him for the inauguration on October 19.

"I was so blown away by that academy and by what Rafa was able to build there," Federer told me. "I think it's so brave and cool that he did this for his home island and home village, and everybody is involved— his girlfriend, his sister, his parents, his agent, whoever. Everybody is full on into it, and I just felt it was only the right thing to do, to help him out, because I asked myself, 'What would I hope for?' And my answer was that I would hope my biggest rival would call me up and say, 'You need my help? I'm there.'

"And that's what I did to Rafa. I said, 'You need my help? You let me know. You got me for a day: kids' clinics, press, opening, whatever.'"

Anything but tennis, which neither of them was healthy enough to play at that stage.

"I told him I wish we could do a charity match or something, but I was on one leg and he had the wrist injury," Federer said. "We were playing some mini-tennis with some juniors, and we're like, 'That's the best we can do right now.'"

It seemed reasonable to think that their time at the very top had passed, but just three months later, they were both ready when the 2017 Australian Open began.

It turned into one of the most surprising major tournaments of the Open era. Djokovic was stunned in the second round by the 117th-ranked Denis Istomin, an Uzbeki who wore wraparound sunglasses on court and had a losing career record.

It was a shock, but Federer did not seem in much position to bene-fit. He was in the other half of the draw, had not won any title in more than a year, and was seeded 17th: his lowest seeding since the Grand Slam tournaments had gone from sixteen to thirty-two seeds at Wimbledon in 2001.

He had beaten qualifiers in the first two rounds: veteran Jürgen Melzer and newcomer Noah Rubin. But he faced a more demanding test in the third round against No. 10 seed Tomáš Berdych, the angel-faced Czech who was one of the game's biggest, flattest hitters. Regrettably for Berdych, he did not have the same steel in his nerves that he had in his groundstrokes. There was also a mechanical quality to his footwork, but he had beaten Federer at Wimbledon, the US Open, and the Olympics.

This time, Federer overwhelmed him in just ninety minutes: 6–2, 6–4, 6–4, keeping him off balance with surprise attacks, sharply angled strokes, and half-volley drop shot winners.

"I played him so many times, and I almost want to say this was the best I saw him play," Berdych said. "I was not in charge of almost any shot, no matter if I served or not. That was quite unusual. After the match, I was positive that he could go all the way and win it."

It was one of those nights when Federer's racket looked more like a wand. He had forty winners to seventeen unforced errors, feasted on Berdych's second serve, and won twenty of twenty-three points at net. He never faced a break point.

"The tennis ball doesn't know how old you are, and it certainly didn't recognize that he was thirty-five years old out there at all," said Jim Courier, a two-time Australian Open champion, as he left Melbourne Park that night. "That was pretty sweet. Magical, actually."

Federer was upbeat but measured.

"I knew from the start I could be dangerous," he said. "In terms of the tournament, I felt the road was long and very difficult, but for one match, I thought before the tournament that I could do something against nearly anybody. Now, can I do it match after match? I still doubt it, but in any case, this result gives me confidence."

His draw still looked like a boot-camp obstacle course, but a major obstacle was about to be removed. Murray, in his first Grand Slam tournament as the No. 1 seed, was upset in the fourth round by Mischa Zverev (older brother of Alex), who played a throwback serve-and-volley style.

In his fourth round, Federer prevailed in a high-quality five-set duel with No. 5 seed Kei Nishikori, an excellent counterpuncher from Japan who had forged his game on the hard courts of the IMG Academy in Bradenton, Florida.

When it ended with Federer winning the final set 6–3, he reacted with the sort of wide-eyed, arms-by-his-sides leap that he usually reserves for much later in a tournament.

With Djokovic and Murray both out, it was the first time since 2004 that the top two men's seeds had both failed to reach the quarterfinal at a Grand Slam tournament.

"Two huge surprises, no doubt about that," Federer said.

Both Murray and Djokovic were apparently paying the toll for their big, draining 2016 seasons. But Federer was brimming with desire and also enjoying the rare feeling of playing without Alp-sized expectations on his shoulders.

He rolled past Mischa Zverev in straight sets to set up a semifinal match with his friend and compatriot Wawrinka, who had won three major titles in the previous three years while Federer had won none.

It was an intense Thursday night clash with big shifts in momentum on a court that Federer and others believed was playing faster this year. Federer won the first two sets with a disgruntled Wawrinka cracking a racket over his knee as if it were a twig.

Wawrinka took an off-court medical time-out and returned in a better mood with tape under his right knee and proceeded to win the next two sets with Federer looking weary near the end of the fourth. Federer said later that he had been expecting his form to dip at some stage during the tournament against the world's best players, but it was his turn to leave the court for medical treatment: an even rarer move for Federer than taking an injury time-out on court.

He had been dealing with pain in the adductor muscle on the inside of his thigh, and Troxler treated it with massage during the break, which lasted a lengthy seven minutes. When Federer returned, he fought off a break point in the third game and then seized the opportunity when Wawrinka played a shaky game to lose his serve in the sixth.

Federer held firm, very firm, to win 7–5, 6–3, 1–6, 4–6, 6–3 and become the oldest man to reach a Grand Slam singles final since Ken Rosewall lost in the 1974 US Open final to Jimmy Connors at age thirty-nine.

"It's gone much better than I thought it would; that's also what I was telling myself in the fifth set," Federer said. "I was talking to myself, saying, like, 'Just relax, man. The comeback is so great already. Let it fly off your racket and just see what happens.'"

Federer did not yet know whom he would face in the final. The Australian Open was then the only one of the four Grand Slam tournaments to play its semifinals on different days. Nadal, putting together quite a comeback of his own, would not play young Bulgarian Grigor Dimitrov until Friday.

Federer, Lüthi, and Ljubičić settled in at their hotel to watch and analyze the match live. There was plenty to dissect: Nadal and Dimitrov played for four hours and fifty-six minutes before Nadal finally prevailed 6–4 in the fifth set.

It was a classic match, the best of this great tournament (for now), and it was instructive to both Federer and Nadal.

For Nadal, facing Dimitrov was the closest thing to facing Federer, from his one-handed backhand with the elastic follow-through to his feathery footwork and all-court instincts. Dimitrov had even been dubbed "Baby Fed," a nickname he grew to dislike. But his similar style also meant that the patterns Federer and his coaches were studying were directly relevant to the final, and it was telling that Dimitrov had consistent success hitting flat and down the line with his backhand. The caveat was that for all his bold brilliance, he still lost.

"It is special to play with Roger in a final of a Grand Slam, I cannot lie," Nadal said. "It's exciting for me, and for both of us, that we're still there, and we're still fighting for important events."

The rematch would be their first meeting in a Grand Slam final since the 2011 French Open, and the first time they had ever met as the lowly 9th and 17th seeds.

Though it was easy to think Federer had an advantage with an extra day's rest, it was worth remembering that Nadal held a 23-11 career edge over the Swiss and a 3-0 edge at the Australian Open. Nadal had been in the same situation in Melbourne in 2009, only to bounce back from an even longer semifinal victory on a Friday over Fernando Verdasco to defeat Federer in the final.

"That was a long time ago," Nadal said. "I think this match is completely different than what happened before. It's special. We have not been there in that situation for a while, so that makes the match different."

For so long, Federer and Nadal meeting in a final had seemed preordained, but this match had come as a big surprise in the midst of what was supposed to have been Djokovic's and Murray's moment. Federer and Nadal had surpassed not only the public's expectations but their own.

"I would have said a great event would be quarters," Federer said. "Fourth round would be nice."

Instead, he was on the brink of an eighteenth Grand Slam singles title. Nadal had been his toughest opponent historically, but it must have been refreshing not to see Djokovic across the net with a big trophy at stake.

The time-machine feeling in Melbourne was not restricted to Federer and Nadal. The night before, Serena Williams, now thirty-five years old, had defeated her sister Venus Williams, thirty-six, in the women's final: their first duel in a Grand Slam final since 2009. Serena, unbeknownst to everyone but Venus and a few others, had won her twenty-third major singles title while two months pregnant.

There was no topping that, but Federer versus Nadal, sometimes an anticlimax, certainly did not fail to inspire this time.

The core of Federer's game plan was quite simple: Hit through the backhand aggressively without retreating deeper behind the baseline over the course of the match. It was a familiar challenge, and through the years he had started with a similar intent against Nadal and then gradually given ground under the cumulative pressure of his wrenching topspin. But he now had a weapon better suited to the task after his switch to a racket with a ninety-seven-square-inch head. He had definitively made the move in the summer of 2014 after more than a year of exhaustive experimentation and fine-tuning. The change from his ninety-square-inch model gave him more power and 8 percent more surface area, increasing the "sweet spot" and reducing mishits. His racket was now similar in size to the hundred-square-inch models used by Nadal and Djokovic, and though Federer's initial concern was that he might be sacrificing feel, he sensed that he had truly become one with the racket during his long break from competition.

He already had beaten Nadal with the 97 in their most recent match in 2015, but that had been indoors in Basel on a quick hard court over best-of-three sets. This final would be played on more neutral ground even if Federer, in light of his underdog status and elder-statesman appeal, would again be the crowd favorite in Melbourne.

Federer was committed to reducing his use of the backhand slice and his use of the blocked return. He needed to keep Nadal off balance, to deprive him of the time to set up properly for his own world-class forehand.

Paul Annacone ran into Federer and Lüthi in the player restaurant a few hours before the final. Annacone, who was calling the match for television, sat down and said, "All right, pal. What am I going to see today?"

Federer responded: "You're going to see RF standing up on the baseline, and I'm going to swing."

Annacone said: "You're going to swing the whole time, right? All three sets, all five sets, whatever it takes?"

Federer said: "Yep. I'm staying there, and I'm not going to be the defender. I'm just going to commit to that backhand side."

It worked well for the better part of two hours as Federer took a two-sets-to-one lead. But Nadal rallied to win the fourth set, at which point Federer took another off-court injury time-out for his adductor problem.

That sparked criticism from the outspoken Australian former star Pat Cash, seldom afraid to criticize, who accused Federer of "legal cheating" for disrupting the flow of the match.

But Nadal hardly seemed destabilized. He broke Federer's serve in the opening game of the fifth set and jumped out to a 3–1 lead.

The score line looked dire for Federer and familiar, but the reality was that Nadal was leading, not dominating. He had needed to save three break points in his first service game of the set and another break point in his next. Federer was still slapping backhand winners with authority and even hitting through his backhand returns when Nadal served tight to his body. Above all, Federer's internal dialogue was new.

"I told myself to play free," Federer said. "You play the ball. You don't play the opponent. Be free in your head. Be free in your shots. Go for it. The brave will be rewarded here. I didn't want to go down just making shots, seeing forehands rain down on me from Rafa."

In a flurry of brilliant, rip-the-ball-early shot making, Federer did not lose another game, breaking Nadal's serve in the sixth game to get back to 3–3 and then again in the eighth, surprising him on the opening point with a wickedly chipped backhand slice that Nadal, so accustomed to Federer's drives at this stage, was slow to read.

But Nadal rallied from 0–40 to get back to deuce, and then came the point that would encapsulate the final: a twenty-six-shot fast-twitch baseline rally of bold strokes and full-stretch defense that Federer won with an open-stance forehand slap winner down the line off a Nadal backhand that had plenty of sting but not quite enough depth.

It was top-this tennis at its best, and it speaks to Nadal's resiliency that he hit a service winner on the next point to keep the game alive. But Federer was really rolling now, and on his next break point, Nadal delivered his classic hooking slice serve wide to Federer's backhand. Federer typically chipped this serve back into play. This time, he ripped a tightly angled backhand that caught Nadal by surprise again.

It was time to serve for the title at 5–3 (with new balls), and though Federer fell behind 15–40, he saved the first break point with an ace and the second with a forehand inside-out winner falling away.

He did not convert the first championship point, but the second was a different matter. He hit a fine first serve down the T and a midcourt forehand crosscourt that Nadal could not reach but immediately challenged.

The celebration was delayed as both stared up at the big screen, Nadal with his hands on his hips. But the electronic review soon confirmed that the shot had indeed landed on the sideline.

Final score: 6–4, 3–6, 6–1, 3–6, 6–3 for Federer, who pumped his arms overhead and leaped with his eyes locked on his team before walking to the net for a handshake and an embrace with Nadal.

Nadal would get his own stunning and reaffirming late-in-the-game moment in Melbourne five years later when, at age thirty-five, he rallied from two sets down to beat Daniil Medvedev and win the 2022 Australian Open after returning from a long layoff linked to his recurring foot condition.

But this was Federer's time to beat the biological clock, and Rod Laver Arena has perhaps never been louder for a tennis match (it is also a rock concert venue). The tears came quickly as Federer saluted the crowd and dropped to one knee.

It had been a long road to his eighteenth and most unlikely Grand Slam title, which was even more surprising than his run at the 2009 French Open, the only other victory that was remotely comparable in his mind.

But he was eight years older now, had not won a major title in nearly five years, and had not played an official tournament in six months. And unlike in Paris, he had needed to beat Nadal for the title.

It was a match that, like the 2008 Wimbledon final, will bear rewatching after both are long retired. They had inspired each other into the gloaming at the All England Club in their twenties. Now they had challenged each other under the lights at Melbourne Park in their thirties.

"Being honest, in these kinds of matches I won a lot of times against him," Nadal said. "Today he beat me, and I just congratulate him."

It was a rivalry with remarkable staying power, with quantity and quality, and Federer's victory in Melbourne signaled a new dynamic.

Though Moyá would tell me much later that Federer's tactics and execution had startled them in 2017, Nadal was not prepared to concede as much on the night of the final.

"He did not surprise me," Nadal said. "He was playing aggressively, and I understand that in a match against me. I don't think it would have been intelligent to try to get into too many long rallies from the baseline. I don't think he would have won. He went for it, and it was the right thing for him to do."

I asked Federer a few weeks later if this out-of-the-ether title had felt like it was meant to be.

"Honestly, I felt the French Open was more meant to be," he said. "I had to work for this one."

"There were tough matches with DelPo and Haas, of course," he said of his five-set victories in Paris in 2009. "But this one didn't feel like it was meant to be in that same way. I felt I was too fresh in the mind, wanted it too badly in the end, felt too good in the end about everything and riding that wave of the comeback with nothing to lose. I felt it was more one of those things. It was such a surprise. Meant to be doesn't come with nothing to lose. This one was different than any other one I've ever experienced."

My next question was how much more tennis he wanted to experience.

Federer had made an intriguing comment to the crowd at the awards ceremony in Melbourne: "I hope to see you next year," he said. "If not, this was a wonderful run here, and I can't be more happy to have won here tonight."

The last 17th seed to win a men's Grand Slam singles title was Pete Sampras at the 2002 US Open. Sampras retired without playing another tournament. Was it tempting to follow Sampras's lead?

"I guess in a faraway place it did cross my mind: How could I ever top this?" he told me. "But then again, the joy was so big, and I kept on watching the reaction of my team when I won the match point in Australia and how they were jumping for joy. Unbelievable. So much fun. I feel like I want to go through it again."

He had invested too much effort into his comeback to stop now, and— no small matter—he was also preparing to play later in the year in the Laver Cup team event that he and his agent, Tony Godsick, had created.

"The goal, when I took my break of six months, was doing this for the next couple years, not just for one tournament," Federer said. "I understand people who say, 'Oh, this would be a perfect moment to go.' But I feel like I've put in so much work, and I love it so much, and I still have so much in the tank."

He would prove that beyond a doubt after celebrating his victory in the Alps by lugging his replica copy of the Norman Brookes Challenge Cup to a mountaintop chalet in Lenzerheide for family fondue and photos. That was not the trophy's only adventure.

"I call it Norman," he said. "I've had dinner with Norman, spent a lot of time with Norman. I know it's just a replica, but that's all right."

He returned to Dubai and lost in the second round to Evgeny Donskoy, a Russian qualifier. But he then came to the United States and swept to the titles in Indian Wells and Miami, defeating Nadal in straight sets in both tournaments.

I once asked Brad Gilbert, one of the game's sharper coaching minds, what he considered peak Federer.

"Obviously the results will tell you that from 2004 to 2006 he was at his best," Gilbert said. "But I have never seen him come close to being better than in 2017 at Indian Wells and Miami. I sat courtside in both those tournaments, and he rolled Rafa twice. I thought that was the highest level I have ever seen him at. It was comical how well he was hitting his backhand. The final in Miami, I am sure Rafa was thinking, 'Wow! What happened to this guy?' But then it forced Rafa to get better. It might seem crazy to say that about Roger when he was ten years from being invincible, but I think now he was playing against some guys I think who were better than in '04, '05, and '06."

But Federer's timing was also excellent in that both Djokovic and Murray fell back during his renaissance.

They were No. 1 and No. 2 as the year began, but remarkably— maybe even astoundingly—he did not have to face either man in 2017 on his way to seven titles. He would not play Murray in 2018, 2019, or 2020, either.

Djokovic's issues were a combination of marital discord, burnout, and a right elbow injury that eventually required surgery in February 2018. Murray's problem was a severely damaged hip that forced him to stop his 2017 season after Wimbledon.

This was hardly Federer's fault or his problem, but it certainly made his task easier. Instead of having to get through two or three members of the Big Four at full strength to win a major, he had to get past Nadal.

Even that was not the case at Wimbledon. The Spaniard, who had just won his tenth French Open, lost in a marathon fourth round to Gilles Müller that stretched to 15–13 in the fifth set. Djokovic later retired from his quarterfinal against Berdych because of his elbow.

Federer had skipped the clay court season entirely to preserve his body and optimize his chances on grass. It paid off handsomely as he swept through the draw at the All England Club without losing a set, beating Raonic without so much as a tumble in the quarterfinals, and then dispatching Berdych in the semifinals and Marin Čilić in a strange and underwhelming final.

Čilić, who had come so close to beating Federer at Wimbledon in 2016, started the match with a deep blister on his left foot, and when he was down 0–3 in the second set, he began sobbing in his chair as he was treated during a changeover.

It was about disappointment, not about pain.

"Obviously it was very tough emotionally because I know how much I went through the last few months in preparation with everything," Čilić said.

Federer, showing the limits of his empathy, closed him out 6–3, 6–1, 6–4 to break his tie with Sampras and William Renshaw and become the first man to win eight Wimbledon singles titles.

Federer was soon in tears in his own chair as he looked up at the player's box, where his seven-year-old twin daughters had been joined by his three-year-old twin sons.

He told me afterward, as we navigated the corridors of the All England Club from television studio to television studio, that he had not seen that reaction coming.

"That was really the first moment I had to myself out there," he said.

"And I guess that's when it sunk in that, man, I was able to win Wimbledon again, and I broke a record, and my family is there to share it with me. I was hoping the boys were going to be there, too, not just the girls. And so I just felt so happy, and I guess I also realized how much I had put into it to be there. It was all those things together."

He had his nineteenth major title, and though he would lose in the quarterfinals of the US Open to del Potro with his back nagging him again, it was a season to savor.

Most of what he touched seemed to go just right, including the inaugural Laver Cup in Prague in late September. It was Godsick and Federer's pet project, inspired by golf's Ryder Cup, which Godsick had studied and attended, with a team representing Europe playing a team representing the rest of the world.

"Go Rest of the World" is not the catchiest battle cry, but the players embraced the spirit of the new event (and the lucrative appearance fees and prize money). It was well conceived, with its punchy three-day format and the value of the matches increasing each day to guarantee a meaningful final day. It had its own look with the black court, mood lighting, and elevated players' boxes that allowed for easy interaction and showboating for the cameras and, in 2017, for social media content.

But what really carried the sold-out inaugural edition in the O2 Arena was star power, with Federer and Nadal teaming up in Prague in the midst of their dual revival. They had split the year's four Grand Slam titles, with Nadal back at No. 1 after winning the US Open and Federer now at No. 2.

After the draw in Prague's packed Old Town Square, I shared a van ride with them back to the team hotel (tennis journalism involves a lot of interviews in moving vehicles). Both had not shaved in a few days. Nadal was in a good mood. Federer was giddy, as enthusiastic as an entrepreneur who had just secured his start-up's latest round of funding and giggling at just about anything Nadal said.

It was a joy ride despite the cobblestones, in the same upbeat vein as their seasons, and one of the most striking things about it was that Björn Borg, the European team captain, was in the backseat silently listening in. Decades before, Borg had been the superstar who was part of a transcendent rivalry, but Federer and Nadal had gone long-form with the concept and were about to team up for the first time to play doubles (if you don't count a few games in a flood relief charity match in Australia in 2011).

"I hope we didn't wait too long, because we're too old now," Federer said.

But the symbol seemed more important than the result at this stage.

"Look, we are, I think, all our lives rivals, so to be together now is going to be something very special, I think unique," Nadal said. "I think it's going to be a great feeling."

We talked about how much they owed each other for their enduring excellence, if they would have achieved as much for so long without the other for fuel.

"In some ways I believe yes, and in some ways I believe no," Federer said. "I believe that because of Rafa, maybe I achieved less, but at the same time, I feel like he made me a better player."

Nadal agreed, which was a surprise considering that he usually is adamant that his drive is internal.

"I have my personal motivation, but of course to have somebody in front of you, it is easier to see the things you need to improve," he said.

"They uncover you; they undress you," Federer said.

"Exactly," Nadal said. "If you're the best and you don't see the things that other people are doing better than you, it's difficult to go on court and understand exactly what you need to do to be better. Having somebody like Roger in front of me for so many years of course helped me to go on court and understand and let me practice with a different perspective on the things I have to do."

There were some details to resolve, however, before Saturday's doubles.

"Where do you play normally?" Nadal asked Federer, who seemed delighted by the novelty of the question.

By Saturday, they had decided on Federer in the deuce court and Nadal in the ad court, and they meshed very well despite one near collision as Nadal retreated to smash an overhead. Side by side in matching blue shirts, white shorts, and white bandannas, they seemed more alike than usual. The left-handed Nadal and right-handed Federer were mirror images: both six foot one, both quick off the mark, and both happy to talk doubles tactics at length on the miked changeovers with Borg, still a man of few words, proving a good listener.

They won, too, defeating a strong team in Sam Querrey and Jack Sock; and Europe prevailed as well, with Federer winning the decisive match on Sunday against Nick Kyrgios in this hybrid event, somewhere on the border between an exhibition and more serious business.

Federer went right back to winning, traveling to Asia, where he won the Shanghai Masters, again beating Nadal in straight sets in the final. He then won his home city event in Basel for the eighth time before surprisingly losing in the semifinals of the World Tour Finals in London to David Goffin. But he recharged in the Maldives with his family, running into the vacationing Čilić at the same resort, which was quite a coincidence even if tennis stars make the Maldives a habit. Federer then returned to Dubai and his court at the Madinat Jumeirah club to get ready for more in 2018.

He rolled into the Australian Open final without dropping a set and again did not face Nadal or Djokovic (or Murray) in a major. But this time Čilić was ready to push him hard with a Grand Slam trophy at stake.

They had practiced together during their holiday: hitting twice for forty-five minutes with no coaches, fitness trainers, or agents in sight. They met for drinks and dessert, Federer with his family and Čilić with his fiancée.

Now they were playing for the Australian Open trophy.

It was all classic Federer: friendly with his competitors but also ruthlessly able to switch off the charm with the ball in play and focus entirely on the challenge (remember James Blake at Indian Wells).

Čilić took him to a fifth set and had what turned out to be his big chance with two break points on Federer's serve in the opening game. But Federer fought them both off and then broke Čilić's serve, offering a reminder of his versatility by using the backhand chip repeatedly and effectively against the six-foot-six Čilić after using it so little against Nadal on the same court in the 2017 final.

Federer had come back a long way in a year: from genuine outsider to clear favorite, even if he had resisted that label before the Open began.

"I don't think a thirty-six-year-old should be a favorite of a tournament," Federer had said.

He had done it to himself and had now made one of the best late-career runs in any sport: winning three of the last four Grand Slam singles tournaments he had contested to run his record total to the easy-to-remember figure of twenty.

Back in Switzerland, Christian Marcolli, his former psychologist, lit up his twentieth cigar on the terrace of his home in Kuettigen in the Swiss countryside, still thinking of Peter Carter.

"I have kept all the cigar butts as some kind of proof," Marcolli told me. "As you can imagine, these were all special, unique, and very emotional times. I have always sought a moment of solitude after each win to smoke that cigar."

Federer was not alone in enduring with excellence. Serena Williams was about to return to tennis at thirty-six after the birth of her daughter, Olympia, and would reach four major finals in the next two seasons. NFL quarterback Tom Brady and Italian goalkeeper Gianluigi Buffon were among those excelling into their forties.

Sports science and a better understanding of nutrition, training, and recovery were all factors. So was the ability for a player like Federer to put together a personal, highly qualified team and afford to bring his family on the road. But it was also useful to know that others were pushing the limits, too.

"I love hearing these stories," Federer told me of Brady, Buffon, and NHL star Jaromír Jágr. "I've always wanted to be a great athlete or great player for a long time, and I was able to achieve that, but seeing that guys were doing it before me and are still doing it, for sure it's inspiration and help and motivation."

Federer had played Agassi in the 2005 US Open final when Agassi was thirty-five, but Agassi never won a major at that age, much less three majors.

To find a precedent in men's tennis, you need to go all the way back to Rosewall, the diminutive Australian ironically nicknamed "Muscles," who won the 1970 US Open at thirty-five, the 1971 Australian Open at thirty-six, and the 1972 Australian Open at thirty-seven. Rosewall also reached the 1974 US Open and Wimbledon finals at thirty-nine, losing to Jimmy Connors in a hurry in both matches.

At five foot seven and 143 pounds, he had a different build than Federer and could thrive because he played mostly on grass courts, where the ball stayed low. Playing with a wooden racket, he hit his forehand with little topspin and his backhand with no topspin at all, driving it or slicing it with supreme control.

"He could hit it on a dime and then look for the dime," said Rosewall's contemporary Fred Stolle.

What Rosewall and Federer shared was smooth footwork and sound technique.

"I'd like to think it was the way we moved around the court, fairly gentle but quick; we moved the right way," Rosewall told me when we met for coffee in Melbourne in 2020, as we had done in the past. "I am sure that Roger would have been excellent if he had played with our wooden rackets," he said. "His technique would have worked very well. That's not true of a lot of today's players."

At age eighty-five, Rosewall still weighed 143 pounds and had a firm handshake and an easy, unpretentious manner that was surely due in part to having spent decades meeting new people in new cities as part of the professional barnstorming circuit.

"We would change locations every night," he said. "There was a canvas court that they would put on the gym floor or on the ice if we were playing in a hockey arena. Our feet used to get cold."

Constant promotion was part of the equation.

"We had to battle to get exposure," he said. "In our pro game, we had no sponsors or marketing to speak of, so we were ready at any time to speak to anybody, to do a TV interview or anything like that."

Like many of the great Australian players of the past, he appreciated Federer's game and respect for the sport's history, and he had taken to writing him a half-page letter of support each year and dropping it off at the players' locker room during the Australian Open.

"Sometimes it's hard to get in the locker room these days," Rosewall said. "I don't really like to bother him, but I think he's been fantastic for the game. I'm a great admirer of his attitude both on and off the court. He's handled the pressure, and he seems not to have that burden that makes him tired of it all."

Rosewall, like his own friendly archrival Rod Laver, bridged the amateur and Open eras, turning professional as a young man, which made him ineligible for Grand Slam tournaments and the Davis Cup until the sport changed its policies for good in 1968.

Rosewall immediately won the 1968 French Open, the first Grand Slam tournament "open" to both amateurs and professionals. He won eight majors in all and most regrets never winning Wimbledon. Muscles would have surely won many more majors if he had not missed eleven years of Grand Slam tennis after turning professional in his physical prime in 1957. Like Federer, he excelled in his teens and in his late thirties. But not even Federer has been able to match the nineteen-year gap between Rosewall's first Grand Slam singles title and his last.

Rosewall never had a significant injury during his career and only began having rotator cuff issues at fifty-five. He played recreationally into his late seventies.

"What Ken did is just incredible," Federer told me in Australia in 2016, shortly before his first surgery. "I certainly look up to him, and what he did gives me hope that if I remain healthy, I can play for many more years to come."

With remarkable men like Rosewall in mind, Federer and Paganini had made a long-term plan for Federer to endure in 2004, shortly after he reached No. 1 for the first time. They were convinced that less tennis could lead to more. They were correct, although the template worked only because Federer had the talent to flick half-volley winners from the backcourt and smack serves under great pressure on the line.

He was still doing that at thirty-six, just as he did at twenty-two, and in February 2018, two weeks after he defeated Čilić in Melbourne, he interrupted his planned vacation and traveled from Switzerland to the Dutch port of Rotterdam to play an indoor tournament.

Federer's love of the game was not the explanation this time. He was on the verge of passing Nadal to return to No. 1. Reaching the semifinals in Rotterdam would give him enough points to manage it, and so he requested a wild card from tournament director Richard Krajicek, a former Wimbledon champion, and seized the moment.

With Rotterdam's draw of thirty-two players, Federer needed to win three rounds. He beat Belgian qualifier Ruben Bemelmans in the first, German veteran Philipp Kohlschreiber in the second, and Dutchman Robin Haase in the third after, in a nod to the significance of the occasion, dropping the first set.

Federer then earned extra credit by winning the tournament, beating Dimitrov 6–2, 6–2 in the final.

When Federer's comeback began, he would have been content with winning one more Wimbledon, but he had done rather more than that, rather more than he or even anyone close to him had expected.

"When I started with him, I made many more predictions than I do now, and I was very often wrong," Lüthi told me. "I am ready to be surprised by him. I'm actually expecting to be surprised by him, and I think the best thing is to leave it open and not try to put fences around it. For sure, me, too, I'm thinking sometimes how much longer is he going to play, but I think the best thing at this stage is just to live and enjoy the moment. When you do that, it can give you strength and power. On the other side, it can be a problem if you're not staying hungry, so you need to always find the balance."

For Federer, the challenge was more mental than physical at this stage, even on a postoperative knee.

"You need to know yourself, and you need to be honest with yourself," he told me. "When you go to, say, Rotterdam, you need to go there with fire. If you're not excited at this age, don't do it. It's that simple."

He had gone with just the right degree of fire, and the Monday morning after the tournament, when he clicked on the ATP website, he was back at No. 1, the oldest player to hold the spot since the ATP published its first rankings in 1973.

CHAPTER FIFTEEN

———◆———

INDIAN WELLS, California

It was moving day in the desert, and Roger Federer was up before dawn. We met on the tarmac in Thermal, a short drive from Indian Wells, where Federer had lost in the final of the 2018 BNP Paribas Open the previous day to Juan Martin del Potro.

Federer, back at No. 1, had more than the usual regrets. He had served for the title at 5–4 in the third set and failed to close the deal despite holding three match points, the sort of reversal of fortune that happened rarely but more often to Federer than to his rivals at the top of the game. He has lost more than twenty times after holding match point, while Nadal and Djokovic have lost fewer than ten such matches.

"I know it's bad to say this, but I sometimes call Federer an under-achiever in tennis considering all the matches in big tournaments he lost being already up," said Günter Bresnik, one of tennis's top coaches. "The guy should be at thirty Grand Slam tournaments if you're talking about del Potro, Djokovic, Nadal, and all these matches he lost where he was clearly ahead."

The reasons were unclear. His underlying sensitivity? His low margin for error? A bad habit that had become hard to break? "I think it's because his style is so offensive," said Paul Annacone, his former coach. "When he was younger and moved differently, he could get away with more. But now that he's older, he has to be more offensive against the great players, and that's tough to do in big, pressure moments. Rafa, when he's nervous, he's got so much margin on every shot, and he's a great mover. Novak, even though his ball is so flat, he's so precise, and there's not a lot of risk in how he hits the ball. Roger, there's a lot more risk."

But Federer, with his hard-earned perspective and ability to compartmentalize, did seem well equipped to cope with the aftermath. He was far from grumpy as he chatted and yawned in the cool of the early morning on too little sleep.

"Five hours," he said. "Not enough after a match like that."

He was soon cleared to board the private jet that would take him to Chicago, and I was along for the four-hour ride: a chance to get an extended look at a day in Federer's business life and the next Laver Cup venue. That I had been invited to report from one of his sanctums was a sign that Federer and I had a good working relationship, but above all it was a sign of how eager Federer and his agent, Tony Godsick, were for their brainchild to succeed.

The Laver Cup, named in honor of Rod Laver, seemed straightforward enough as a concept: three quick-hitting days of tennis each year matching the best of Europe against the best from everywhere else, with Federer getting the unprecedented chance to play on the same team with Nadal and Djokovic.

But in practice, it had been complicated because of all the competing interests in the game. For a comparatively small international sport that allows only about two hundred men's and women's touring pros to make a good living, tennis has a surfeit of governing bodies: seven if you count the men's tour, women's tour, the International Tennis Federation, and the four Grand Slam tournaments, which often act in concert but remain independent entities.

Reaching consensus is harder than it should be, and the fragmentation has made it harder for tennis to innovate and create meaningful change. It has held the sport back significantly. Every new event, every modification to the overstuffed schedule, trespasses on someone else's turf.

Federer and Godsick knew all this when they created the Laver Cup in Prague in 2017, and they understood it all the more when they committed to Chicago for the second Laver Cup in 2018.

"That's the craziness about tennis," Federer told me before Prague.

"Whatever you move it's like, arghhhh, the whole building starts to shake. Anything new puts shock waves into the current system that tennis players have gotten used to, but that doesn't mean it's negative necessarily."

For a superstar, Federer had gotten heavily involved in the governance and politics of the game, first showing the inclination when he took a leadership role with Switzerland's Davis Cup team early in his career. He later served as president of the ATP Player Council from 2008 to 2014 when it successfully pushed for big prize money increases at the Grand Slam tournaments and regular tour events.

Men's tennis was once a hotbed of activists. Leading players such as Arthur Ashe, Cliff Drysdale, and Stan Smith all worked during their careers to increase the players' influence and bargaining power in a microcosm dominated by the national federations and tournament owners. But Sampras, Agassi, and Boris Becker—the major stars who ruled before Federer's emergence—were much less interested in spending precious energy on governance issues.

"Maybe it's a generational thing, but no great top-tier player in my time would ever take the time to get involved in any of these things," Sampras told me. "I didn't want the distraction of getting involved in politics or prize money or different federations. I had a hard enough time playing and winning."

But Federer would become much more engaged, and Nadal, Murray, and Djokovic all joined in to varying degrees. There was even rare tension between Federer and Nadal in 2011 and 2012 when they disagreed on changes to the ranking system and on the choice for the ATP's next chief executive. Their dispute became public at the 2012 Australian Open when I mentioned to Nadal in a news conference that Federer did not like it when top players spoke negatively about the tour in public. "I totally disagree," Nadal snapped. "He has it easy: 'I say nothing. Everything positive, I come off looking like a gentleman and let the others burn themselves.'"

In more acrimonious eras, when the stars were infrequently aligned, such a comment would have been business as usual, but for Nadal to go after Federer in that manner was akin to a shouting match at the net. Order and politesse were soon restored, but Nadal's outburst was a reminder that even the friendliest of archrivals were still, at the core, competitors for influence as well as for titles.

Djokovic ultimately became the most radical of the Big Three. He took on the establishment overtly and even led the launch of a new player group in 2020, the Professional Tennis Players Association (PTPA), that sought to be an independent voice from the traditional men's tour and faced strong resistance from some sectors in the sport.

Federer and Nadal were among those who did not back the PTPA. That was not surprising.

Federer consistently preferred to work within the system, lobbying and cajoling behind the scenes. Fittingly, he chose two coaches in Paul Annacone and Ivan Ljubičić, who were deeply involved in ATP politics during their playing careers and understood all the main issues. "We talked through a lot of that stuff together," Annacone said.

But the Laver Cup created plenty of tension in the open and behind closed doors, surely more tension than Federer would have wanted to deal with in his golden tennis years.

The International Tennis Federation viewed the Laver Cup as a drag on its Davis Cup team competition, which was struggling to get consistent participation from the biggest men's stars, including Federer, and was about to change format. The Laver Cup's dates in late September also conflicted with existing men's tour events in that same window, depriving them of attention and the chance to lure top players.

The Grand Slam tournament leaders had diverging views. The All England Club and French Tennis Federation kept their distance, but Tennis Australia and the United States Tennis Association actually invested in the Laver Cup, with the Australian Open media relations team even traveling all the way from Melbourne to Prague to work the event as part of the arrangement.

My belief was that tennis had a glut of tournaments but not a glut of transcendent tournaments. There should be room for an event like the Laver Cup that, with Federer involved, had a good chance of generating international buzz instead of merely local or regional interest. I also had covered many a Ryder Cup, the inspiration for the Laver Cup. For me, the Ryder Cup was one of the most consistently compelling events in sports: a nerve jangler from the first shot on the opening morning with its match play format. The Ryder Cup, like the Laver Cup, was an exhibition in the sense that it offered no ranking points, but it had come, over many years, to carry great weight with the players. It also provided a still-rare vehicle for European athletes to compete together. The difference was that the golfers represented the European tour as well as their continent. There was no separate European tour in tennis, but Europe was no doubt the dominant force in the men's game: perhaps too dominant for the Laver Cup's long-term good.

The first Laver Cup in Prague turned out to be a smash hit in terms of entertainment value, with close matches, sellout crowds, and Federer and Nadal joining forces. But the event also lost significant money because of the start-up costs and the rich participation fees and prize money paid to the players.

It was important to Federer that the second edition build on the positive first impression, which was why he was heading to Chicago while Mirka and the children traveled separately to Florida to set up base camp for the Miami Open.

"Laver Cup is something that is very dear to me, so clearly I always have extra energy for the Laver Cup," Federer told me. "For my own career, I don't play as much anymore, and when I am there, it's all-out and full speed, and then I need the time away again."

Federer did not own his own plane but was traveling on one provided by a company that sells fractional private jet ownership. Federer used the service when he traveled within North America and often within Europe.

It was all part of the plan to reduce the friction in his complicated global life: to make the transitions, the jet lag, and the rest of his off-court existence as smooth as possible for himself and his family.

"I don't need all this," Federer told me, gesturing toward the plane. "It's just so easy, so simple. It's just an investment in yourself in terms of energy and management. Not having to beat so many checkpoints and lines and people and pictures, so I can get into the plane, and I can relax already now."

He had the means at this stage to reduce a great deal of friction. He was on his way to becoming the first tennis player and one of the few athletes to earn $1 billion during his playing career: joining the golfer Tiger Woods and the boxer Floyd Mayweather. Only about $130 million of Federer's earnings has come from official prize money. The rest has come through sponsorships, endorsements, appearance fees, and special events like the lucrative exhibitions that Godsick had organized in South America.

Federer's performance in this domain has been every bit as impressive as his performance on court, and though his business and tennis results are inextricably linked, he started with disadvantages in off-court earning power.

He was from a wealthy country but not from a major market like the United States, Japan, Germany, or France. That limited his appeal at the beginning to potential sponsors.

"When you are Swiss, you represent a small country," said Régis Brunet, Federer's first agent with IMG. "If you want to make serious money, being number ten in the world does not suffice."

Brunet, a former French player, knew this firsthand, because he had represented Marc Rosset, the Swiss star who had peaked at No. 10.

"You have to be number one in the world to go global," Brunet told me. "If you are number one and American, you are going to make a ton of money, but at that stage, being Swiss, you could only make the same kind of money as the American by being a lot better than the American, by being a truly exceptional number one."

Brunet first saw Federer at the Junior Orange Bowl in 1995, when Federer competed in the fourteen-and-under division at the Biltmore Hotel in Coral Gables near Miami. There was no shortage of agents on their perpetual search for the next big thing. Brunet's main target that year was Olivier Rochus, a promising Belgian, but Brunet's close friend Christophe Freyss told him he should take a look at Federer as well. Freyss was the French coach who oversaw Federer's training at the Swiss national training center in Ecublens.

"Christophe told me that Roger was not easy to handle because he was very high-strung, but he had quite a bit of talent," Brunet told me. "So, I went to watch, and after five minutes, maybe it was ten, I rushed to the first telephone booth I could find, because in those days there were no mobile phones, and I called Christophe and asked him if he could organize a meeting in Basel with Roger's parents. I knew that I needed to move fast, because I knew the other agents would not take long to see Roger's abilities."

Brunet was not troubled by Federer's temper and was particularly impressed by his precocious technical proficiency, above all his ability to hit different kinds of backhands at age fourteen.

"Everybody hit good forehands, but that backhand really set him apart for me," Brunet said.

He returned to France and traveled to Basel to see Lynette and Robert Federer. He had met Lynette during her years in the accreditation department at the Basel ATP event. Brunet said the Federers knew IMG and were reassured by the fact it was "an American company" with international reach.

"At that stage, as agents, we talk much more with the parents than with the player," Brunet said. "And I can tell you Roger's parents were extraordinary. They were well educated and asked the right questions, and when they gave you their confidence, they gave it to you all the way. If all the parents had been like them, it would have been a much better business. It's tough to be an agent, because the grass is always greener elsewhere."

There was no formal agreement at first, but the Federers made the commitment. Brunet was able to secure a deal with Nike in 1997 for Federer to wear its tennis apparel and shoes. There was also interest from Adidas, which provided some leverage, and Brunet said the base value of the Nike contract was $500,000 over five years: a significant sum to commit to a junior.

"It was the biggest contract we had signed for someone that age," Brunet said. "The level for a very good Swiss junior player would have been perhaps $20,000 a year for a couple years and then we'll see. But Nike multiplied that by five and went for five years, because they believed in

Roger a lot. I pitched him to Nike as a future number one, but to be honest I pitched all of the players to Nike as a future number one. The most important thing was not the total, it was that it gave Roger protection in terms of the way it was structured so that if he arrived quickly in the top 50 or 20 his financial level would reflect his tennis level."

Though some players feel obliged to choose a racket company based on the size of the financial offer rather than their preference, Federer was able to sign a deal with Wilson, which made the racket he used and liked.

In 1998, he finished as the world's No. 1 junior, and Paul Dorochenko, the French physiotherapist, remembers a celebration at Federer's residence in Switzerland after he won the Orange Bowl eighteen-and-under title.

"It was the end of the year," Dorochenko said. "Roger's father gave me, Peter Carter, and Peter Lundgren each an envelope with some money. The Federers were not rolling in it. They were hardly poor, but they were not rich, and they gave us a generous amount, something like 1,000 Swiss francs, which is about 1,000 euros."

Above all, Dorochenko remembers what happened next.

"I drove back home and there was a winter storm, and the windows were all fogged up, and so I rolled the windows of my car down, and when I took the bills out of the envelope, there was a huge gust of wind and most of the bills went out the window," he told me. "I tried to use the headlights to find some of it, but it was snowing so hard it was really tough. The next morning, I got up and went back out and a bunch of the bills were up in the tree."

There is a metaphor in there somewhere.

Brunet and Robert Federer would often discuss Roger's future. Robert believed in his son's talent, but as he was only a recreational tennis player, he sought expert opinions.

"Robbie would ask me, 'Do you think he's going to be big? Is he going to be good?'" Brunet said. "And I would say, 'Robbie, come on! Your son is exceptional but to know if he's going to be top 10, top 20, top 100, it depends on so many things: injuries, motivation, girls.' It really was so hard to tell which juniors were going to make it big."

One of Brunet's main tasks was to secure wild cards for Federer into professional tournaments to accelerate his transition to the tour. He did this effectively but not without difficulty.

In 1999, Brunet had two wild cards available into the IMG-owned indoor event in Marseille. His quandary was that he represented three promising young players: Federer and Frenchmen Arnaud Clément and Sebastien Grosjean, who both would eventually break into the top 10. Brunet had to pick two of the three and eventually settled on Federer and Clément. Federer made Brunet look very good in Marseille by upsetting reigning French Open champion Carlos Moyá in the first round, but Grosjean dropped Brunet as his agent.

"He was angry with me and stayed angry with me," Brunet said. "We joke about it now, but I lost Grosjean because of Roger."

Federer's victory over Moyá, who would briefly rise to No. 1 just a few weeks later, certainly made it easier to secure him a wild card into the IMG-owned Miami Open in March ahead of players from bigger markets.

But wild cards, however useful, would soon be unnecessary. The last one Federer required was in Marseille in February 2000. This time, he reached the final.

"I always thought Federer and the family had a good relationship with money," Dorochenko said. "I remember when he got to the final in Marseille, and when he came back, he gave the check to his mother and said, 'Here you go. It's starting to come.'"

That was true, but the relationship with Brunet and IMG eventually soured. Federer and his parents were upset to learn that Stephane Oberer, Rosset's longtime coach and now the Swiss national technical director, had been receiving commissions from IMG without their knowledge from Federer's sponsorship contracts. That was because Oberer had played a role behind the scenes in bringing Federer and IMG together.

Many coaches avoided this kind of arrangement because of concerns about conflicts of interest, but Brunet said that paying the equivalent of a finder's fee was common practice but usually stayed "confidential."

Brunet said the person who revealed it to the Federers was Bill Ryan, an American who was Lundgren's and Borg's agent with IMG and who represented Federer after he split with Brunet.

Ryan confirmed to me that he had informed the Federers and said he was surprised that no one had told him of the arrangement when he began managing Federer's affairs. He said he discovered it on his own.

"I would never do a deal like that," Ryan said. "Basically, you are taking money away from the player."

Brunet told me that Federer was never shortchanged because of what Oberer received.

"Roger did not pay more in commissions," Brunet said. "It was perhaps less money for us at IMG. It was not against Roger. He was not penalized. It was just a commercial agreement you can have when someone brings you business, and you want to reward them."

Ryan could be an abrasive figure. Though he inspired loyalty from the many players he represented, he was unpopular with some in the industry, including Mike Nakajima, a former director of tennis at Nike who had known Federer since his teens.

"I never saw eye-to-eye with the guy, and I was saying to myself, why is the world's biggest asshole representing the nicest guy on tour?" Nakajima said.

In 2002, Federer's initial five-year contract with Nike was expiring, and Ryan said he refused to accept a renewal offer from the company that he felt was far too low.

"They were only offering him $600,000 a year," Ryan told me. "Roger's father was begging me to take the deal, and I said, 'Robbie, your son is going to be the best player who ever walked the face of the earth. Why would I accept a $600,000 deal?'"

Based on other players' contracts, Ryan felt that Federer should be getting a base of at least $1 million annually from Nike. "Roger was on board," Ryan said. "But I still have the email from Robbie saying, 'Bill, you have to talk Roger into taking this deal. He needs the money.'"

Ryan would not budge, and when he left IMG on contentious terms in late 2002, the Nike contract had not yet been renewed. That was partly due to Federer's shaky start to 2002, with his first-round losses at the French Open and Wimbledon.

"The contract was up, and Adidas was also in the picture, but all the brands were hesitant because Roger really was struggling at that time," said a friend who knew the couple well. "That was a tipping point in Roger's career. But Mirka really stepped up her role and took more responsibility and led Roger towards a structure that would get him through this tough time."

Ryan told me that he was stunned that other companies were not ready to sign Federer when Nike balked. "There wasn't a company I didn't call: the Japanese, Fila, Diadora, Lacoste, everybody," he said. "I was begging them to do it. It was, 'Look, I'm handing you the best player ever.'"

Nakajima said the delay on the Nike renewal was more a matter of money than doubt about Federer's game. Nakajima had been courtside at Wimbledon when Federer had defeated Sampras in 2001. "I just sat there mesmerized at the way he glided over the court," Nakajima said.

But business was business. "It was a negotiation," Nakajima said. "Sometimes agents want more. We say internally at Nike anytime you meet to negotiate the price goes up, so the less we meet the better. And we were just too far apart."

Ryan said he told Federer he could no longer represent him during the 2002 US Open but could not offer an explanation because of the terms of his departure from IMG. He had a noncompete agreement.

Ryan and Federer had developed a good relationship. They called each other "Kenny" after a lyric in an Eminem song that Federer played (and played). Federer and Mirka had stayed with Ryan and his family at their home during the US Open in 2001, and Mirka had trained with Ryan's wife, the former Swedish player Catarina Lindqvist.

"I just felt horrible," Ryan told me of the split. "Roger came down to my room, and he had his mouth open, and he said, 'What happened?' I said, 'I can't talk about it, but it has nothing to do with you.' He was sad. He was upset, and the thing I regret is I couldn't explain it to him."

Federer, just twenty-one years old, decided with Mirka and his parents to break ties with IMG and set up his own management team.

"When Bill left IMG, we weren't allowed to work with him," Federer explained to me later. "I don't know what the reason was. We thought about looking for another manager, and I finally said, 'I think we should try to handle things on our own for a while.'"

His parents played a leading role, with Lynette Federer leaving her job in the Swiss pharmaceutical industry and Robert Federer negotiating appearance fees and new commercial deals with the help of Bernhard Christen, a Swiss lawyer.

"I wasn't prepared in the beginning," Roger told me in 2005. "There were times, of course, where you think, 'Jesus, if I would have known that,' or 'Oh, man, I wasn't planning on coming back to Basel and having meetings to sort things out' and decided on business things. But the bottom line is I feel very comfortable with it, because I have the feeling I am in control of everything."

Federer recognized that the learning curve would mean that mistakes were made.

"The thing that makes me feel good is I'm taking decisions by myself, and I used to hate taking decisions," he said. "And I think that is also what has helped me to maybe even become a better player and to become a better person maybe, more of a grown-up person. Because I cannot just say, 'Well, you guys decide' when someone asks me, 'What do you think, Roger?' I have to give my opinion and have a strong opinion, because I know my opinion counts most."

For Federer at that stage, the chance to focus on business was a healthy escape from the tennis court. He also believed that understanding the business side of his career could make him less vulnerable to trusting the wrong people and losing what he had earned.

"You see and hear that and always wish that it's not going to happen to you, but you hardly ever have a guarantee except, of course, if you really take it in your own hands like I did," he told me.

But Federer's homespun management approach was a cause for concern for many within the tennis industry, including rival agents like Ken Meyerson, a hard-charging, quick-thinking American who represented Andy Roddick before dying in 2011 from a heart attack at age forty-seven.

"I feel Roger is terribly inadequately represented and feel there are millions and millions being lost," Meyerson told me in May 2005, when Federer already had been No. 1 for more than a year and won four Grand Slam singles titles.

Roddick had won one major title at that stage and was ranked No. 3, but Meyerson had just closed a lucrative long-term deal for him with French apparel manufacturer Lacoste. It reportedly paid Roddick about $5 million annually and compared very favorably with the multiyear Nike renewal that Federer had finally signed in early 2003 with his father deeply involved in the negotiations.

"I can honestly say we've got a substantially bigger deal than Federer and yet Andy is clearly lower ranked," Meyerson said. "Whoever negotiated his current Nike deal certainly did a disservice to those who are out there representing commensurate talent. It brings down the entire market if the father, because of his inexperience, thinks a deal is worth X, and it is really worth ten times that."

Meyerson estimated that Federer's Nike deal paid him at best between $1.75 million and $2 million annually.

"It should be worth $10 million per year," Meyerson said. "Regional management is only good if you want to be a regional player...Does that translate into lost dollars? I think so."

It was also instructive to compare Federer to new women's star Maria Sharapova, who had won Wimbledon at age seventeen in 2004. Her off-court sponsorship deals were approaching $20 million a year by the end of 2005, according to IMG executives, who said that Federer's did not even total $10 million.

"We were crushing deals, and we were miles ahead of where he was," said Max Eisenbud, Sharapova's longtime agent at IMG. "But he was a different Roger Federer then."

In 2005, the year after Federer won three of the four major tournaments, *Forbes* estimated his annual earnings at $14 million—a figure that placed him well behind Andre Agassi ($28 million) and Sharapova ($19 million).

Federer explained to me then that he enjoyed his independence and did not want to overcommit to sponsors because of the demands that

would generate on his time. But he clearly took note of the dispari-
ties and of the demands on Mirka, who was busy managing his media
relations and agenda.

In August 2005 when Federer came to North America, he decided to
meet with management agencies. IMG had a new chairman and chief
executive: Ted Forstmann, a billionaire and tennis aficionado whose
private equity firm Forstmann Little had acquired IMG in 2004.

Forstmann was aware that other IMG executives had tried without success to bring Federer back into the fold. He knew former No. 1
Monica Seles and asked if she would help arrange a meeting. Seles
agreed, reached out to Mirka, and took part in the meeting. It went
well: Forstmann and Federer connected over South Africa. Forstmann
had adopted two sons from South Africa after visiting an orphanage
during a tour of the country with Nelson Mandela in 1996. Federer
had recently started a foundation to help improve early childhood
education in the country.

The question was who would work with Federer day to day. Godsick,
then in his midthirties, already represented Seles and the current wom-
en's No. 1, Lindsay Davenport, as well as Tommy Haas. But Seles was
essentially retired, and Davenport would soon start a family and curtail
her playing career. Godsick's own career was coming to a crossroads,
and he was even exploring opportunities at IMG outside of tennis.

He already had been in the right place at the right time once in his
career. An Ivy Leaguer who played football at Dartmouth, he was a
summer intern in 1992 in New York at Trans World International,
the broadcast arm of IMG, when a call came in from the Cleveland
office that Seles needed someone on short notice to work with her at
an exhibition in Mahwah, New Jersey.

Godsick, who was working late, jumped at the chance. "I said, 'I
don't know what I'm doing, just tell me what to do,'" he remembered
with a laugh.

He got into an argument on his first day with the tournament pro-
moter about Seles's scheduling demands. Seles, who was receiving a
then-hefty appearance fee of more than $250,000, ended up getting

the time slot she wanted, and the eighteen-year-old Seles soon gave Godsick another challenge.

"Guns N' Roses is playing tomorrow," she said. "Get tickets."

Godsick managed that, too, and even secured backstage passes at Giants Stadium because the band's lead singer, Axl Rose, was a Seles fan.

"The whole thing felt pretty surreal," Godsick said.

Seles asked him to work with her on the road, but Godsick still had his senior year at Dartmouth to finish. He juggled his studies and working with Seles until March 1993, when he accepted an offer from IMG for a full-time job as Seles's road manager that would start after graduation. His base salary was just over $20,000 per year.

But just a few weeks later, he returned from the golf course in Hanover, New Hampshire, and saw that he had an unusual number of messages on his answering machine. It was April 30, and the No. 1–ranked Seles had been stabbed in the back on a changeover with a nine-inch knife by a deranged Steffi Graf fan in Hamburg, Germany. Seles underwent surgery and recovered quickly from her physical wounds, but the psychological ones were much deeper. She experienced depression and did not return to action until the summer of 1995 with Godsick as her agent.

"It was a horrible thing that happened to her, obviously, but to be honest, it really helped me that she was out for those two years," Godsick told me. "It allowed me to learn the business and handle things properly or at least try to handle the big crush of her comeback."

Godsick went on to become one of the leading agents in tennis.

"If I hadn't answered that message, if I had been away from my desk for a couple more minutes or not been working late, it all might never have happened," he told me. "Really."

Seles introduced him to her friend Mary Joe Fernández, the former American tennis star, and encouraged the two of them to start dating. Godsick and Fernández married in 2000. Seles also vouched for Godsick with Mirka and Roger.

"Monica was the one who ended up getting me connected with

Roger," Godsick told me. "I owe her so much in my career, and I owe my wife, too, who has really helped me."

Godsick's arrival in late 2005 marked a major change in Federer's bottom line. By mid-2010, his annual earnings had more than tripled to an estimated $43 million, according to *Forbes*. That included deals with German automaker Mercedes-Benz and internationally focused Swiss brands like watchmaker Rolex, chocolatier Lindt, and the bank Credit Suisse.

In 2008, Federer renewed his Nike deal for ten years at more than $10 million per year: a record for a tennis endorsement. This time, there were no complaints that he was bringing down the market.

Godsick was also attempting to bring Federer into the mainstream in the United States, perhaps the toughest market for a European tennis player in part because tennis is a niche sport in North America compared with the major team sports.

"In the beginning of the career, everybody talks about America," Federer told me. "'Have you done it in America? Are you famous in America?'"

I was under no illusions. My frequent access to Federer was deeply connected to his desire to broaden his reach in the United States. But the *New York Times* was just one small part of a broader strategy. Some sponsorship contracts stipulated that Federer get exposure in the United States. Federer also developed a link with one of the most prominent American celebrities: Tiger Woods.

Both were represented by IMG and were sponsored by Nike, and in 2006, Godsick and Woods's agent, Mark Steinberg, who were friends, arranged for Woods and Federer to meet at the US Open tennis tournament in New York. At that stage, both were six victories short of the men's record for major championships in their sports: Federer with eight Grand Slam singles titles to Pete Sampras's fourteen; Woods with twelve majors to Jack Nicklaus's eighteen.

Their mutual admiration seemed genuine. Woods declared himself a "huge Federer fan" during the British Open that he won at Royal Liverpool in July 2006, and when I interviewed Federer several weeks later in New York ahead of the US Open, he spoke at length about being inspired by Woods.

"I do draw strength from it," he said. "The idea is that you want to prove to yourself you can do it, and not to other people. That's why for me, this rivalry with Rafael Nadal, okay, it's interesting maybe, but in the end, I care about winning tournaments. That for me is the bottom line, and if Rafael Nadal happens to be on the other side, even better. Because then I can beat the main rival or make a great story on top of that. But I think what people like Tiger and I are more interested in is not who we're playing or racing against. You want to do it the best *you* can. It's important you can wake up in the morning and go to bed feeling good about yourself and your effort."

"So how are you sleeping these days?" I asked.

"I'm sleeping well, thank you," he answered.

Federer and Godsick were also interested in getting the best out of his commercial potential. Gillette, the Boston-based razor company, was looking for global brand ambassadors to replace soccer star David Beckham. It already had decided on Woods and had winnowed the final candidates to a small group that included both Federer and Nadal. A real-life connection with Woods surely could not hurt. When Federer faced American star Andy Roddick in the 2006 US Open final, Woods came to Flushing Meadows and met Federer before the match. When the final began, Woods was in the front row of Federer's box with his wife, Elin Nordegren, on one side and Mirka on the other.

"It wasn't some stunt to get the Gillette deal," Godsick said. "Tiger and Roger just wanted to meet. The US Open was the only time we could make it work."

But the optics were certainly helpful to Federer with Woods at the peak of his fame. When Federer won the title, Woods visited the locker room, his white backward ball cap in place, to help Federer celebrate with some champagne.

"It's funny, you know, because many things were similar," Federer said. "He knew exactly how I kind of felt out on the court. That's something that I haven't felt before, a guy who knows how it feels to feel invincible at times."

Roddick certainly took note of his fellow American cheering in the front row for a Swiss he had just met.

"I would say that that was kind of surprising," Roddick told me. "I didn't know it was happening. I looked up. Sitting in someone's box is a different type of thing, and I was surprised to see that at the US Open. I understand the Nike and the IMG thing, I guess, but yeah, I don't have a right to be upset with someone I don't know but maybe 'unnecessary' is the right word."

In January 2007, Federer was named a global ambassador by Gillette, along with Woods and soccer player Thierry Henry.

Federer and Woods kept in touch, and when their tournament schedules coincided, they would watch the other play in person. But the high-profile sponsorship deal with Gillette lasted longer for Federer than it did for Woods, who in 2009 had to deal with revelations of his serial infidelity and the subsequent collapse of his six-year marriage. The scandal generated massive international media coverage and cost Woods numerous endorsement deals.

He and Federer would not share in a victory party again, but Woods did share one with Nadal in 2019 at the US Open, when Woods watched from Nadal's box as the Spaniard won the title.

Nadal, as it turned out, was a much bigger golf fan than Federer and a much more serious golfer, even though he played the game right-handed.

I asked Federer about Woods in May 2010 when we met in Paris a few months after the infidelity scandal broke.

"I tried to reach out, but it's hard," he said.

He said he had seen Woods's soon-to-be-ex-wife, Elin, in Miami in March with their daughter, Sam.

"It was sweet, nice catching up with her and seeing how she is doing as well," he said of Elin. "I'm looking forward to seeing Tiger again. I haven't seen him in a while."

Federer was more interested in discussing the tenor of the coverage than Woods's behavior.

"People like shocking news and then they follow up on it, and it becomes this reality TV show, which is so common now," he said. "I'm surprised how long these stories last and how big they get."

I asked if he felt the Woods story had deserved so much coverage.

"For me this is a bit exaggerated, to be honest," he said. "I don't care especially about making sure that everything is perfect or whatever. It is what it is, and I don't think you should try overly crazy to protect your image. It should happen naturally, and that's the approach I've had.

"If people love you, they love you," he added. "If they don't, they don't. I'm not going to change my character to please everyone, because I know everyone won't be pleased, and I know they shouldn't be, because there are plenty of other characters out there and other athletes. So I just think the natural way with the media and the fans was for me the way to go. I'm happy I can speak so openly and honestly to everyone without being too controversial, but I guess I try to be interesting for the fans, because I want them to read a good story instead of all these controversies."

I noted that he was, in some respects, the last superstar standing when it came to avoiding image-tarnishing behavior.

"There's a feeling out there of, 'Don't screw it up, Roger,' " I said. "Do you think about that?"

Federer chuckled.

"You can't think about that," he said. "Because sometimes stuff happens, and you deal with it then."

Agents within the sports industry believe that Federer inadvertently benefited from Woods's image implosion.

"It took Roger a while, many Grand Slam victories to get it going," said Max Eisenbud, Sharapova's longtime agent at IMG. "But I've just never seen a more complete package than him, and I think when a lot of things started to happen, the Tiger Woods controversy, and brands started to get really uptight and worried about brand associations, Roger really catapulted himself because he was as safe as safe could be. The Tiger Woods situation really rocked the world, because Tiger was viewed as bulletproof. I think brands were really starting at that moment to look at maybe not even doing associations, or if they were doing associations it had to be so clean."

In this context, it was both troubling and poor timing that in late 2010, a lawsuit against Ted Forstmann in Los Angeles County Superior Court charged that Forstmann had increased a bet on the 2007 French Open final after consulting with Federer.

Match fixing had become an increasing concern in professional tennis, amplified by the rise of internet gambling and the paltry prize money on offer in the game's minor leagues, which created considerable incentive for cheating. The sport was slow to act, but in 2008, it created the Tennis Integrity Unit, an investigative and sanctioning body. Though players had long been banned from gambling on tennis, it was not until 2009 that others who worked in the sport—player support staff, tournament officials, and such—were expressly banned from wagering on the game.

Forstmann's bet on the 2007 final, which he acknowledged making, predated the new rules. But the lawsuit, which claimed that Forstmann had placed millions of dollars in wagers on a variety of sports, still put Federer in an uncomfortable position, suggesting that he was providing a gambler with inside information.

"I would never do such a thing," he said when he spoke with me and a small group of reporters at the Paris indoors event in November 2010.

It was the only time I can recall Federer being put in a position to have to rebuff a story on such a potentially volatile subject. But Federer said he had no idea that Forstmann was betting on his matches and denied any involvement with gambling. He said he had directly contacted Forstmann, the then-seventy-year-old financier who had helped lure him back to IMG.

"I reached out and told him I want to know everything about it, how this came about," Federer said. "And he's been, you know, nice enough obviously to tell me from his side and has been very open in the press already. So that's okay. He's not my agent. Tony is my guy, but still, it's a firm that does a lot in sports, so it's just something that for me is important to know what is going on from their side, too."

The lawsuit, based on a business dispute, charged that Forstmann had placed bets of $22,000 and $11,000 on Federer to win on June 9, the day before the 2007 French Open final that Federer lost to Nadal, another IMG client. The situation would have been more problematic still if Forstmann had bet on Federer to lose.

At first, Forstmann told the *Daily Beast* that he might have called Federer before the final, but only because he was "a buddy of mine."

"All I would be doing is wishing him luck," Forstmann said. "How is that insider information?"

But after consulting his phone records, Forstmann maintained that he had not called Federer at all before the final. At the least, the pattern of gambling on his own clients showed remarkably poor judgment. IMG not only represented dozens of tennis players; it owned tournaments and special events.

Federer was rightly concerned, as were members of IMG's board of directors.

"I just think it's really important to keep an eye open, I guess, for what are the players doing and what are the entourages doing, how much betting and stuff is going on," Federer said. "We should cut that out to the absolute maximum, obviously.

"That names get thrown around, that you can't help sometimes. That's just the way it is. So, for me, from that side it was crazy news to hear that. But obviously it's not a good thing when IMG or Ted Forstmann is involved in it, but I'm sure he has learned his lesson."

That did not seem entirely clear, but there ultimately were no sanctions against Forstmann. He was diagnosed with brain cancer about six months later and died in November 2011. He never testified in the lawsuit, which was eventually dismissed.

Federer Inc. continued on its upward trajectory. By 2013 Federer's annual income had reached an estimated $71.5 million, boosted by his first South American exhibition tour and a new five-year deal with champagne brand Moët & Chandon. That put him second on the

2013 *Forbes* list of the world's highest-paid athletes, behind Woods and ahead of basketball star Kobe Bryant.

The *Forbes* list is an imperfect vehicle. Agents will tell you that it is, at best, an estimate and often inflates the numbers, relying on the agents themselves to confirm the figures. The incentive for agents to exaggerate is high because it is good for business.

But there is no doubt that what has separated Federer from so many great athletes is not just his performance on the court but his performance in boardrooms and corporate suites. He takes pride in delivering personalized service. Even in his early years, he would visit all twenty-one of the sponsor suites at the Swiss Indoors to meet and greet. He has stuck with that philosophy.

"He's just so good if you've seen him with sponsors, with CEOs," Eisenbud said. "He just has the ability to make you feel like he really cares what you are saying, and he has time for you. He's never rushing you. If you're a fan at a hundred-person event that one of his sponsors puts on and you are talking to him, he makes you feel he has all the time in the world to talk to you and hear what you have to say. I think it's genuine, and I've never seen another athlete like that, and I think it has a lot to do with how he was brought up."

Andy Roddick told me that Federer came to Austin, Texas, in 2018 as a personal favor to help him with an event for his charitable foundation, which funds educational programs and activities for lower-income youth.

"I pick him up at the airport, we're driving in, and he's like, 'Okay, what's the run of show?'" Roddick said. "And Roger said, 'Be very specific about what you guys do. I don't just want to say you help kids because that's lazy.' And then he goes, 'Okay, how can I add the most value to you all today?' There wasn't a conversation about what time will I be able to leave, how much time do I have to spend?"

When they arrived at the event, Roddick expected that he would be Federer's escort, introducing him to guests and donors. But Federer took the initiative.

"He breaks away from me and literally goes up to the first two people he sees, introduces himself, and works the room by himself with no agent, no manager running interference," Roddick said. "I watched him do it for an hour, straight into a room full of strangers and just engaging with people. One of our board members has twins, and they are talking about twins. He's able to find the parallels and the common ground. I was really impressed by that. The person who needs to do that the least is the best at it. We finished the event, and his plane was delayed, and he walked back into the donor room and started going again. He didn't get out of Austin until one or two in the morning, and if he was pissed no one would have known."

I asked Roddick how unusual that sort of approach was compared to other elite athletes.

"The thing I'm most jealous of is not the skill and not the titles, it's the ease of operation with which Roger exists," Roddick said. "There are people who are as great as Roger in different sports, but there's no chance that Jordan or Tiger had the ease of operation Roger has day to day."

Nakajima remembers Federer coming to Nike's headquarters in Beaverton, Oregon, one year for shoe testing at Nike's research lab. They walked out of the building and were headed for their next meeting when Federer stopped in his tracks and said, "I've got to go back."

Nakajima asked him if he had forgotten something, and Federer said he had forgotten to thank the people who had helped him with the shoes.

"So we ran back into the building, downstairs, through security so he could say thanks," Nakajima said. "Now what athlete does that?"

Federer was at Nike headquarters for "Roger Federer Day," in which all the buildings on the sprawling campus were temporarily renamed for him. But Nakajima said the day was not simply a celebration of Federer's achievements. Federer, often up for a prank, agreed to play a few on Nike's employees.

They brought the advertising team together to watch a new advertisement. Federer surprised them by wheeling a cart around the room and serving coffee and doughnuts. At the company gym, he sat behind the front desk and handed out towels to the employees. At the company cafeteria, Federer did a shift as a cashier and then as a barista.

"Of course, he didn't know how to make coffee, so what he ended up doing was he just went around, going table to table, saying, 'Hello, my name is Roger Federer, nice to meet you,' as if people didn't know who he was," Nakajima remembered. "I mean, it was unbelievable. What other athlete could you do that with and have the athlete say, 'That's a great idea'? You think you could get Maria Sharapova to do that? No way. And Roger did that with a smile on his face, and then he played Wii tennis with anybody who wanted to play with him."

In 2011, the University of Oregon opened a new $227 million basketball arena named for Matthew Knight, the late son of Nike cofounder Phil Knight. Matthew had died in a scuba diving accident at age thirty-four, and Nakajima thought a tennis exhibition that March would be a fine way to help inaugurate the arena because both Knights loved the sport.

"The first person we called was Roger, and Roger already had a seven-figure commitment to be somewhere else," Nakajima said. "And Roger said, 'Is this for Phil?' And I go, 'Yeah,' and Roger goes, 'I'm in.'"

At the end of 2013, I broke the story for the *Times* that Federer and Godsick were leaving IMG to form their own boutique management firm called Team8. The name was largely a nod to Federer's talismanic number (he was born on the eighth of August, the eighth month of the year, in 1981). According to executives familiar with the deal, they were able to leave "clean" without paying penalties or fees to IMG, which was something Forstmann had agreed to before his death.

The breakaway move was part of a high-end trend. Tiger Woods and Steinberg had left IMG in 2011. Nadal had left recently as well, with his longtime agent, Carlos Costa.

The Federer and Godsick families have become deeply connected. Fernández is a godmother of Federer's children, and Godsick's and Fernández's son Nicholas, a promising tennis player, has received counsel from Federer and had a prime seat for many of his matches.

Team8, which also had backing from American investors Ian

McKinnon and billionaire Dirk Ziff, aimed to represent athletes other than Federer. Younger tennis stars Juan Martin del Potro and Grigor Dimitrov signed on as Team8 launched.

"Roger is going to have a legacy and a business that is going to live on well past his playing days, similar to a guy like Arnold Palmer in golf," said John Tobias, then the president of Lagardère Unlimited Tennis, a rival agency. "I figured that would be enough, and I had to figure those figures postcareer would be so solid that Tony would be just fine financially. Why he wants to take on additional responsibility, I'm not sure. I'm guessing it's because Tony is a pretty competitive guy."

Godsick told me he wanted to innovate and create new value, not just manage Federer's existing business. It was a bold but far from illogical move in light of Forstmann's death, the impending sale of IMG, and Federer's experience operating on his own earlier in his career.

He got more involved in player recruitment than expected, using his star power and communication skills to connect with young Australian Nick Kyrgios and his family, young German star Alexander Zverev, and American teen phenom Coco Gauff.

Zverev and Gauff formally joined Team8 while Kyrgios did not. One rival agent called some of the new agency's recruiting tactics "shocking" and expressed surprise that "Roger would want to get involved in all that."

It has not been the smoothest of rides. Despite Federer's appeal, recruitment has been challenging, and there has been considerable attrition among clients and employees. Dimitrov, Zverev, and del Potro eventually left. Team8 also split with Tommy Paul, a young and talented American player.

Andre Silva, a highly regarded former ATP executive hired by Team8, left in 2016 to become a tournament director. Chris McCormack, the grandson of IMG founder Mark McCormack, left and joined a rival agency.

But Federer's earnings have continued to climb, and in 2018, when he and Nike surprisingly could not come to terms on a renewal, he signed a long-term, ten-year apparel deal with Uniqlo, the Japanese mass-market retailer. The agreement has been reported to pay Federer $30 million per year, though some other agents in the industry believe the guaranteed amount is lower.

Either way, it is far more than Nike was prepared to pay an aging superstar, no matter how spotless his image.

"I'm glad it happened after I left because I never would have lived with myself," said Nakajima of the Nike-Federer split. "Unfortunately, it comes down to numbers. But I mean, are you kidding me? You're going to let Roger Federer go? It was sad this happened. For me, he's like a Michael Jordan. He's already thinking about what's going to be happening next, and he could potentially be more successful post-career if he does things right. Who wouldn't want to attach your name to that if you're a company?"

John Slusher, Nike's executive vice president for global sports marketing, was the lead negotiator for Nike. He is the son of Howard Slusher, a leading sports agent who was nicknamed "Agent Orange" for his red hair and scorched-earth negotiating tactics and who worked late in his career directly for Nike cofounder Phil Knight.

John Slusher, like Godsick, is a Dartmouth alumnus and also played on the football team, graduating three years before Godsick in 1990. But old school ties did not help the deal get done. Nor did Slusher's face-to-face meeting with Federer or all the goodwill gestures that had been made through the years. Massimo Calvelli, who left Nike to become the ATP's chief executive officer, was also involved in the negotiations.

"We had some tough negotiations ten years ago, fifteen years ago, so you get used to it," Federer told the New York Times. "But it's all good. We tried to work it out for a year, maybe even more than a year, and from my point of view I thought I was being reasonable."

Tennis is not a major money spinner for Nike. It is a small division within the large, global company. Nike is closing in on annual revenue of $50 billion. "The tennis business is about $350 million, so you do the math," Nakajima said.

The rule of thumb, according to Nakajima, is not to spend more than 10 percent of revenue on athlete sponsorship. Nike already was committed to stars like Serena Williams, Nadal, and Sharapova, who had not yet retired in 2018. It also had rising stars under contract like Kyrgios, Denis Shapovalov, and Amanda Anisimova. To come closer to meeting Federer's demands, Nakajima said the company would have had to break that 10 percent ceiling.

In 2008, when Federer had signed his lucrative ten-year renewal with Nike, Phil Knight was directly involved in the negotiations. This time Federer hoped that Knight would again intervene on his behalf, but Knight was in a chairman emeritus role by 2018 and had stepped away from day-to-day management at age eighty. Slusher and former chief executive Mark Parker took the lead and might not have thought that Federer would really leave a high-performance sportswear company for a more down-market, fast-fashion brand. But if it was a bluff, Federer called it, and though Nike had the right to match any offer, the Uniqlo deal was, in Nike's view, too big to match.

"There's no way Roger wanted to leave Nike, no way," Nakajima said. "I heard Massimo cried when Tony told him the deal was done with Uniqlo. I would never, never have let that happen."

Some in the tennis industry were surprised that Federer did not accept less money up front from Nike in exchange for guarantees that Nike would build the "RF" brand for the long run, as it has done with Michael Jordan's brand.

"It was always a dream for me," Federer once told me. "Agassi had a line, right? Jordan had a line. I think it's so cool, and it's not for myself, so I can go around and go, 'Look, I have my own line' to another tennis player or another athlete. This is, for me, not so important. For me, it's important that a fan can buy something that is related to me, like in soccer, you buy a shirt and it's got somebody's name on the back. That's what I like about the RF logo. I'm really proud Nike was willing to go that direction, because I know it's always hard for them because if they do it for me, another fifty will come knocking on their door and say, 'What about me?'"

But after more than twenty years, Federer embarked on a new

direction, even if it would take him more than two years to regain control of the "RF" logo from Nike.

"What you see as your value may not be what they see," he said of Nike. "I'm happy to be proven right with this long-term deal with Uniqlo."

The Uniqlo deal put Federer on a level of his own financially. In mid-2020, *Forbes* named him the world's highest-paid athlete, estimating his annual income at $106.3 million, only $6.3 million of which was official prize money.

It was the first time Federer or any tennis player had topped the list. He finished ahead of soccer stars Cristiano Ronaldo, Leo Messi, and Neymar and NBA stars LeBron James, Stephen Curry, and Kevin Durant. Federer's preeminence at age thirty-nine was due in part to the pandemic that shut down professional sports and curtailed earnings for a significant chunk of 2020.

Because the Uniqlo agreement did not cover footwear, Federer also invested in On, a Swiss running-shoe company based in Zurich. He worked with them at length to develop a tennis shoe that he wore in competition for the first time in 2021 and whose sole pattern and rubber compound were developed specifically to limit squeaking on hard courts.

On Holding AG went public later in the year, and after its initial public offering on the New York Stock Exchange on September 15, 2021, Federer's investment stake, estimated at 3 percent, was worth over $330 million. Although On's share value has fluctuated significantly since the I.P.O., Federer clearly has done very well for himself by leaving Nike, making two deals potentially worth over $300 million apiece.

He lives in luxury no doubt, but Lüthi, who knows him as well as anyone at this stage, does not think great wealth has changed his nature. "I honestly think he would have been happy painting houses in Basel," Lüthi told me. "I think money can create a lot of problems. Everybody likes to have more, but not everybody can deal with it. I think Roger deals with it pretty well."

Beyond Federer's lucrative individual pursuits and Gauff's portfolio-in-progress, it is the Laver Cup that remains Team8's focus—an event that, if it prospers, could serve as both a legacy for Federer and a vehicle for him to remain involved in the game as a team captain or organizer.

To protect it, he and Godsick pushed insistently behind the scenes for it to become an official part of the ATP Tour. They also have fought fiercely to preserve its late September dates, which are appealing to the revamped Davis Cup. Federer and Godsick could not, however, prevent edgy French Open leaders from making a landgrab during the pandemic year of 2020 by unilaterally moving their tournament into the Laver Cup's week on the calendar. But then the 2020 edition of the Laver Cup in Boston's TD Garden would very likely have been postponed in any case because of the restrictions on public gatherings.

<hr />

After taking off from the California desert at 7:00 a.m. in March 2018, Federer spent the first part of the flight having breakfast and talking tennis politics with me, Godsick, and Lüthi, who looked even sleepier than Federer. It was a long, involved discussion. Federer listened more than he talked, asking questions about everything from the potential changes to the Davis Cup to the impact of social media on the journalism business. Federer and Godsick bantered with familiar ease, raising their voices slightly when their opinions differed. This did not feel like Federer with a traveling band of yes-men.

"It's just like the rest of his disposition. You can disagree with Roger, and he doesn't take it personally, his pulse rate doesn't get up," Paul Annacone once told me. "He's happy to sit and talk about it and go, 'Okay, I get that,' but he can take a step back and really objectively evaluate things well."

Lüthi said that he and Annacone realized when they were both coaching Federer that it was more effective to give him two different takes than to reach a consensus view and present Federer with a single piece of advice.

"Other players, when they are hearing different things, they might be getting nervous," Lüthi told me. "Roger is just not like that. He likes to hear the different opinions and then decide for himself. He always gives you the possibility to be yourself and express yourself and be honest, and for me that's key. I think that's one of Roger's great strengths. We don't agree on everything all the time, but I think that makes it interesting."

After a brief nap in a separate cabin, Federer warmed up for his first visit to Chicago with a quiz.

"NFL team?" "Bears," he answered.

"NHL team?" "Blackhawks!"

"Baseball team?" "Cubs!"

"And?"

There was a pause before Federer came up—correctly—with "White Sox."

Not bad for a Swiss who surely had watched a lot more soccer than baseball, but Federer is a sports fan and was also, in his youth, a big NBA and Chicago Bulls fan. When he was seventeen, he had posters of Michael Jordan and Shaquille O'Neal in his room (as well as a poster of Pamela Anderson in a swimsuit).

A big part of Chicago's appeal to Federer was the chance to play the Laver Cup in the United Center, the home arena of the Bulls. We soon made our way there after landing at Chicago's Midway International Airport. Federer visited the United Center with Kyrgios, the Australian who was a lock to play for the World Team in the Laver Cup but, considering his ambivalence about tennis, would surely have preferred being an NBA star.

The surprise was their tour guide: Scottie Pippen, a fine complement to Jordan on those Bulls championship teams. Federer got goose bumps as Pippen escorted them into the Bulls locker room and into the arena.

"That was special, meeting Scottie," Federer told me. "Nick follows basketball now a lot. I still do as well but way back when Scottie played, that was when I was really following basketball."

The four hours in Chicago felt like an extended fast break, with visits to a deep-dish pizzeria, the Chicago Theatre, Millennium Park, and the Chicago Athletic Association Hotel for a news conference with Rod Laver, Team World captain John McEnroe, Kyrgios, and Chicago mayor Rahm Emanuel.

"Roger's life, if it's not hectic, it's not Roger's life, because it's all he knows," Godsick said.

I joined Federer in the backseat for the long car ride back to Midway Airport, back to the private jet and his flight to Miami. I asked him if at this stage of his life, he ever spent time alone.

He laughed and seemed surprised by the question. "Not often," he said. "But I do travel without Mirka and the kids once in a while and so I'll get time in my hotel room."

But he confessed that he had no particular need for solitude even if he did feel the need to reconnect with nature and a more peaceful environment after too much time on the circuit. He made it clear, though, that he was not yet weary of the travel.

"Think about today," he said. "We left with the sunrise, beautiful weather in Indian Wells, and we get here, and it's cold and a totally different vibe. That's the beauty of travel, of seeing different places. I love it. I do. I still love it."

Skipping airport security lines and airline boarding procedures certainly made it easier to see the beauty of travel, but Federer still seemed preternaturally equipped to be the ultimate tennis pro with his love not just of the game but of most of the stuff that came with the game and nagged at his peers. Laver Cup was for him a bridge between generations: between the pro circuit barnstormers of Laver's day and the future wave of stars.

"I feel like the wheel keeps turning in tennis and you get lost as a legend sometimes," he said. "I think it's nice that the retired legends still have a platform. In this day and age, tennis can use that, too. The legends have many stories to tell, so that's one of the big reasons I liked the idea of the Laver Cup. For me Laver really stands out, but he was not the only one of his generation. There was also Lew Hoad and Ken Rosewall. These guys really had to grind. Tony Roche told me many of their stories, and I thought it would be nice to thank them in a way for all their contributions. Nobody really knows their story and if you dig into it, it's quite remarkable. They played in, like, 150 cities in 200 days. It was like a circus, really."

But Federer also wanted to play a mentor's role: to remind the game's young stars of their place in a continuum and to help them avoid the pitfalls of youthful fame and fortune.

"My credo is always 'Just be interested; be interested in all your things,'" Federer said. "It could be your finances, could be your agency, communication with your agent. It could be your sponsors, your taxes. Whatever it is, don't have other people make all those decisions for you. At the end of the day, if there is a problem, it's you who is at fault. That's my biggest advice to anyone."

I asked Federer what he saw in the younger players' eyes when he explained the credo.

"I feel they are thinking, 'Good idea,'" he said. "And then you're like, 'Well, yeah, then do something about it.'"

The chauffeur drove the car straight onto the tarmac at Midway Airport, stopping next to the plane. Federer's first trip to Chicago was just about over, but it delivered one more authentic Chicago experience as the strong winds made it a genuine struggle for him to open the car door.

After winning that battle, he politely bade farewell and fought another gust or two of wind on his way up the boarding stairs before finally ducking inside the jet.

My travels with Federer were over, and after writing a column the next day, I was soon back in the air in very different style: in a middle seat in economy class on an overbooked American Airlines flight headed for Boston. As I ate dinner on my tray table and shared both armrests with my neighbors, it all seemed like payback: an abrupt reality check after an extended stay in Federer's low-friction world.

Upon arrival at Logan Airport, I caught a bus north to my town near the New Hampshire border but arrived past 2:00 a.m., which meant that it was too late to call a local taxi.

I ended up walking the three miles home along the side of the road, rolling my suitcase behind me and occasionally laughing out loud in the darkness at the contrast between the glamorous start of my journey and the pedestrian finish.

This, it struck me, was the sort of solitude that Federer so rarely experienced.

CHAPTER SIXTEEN

FELSBERG, Switzerland

The court was named "Roger," and Federer was sweeping the red clay, like a woodworker cleaning the workshop floor after a busy day at the lathe.

He had been away from his first tennis surface long enough to miss the sliding, the muffled bounce of the ball, and the rituals, like dragging a thick net across the clay to erase the marks and prepare it for the next players.

Nadal often sweeps his own practice courts, too, and there is a certain humility in the gesture. It also never gets old to see superstars acting just like the rest of us.

"Even Roger Federer cleans the clay," said Toni Poltera, president of Tennisclub Felsberg, as he watched Federer at work. "This is why Roger is popular here. He's not over the top. He has the human touch."

I had come to the Alps in April 2019 to spend a day watching Federer train and interview him for the *New York Times* about his return to clay after a three-year break but also to talk about his connection to Switzerland.

He could certainly have paid lower taxes (or no taxes) elsewhere, but he was anchored there despite all his travels and options, despite his apartment in Dubai and property in South Africa and affinity for laid-back lifestyles.

"I feel very Swiss at the end of the day," he said. "So that's why I would like to bring my kids up here. When we talk about home this is it. As much as Mirka has a Slovakian background, and I have a South African background, I think we feel most happy here."

Federer was speaking over lunch at the Rheinfels restaurant, a family-style pizzeria in Chur, where we had driven in his Mercedes between practice sessions. The main dining area was close to full when we entered, but though heads turned, there were no gesticulations or exclamations from the other customers as the hostess escorted us to a table in the adjacent room, where we could have a quieter setting for a tête-à-tête.

Clearly, Federer had not gone unnoticed, but he had gone unharried, at least for a little while. Not long after we ordered, a family came toward our table, practically on tiptoe alongside the hostess, and asked in Swiss German for a group selfie. At first, Federer, who had been midsentence, looked mildly annoyed at the interruption, but he got up from his wooden chair, smiled, laughed, and complied.

Still, this was hardly Beatlemania and the relative calm was remarkable, considering that Federer is by far the most famous Swiss at home and abroad.

Severin Lüthi, Federer's longtime coach and friend, knows it too well.

"If you're going to Thailand or wherever, even if you go for holidays, and they ask you where you are from, and you say Switzerland, then they say 'Roger Federer!'" Lüthi said. "That happens pretty regularly."

A less tactful person might respond that he actually knew Federer.

"I don't tell them," Lüthi said. "I'm happy just to see how they react. Otherwise, it looks like you want to show off."

As that comment suggests, Switzerland is a country that emphasizes discretion and egalitarianism from early school days onward, and Federer believes the respectful, understated atmosphere has helped him prolong his career.

"I really feel I can come back to Switzerland and decompress," he said.

And yet with a professional career lasting more than twenty years, he is part of the collective memory bank, so he does often feel as if he owes the Swiss who cross his path some sort of acknowledgment, no matter how cool they try to play it.

"People look at me sometimes in a way like I'm almost a politician," he said with a laugh. "I'm almost supposed to greet everybody because they know me so well from TV and ads and interviews."

I asked Federer: What, for him, is the Swiss mentality?

"Um, reserved, you know, in some ways, but if you get to know a Swiss he's very open and very inviting, and you will find probably a friend for life," he said. "I think because we also have four national languages, we are quite international naturally. We have a lot of German, French, Italian, Austrian influence, so I feel we are very much a melting pot. And it's an easy place to get around and change your world. We're here now, and you can drive two or three hours and you are in Milan, just a completely different place."

Though Federer certainly does not have a "normal life" in Switzerland, his life does feel manageable. We went to lunch—just the two of us, without handlers or security guards. Despite the photograph request, the rest of the two-hour meal was tranquil: from soup to pasta to espresso (Federer is not much of a carnivore).

"I'm not a huge believer in star signs and all that stuff, but I am a Leo," he said. "And I think the Leo, he likes to be the center of attention but when he likes to be. So for me, the tennis world works perfectly. I'm happy to face it all: the music, all the big stadiums, the media, the attention. But then I need to get away from it all."

That seemed a particularly revealing comment, one that I could relate to on some lower-grade level. As a sportswriter, you need to plunge into the stress, the ruckus, and the crowds, write your deadline pieces in press boxes with thousands cheering, booing, or chanting. All that energy and emotion seeps into you and eventually drains you, even as a mere observer. Though I am a Sagittarius, not a Leo, I have often finished covering a series of Grand Slam tournaments, an Olympics, or a World Cup and found myself searching out the quietest life possible: forests, farmland, mountain trails, anything with chirping crickets instead of roaring fans. It is as if you need to swing from one extreme to the other to find some semblance of balance.

Federer nodded at this.

"Here I feel I can find my equilibrium and find my peace and all that," he said, making a sweeping gesture with the hand that was not holding the coffee cup. "So it was actually a lucky idea to have the family grow up in the mountains. This was not a plan of ours at first. It just happened that we found a piece of land and were able to build, like, five, six, seven years ago and come away from the big cities into this more remote area."

They built in Valbella, within easy reach of the ski runs and hiking trails of Lenzerheide and only a forty-five-minute drive from Davos and an hour from Saint Moritz.

Living here means training at altitude. Felsberg is at 572 meters, which is about 1,900 feet—enough to make a tennis ball move faster through the thinner air. It also means playing in cozy, unpretentious places like Tennisclub Felsberg, which lies close to the Rhine River. Symphonies were not written about this narrow section of the Rhine, but lift your gaze, and there is plenty of majesty: snowcapped peaks even in late April.

The soundscape on this Tuesday was a mix of birdsong, lowing cattle, passing traffic, and crisply struck tennis balls. The club has a hitting wall and a rustic wooden clubhouse that looks like it was decorated by someone who was in a hurry to get on one of the three clay courts. When I visited, there was a photo on the wall of Federer and his friend and frequent training partner Tommy Haas.

A broken racket hung over the entrance.

"That's not mine," said Poltera, the club president, a jovial extrovert in jeans and a hooded sweatshirt who takes understandable pride in his modest facility's link with Federer.

"This is the fifth or sixth time they've been here this year," Poltera said. "You never know. It depends on a lot of things, including the weather."

It also depends on word of mouth. Go to one place too often, and the fans will start to flock to that club. The Swiss might be discreet, but they are not going to pass up a chance to watch Federer for free.

"We like to mix it up," Lüthi explained after picking me up at the train station in Chur that morning. "It's good to change. People don't need to always know where we practice."

They also mix sparring partners, often bringing in young Swiss players like Jakub Paul, who grew up in Chur and now trains in Biel/Bienne at the national center.

"I was at home once on holiday, and Lüthi called me up out of the blue and asked would I have time for practice," Paul told me. "And I said *of course* I have time. So I got to play with Roger at the little club."

This week the practice partner was Dan Evans, the tattooed British veteran who, like Federer, has a one-handed backhand and played squash frequently in his youth. In 2019, Evans was still working his way back into the rankings after being banned for a year for cocaine use. Normally, his varied and creative game is the most stylish on any court, but not when he is practicing with Federer.

This was hardly classic, grinding clay court tennis, but it was a treat.

"We're going back to the '80s: slice winners!" shouted Federer after one particularly flashy rally on Roger-Platz, the court named for him.

He had done his preparatory stretching and warm-up at home in Valbella, which is a short drive away, but before practice began at 10:00 a.m., he did some footwork, sliding on the clay without his racket as if he were testing his range.

"Sometimes the challenge for me on clay is not to slide just to slide," he said. "I think that's what Rafa does so well or the top clay courters, they only slide if they really have to. Naturally you think, 'Oh, sliding is fun,' so you just start sliding to every ball even though you have maybe less control when you're sliding."

After our long lunch, he did not stretch or warm up again but started back up quickly. I found that surprising for a thirty-seven-year-old with a history of back and knee problems.

"He should have done a bit more, and normally he does," Lüthi said.

Fitness trainer Pierre Paganini, typically part of such practices, was absent today, but both Federer and Lüthi said it is important for Federer's mental freshness to not turn preparation into drudgery.

"Sometimes before the matches, the physio wants to do his job perfectly, and I have to tell him we're not doing a back exercise for ten minutes," Lüthi said. "Sometimes we have to do just a compromise. It's different now with a body that's been on tour for twenty years. But Roger used to jump twice and then start his match, so you can also overthink things and do all kinds of taping and go nuts."

Federer said he was paying much more attention now to off-court preparation. "For a few years now, I'm warming up more than ever, doing more stretching and massage," he said. "But I told the team, 'Look, I can only do so much, because I need to have a life. I need to be here for my kids, need to be here for my wife. I need to enjoy it. I can't be practicing for one hour and then spending three or four hours doing other things just to cope with the physical strain.' So we found a good plan that works for me and for them."

It goes back to the metaphor of the clenched fist that Roger likes to use. Stay intense and on task for too long, especially away from the courts, and you will eventually break down and burn out.

We will see how Nadal feels when he is in his late thirties—he has prospered far longer than most of us expected with his full-throttle approach—but it is hard to argue with Federer's results and durability.

The French often use the world *relâchement* when they talk about Federer's game. It can be translated as "relaxed," but the better translation is "looseness." For me, that elasticity is the key to so much: his smooth movement, his unforced power, his ability to come up with wizardry on the move and under duress.

"If you put another twenty pounds of muscle on Roger, it's not going to guarantee that he's going to hit the ball bigger," his former coach José Higueras told me. "He may actually hit the ball slower. It's not about the strength. It's about the timing."

Ella Ling, one of the best tennis photographers, used to resist taking pictures of Federer in her early years because he kept his emotions so tightly under wraps. But she has changed her perspective. "The lack of facial contortion when he hits the ball speaks volumes," she told me. "Playing tennis is natural, effortless to him; an extension of his body and mind. It is unique, and I doubt we will ever see the likes of it again."

His *relâchement* certainly played a role in helping him endure when so many of his peers already had retired. Of the 128 men who played singles at the 1999 French Open, his debut Grand Slam tournament, he was the last one still playing singles on tour.

"Come on!" he said when I offered up that stat. "Nobody else left?"

A few other players his age, or even older, were still competing in singles: Feliciano López, the left-handed Spaniard who was once his junior rival; and Ivo Karlović, a towering Croatian with a massive serve and flecks of gray in his beard.

But Federer's wild card in Paris in 1999 had put him ahead of the curve, and he was still ahead of it twenty years later, contending for majors and racking up tour titles: he had won his 100th in Dubai earlier in 2019 and his 101st in Miami.

Nature or nurture?

"Maybe where my talent maybe has helped me a little bit is to shape and get the technique I have today that puts maybe less wear and tear on me," he said. "But I think I've earned it by my schedule and my buildup and maybe my mental side of the game as well. As much as I take things very seriously, I'm very laid-back, so I can really let go very quickly. This lunch, for example, is like a break for me. In my head, I'm able to say, 'Look, we just had a full-on practice and here I am actually able to relax and chill. And then we're going back to work again.' I think having that approach is really key."

Federer is an intriguing blend of order and spontaneity, or perhaps it is not a blend but more like an alternating current. It is as if all the planning is what allows him to be in the moment, fully present, and he seems particularly resistant to outside influences interfering with his natural cycle.

The retirement question had been hanging in the air since 2009 and yet he insisted, even ten years later, that he had not allowed himself to think about it in detail.

"What I'm trying to do is really keep it as flexible as possible for afterwards, to really see what shall we do," he said. "How much tennis? How much business? How much family? Of course, I'd like to have all the options open for my kids and Mirka first, and then we go from there. What I don't want to do is commit to something too soon and then regret it. So yeah. I don't know. I really don't know. I've always said the more I think about retirement, the more I am already retired. I feel like if I plan everything for my postcareer, I feel like I'm halfway there, half retired."

"And that would affect your performance?" I asked.

"Well, not my performance per se, but maybe my overall desire to want to do well," he said. "I can figure it out when I'm retired. I'm not feeling stressed about it."

He had been thwarting other people's timelines for him for years.

"'You have been world number one, you've won all four Slams, so what's next? I guess it's over, right?'" said Federer, mimicking the questions and the assumptions. "That was a common theme, definitely."

At this stage, he could sense people positioning themselves for the finish, which is, for better or worse, what journalists like myself are hardwired to do.

"They have to capture extra stuff, so I can feel it, like the net is tightening around me," he said. "Everybody is asking for the extra interview, and can I interview that guy? I can tell that it's just in case. But it's okay. It is what it is, you know. It's all good."

Another part of Federer's legacy is that he will spare future champions the same sort of repetitive interrogation until much later in their timelines.

"I hope so," he said.

"I mean, Stan now said he would like to play for a few more years," he said, speaking about Wawrinka. "He's just turned thirty-four, and thirty-four was, like, old back then, and now it's like I'm gonna still play for hopefully another three, four, five years."

Federer's voice was rising, and he was waving his hands.

"I mean, five years, that's, like, thirty-nine, man!" he said. "But it's tough, because the top guys are strong."

Federer is hardly *aprés moi le déluge*—or, in the era of the Big Three, *aprés nous le déluge.* He has an acute interest in the next generation, and not just because he still has to play them. He is genuinely curious to see who will come through to reach No. 1, win multiple majors, and carry his sport forward and hopefully not backward.

Much of the end of our lunch, with the coffee cups sitting empty on the table, amounted to the two of us speculating on which of the youngsters had the right stuff.

"[Alexander] Zverev, maybe? [Stefanos] Tsitsipas, maybe?" he said, sounding more curious than convinced.

Several other players came up, too, including young Canadian Felix Auger-Aliassime.

"You know how it is, the game always produces superstars, so I don't worry about that," he said. "Maybe also when this generation has gone that will also free up and actually unlock some of their potential. Maybe they need a big tournament win that then is going to make them believe. It's like what I needed. I needed to win Wimbledon to say, like, 'Okay, I can do this every week.' And maybe they also need to overcome that, because maybe for the time being, these guys can't come out and say, like, 'I want to be world number one' because every-body's gonna go, 'Ha! Novak is number one,' or 'Yeah, how are you going to get through Rafa, buddy?'"

Federer had not played a clay court match on tour since 2016. He had skipped the 2017 clay season to preserve his energy and post-operative knee during his successful comeback. He went on to win Wimbledon without dropping a set. He had skipped the 2018 clay season because he wanted to maintain the same routine that had worked so well for him. Above all, he wanted to celebrate Mirka's fortieth birthday in style in April.

"She has done so much for me, and I thought instead of giving her something that you could take with you, I thought I would like to give her memories, experiences," he said. "My dream was always for her to know about the vacation or a place we're going but not to know all the details, because normally she organizes everything. So I thought, 'Let me reverse it.' "

After a family vacation, they ended up taking an adults-only trip to Ibiza with about forty friends, with Federer generally avoiding tennis but still catching most of Rafael Nadal's three-set victory over Alexander Zverev in the final of the Italian Open.

"I was in one of those beach clubs, watching it on television," he said. "We have a great group of friends; Mirka has done so much to stay in touch with so many friends. She knew about Ibiza. She knew we were going to invite friends, and she decided the list, and so I said I'll decide all the small stuff. All the daily surprises she didn't know about, so that was great."

But by 2019, Federer was ready again for a fuller season instead of taking a two-month break in the spring. His belief was that playing on clay would also help his chances on grass at Wimbledon, where he had lost in the quarterfinals to Kevin Anderson in five sets in 2018 after holding a match point.

"I think I was too long on the grass last year," he said. "I think playing on clay will help me just hitting through the ball full speed. When you play too much on grass, I feel you start guiding the ball, whereas on clay, you go with full swings. You have to earn it, so I think this could benefit me down the stretch. The biggest thing is I want to go back to Paris. I want to go back on the clay."

It would go well. He reached the quarterfinals in Madrid in his return to the surface and went on to reach the semifinals of the French Open in his first appearance since 2015. Not much had changed in his absence. Nadal was still the man to beat, and for the sixth time in six attempts at Roland Garros, Federer could not manage it. He lost in straight sets on one of the windiest days in the tournament's long history, with clouds of red clay swirling into the players' eyes and ripping Panama hats off spectators' heads.

It was a desert storm in Paris.

"You get to a point where you're just happy to make shots and not look ridiculous," Federer said.

But Nadal, with his deeper court positions and heavier topspin, was better equipped to handle the conditions. Even in freakish weather, he is in his element at Roland Garros.

"He has incredible abilities on clay," Federer said. "I knew that ahead of time. I don't look like I fight, but I do, and I tried to believe in it. I tried to turn the match around until the end. But the longer the match went on, the better he seemed to feel in the wind."

Still, Federer's clear goal was Wimbledon, and he arrived in the right form and frame of mind, having won the title in Halle on grass for the tenth time. At Wimbledon, he won his first five matches to set up another semifinal with Nadal.

It was their first match at the All England Club since the 2008 final. It was a time to reflect on how great that duel had been and on how surprising it was that the thirty-three-year-old Nadal and the thirty-seven-year-old Federer were still facing off regularly more than a decade later in the business end of the majors.

They had gone from dominating the game together in the late 2000s to struggling to keep pace with the multisurface threat posed by Novak Djokovic. They had become part of the "Big Four" with the rise of Andy Murray and then part of an even larger lead pack with the emergence of Wawrinka. But by 2019, with Murray and Wawrinka diminished by injuries, they were back to being the Big Three. Djokovic, who had winning records against both of them, had returned to No. 1 and was already into the Wimbledon final after beating Roberto Bautista Agut earlier in the day on Centre Court.

Federer and Nadal's long-awaited Wimbledon rematch would not rise to the level of their 2008 mutual masterwork. This duel went four sets instead of five, failing to generate the same sort of consistent suspense or twilight memories. It ended well before dark.

But their fortieth match was still quite a spectacle as they both covered ground astonishingly well, with Nadal often tighter to the baseline than usual in an attempt to be the first to seize the initiative. He and his coach, Carlos Moyá, were all too aware that Federer had dominated their matches on faster surfaces since his 2017 comeback.

"Roger's backhand has improved a lot, and he caught us by surprise in Australia," Moyá said of the 2017 Australian Open. "After that, we knew we had to change something, and for sure on clay it is easier for Rafa to change a few things against these guys who are trying not to give him any rhythm."

Grass remained a bigger challenge. Federer won the tight first set by winning the last five points of the tiebreaker. He then lost his timing in the second set, losing his serve twice and twenty of the final twenty-three points as he repeatedly shanked shots off the frame.

But he fought through more trouble to win the third, and then both seemed to peak at the same time in the fourth. Winners, not errors, were the rule as both looked to run around their backhands and smack inside-out forehands.

"You expect magnificent shots from him; it's what he does," Federer said of Nadal. "What you need to do is make him keep having to hit magnificent shots. The problem is when you have to always play close to your limit, to take a mega risk for a break point. It's hard to say, 'I'm just going to go for it,' because you know it's difficult. You have to find the balance, and today I found it quickly. I was a bit zen and calm."

It had long been hard to know from looking at Nadal whether he was winning or losing, whether he was satisfied or frustrated. But with age he had become more transparent, and in the sixth game, after missing a forehand return, he smacked himself in the forehead with his palm. Later in the game, after missing a sliced backhand, he leaned forward and berated himself.

Nadal was not done being Nadal, however. Down 3–5, he saved two match points in a titanic, five-deuce game. He then fought off two more match points with Federer serving for the match in the next game. Both were saved with winners: a forehand inside out to end a high-velocity, twenty-four-stroke rally, and then a cocksure backhand passing shot off a soft Federer approach. But Federer did convert his fifth match point to reach his twelfth Wimbledon final, extending both arms triumphantly and then extending them again in Nadal's direction for a warm exchange at the net.

"It lived up to the hype," Federer said of the rematch.

I agreed, as I wrote in my *Times* column that night:

"The match was mesmerizing in the fourth set, not because Federer and Nadal were defying time, but because they were defying each other."

When Federer's 7–6 (3), 1–6, 6–3, 6–4 victory was complete, I spoke with Jarkko Nieminen, the retired Finn who is close with Federer and, being a left-hander with a good topspin forehand, had helped warm him up for the match.

"The level of tennis was ridiculously good," Nieminen said. "At some stages, I was speechless. I couldn't believe how early they took the ball, how hard they were hitting, how close to the lines. They aren't thinking about their age out there, I can tell you that."

But unlike in 2008, this duel would not finish with a trophy ceremony. Djokovic awaited Federer, and at this stage, Djokovic, not Nadal, was Federer's bête noire. Federer had beaten Nadal in seven of their last eight matches but had lost five of the last six to Djokovic.

"I know it's not over yet," Federer said of the tournament. "There is, unfortunately or fortunately, one more."

It was an unusually frank way to put it, but Federer knew too well that he had not beaten Djokovic in any major since the 2012 Wimbledon semifinal.

What was clear was that Federer was playing and managing risk particularly well. His springtime decision to play on the clay before the grass looked like the right move.

But Djokovic had also become a master scheduler and was now firmly reestablished at the top of the game. Federer had spent his last week at No. 1 in June 2018, running his career total to 310 weeks. Djokovic would eventually pass him for the men's record in 2021, part of his renewed assault on tennis's most prestigious records after emerging from his slump in 2018.

He was a formidable, shape-shifting opponent on any surface and all the more a challenge considering that Federer had never managed to beat Nadal and Djokovic in the same major tournament.

"Rafa, as a lefty, poses very different problems to me or others than Djokovic," Federer said. "Djokovic stays on his line, hits flat, moves differently, and covers court differently. You have to adjust tactically. Today, Rafa was serving faster than before. Novak serves in the same zone in terms of speed, so that helps a lot because the adjustment used to be more extreme. But the most important thing is the confidence. If you don't have the confidence, or I don't, it's very difficult to beat Rafa or Novak back-to-back."

The use of "Rafa" and the alternating use of "Novak" and "Djokovic" seemed a fair reflection of the state of Federer's relationship with each rival: warm and familiar with "Rafa"; cooler and more conflicted with "Novak" and "Djokovic."

But Federer's countenance remained similar during both matches. Zen was his mode at 2019 Wimbledon, and one of the more intriguing elements of the final was that Djokovic, who often runs on bellicosity, chose to adopt the same approach.

"One of the tactics that we talked about before was that he needed to stay very, very calm and positive," said Goran Ivanišević, one of Djokovic's coaches. "The goal was just put the crowd aside. There's no crowd. Only you and Roger on the court."

That was because the Centre Court crowd was, as usual, heavily in favor of Federer, the aging (or ageless) underdog with the elegant game and manners to which Wimbledon's upscale clientele can relate.

Just as he had against Nadal, Federer opened with an ace and a quick hold. Djokovic then held at love, which set the tone for a finely balanced, break-free first set full of tight-to-the-baseline power and guile. In the tiebreaker, Federer jumped out to a 5–3 lead on his serve, but then came trouble as Federer closed on a midcourt forehand and missed it wide. He would lose the next three points as well and the set.

But Federer showed no sign of a hangover, breaking a suddenly shaky Djokovic three times in four service games to sweep through the second set in just twenty-five minutes. Such one-way traffic would turn out to be an anomaly, and the taut third set was a repeat of the first. Federer had a set point with Djokovic serving at 5–6, 30–40, but Federer missed the backhand return wide off a good first serve.

Into a tiebreaker they went, and Federer had a calamitous start, mishitting more backhands and falling behind 1–5 before rallying to 4–5. Djokovic gave him a chance to play, hitting a second serve, but Federer missed another backhand, this one sliced. It was another opportunity gone, and it was soon two sets to one for Djokovic, even though Federer's point-to-point level had been consistently higher.

So it remained in the fourth set, but this time Federer got the reward, and they moved stoically into the decisive fifth but under a new set of rules.

For 2019, the All England Club had decided, for the first time, to institute a fifth-set tiebreaker at twelve-games-all. The club had made the move in response to an increasing number of ultramarathon men's matches, some of them involving big-serving American John Isner, and one of them involving Federer when he had defeated Andy Roddick in a fifth set that stretched to 16–14 in the 2009 final.

This year, if necessary, there would be a clear finish line. After Federer broke Djokovic at 7–7 in the fifth with a forehand passing shot, it appeared that no tiebreaker would be required. Once the crowd had been quieted, Federer served for the championship at 8–7. Mirka, his wife, was hunched forward in the player's box, her forehead resting on her clasped hands as if she could not bear to look.

At 15–15, Federer smacked an ace up the T. At 30–15, he sliced another ace up the T.

It was 40–15. Two match points. Reassuring news against most opponents, but certainly less comforting for Federer against Djokovic in light of those back-to-back US Open semifinals.

Mirka popped her head up, blinking in the late-afternoon sunlight, took note of the score, and then went straight back to not watching.

Federer smartly hit his first serve up the T again. Djokovic was leaning the wrong way, but instead of a third consecutive ace, the ball struck the tape and fell back.

"Novak was totally guessing wide," said Paul Annacone, Federer's former coach. "Roger, anything over the net anywhere close to the middle wins the match, and instead it hits the net cord. When that happened, I had a total flashback."

Federer had to hit a second serve and he was a beat slower than usual to respond to Djokovic's deep forehand return, missing his own forehand wide.

It was 40–30. Federer made the first serve this time. Djokovic blocked back a forehand return that landed fairly short. Federer decided not to die wondering and hit a topspin forehand crosscourt and rushed forward to the net. But it was not a particularly crisp or well-placed approach shot, and Djokovic moved right and did not even have to stretch to hit a forehand crosscourt pass that dipped out of reach of the lunging Federer.

Two championship points saved, and Federer, surely more shaken than his poker face revealed, played the next two points conservatively and lost them both. He flicked the ball away in disappointment as the electronic scoreboard ticked to 8–8 at 6:23 p.m.

It was haunting for Federer and his fans, some of whom had been pointing a single finger to the sky on his first championship point. It was exhilarating for Team Djokovic, but there was still much work to do, and Federer, to his credit but not to his benefit, hardly staggered to the finish.

Tennis is always, on some level, a contest of concentration: two internal tussles divided by a net. This match exemplified that.

"True," Djokovic told me months later when we met in Monte Carlo. "Every aspect of your life translates into being match point down in a final, and am I able to handle this or not? It's more complex than just a simple thing, but it can be boiled down and explained in a simple sentence, which is: Be in the present moment, and trust yourself, believe in yourself."

Djokovic was not entirely sure what he was up against. At one stage, he actually had to confirm with Damian Steiner, the chair umpire, that the tiebreaker, if necessary, would happen at twelve-games-all.

To me, the most impressive game Djokovic played all match came when he was serving at 11–11. Up 40–0, he lost four straight points to allow Federer a break point. Djokovic saved it by attacking, and Federer's chipped backhand pass landed just wide. Federer soon had another break point, and Djokovic attacked again, hitting a less-than-textbook forehand volley and a shaky overhead behind the running Federer to finish off the point. As Djokovic turned to walk back to the baseline, he shook his head and smiled wryly. He knew that had been close and ugly, dangerously close and ugly.

Still, it was resilient, gutsy, take-the-initiative tennis from Djokovic with the crowd and the flow of the game against him. Federer was still striking the ball so cleanly, mixing chips and drives on his backhand and looking as fresh late in the fifth as he had late in the first.

But his best chance was gone. At twelve-games-all, Djokovic seized command of yet another tiebreaker, taking a 4–1 lead as Mirka watched through splayed fingers. Federer closed the gap to 4–3, but Djokovic won the next two points like a champion, hitting a clean forehand winner and then a flat blast of a backhand winner down the line to end an extended rally.

It was 6–3, and Djokovic had his first match point, forty-four minutes after Federer had had his last.

Federer hit a second serve, Djokovic hit a crosscourt backhand return, and Federer moved to his left and mishit his final forehand: The ball flew off the top of his racket frame and into the crowd, which had been ready to celebrate but was now much more subdued.

Djokovic's parents, uncle, agent, and coach Marián Vajda were jumping in place and embracing, but Djokovic maintained a notably even strain, walking to the net for the handshake with a me-against-the-world grin that struck me as sardonic. He then squatted on the grass and selected a few blades of grass for his now-traditional, still-unusual, postvictory Wimbledon meal.

As Djokovic chewed, Federer stewed. The Swiss had been one point away from what would rightly have been seen as his greatest victory, one that would have made him the oldest men's singles champion in Wimbledon's modern era and given him a twenty-first major singles title, widening the gap with Djokovic and Nadal.

"I just feel it's such an incredible opportunity missed," Federer said later, his baritone voice a bit lower than usual.

Asked where it had gone wrong, Federer answered: "One shot, I guess. Don't know which one to pick. Your choice."

It was one of the best finals in tennis history, as compelling in many regards as the 2008 Wimbledon final and with superior continuity and visibility.

"This one is more straightforward maybe in some ways because we didn't have the rain delays, we didn't have the night coming in and all that stuff," Federer said. "But sure, epic ending, so close, so many moments. I mean, sure, there's similarities. But you've got to go dig, see what they are. I'm the loser both times, so that's the only similarity I see."

Djokovic's 7–6 (5), 1–6, 7–6 (4), 4–6, 13–12 (3) victory was also the longest Wimbledon men's singles final, at four hours and fifty-seven minutes, at a tournament that dates to 1877.

"I thought most of the match I was on the back foot," Djokovic said. "I was defending. He was dictating the play. I just tried to fight and find a way when it mattered the most, which is what happened."

Federer finished with 91 winners and made 61 unforced errors; Djokovic had 54 winners and 52 unforced errors, many of them in his walkabout of a second set. Federer hit more aces (25 to 10) and had fewer double faults (6 to 9). He converted more break points (7 to 3) and won more points overall (218 to 204). But tennis, as Federer knows as well as anyone, is about winning the critical points.

It was not just about the choices he made on the two match points. It was about the tiebreakers, typically Federer's territory.

"Roger was pushing Novak around but not in the three tiebreakers, not at all," said Craig O'Shannessy, the analytics expert who was a consultant for Djokovic. "Novak actually ended up at the net more than Roger did, which is a massive mistake. Roger should have served and volleyed, should have chipped and charged, should have come in on second serves, should have been approaching down the middle of the court. He should have been all over the net in the tiebreakers, and he just kept hesitating and staying back and letting the rally extend."

It is cruel but unavoidable that Federer, one of the most prolific winners in tennis or sports, will also be remembered for losing two of the greatest matches ever played, perhaps *the* two greatest matches in which he played. His 2017 Australian Open victory over Nadal was spectacular, but Wimbledon remains the most historic and globally prestigious of the majors, the grassy place that suits his style and image best.

He has inspired many with his tennis but also inspired the opposition.

"I hope I give some other people a chance to believe at thirty-seven it's not over yet," Federer said gamely during the awards ceremony on Centre Court as he spoke with Sue Barker of the BBC.

It was soon Djokovic's turn to join Barker.

"Roger said he hopes that he gives some other people a chance to believe they can do it at thirty-seven," said Djokovic, then thirty-two. "I'm one of them."

There is a seductive school of thought that Federer has had an easier path to greatness, that he amassed the bulk of his Grand Slam titles when Nadal was not yet a true all-court threat and Djokovic had not yet clicked into top gear. You could make a strong argument that the only major Federer won with both those men at something resembling full throttle was the 2008 US Open. But that is forgetting that Nadal and Djokovic became as fabulous as they did only because they had Federer for a measuring stick. Federer managed to remain a true contender even when Nadal and Djokovic were in their physical prime and he was in his mid- to late thirties.

But while Sampras had to deal with the surprise of his records being broken less than a decade after he retired, Federer endured so long that he had to cope with his records being broken before he retired.

It is a poignant development, and I asked him about it once.

"As much as I like the records, to break those or own them, I guess for me it's really the breaking part which is beautiful, not the owning part," he said. "Because no one can take away that moment. All the records are there to be broken anyway at one point, but that first moment when you take that step or that leap into that sphere where nobody has been before, that really is inspiring."

It is surely all the sweeter to savor when you have tasted the bitterness of big-match disappointment. His hallmark resilience has certainly been put to the test even when he had very little left to prove.

If you falter, it helps if your family knows how to help you move on quickly. Mirka, who had so clearly sensed the danger on Centre Court, understood perfectly. The day after the defeat, the Federers were back on the move for a family camping trip.

"Look, I struggled a little bit the first couple days," Roger said. "At the same time, I was caravanning with my kids. I didn't have that much time thinking about all the missed opportunities. I was organizing my life for my four children, driving around the beautiful countryside in Switzerland. Sometimes you have flashbacks, things like, 'Oh, I could have done that, should have done that.' The next day you're having a glass of wine with your wife thinking, 'The semis was pretty good, even the finals was pretty good.' You go in phases."

EPILOGUE

SOUTH AFRICA

I had traveled by train to Basel, with its orderly streets and well-tended tennis courts. But tracing the Federer origin story to its true beginnings required rather a longer journey.

In February 2020, after covering the Australian Open, I caught a day flight from Melbourne to Perth, a red-eye flight across the Indian Ocean to Johannesburg, and an Uber ride from the international airport to an industrial zone in Kempton Park with an expatriate Zimbabwean driver in a rusting sedan that, like the neighborhood, had seen better days.

Without South Africa, there would be no Roger Federer.

It was in Kempton Park in 1970 that Federer's father, Robert, then a twenty-three-year-old chemical engineer, met Federer's mother, Lynette, then an eighteen-year-old secretary, when both were working for the Swiss chemical company Ciba-Geigy.

"My husband lost his heart in South Africa," Lynette told me many years later with pride.

She lost hers, too, and though the young couple soon moved to Robert's home country of Switzerland, they returned often to Lynette's home, both as newlyweds and later with their two children.

"We spent most holidays there for many years," Lynette told me. "Roger went for the first time when he was three months old. He was really a baby, and my daughter was two. I loved going with the kids. Before the children started school, we used to go for three months at a time. They got a feel for South Africa, even though they were very young."

The connection remained strong for Roger, who has dual Swiss and

South African citizenship, even if the visits became much rarer as his tennis career gathered pace.

But he was returning to South Africa on a mission now: for an exhibition match with Rafael Nadal in Cape Town's fifty-five-thousand-seat soccer stadium with Microsoft cofounder Bill Gates and comedian Trevor Noah joining in for doubles.

The tickets had sold out online in less than ten minutes.

"I think it's going to be quite emotional, to be honest, because I've wanted to play in South Africa for many, many years," Federer told us at his prematch news conference. "I can't believe it's taken this long."

Federer had just reached the semifinals of the Australian Open, where he had faded in a lopsided loss to Novak Djokovic, struggling with a leg injury that had forced him to consider withdrawing before the match. He played anyway, jumping out to a quick 4–1 lead before reality set in and Djokovic won in straight sets.

Little more than a week later on a different continent, he was ready to go back on court for the "Match in Africa," the latest in the exhibition series benefiting Federer's foundation, which helps fund early childhood education.

He had started the charity with his parents' help and encouragement in 2003, the year in which he won his first Grand Slam title at age twenty-one.

"When Roger was starting to earn good money, we said, 'We think it's a good thing you give back a bit of your own fortune to those who are less advantaged,'" Lynette told me.

Lynette, the youngest of four children, grew up in South Africa during the apartheid era. Her father had fought in World War Two for Britain and had long been stationed in Europe. Her mother was a nurse, and Lynette said she and her siblings were raised to see Black people as equals. Lynette, like her son, was careful to avoid politics in public, but she was clearly a driving force in the foundation and its focus.

"A lot of people were interested in Roger supporting projects," she said. "The Red Cross and others were all interested, but we were looking for something not too big and where you can really see and feel the change it makes."

Roger had been motivated in part by Andre Agassi, the American champion who had started his eponymous foundation in his thirties. Agassi often said he wished he had done so earlier.

"I remember hearing that quote," Federer told me. "I definitely got inspiration from Andre. I can say I started it way before I was really good, and this shows that it really meant a lot to me to do something like this."

It was intriguing that both he and Agassi gravitated to charitable work in education even though both had stopped their formal schooling in their midteens. Federer was, by his own admission in his early adulthood, not much of a book reader, although he clearly developed a fondness for record books.

But Federer's foundation did fine work, beginning by funding projects in South Africa and then expanding to other African countries and Switzerland. Before arriving in Cape Town, Federer had traveled to Namibia, where he had met with the country's president, Hage Geingob, just as he had met with Zambia's president, Edgar Lungu, on a trip to Africa in 2018.

The five previous Matches for Africa had raised about $10 million for the foundation's work, and the Cape Town match would raise about $3.5 million more. In total, according to Godsick, Federer had generated more than $50 million through the years for projects in Africa.

It was clear that Federer intended to focus more on the foundation in retirement.

"Until now, I haven't had a lot of time," he told a group of Swiss reporters before arriving in South Africa. "I've always said that these years would serve as an apprenticeship, but it's true that down the road, my dream would be to be as well-known for the foundation as for tennis."

That will be quite a challenge but was certainly one of the reasons Federer had sought out the mentorship of Gates, a tennis fan and one of the world's richest men. Gates had transitioned from running Microsoft to philanthropy through the Bill & Melinda Gates Foundation, which had become the world's largest private foundation, with assets approaching $50 billion, and had done extensive work in Africa on problems like malaria.

Godsick had reached out to Gates when Federer was organizing an exhibition in Seattle in 2017, and Gates had agreed to take part. Federer, from a modest background, was now as comfortable in the company of billionaires as he was with baseliners. He and his family have vacationed with Frenchman Bernard Arnault and his family. Arnault is the chairman and chief executive of the world's largest luxury goods company: LVMH Möet Hennessy Louis Vuitton SE. Möet & Chandon, a division of the company, is one of Federer's sponsors and in May 2015, according to French journalist Thomas Sotto, Federer surprised Arnault on his private tennis court in Paris and played doubles with him against two of his sons.

Federer also has close ties with Jorge Paulo Lemann, the Swiss-Brazilian businessman who played at Wimbledon in his youth and is an investor in the Laver Cup (Federer sometimes practices on Lemann's grass court).

"Look, Bill Gates has been amazing for my foundation," Federer said. "It's just so interesting to learn from him, speak to him, get to know his wife as well. All the team behind his foundation is a completely different size to my family foundation, to be honest, but to be spending some time with him and seeing his support has been truly important for us."

Those roles were reversed on the tennis court, where Gates, consistent but limited, was delighted to defer to his doubles partner. Federer nicknamed their team "Gateserer," which did not exactly roll off the tongue.

"If somebody has a better name, we're open to it," Federer said with a laugh.

But at least Gates was an avid tennis player. Trevor Noah, the South African comic who had become a star in the United States as the host of *The Daily Show*, was a great fit for the event in several respects. He, like Federer, had a South African mother and a Swiss father. He was also a big draw in South Africa. The problem was Noah did not know how to play tennis.

"I didn't want to tell them, because you know when cool people invite you to things, you're like, 'I'm in!'" Noah later explained in an appearance on *Ellen*. "In two months, I had to learn tennis from scratch, one of the craziest things I've ever done in my life."

There were many remarkable things about the Match in Africa, but that Noah managed to keep it together in front of 51,954 spectators while playing a game he had just learned might have been the most remarkable. The man clearly has no stage fright.

Neither does Lynette Federer. She was introduced inside the stadium as "Roger Federer's proud mother" and jauntily walked up the ramp to perform the prematch coin toss with the crowd roaring. She was beaming, reveling in the moment, and her son greeted her on court, held her close, and kissed her on top of the head.

Watching the scene from the stands, I thought of my brief visit to Kempton Park two days earlier and the walk around the former Ciba offices where Robert and Lynette had once worked. Inside the main gate topped with coils of barbed wire, a Swiss flag fluttered in the breeze next to a South African flag.

There are elements of randomness to all of our lives: the unexpected fork in the road. But the Federers' chance meeting certainly had larger consequences than most. Robert, brimming with wanderlust in his youth, so easily could have ended up elsewhere on his professional adventure: the United States, Australia, even Israel, which was recruiting foreign workers.

Instead, he traveled all the way to South Africa, where he and his future wife enthusiastically played recreational tennis and then introduced the game to their children back in Basel.

Their energetic son grew up to be one of the greatest players of all time: a creative and often overwhelming force, a crowd favorite but also a resilient competitor, a relentless optimist with a pragmatic streak who was capable of making tough decisions and adapting to great success and brutal defeat.

It is quite a package—not perfection but still quite a package, one that allowed him to win on tour in the 1990s, 2000s, 2010s, and 2020s.

"I never fell out of love with the sport," Federer told me. "Never."

There have been times when that seemed more stubborn than logical, but I believe him. His job satisfaction came through unmistakably, from the practice court to the match court to the makeshift court on a platform in the center of a blustery South African stadium with the largest crowd in tennis history watching Federer play his defining rival.

"Through time, we've left behind a bit of that hard-core rivalry on court for a rivalry that we both value and understand has been part of something special within the world of sport," Nadal shared with me ahead of the match. "And I think we also understand that both of us have benefited from it, and we have to take care of it. I think it's beautiful to take care of this story we have lived together, and I think we both understand that to take care of it, one of the important things we need to do is to have a really good relationship."

Federer could not have imagined Cape Town without Nadal. In his mind, it was the matchup the South African public deserved. It was quite a conundrum to find a date that worked for both men to make the journey. When the match finally happened, Federer had to rely on his tolerance for pain: merrily chasing down lobs and flicking trick shots on an ailing right knee that, unbeknownst to all but his inner circle, would require surgery later in the month.

Gates, deeply involved in public health issues, was well aware of the potential for the coronavirus that had recently surfaced in China to create global upheaval. He spoke with Federer and Nadal about the gathering storm during dinner at their intimate, elegant, and very well-guarded hotel. They were staying at Ellerman House, with its view of Bantry Bay and Robben Island, where Nelson Mandela once counted the days in prison.

"We were very lucky and very thankful that we were able to host the event," said John-Laffnie de Jager, the former South African tour player who was one of the exhibition's promoters. "A couple weeks later, with the virus, we would have been gone."

A couple of weeks later, there would have been no full-circle moments in Cape Town Stadium, no embraces at the net, no pride and joy in the stands, no postmatch celebration with the players, ball kids, and dancers all tightly packed and bouncing in time with the music as tears again streamed down Federer's cheeks.

As so often, his timing was excellent.

Acknowledgments

"So how long did it take?" is the question I have heard most upon completion of this book.

More than a year is the simple answer if you are talking about the planning and writing process. I talked it through with my new and intuitive literary agent Susan Canavan, who liked the idea from the first time we discussed it over lunch on the north shore of Boston in 2019. It sounded so simple then! I went on to conduct more than eighty interviews for the project and watch or rewatch scores of Federer matches.

But the real answer is that this book started more than twenty years ago, in the stands of the Suzanne Lenglen Court at the French Open in the spring of 1999 as Federer made his Grand Slam debut.

He held your interest as a teenager and has never surrendered it. There have been more flamboyant and fascinating tennis champions but never one whose game was so pleasing to the eye and, as I realized in reporting this book, never one who embraced all aspects of the sport with such unquenchable enthusiasm.

Getting the chance to cover Federer's career so closely was a matter of being in the right place—usually Europe—at the right time.

Thanks to Barry Lorge and Bob Wright, my late and great bosses at the *San Diego Union* newspaper who opened the door to journalism and then sent me to cover tennis tournaments, including Wimbledon in 1990.

Thanks to Neil Amdur, a former tennis correspondent at the *New York Times*, who went on to become its sports editor and took a chance on me not long after I had moved to France as a newlywed freelancer. *Merci* to Peter Berlin and Michael Getler, who hired me in Paris for my dream job as chief sports correspondent at the *International Herald Tribune*, and *merci* to the remarkable David Ignatius, who made me a columnist with a free rein. Who could ask for more?

These have been pinch-yourself years, roaming the globe to cover the biggest events: Olympics, World Cups, world championships, America's Cups, Champions League, golf majors, and, always, a great deal of tennis. Thanks to all the editors at the *IHT* and the *Times* who have made it possible, including Tom Jolly, Alison Smale, Sandy Bailey, Jeff Boda, Marty Gottlieb, Jason Stallman, Dick Stevenson, Jill Agostino, Naila-Jean Meyers, Andy Das, Oskar Garcia, and most recently Randy Archibold, who supported the leave I needed to write *The Master*.

I could not have written it properly without those who spoke with me. Thanks to all eighty-two of you for the time and the trust, and many thanks to Andy Roddick, Marat Safin, Pete Sampras, Rafael Nadal, and Novak Djokovic, for going deep on what it was like to face Federer, and to Peter Lundgren, José Higueras, and, in particular, Paul Annacone, for going deep on what it was like to coach him.

A special thank-you to Federer and his longtime agent Tony Godsick for granting me and the *Times* so much access through the years. Such opportunities have become too rare with many superstar athletes, but Federer understands and respects the role of the news media and has been willing to share more of himself than most.

"So how long did it take?"

"Longer than it should have," Sean Desmond, the publisher at Twelve, might have said. But he refrained. With warmth and Federer-esque empathy, Sean, an author himself, gave me the time and the peace of mind to finish the job right.

I am grateful to him for believing in this project and to Rachel Kambury, Megan Perritt-Jacobson, Estefania Acquaviva, Joelle Dieu, and the rest of Sean's team for supporting it. I am also grateful to my family and friends for their forbearance as I disappeared into deadlines and tennis seasons past. Above all, *un grand merci* to my own rock, my wife of thirty years, Virginie, who never faltered, not even in the midst of a pandemic, and who reminded me when the task seemed a bit too much that this was what I had always wanted to do.

As so often, she was right, or, as the hard-to-impress French like to say, not wrong.

Index

About the Author

Christopher Clarey has covered global sports for the *New York Times* and the *International Herald Tribune* for thirty years from bases in France, Spain, and the United States. He is one of the world's leading authorities on tennis and covered his first Grand Slam tournament in 1990 at Wimbledon. In 2018, Clarey received the Eugene L. Scott Award from the International Tennis Hall of Fame, a career prize awarded for "communicating honestly and critically about the game" and "making a significant impact on the tennis world." He is a past winner of the Associated Press Sports Editors contest in the breaking news category. A former collegiate tennis player at Williams, he has traveled in and reported from more than seventy countries on six continents.